The Washakie Letters
of
Willie Ottogary

Northwestern Shoshone Journalist and Leader
1906–1929

"William Otagary," photo by Gill, 1921, National Anthropological Archives, *Smithsonian Institution*.

The Washakie Letters
of
Willie Ottogary

Northwestern Shoshone Journalist and Leader
1906–1929

Edited by

Matthew E. Kreitzer

Foreword by Barre Toelken

Utah State University Press
Logan, Utah

Copyright © 2000 Utah State University Press
All rights reserved

Utah State University Press
Logan, Utah 84322-7800

Manufactured in the United States of America

Printed on acid free paper

07 06 05 04 03 02 01 00   1 2 3 4 5 6 7 8

Ottogary, Willie.
   The Washakie letters of Willie Ottogary, northwestern Shoshone
journalist and leader, 1906–1929 / [compiled by] Matthew E. Kreitzer.
      p. cm.
Includes bibliographical references and index.
   ISBN 0-87421-401-7 (pbk.) — ISBN 0-87421-402-5 (hardback)
   1. Ottogary, Willie—Correspondence. 2. Shoshoni
Indians—Utah—Washakie Indian Reservation—Biography. 3. Indian
journalists—Utah—Washakie Indian Reservation—Biography. 4. Shoshoni
Indians—Utah—Washakie Indian Reservation—Social conditions. 5.
Washakie Indian Reservation (Utah)—History. I. Kreitzer, Matthew E.,
1957- II. Title.
   E99.S4 O77 2000
   979.2'42—dc21
                            00-009792

To my parents, Melvin and Ann Whitenack Kreitzer
for teaching me to love people and history.

To the Ottogarys, Clyde and Cecelia, and family,
for allowing me the privilege of studying
their grandfather and great grandfather, Willie.

To my wife, Shelle, and our children,
Joshua, David, James, Kalani, Nathaniel, and Samuel,
for their unwavering support and love.

To A. J. Simmonds, mentor and friend.

To the Northwestern Shoshone.

To God, who has given me life.

Contents

Illustrations

Foreword

Barre Toelken

IN MANY WAYS, WILLIE OTTOGARY IS EXEMPLARY of what early Japanese folklorist Yanagita Kunio called "the invisible culture"—that uncountable mass of everyday people whose lives and expressions, while never becoming "visible" in museums, libraries, and other elite venues, nonetheless actually constitute the ongoing, dynamic force of their own society. Usually such people—for all their importance to historical movement—remain personally unknown, anonymous, unrecognized. Under typical circumstances, Ottogary would have been even more invisible than most, for he was a Shoshone Indian with a limited command of English. If it had not been for the fact that he steadfastly refused to be invisible, we would know virtually nothing of him today. But with a resolute and stunningly friendly insistence on being heard, he left a trail of vernacular journalism in the newspapers of northern Utah and southern Idaho during the early 1900s.

His columns were apparently quite popular in their day. Perhaps they served some as an indication that Indians were educable; to others, they may have registered as unintentional cultural parody. In later years, his columns—known to a handful of archivists for their humorous local color—languished in yellowing stacks of old newspapers on the special collections shelves of a few university libraries. Ottogary might have decayed into obscurity along with hundreds of other local columnists of the West if it had not been for the keen eye and ear of Matt Kreitzer, who recognized the columns (through a chance encounter) as a potential window on Native attitudes and ideas that have otherwise escaped our attention. Kreitzer not only searched for Willie Ottogary in the dusty backrooms of libraries, but on the land and among the man's Shoshone relatives and descendants. Every new discovery yielded still more fascinating aspects of this remarkable person, and the resultant picture is a wonderful example of how rich the vernacular record is—if one has the dedication and the energy to find it and pay serious attention to it.

In a curious way, Ottogary's ostensibly humble accounts of Shoshone everyday life in the early twentieth century leap out from the newspaper pages today with an honesty and freshness that contrasts with sober accounts of church conferences, dull reports on town council deliberations, stilted social calendar reports, and boring discussions of feed and grain prices. Defective grammar and unique idiom notwithstanding, Ottogary's down-to-earth comments are a delight, a treasure for anyone who wants a richer, more diverse account of life in turn-of-the-century Utah.

Preface

EIGHT YEARS AGO I EMBARKED ON AN INCREDIBLE JOURNEY. This journey allowed me to follow the trail of an amazing individual named Willie Ottogary. It began in 1992, when I took a sabbatical leave from my teaching position at Pine View High School in St. George, Utah. My wife and I had discussed the plan for years, and when I finally gained the required seven years of experience, we uprooted our young family and moved to Logan, Utah, where I entered a master's program in American studies at Utah State University (USU). I had searched carefully for the right institution—a university that had outstanding faculty, unparalleled research opportunities in my field, and breathtaking scenery. I was pleased on all counts, beyond my fondest wishes.

My research focus was on Native Americans, but in what direction my thesis research would take me, I was not sure. I enrolled in a standard research and bibliography course. During a class excursion to the USU Special Collections and Archives, I was introduced by Brad Cole, keeper of manuscripts, to a small blue-grey pamphlet titled *Willie Ottogary's Letters to "The Journal" Logan, Utah.*[1] I read the pamphlet and determined to do my thesis on the subject. On a subsequent trip to the Special Collections department, I mentioned my desire to A. J. Simmonds, director of special collections. A.J. said, "Good, it's about time." He then disappeared for several minutes. When he returned, he had a stack of dusty 3 x 5 index cards held together by an old rubber band. He handed me the stack and said something like, "Here, this should get you started." The stack contained dates and notes regarding Ottogary's letters that A. J. had recorded as he had gone through hard copies of *The Journal*. I was thrilled. This experience marked the beginning of a student-mentor relationship that was maintained until A. J.'s unfortunate death in 1997.

At Special Collections I gained access to the appropriate microfilmed copies of *The Journal* and began locating Ottogary's published letters. At first I searched only for the dates on A. J.'s cards, but when I noticed a letter in microform copy that was not mentioned on a card, I decided to search each page of the microform collection until I was sure all the letters were found. When I began doing this, I did not completely understand the amount of time and effort this would represent, but after reading just a few letters, I was hooked; time and effort became secondary concerns. There was nothing that would keep me from my quest to locate every letter Willie Ottogary wrote to *The Journal*. I spent months in front of the microform reader and became closely acquainted with every employee in the department. I soon branched out to other newspapers that were published near Ottogary's home. I was amazed to find more letters published in four other papers. My major professor, Barre Toelken, shared my enthusiasm with each new discovery, and we spent many office hours discussing the significance of Ottogary's work.

Just over a year after my sabbatical began, I finished the thesis and submitted it. In it I included an introduction to the Northwestern Shoshone, an account of Ottogary's life and writings, discussion of key aspects of his journalism, and a conclusion regarding his significance as a journalist, historian, and leader. Several people approached me hoping to get more information about Ottogary and his writings. My thesis committee, which consisted of Barre Toelken, A. J. Simmonds, and Clyde A. Milner II, felt the wealth of information contained in the Ottogary letters ought to be mined further. With their encouragement, I began. Two books (at least, and numerous articles) seemed obvious follow up projects: an edited collection of the letters and a biography. The former is represented in this volume, while the latter is next on my agenda.

As I collected the letters, I organized them chronologically and separated them by newspaper. I next turned my attention to the people mentioned in Ottogary's letters. One of the most fascinating aspects of the letters is the wealth of information they contain about the citizens of Washakie. I spent over a year creating a biographical register and index that would provide information about the people Ottogary mentioned most consistently. Commenting on the letters themselves was a difficult task. After sharing my concerns with John R. Alley, Utah State University Press editor, we decided on a method with which both of us felt comfortable (see the section on editorial methods at the end of the introduction for more information).

My research took me through thousands of pages of books, articles, and manuscripts. I read everything I could that would give me a clearer understanding of the Northwestern Shoshone and related Shoshone groups. I interviewed living descendants of the original Washakie residents. I also interviewed Ottogary neighbors who still reside in Elwood, Utah. I was amazed at the reception I received from elderly white residents of Cache and Box Elder counties. Many of these wonderful people knew of Ottogary's letters and graciously commented on them; sometimes they even pointed me in other directions where I could locate more information.

As I narrowed my focus, I went to the National Archives in Washington, D.C., where I located valuable information that corroborated much of what was written by Ottogary. When I focused on the Latter-day Saint (Mormon) influence at Washakie, I located great stores of information at the LDS Church History Department in Salt Lake City, Utah. County clerk offices, district courts, and other local government agencies as well as several universities throughout northern Utah and southern Idaho also proved helpful as I compiled the necessary information for this volume.

Of special significance to my research were trips I took to places discussed by Ottogary. I wanted to see and feel some of what Ottogary saw and felt about his homeland and his people. I spent hours at the ruins of what was once the Washakie settlement. Not being satisfied with one trip, I returned again and again, trying to see the area in each of the four seasons. I also hiked over the ground that was once the Ottogary homestead. I visited Willie Ottogary's grandson, Clyde S. Ottogary, at his home on Bannock Creek in Idaho. I visited with a grandnephew at Brigham City. I attended several Sun Dances held near the Portneuf Bottoms area of the Fort Hall Reservation and was moved by the beauty of this ceremony. While there

Clyde S. Ottogary (*center*) and part of his family with the editor and one of his sons, summer 1993. *Clockwise from right:* Cecelia Moon Ottogary, Clyde S. Ottogary, William Wayne Ottogary, Shaneá Tobi Morning Dove Ottogary Deppe, Jodell Fayette Wetchie, Dianne Ottogary, and Matthew E. Kreitzer holding Nathaniel L. Kreitzer. *Photo by Matthew E. Kreitzer.*

I was also able to visit with Shoshone (as well as Utes and Paiutes) from other areas. I was invited, and attended, a Northwestern Shoshone Tribal Council meeting, where I met other descendants of the original families of Washakie. As much as possible, I wanted to immerse myself in the physical and cultural landscape to which Ottogary was accustomed and spend time with the people for whom he cared most deeply.

One fundamental objective motivated the writing of this volume: to honor Willie Ottogary and the Northwestern Shoshone whose lives he preserved through his journalism. This book, arranged chronologically from first letter to last, is not a thorough enthnography or history. It is, however, part ethnohistory, social history, and biography. Since few other Native Americans have undertaken a task such as Ottogary did, this volume will find few peers. It offers a unique contribution to Western American history in general and Great Basin cultural history specifically.

I am grateful to the many individuals who gave their support throughout this project. I would like first to thank the members of my thesis committee—Barre Toelken, A. J. Simmonds, and Clyde A. Milner II—for their initial advice and constant support and for allowing me to bend their ears in my direction when I needed special help. For help with the Shoshone language I am indebted to Mae Timbimboo Parry, Alene Menta, and Richley Crapo of USU. I also thank my dear friend and sounding board, Charles S. Peterson, emeritus professor of history, USU. Chas has been a constant support. He has carefully proofread early drafts, given me advice in obtaining financial support, and in other ways allowed me to upset his so-called retirement. Thank you also to Scott R. Christensen of the LDS Church Historical Department, a scholarly associate with whom I share an affection for the Northwestern Shoshone and Washakie, Utah.

I would also like to thank the many Shoshone individuals who have assisted me with information and support. I will not attempt to mention them all for fear of leaving someone out but will mention only those who either knew Ottogary personally or are related to him. I am deeply honored by the Ottogary family's consistent support and friendship. Also important was Mae Timbimboo Parry, who gave me countless interviews and loaned numerous photographs to me for the book. Thank you as well to Leland Pubigee (Ottogary's grandnephew) for the several interviews he so graciously allowed me and for the many Christmas cards over the years.

Many archivists aided me in many ways. I especially thank the staff of USU Special Collections: Brad Cole (who has since moved on to Northern Arizona University), Peter Schmid (who also has moved on), Anne Buttars, Robert Parson, and the rest of the crew. I am also appreciative of the archival staffs at Brigham Young University, Provo, Utah; the LDS Church History Department, Salt Lake City; the National Archives and Records Administration, Washington, D.C.; the University of Utah and Utah State Historical Society, Salt Lake City; and Idaho State University, Pocatello, Idaho.

As I look back at how this project came together, I am especially cognizant of those who provided financial support. I am grateful to a dear neighbor, William McCall, for purchasing a room air conditioner so I could think more clearly and hopefully write more effectively in the desert heat of St. George, Utah. I am also appreciative of the American Philosophical Society for a Phillips Fund Grant for Native American Research, which allowed me to collect oral histories of Shoshone. I am very grateful for the generous support of BYU's Charles Redd Center for Western Studies Faculty Fellowship for 1996–97. That support allowed me to focus my time and effort on research and writing. I am also obliged to the National Endowment for the Humanities for their Independent Study in the Humanities Research Fellowship (from the Council of Basic Education), which allowed me to study, in depth, the topic that I loved so much.

I am also thankful for family and friends whose constant questions about how my book was coming gave me added incentive to forge ahead, while at the same time making me feel that I was doing something that was of extraordinary significance.

Any interpretations proposed and errors remaining herein, regardless of intense effort and intention to minimize them, are my responsibility.

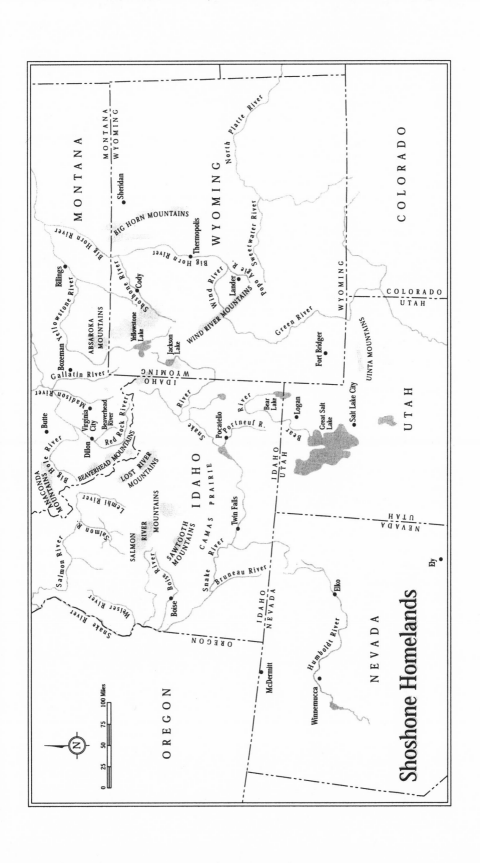

Shoshone Homelands

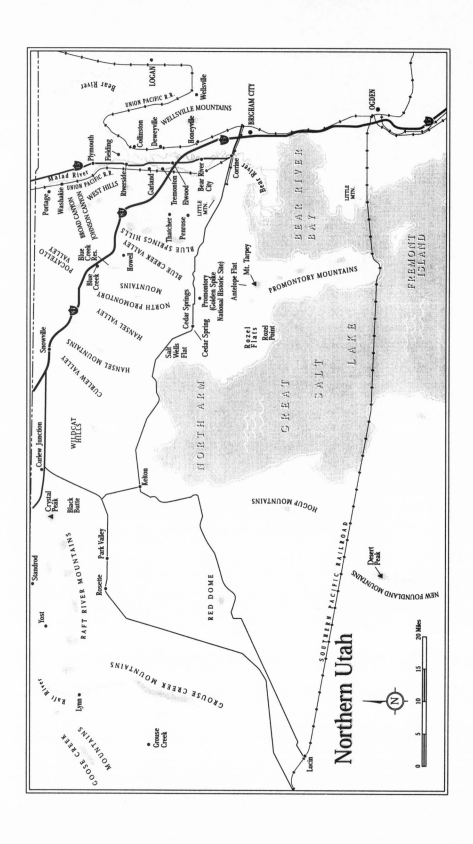

Northern Utah

Introduction

THE BUFFALO WERE LONG GONE. As Mormons and other non-Indian settlers had expanded their respective kingdoms throughout the Great Basin, indigenous seeds and other food sources had rapidly disappeared or become unavailable. The native Shoshone bands had to adapt to the settlers' intrusion as best they could. Some fought back against the tide of immigrants, but none were able to stop the inevitable flood.

Early in 1863 settlers and travelers begged the government to put an end to recent Indian depredations. Colonel Patrick E. Conner and his command, the California Volunteers, mustered into service to deal with the situation. The soldiers marched from Salt Lake City to southeastern Idaho, finding the Northwestern Shoshone at their wintering grounds where Battle Creek (as it is now called) meets the Bear River. Chiefs Bear Hunter and Sagwitch led the Shoshone.[1] The date was January 29, 1863. The temperature was below freezing, and sheets of ice choked the flow of the Bear River. The Shoshone had heard that soldiers were coming but may have doubted the seriousness of the reports. They believed they were innocent of the recent depredations, and some knew that soldiers occasionally paraded about to coerce or intimidate Indians.[2] Perhaps they thought what was coming was just another parade. It was not.

The soldiers arrived in the early dawn and followed their orders of retribution with fervor. Their firepower, tactics, and numbers took a terrible toll as the Indians waged a desperate struggle. As the volunteers were about to consummate their mission of death, those Shoshone still living made desperate attempts to escape the carnage. Many were killed in the act. Those who succeeded used a variety of means. A few feigned death, some dove into the frigid water of the Bear River and swam to safety, and others mounted their ponies, charged up the hill through the encircling troops, and disappeared over the other side. Details of the attack and the escape narratives of the survivors were passed down orally to their descendants. Of key importance to this book is the story of how Willie Ottogary's father, O-Ti-Cot-i, escaped death.

In the early years after the arrival of Mormon pioneers, Willie's father roamed what is now northern Utah, western Nevada, southern Idaho, and western Wyoming and possibly ranged even further east. Besides being a *buhagant*, or *pohakanten* (shaman, doctor, or medicine man), O-Ti-Cot-i was a distinguished warrior. At the time of the massacre, he was camped with his familial band at Bear River, where they traditionally wintered. During the attack, O-Ti-Cot-i used himself as a diversion. Family lore relates that his medicine was very powerful, and because of his protective buffalo-robe shroud, he was able to ride through a hail of bullets, and even be hit, without receiving any bodily harm. Well into the fighting, he realized that little else could be done and made his escape, though he and others

1

returned later to assist survivors. The story of O-Ti-Cot-i's bravery and escape passed down to his descendants, and the retelling of these harrowing events and others undoubtedly helped shape Willie's mind and prepare him for his future.[3]

In the aftermath of their devastating punishment, O-Ti-Cot-i and other Shoshone dispersed. In July 1863, surviving Northwestern Shoshone leaders signed a treaty with the United States in Box Elder County, Utah.[4] Their lives would never be the same. The events of the previous several years had made it very clear that in order to survive as a people, the Northwestern Shoshone would have to learn the ways of whites. In order to maintain any expressions of their culture, they would have to make extraordinary adjustments. The massacre at the Bear River was a terrible catalyst for change, a crucible of cultural transformation.

For several years after the massacre, the scattered bands continued, as best they could, their traditional lifestyle of hunting and gathering. Family groups once again scattered throughout their home territory in northern Utah. However, due to a constant influx of immigrants, relatively little ground was left on which the Shoshone could survive.

Soon after the Bear River Massacre, O-Ti-Cot-i and his wife, Sots-Ze-ump, may have moved on to Wyoming, as records indicate that three children were born to them there.[5] One of them, a daughter later known as Eliza, was born about 1867. In July 1869, in a valley named Mantua, in Box Elder County, Utah, Sots-Ze-ump bore a son. In time the child would be known as Willie Ottogary. Eliza and Willie were the only children of O-Ti-Cot-i and Sots-Ze-ump known to have survived to adulthood.

Mormon culture blanketed northern Utah, and its influence deeply affected the Shoshone. In 1875, a devout Mormon missionary named George Washington Hill preached to—and baptized—hundreds of Indians in the region. O-Ti-Cot-i was among a group of Shoshone baptized in August of that year. According to a descendant, O-Ti-Cot-i (soon known as Peter Otahgary) truly converted to the Mormon Church, officially called the Church of Jesus Christ of Latter-day Saints (LDS). His great-grandson Leland Pubigee has stated that Peter hid up his "medicine" and followed the LDS faith completely. Peter felt that he could not live essentially torn between two spiritual worlds.[6]

After conversion, Peter and the other Northwestern Shoshone cautiously followed the plans laid out by LDS missionaries to settle on arable land, where the Shoshone would be taught to farm, educated, and "civilized" according to white values. An early settlement for the Indian converts was near Corinne, Utah, but it failed because the people of Corinne (a "gentile," or non-LDS, community) viewed the Indian settlement as a potential threat. Rumors led the citizens of Corinne to believe an Indian attack was coming. Fearful that the LDS Church was using Indian allies to rid the territory of gentiles, the people of Corinne asked the military to help uproot the Indian community and move the Shoshone out. The harvest had just begun, and the Indians were gathering in their crops when the eviction took place. After the Shoshone dispersed again, the aggressors plundered the crops and whatever else the Indians left behind.[7]

After the Corinne incident, the Mormon missionaries chose a new location and persuaded some of the Indians to try again. The site, near present Elwood, Utah, lacked access to open space, traditional foods, culinary water, and fuel, which

Washakie, Utah. The log house at left was the first house constructed
at Washakie. It was built by Ammon Pubigee, Jacob Peyope, and others. Soquitch Timbimboo moved into the house, although he preferred to live in his nearby tipi. *Courtesy Mae Timbimboo Parry.*

dictated yet another move.[8] LDS Church president John Taylor and other church
leaders proposed a new site be found. A fifteen-hundred acre tract in the Malad
River Valley, near the present town of Portage, Utah, and about seven miles south
of the current Idaho border, was chosen.[9] It was called Washakie, in honor of the
famous Eastern Shoshone leader. Eventually a school, church, and small homes
were built. However, many of the Indians preferred to live in their tipis or tents.[10]

With the conclusion of the major Indian Wars of the late nineteenth century, the federal government, acting on the advice of countless progressive-minded
scholars and religious leaders, determined that the best way to deal with Indians
was to civilize and assimilate them, compelling them to be like their white neighbors. The goal of civilizing the Indian was to be achieved through the allotment of
tribal land holdings to individual Indians, agricultural instruction, education, and
conversion to Christianity. The Mormon Church as well as the federal government pursued these goals.

Mormon beliefs, though, held that the church's mission was to care for Indians
as though they were literal brothers, not an alien race. This belief motivated those
faithful Mormons who followed their leaders' counsel to feed the Indians, rather
than fight them. Believing that it was fulfilling prophecy regarding the descendants of the Lamanites of the Book of Mormon, the Mormon Church sent missionaries to teach both the LDS gospel and agrarian arts. Mormon families were
eventually called to go to Washakie, live among the Shoshone, and teach them
Christianity, farming, home construction, livestock raising, and other skills. With
this strategic support, the Mormon-led Washakie Colony succeeded where countless federally supported efforts failed.

Throughout the early twentieth century, the federal government met with very limited success in meeting the needs of its Indian charges. The principal legislation alloting tribal lands to individual Indians was the Dawes Act of 1887. Because of its inherent weaknesses, which included allowing the eventual transfer of millions of allotted Indian acres to white opportunists, it proved a failure. Problems with the Dawes Act and other weaknesses in federal Indian policy were exposed at length in the Meriam Report of 1928. In it, the Meriam Commission listed recommendations for future Indian policy, which culminated in the Indian Reorganization Act of 1934 and the abandonment of the allotment policy. Through all these years the Washakie Colony received most of its support through the Mormon Church, its leaders, and missionaries, not through the federal government, its agents, or local officials. The irony that the federal goal of turning Indians into Christian agrarians was largely achieved at Washakie without government involvement is illustrated in Ottogary's letters.

While the Washakie site was being developed, faithful members of the LDS Church in Cache Valley were hard at work on a new Mormon temple in Logan. Following their new convictions, Peter Otahgary and other Shoshone Mormons went with their white brethren to Cache Valley and helped with the construction. They also donated $8,000 to the temple effort.[11]

A Shoshone oral tradition holds that the Logan temple site was always a sacred place: "These hills were known as the most sacred place of worship, from which many miraculous healings were observed."[12] It is likely that the Shoshone were so enthusiastic to build the temple because its site already had special significance to them. It is also probable that the Shoshone more readily accepted LDS beliefs because they already believed in the supernatural, spiritual gifts, and intervention by a supreme being or great spirit on behalf of humankind.[13]

The LDS missionaries did more than preach the gospel. In more secular matters, they guided the Washakie Indians through the muddle of legal work and helped them establish numerous homesteads at Washakie and along the lower Bear River Valley. The Indians could farm their own property like their white neighbors, and their descendants would have a remnant of the Shoshone's former lands to call their own. O-Ti-Cot-i received a patent for a lot in section 18 of township 11 north and range 2 west, Box Elder County, Utah.[14] This property was located near the town of Elwood, Utah. The Otahgarys (or Ottogarys), according to census records, also had property in Washakie.[15]

Young Willie Ottogary spent time with his immediate and extended families at both locations. When he was about eight years old he was baptized into the Latter-day Saint faith. His childhood experiences were undoubtedly influenced by a mixture of Shoshone culture (both traditional and transitional), white civilization (as practiced by the LDS missionaries at Washakie), the LDS faith, and a secular education gained at the Washakie Day School.

It was in school that Ottogary developed proficiency at writing. Published evidence records that "Billy," as he was sometimes called,[16] "[was] one of the most enlightened of the Indians . . . [and] is perhaps the best scribe."[17] During his early adulthood he utilized his writing skills as he served in various secretarial and clerical positions in the Washakie Mormon Church organization. A journalistic bug apparently bit Ottogary in 1906. In August of that year he began a series of columns in the *Tremont Times*, a local newspaper that began publishing in 1904. The editor apparently sought social information from all the communities in the area and asked Ottogary to offer a glimpse into the lives of the Shoshone at Washakie. Subsequently, their customs, struggles, successes, whatever Willie felt was important, made it into print. Over the next twenty-three years he maintained correspondence with newspaper editors, writing columns in at least five newspapers: *Tremont Times* (hereafter TT), Tremonton, Utah; *Oneida County Enterprise* (hereafter OCE), Malad, Idaho; *Box Elder Journal* (hereafter BEJ), Brigham City, Utah; *Box Elder News* (hereafter BEN), Brigham City, Utah; and *The Journal* (hereafter LJ), Logan, Utah. His most extensive writings appeared in *The Journal* from 1909 to 1929.

In Cache Valley, where *The Journal* was published, Ottogary found a lasting audience. His articles apparently fulfilled locals' desire for information about the Shoshone who once lived throughout the vast area. As Stan Andersen, a neighbor to the Ottogarys in Elwood, suggested, some may have found Willie's writings "more amusing than significant."[18] Ottogary's distinctive style, with its occasional misspellings and nonstandard grammar, represented his learning of English as a second language, but his writing was nevertheless expressive and informative. Some readers may have read his pieces simply for amusement or to fulfill their preconceived stereotypes of Indians, but the columns have enduring value as a history of a community in the voice of one of its spokespersons.

There were people who recognized the historical value of the columns. The editors of the Logan paper appeared to understand their significance. The publication of Ottogary's "Washakie Letters" column probably enhanced the newspaper's circulation. Eighty percent of the time the column was published on the front page of the first or second section of *The Journal*. One local professional, Benjamin Franklin Riter, owner of Riter Brothers' Rexall Pharmacy, was a good friend of Ottogary's. Mr. Riter was also a collector of Western Americana and no doubt recognized the historical value of the column. If Ottogary "forgot" or was too busy to write, Mr. Riter would pen a friendly letter of encouragement. Ottogary wrote his last letter of 1914 in July. In January 1915 he wrote:

> Well, I hope all the Journal readers must be disappointed on account I being not write for such long time.
>
> Mr. B. Riter wrote me a letter. He was kindalonesome he said in his letter. He wants me to write to Journal again once more. I will do my very best in this.[19]

During Ottogary's lifetime, the Shoshone were going through a difficult historical transition. Their traditional ways of life had been radically changed under the influence of neighboring whites. Ottogary was there to chronicle the unprecedented adaptations. He wrote honestly of the problems his people experienced with dry farming. He noted the Shoshone's struggle to keep their lands at a time when whites with dubious morals seemingly hovered over them like vultures, waiting for the old ones to die so they could take advantage of their heirs. The Indians were not trained in the laws of whites, including the legal action required for heirs to retain possession of deceased patent owners' property. Land was a critical issue to Ottogary and ran as a common thread through the entire weave of his journalism.

An important objective for Ottogary was to regain land acknowledged as belonging to the Northwestern Shoshone in their 1863 Box Elder Treaty with the United States but subsequently taken by whites. His efforts, though, usually met stiff opposition. On one occasion he charged Moroni Ward, the former bishop of the local Mormon ecclesiastical unit, the Washakie Ward, of "telling untruth statements" regarding Shoshone land questions.[20] A loyal Mormon, Ottogary usually attacked gentiles involved in shady land operations with more enthusiasm. To Ottogary, as well as other Shoshone, though, selling the land of the grandfathers was simply unacceptable, regardless of who was involved.

As Ottogary's influence in tribal matters grew, the opportunity came to take his concerns to Washington, D.C. The circumstances of his ascent to leadership are not clear, but by 1915 he had the blessing, and the authority, of his people to represent them at the nation's capitol. According to his column, he made two trips to Washington early in 1915 (see 1915-05-06 LJ). His objectives there were to establish positive relations with government officials and seek redress of tribal grievances. The Northwestern band's history compiled in July 1937 records another trip two years later:

> In the year 1917 another committee was sent to Washington, with Chief Ottogary and Chief Annie Tommy, and Assistant Chiefs George P. Sam, Thomas Pabawena and James M. Pabawena. Chief Ottogary again presented the case to the Commission of Indian Affairs . . . but again no action resulted from said meeting.[21]

Clearly, Willie Ottogary was recognized as a leader of the Northwestern Shoshone by at least 1917. After he died, the tribal council signed "An Agreement or Certificate" noting Ottogary's past leadership and appointing his son Custer as new co-chief with Harry Dixon Tootiaina.[22] Since Harry D. Tootiaina was a member of the Western Shoshone, the two groups apparently had banded together to facilitate their hopes of improving conditions for their respective members.

The Shoshone nation was widespread. Reservations had been established in Nevada, Idaho, Utah, and Wyoming for various Shoshone groups. Since social boundaries between the bands were not firm, these areas were populated by blood relatives, and relations among the groups were typically friendly and cooperative. Ottogary's frequent travel to the various reservations and his published comments on each of them show his concern for Shoshone people everywhere.[23]

His political activism on behalf of pan-Shoshone rights got him into trouble with the law on at least one occasion. In 1918 he received word that the Selective Service Act was going to compel Native American men into military service during World War I. Ottogary and others organized a movement to resist the draft, which made many whites near the Goshute reservation at Deep Creek, on the border of central Utah and Nevada, nervous. The perceived Indian threat caused emotions to run high. Federal marshals were called in to arrest the leaders and put an end to the uprising. They arrested Annies Tommy and others at Deep Creek, but Ottogary had already returned home. After some difficulty, however, Deputy U.S. Marshal David Thomas found Ottogary at Tremonton, Utah, and arrested him.[24] Unfortunately, Box Elder County records and local newspapers do not mention whether he was tried, sentenced, or acquitted. Perhaps the arrest of Indians was more interesting news than their guilt or innocence.

Another important issue for Ottogary was the right of Indians to hunt wild game. In February 1925 he wrote that a game warden had arrested Tom Elk for killing deer. In the ensuing court case, the judge released Mr. Elk after hearing arguments based on treaty provisions that noted the right of Indians to hunt anytime of the year (see 1925-02-07 LJ). As a concerned and educated citizen, Ottogary would stand up for his rights. On one occasion he and a friend, George P. Sam, felt they were cheated in a business deal that involved some genealogical research they had done. Their employer refused to pay them for their services, so Ottogary took the issue to court and won.[25]

After his early visits to Washington, D.C., Ottogary made several follow-up trips. In March 1921 he attended President Harding's inauguration, visited with important congressmen, and, with other Indian delegates, voiced concerns over Indian rights (see 1921-03-22 LJ).[26] Land and treaty rights were Ottogary's constant message, especially to anyone in Washington who would listen. As a tribal advocate, he worked hard for recognition of the Northwestern Shoshone and redress of wrongs against them, but his hopes were not realized in his lifetime. One week before he died, his expectations for the establishment of a reservation in northern Utah ran high. In his letter to *The Journal* on March 7, 1929, he reported encouraging news that he had received from Utah senator William King. Ottogary interpreted the news to mean a reservation was coming for the Washakie Shoshone (see 1929-03-09 LJ). The bill in question was signed into law; however, it did not contain a provision for a new Northwestern Shoshone reservation as Ottogary had hoped.

Reporting difficulties with authorities played only a small part in Ottogary's writing. He also recorded and celebrated the many positive experiences he and his people had, such as those of the summer of 1925, which he spent entirely on the Wind River Shoshone reservation in Wyoming, reporting on noteworthy events—including the Sun Dance—visits with other Indians, hunting and fishing, and life in general there.

Ottogary's devout belief in Mormonism also brought him great hope. It has been noted that his father was a strong believer in Mormonism and in spiritual gifts. Willie's sister, Eliza, also had an affinity for the spiritual. When she was a young woman, she had a powerful supernatural experience. In her story, as related in later years by her husband, Ammon Pubigee, she "died" and visited the world of spirits. During her visit she saw God and Jesus Christ and was taught by them how she should live. She was then told to go back to earth.[27] The experiences of his father and sister undoubtedly influenced Ottogary's own testimony of Mormonism.

According to family records, George W. Hill baptized Willie Ottogary into the Mormon Church on August 1, 1875.[28] Unfortunately, an 1887 fire destroyed early records of the Washakie LDS organization.[29] Archival records of the Washakie church begin again in 1905. These documents note in many instances the Ottogary family's expressions of belief by bearing testimony. In the LDS faith,

Ammon Pubigee, *seated at left*, and Willie Ottogary, *standing at right*, before they set out on their mission to Deep Creek, or Ibapah. *Courtesy Mae Timbimboo Parry.*

individual members voice testimonies periodically in church services as prompted by the Spirit. Details of what the Ottogarys said are lacking, but it is recorded that family members bore testimonies often. For example, at the blessing (christening) of Chester Ottogary, Willie, his wife Nancy, his father and mother, and his sister and her husband all bore their testimonies.[30]

In 1907 Ottogary was ordained a seventy (a special missionary position) in the LDS higher priesthood. In the half-dozen years that followed, he went to the LDS Logan Temple and received the highest sacrament available to worthy members, temple marriage, or sealing.[31] All indications are that his belief in the Mormon Church was total. He was always willing to share his beliefs with others. In early 1913, he and a cousin, Charlie Broom, were called on an LDS stake (a Mormon ecclesiastical unit) mission. For two months the pair travelled the region and preached the gospel of Mormonism to fellow Shoshone. They had some success. Ottogary related that on one occasion they taught ninety-six people, who expressed an urgent desire to be baptized (see 1913-04-22 LJ).

In his later years Ottogary remained faithful, continuing to serve his church wherever he was called. Sometime before 1910 he transferred his membership to the Elwood Ward, to be closer to his home. A life-long resident of Elwood, Owen Rasmussen, remembers that "Bill," as he always called him, served as a doorkeeper for the ward. His jobs included greeting people, maintaining reverence, and controlling the temperature in the Elwood chapel. If it was too hot, he would use a long pole, with a hook on the end, to reach up and open the windows. Rasmussen remembered, as a young man, watching Ottogary use the pole to reach over the pews and awaken

Ammon Pubigee, *seated at left*, and Willie Ottogary, *standing at right*, ca. 1892. "Ammon first Sunday School superintendent of Washakie Ward. Willie Ottogary his secretary." This photograph appears to have been staged to illustrate Indians in traditional costume. *Courtesy Mae Timbimboo Parry.*

dozing members by tapping them on the head. He also recalled that certain members would avoid sitting on the same bench with the Indians to avoid sharing sacrament cups with them.[32] The racism of insensitive church members apparently did not shake Ottogary's beliefs. As a religious man, he also firmly believed in the virtues of honesty and moral integrity. At his death, it was remarked in the local paper: "Willie Ottogary was a clean living and honest Indian, his word was his bond, and was faithful and true to every trust and had gained the confidence and respect of all. . . . He was a member of the L. D. S. church and lived faithful to its teachings."[33]

Willie Ottogary was a complex individual. He loved life and drank deeply of its fullness. His own life seemed to be centered on others, and he demonstrated his concern for his people in most of his writings. Family stories also recall that concern: a grandnephew noted that at harvest time, Ottogary would load his buggy with melons and travel from his farm in Elwood to Washakie, where he would distribute them to family and friends.[34] Yet, he was also somewhat self-conscious. Living in two worlds was not easy for him, and on occasion he felt uneasy around whites, especially in awkward situations. He was concerned about how he was perceived by them, but he understood that whites generally held little esteem for Indians. One personal encounter with such prejudice occurred during a visit to Brigham Young College in downtown Logan, Utah, where he received a derisive welcome (see 1912-03-30 LJ). His columns demonstrate that while reporting such scornful reactions, he sought to improve white perceptions of Indians.

Now and then Ottogary expressed his pride quite spontaneously, even flamboyantly. On one occasion he and his wife were attending the Tremonton fair and

Looking northeast across the Bear River from the Ottogary homestead at Elwood,
Box Elder County, Utah, 1994. Wellsville Mountains in background. *Photo by
Matthew E. Kreitzer.*

he saw a chance to demonstrate his strength and possibly impress his wife as well.
A booth offered a prize to anyone who could bend an iron rod with their bare
hands. Ottogary jumped at the chance. He grabbed the rod and strained to bend
it. Feverishly he tugged and pulled without success. At the instant that failure was
evident, a young Indian from Washakie (who possibly was intoxicated) took the
rod and bent it double until it broke.[35] Ottogary, though, had given his best effort,
as he did with all of life, regardless of the risk of failure.

As a farmer, he reached a moderate level of success. After his father's death,
Willie and his two sons, for the most part, farmed the family homestead. Documents
from the divorce proceedings of Willie and Nancy record their jointly owned property as including "about ten head of horses, two wagons, two sets of harness, 3 mowing machines, one rack, one white top buggy . . . single buggy and plow and harrow
and other small farming implements."[36] Ottogary's farming income may not have
made him wealthy, but it provided the necessities for his family. There was also
enough left over to help fund his tribal business trips, which though they were
intended to benefit his people, were not always accepted by his spouse. He also grew
garden vegetables and willingly shared the produce with others.

In his columns he usually noted items of interest to farmers: the weather, new
equipment, the price of hay and grain, the availability of water, crop yields, and
so forth. In 1914, he attended and reported on the Utah Agricultural College's
yearly Agricultural Round-Up in Logan (see his *Journal* columns for late January
and early February 1914). The conference instructed farmers and students on the
latest innovations in agricultural science.

"Co Pe Ka - Alice? Williy Ottogary's first wife. Mother died when girls were young. Oldest 4 yrs. old. . . . Don Carlos Hootchew was married to this lady's sister." The two girls are probably Bertha, *left*, and Pearl (Pe way boo), on her mother's lap. The photo was probably taken in 1902. *Courtesy Mae Timbimboo Parry.*

Ottogary married twice. Both marriages ended unhappily. In the late 1800s he wed a young woman named Alice (known to her people as Pishey-boo-ey).[37] No legal records have been found, so the marriage presumably was according to traditional Shoshone custom. Two daughters, Bertha and Pearl, came from this union; both girls died in childhood. In November 1902 Alice also passed away.[38] Almost a year later, in October 1903, Ottogary married Nancy West.[39] Their first two children, Melton and Florence Christina, also died in childhood. The year 1908 brought good news: another child, Chester Ottogary, was born on January 30. Two years later another son, Custer, was born, and in 1912, a daughter, Louise. These three children all survived to maturity.[40]

Sometime in 1915 or 1916, however, marital dissatisfaction began to affect Nancy. One issue was her husband's trips. By November 1916 the marriage had dissolved. The divorce was a messy one that left deep emotional scars. Nancy received custody of their daughter, Louise, and moved to Idaho, although Louise spent much of her time living with an aunt in Elwood. Willie got custody of the two boys, Chester and Custer, and since Louise spent a lot of time nearby, the three children were rarely very far apart.

Willie was a loving father. The loss of several children and two wives certainly intensified his paternal feelings. He did his best as a single parent to young sons, taking them camping, fishing and hunting, and sometimes on tribal business trips. When they were young, he would toss them up on their horses, strap their feet together underneath so they would not fall off (a traditional horse-culture riding method), and walk them to school. Once at school, he would undo the strap, pull them down, and

Louise Ottogary, 1991, Fort Hall, Idaho.
Courtesy Stan Andersen.

hustle them off to class.[41] The three also worked together on the farm when Willie was not away on business. As his sons grew into young men, they took up boxing and became quite successful at it. Ottogary followed their fighting careers in his newspaper columns. His strong faith provided an example, and Chester, in his sixties, served a full-time mission for the LDS Church from 1971–1973.[42]

As a teenager, Louise was friendly and helpful. A neighbor boy, Stan Andersen, remembered that Louise taught him how to read. Each Sunday Stan would run over to the Ottogary home, where Louise would read him the comics in the Sunday *Denver Post*.[43] Louise matured, got married, and had several children of her own. For many years she passed on the family's oral traditions. She died in the fall of 1992.

Throughout the Bear River Valley of northern Utah, Ottogary was well known and respected. Upon hearing of his death, the Tremonton newspaper observed:

> not many Indians have held a place that Willie, as he was called by everyone, has held during his life time in the hearts of his people, as well as in the hearts of all the whites' who knew him. . . . This is the first death of so prominent an Indian in many years, and the community will miss Willie Ottogary.[44]

The legacy of Willie Ottogary might have been lost to history were it not for his work as a journalist. It was through the pen and/or the typewriter that Ottogary gained prominence. He had learned the English language early, and though he did not have a command of its mechanics, he composed enthusiastically. In the final analysis, he probably understood that the message was more important than the messenger's skill at presenting it. Why he wrote is not completely clear, but there are subtle clues in his letters and in other sources. The most compelling reasons seem to be that he enjoyed it, he received a wage for it, it offered a chance for a native voice to be heard, his columns helped maintain a good circulation base for the newspapers, and he was encouraged to write and record the social history of his people.

Ottogary's first column appeared in the August 23, 1906, edition of the *Tremont Times*. This paper originated from Tremonton, Utah, and its circulation covered much of the Bear River Valley. His first article in this paper covered topics such as the condition of his people, their crop harvesting, visiting Shoshone from Nevada, and the birth of his and Nancy's baby girl, Florence Christina (who died in February 1907). He continued writing for the *Tremont Times* until March 1908. Sometime between March 1908 and May 1909, Ottogary approached or was approached by the editor of *The Journal*, Logan, Utah. In the May 29, 1909, edition of that paper, his first article for Cache Valley readers appeared. Ottogary maintained correspondence to *The Journal* consistently until his death in March 1929.

From May 1911 through February 1923, Ottogary had sixty-two letters published in the *Box Elder News*. *The Journal* also published many of these letters, some simultaneously, with minor variations. During 1924 and 1925, Ottogary wrote, along with his Logan articles, columns in two other papers. From January to July of 1924, he wrote for the *Oneida County Enterprise*, Malad, Idaho, and from March to November of 1925, he contributed to the *Box Elder Journal*. Since all the letters maintain a consistent style, regardless of the newspaper, it is assumed they were published, for the most part, as he wrote them. His original manuscripts no longer exist for comparison.

Ottogary's writing style developed out of several key factors; first, his Shoshone culture and language, with its unique usage and structure; second, his education in the English language at the Washakie Day School; and, third, feedback he received from those who read his published letters and commented on them. He did not master written English, and his letters, though expressive, contain multiple problems with syntax, grammar, and other mechanics, to the extent that making sense of some sentences and phrases is difficult. One obvious, and clever, imperfection is his phonetic spelling of words he did not know. There are many examples in his letters, but one is his comment that a woman had injured her leg and "her was swollen offle [awfully] bad" (see 1914-07-14 LJ).

It is not clear whether Ottogary wrote the letters by hand or used a typewriter and, if the latter, whether typing introduced additional spelling and other typographical errors. Edlef Edlefsen, in the introduction to his pamphlet *Willie Ottogary's Letters to "The Journal" Logan, Utah*, suggested the letters were sent to the newspapers handwritten.[45] Clyde Ottogary, Willie's grandson, said he had been told that his grandfather had an office at Brigham City, Utah, where he typed the letters.[46] Other leads on the subject have proven inconclusive. It is possible that earlier letters were handwritten and later ones typed.

Ottogary's letters were similar to society page articles that reported "local happenings" in other Box Elder and Cache County communities. Just as other society correspondents wrote of community members' important events and accomplishments, of their trips, and of visits by important persons, so did Ottogary. He noted,

Washakie Shoshone planting sugar beets, 1903. *Special Collections & Archives, Merrill Library, Utah State University.*

among other things, the travels of Washakie people. A common line in his column took the form of "so-and-so motored down to such-and-such last week." Many of these excursions were shopping (or "chopping," as it was sometimes printed) trips. He also mentioned when visitors came to Washakie, who they were, from where they came, how long they stayed, and with whom they visited.

Agriculture was an important topic that recurred frequently in Ottogary's columns. Every letter mentioned something about it: planting, harvesting, sheep shearing, sugar beet topping, or marketing a commodity. He was attuned to the yearly agriculture cycle and covered each phase as it came around. He noted when Washakie residents hired themselves out as farm laborers (usually for work involving sugar beets). As Shoshone farm laborers came into the Washakie area from other regions, he noted who they were, where they were from, where they were staying, and for whom they were working. He also commented on the availability and productivity of land and detailed typical farming problems his people faced. These problems included high costs of necessary supplies, low produce prices, and pests such as crickets, sparrows, rabbits, and squirrels. The price of alfalfa hay was a particular concern to a small farmer whose sole power source was his team of horses. The county fair was another key event Ottogary covered. For example, in 1925 he reported that Washakie resident George P. Sam won first place for his oats at the Tremonton Fair (see 1925-10-03 LJ). Ottogary's running observations are a valuable

Shoshone tipis on a demonstration farm, 1903. *Special Collections & Archives, Merrill Library, Utah State University.*

historical record of Shoshone farming—an economy that they had only adopted in the previous few decades—and of northern Utah agriculture in general.

The topic of land occupied much of Ottogary's writing. He often expressed frustration with land-hungry whites. Some of them shrewdly took advantage of Shoshone who did not understand laws regarding land titles, deeds, transfers of property, wills, property taxes, heirship, and probate courts. Ottogary worked to correct these wrongs and wrote about his hopes of rectifying the problem by obtaining a reservation for the Northwestern Shoshone and their heirs.

Much of Ottogary's life was spent on the land. As a farmer he spent countless hours working the soil and tending crops, but he also took the time to appreciate nature. He enjoyed trips for outdoor recreation and commented on similar activities of others. Among other such activities, Ottogary indulged in and reported on camping, fishing, and pleasure rides.

Ottogary's letters must have appealed to a wide readership because some individuals used his column for free advertising. In 1916, F. F. Whitt asked Ottogary to include an advertisement notifying readers of the birth of twin sons (see 1916-09-12 LJ). On another occasion, Ottogary gladly supported his friend Benjamin Riter by urging readers to attend a big sale at Riter's store (see 1924-05-17 LJ). Ottogary also used his column to promote the activities of members of his own tribe. On one occasion he told of George P. Sam taking his grandson to Wyoming to get deer hides so

Sam's wife could make handmade gloves and then commented that she was especially skilled at glove making (see 1922-08-12 LJ).

Ottogary's coverage of events related to the LDS Church reflected his belief in Mormonism. He was aware of the church's role as a promoter of social events and wrote of the many activities held in the Washakie Ward meetinghouse. He reported church-sponsored dances, which usually were held each Friday night at the meetinghouse, as well as Christmas programs, New Year's Day celebrations, and George Washington's birthday observances held there. He mentioned when individuals traveled to Salt Lake City to attend the semi-annual LDS General Conference. Of special interest was an occasion when Washakie Indians participated in the general conference proceedings (see 1922-04-08 LJ). In 1928 he reported that a group of Washakie Indians had been invited to Logan to put on a special gospel-centered meeting (see 1928-04-04 LJ), urging readers for nearly a month to remember that the Shoshone were coming to town. The Indians wore traditional native dress for the meeting.

Expressions of Shoshone culture received consistent support in Ottogary's column, where he reported on them during the appropriate seasons in the traditional Shoshone annual cycle. Among these were ceremonies. Ottogary grew up in two cultural worlds and, while accepting Mormonism, retained an active interest in, and commitment to, traditional Shoshone religious ceremonies. He covered these events as they were held throughout the year. Conserving traditions filled a void in the lives of the Washakie Indians, a void created in part by attempts to deny them the opportunity to participate in customary activities. Dances especially seemed to be an important issue to the local LDS Church leadership. They thought it best for the Shoshone to forget old ways that might distract them from new Mormon spiritual standards. So, they did not allow the Washakie Shoshone to hold their traditional dances, though the Indians could and often did participate in white dances such as those held weekly at the LDS meetinghouse. The restriction did not stop the Shoshone from going elsewhere to celebrate with other Shoshone.

The most significant ceremonial activity that drew Ottogary's attention was the Sun Dance. The Sun Dance, as practiced by the Shoshone, blended aspects of Christianity with native songs, rhythms, and dance steps. The objective of the dancers was a communal blessing achieved through personal sacrifice. Each participant gave up food, sleep, and personal comforts in order to obtain blessings for everyone. For three days and nights the dancers performed. If a dancer desired and was rewarded, he received a vision or other personal gift or blessing.

Over the years, Ottogary reported on many Sun Dances. He traveled to where they were held, observed the proceedings, and commented on the events in his column. He reported on Sun Dances in Elko, Nevada; Fort Washakie, Wyoming; Fort Hall, Idaho; and the Uinta Basin in eastern Utah. At one Sun Dance, he noted, an admission fee was charged to onlookers (see 1923-09-15 LJ). The money was probably used to pay the drum group and singers and may also have helped cover travel expenses incurred by dancers. In another column he wrote that his nephew, Enos Pubigee, planned to attend two Sun Dances in the same summer (see 1923-09-15 LJ). In 1925, while attending a Sun Dance at Fort Washakie, Wyoming, he noted the number and variety of participants (one Ute, two

Bannock, and fifty-seven Shoshone), the varied white audience (some of whom had come from as far away as Chicago and New York), and even the prayer of invocation offered by a local white minister (see 1925-08-01 LJ). The Sun Dance ceremony fostered community and cultural identity among the Shoshone. It is still practiced by many Native American groups in the United States and remains a vital expression of culture.

References to other Indian dances and ceremonies appeared in Ottogary's columns. Apparently, "War Dances" were performed for the curiosity of whites. There are two reports in Ottogary's letters of War Dance performances that involved Washakie Indians; one occurred during a rodeo at Preston, Idaho (see 1922-09-08 LJ), and the other was part of Brigham City's Peach Days celebration (see 1926-09-04 LJ). He also mentioned the Warm Dance, Grass Dance, and other traditional dances. The first two were performed in relation to the weather. The Warm Dance was done during the cold winter months, usually January, to "ask the Maker for help . . . [regarding the weather] be lenient to the people." The Grass Dance was done in the spring, to seek divine intervention "to speed up nature so everything be good in summer, hurry things up."[47] Ottogary provided no details regarding how the other dances he mentioned were performed, by whom, and for what purpose. Because of the names he used for them, it is assumed they were traditional Shoshone dances and not of white origin.

Ottogary only mentioned traditional Shoshone medical practices in a few instances and provided very little detail. He mentioned that on two different occasions, individuals from Washakie traveled to hot springs to take "hot baths." In both accounts, the people went to the springs because they were ill. A few times, he referred to an "Indian doctor." It is not known whether this doctor was a Native American M.D. or someone who practiced traditional Shoshonean medicine, although the latter is more likely.

Shoshone marriages, before whites came, varied from group to group, but generally speaking, they were easily gotten into, easily dissolved, and required only the condition of conjugal living. However, they were an integral part of survival in the Great Basin, and the partners generally held equal status.[48] In 1924, Ottogary reported the marriage of Jim John Neaman and Emmaline Pabawena and noted they were married according to Indian custom (see 1924-07-05 LJ).

Of course, Ottogary also paid attention to many cultural activities that were not traditional among the Shoshone. While the Indians had their own customary games and physical contests, by the time Ottogary wrote, the young people at Washakie were involved in the athletic competitions of their white neighbors. The Washakie community organized a baseball team at an early date, and Ottogary noted where they played, how they fared, and highlights of each game. On one occasion, in a typical mix of personal and social information, he noted that the Washakie team lost, he had renewed an old acquaintance, and Willie Neaman had been injured by an errant baseball (see 1926-06-05 LJ).

Boxing had special significance for Ottogary, who covered it regularly. Several young men from Washakie, but especially his own sons, became quite well known in boxing associations throughout the region. As Chester ("Kickapoo Dan") and Custer ("General Custer") Ottogary gained fame, other Washakie boys took up the pugilistic art. Willie Ottogary reported their bouts, wins and losses, injuries, and training.

Another popular sporting event among the Shoshone was horse racing. Although this was a traditional activity for them, the rules, racetracks, and equipment used by the time Ottogary wrote came from the white world and were fairly new to the Shoshone of Washakie. They readily adapted though. Ottogary recorded that the young men involved prepared well. In 1926 they cleared some ground north of Washakie and built a racetrack on which to train their horses (see 1926-05-22 LJ).

The Shoshone participated in many activities that they had learned about from whites. As Ottogary reported, the Washakie Indians observed Independence Day, George Washington's Birthday, Thanksgiving, Christmas, and New Year's Day. Regional celebrations such as Pioneer Day (the July 24 holiday marking the arrival of the Mormon pioneers in the Salt Lake Valley in 1847) and Brigham City's Peach Days (a fall harvest celebration in Box Elder County) also drew his attention. In the early 1900s, the Washakie Indians typically were invited to participate in the Fourth and Twenty-Fourth of July parades in traditional dress. Ottogary did not publicly express any concern over this, although it put the Shoshone on exhibit. He seemed to feel these were positive experiences for his people.

The Shoshone of Washakie pursued many means of economic development, and Ottogary reported on the varied work of his people. Besides individually farming their own ground, the Shoshone labored in the sugar beet fields that supported the Garland sugar beet factory (see, for example, 1925-10-24 LJ). Ottogary himself participated in a variety of money-making activities aside from his farm, from journalism to selling Christmas trees (see 1928-12-26 LJ). Some of the Shoshone at Washakie sold cedar posts (see 1923-04-02 LJ), and some trapped coyotes for furs (see 1923-02-03 LJ). Others raised sheep or cattle. The younger generation found that there were ways to turn traditional hunting habits into contemporary cash. For centuries the Shoshone had hunted rabbits for meat and skins. When whites came, woven fabric blankets replaced traditional rabbit-skin robes for protection during cold weather. However, the arrival of whites attracted more rabbits. The rabbits were drawn to farms, where they could survive much easier than on the desert. Living off crops and spoiling haystacks, they were a nuisance. The Shoshone were adept at rabbit hunting, and their skill proved both a nutritional and economic boon for their community. In 1914, Box Elder County officials offered 5¢ a "scalp" (a revealing choice of words) for the hides (see 1914-01-01 LJ). This bounty had risen to 9¢ in 1928 (see 1928-12-26 LJ). Individuals earned good money driving and killing literally thousands of rabbits during the winter. Economic ventures, whatever their outcome, were primary subjects of Ottogary's journalism.

The people of Washakie experienced many of the same health problems that beset other Americans but often to a greater degree because of low immunity, genetic factors, living conditions, and inadequate or unavailable health care. Whenever someone was ill, Ottogary reported it. He noted specifically the following ailments, many of which were more common in American Indian communities than in the general population: consumption, kidney trouble, appendicitis, stomach ulcers, alcoholism, eye problems, and smallpox. With regard to eye problems, which like-ly included glaucoma, he mentioned that at least in one case, the cure did more damage than the disease (see 1914-06-09 LJ).

Ottogary also covered births, marriages, and deaths. He was closely involved in the life-cycle events of his people and noted them as they occurred. Sometimes he reported tragedies, as in 1924 when he announced that after a recent birth, both mother and infant died from associated complications (see 1924-11-08 LJ). Accounts of a variety of accidents—shootings, wagon wrecks, train wrecks, auto crashes, and injuries resulting from farm machinery—made their way into Ottogary's columns. The resident whites at Washakie tutored the Indians in the use of farm machinery, but such accidents were a leading cause of work-related injuries throughout the nation.

New technology sometimes came to Washakie without warning, as in Ottogary's report of an airplane flying over the community (see 1916-10-10 LJ and 1922-05-27 LJ). He also noted the influx of automobiles, which brought a new set of problems for Washakie residents. For example, in February of 1924, Ottogary recorded that John Johny had recently purchased a used car but had burned its engine up after running out of oil (see 1924-02-23 LJ).

Technological advances engendered awkward and appealing new experiences, as when Ottogary in 1912 reported that while seeing their first motion picture, he and Nancy both succumbed to fits of uncontrollable laughter. Ottogary claimed embarrassment that he couldn't stop "my ugly laugh," but said he liked "very much to see them kind show" (see 1912-03-21-B LJ). Ottogary also marveled at the new automatic printing press that was purchased by *The Journal* in February 1928 (see 1928-02-11 LJ).

Over the course of nearly a quarter-century, from 1906 to 1929, Willie Ottogary faithfully covered, in over 450 letters, the entire breadth and depth of Shoshone experience as he saw it unfold. He was a complex man whose heritage was extreme-ly important to him. A man of integrity and an effective leader who worked dili-gently on behalf of his people, he demonstrated courage in exercising civil disobedi-ence on their behalf. A responsible husband and devoted father, he was also a suc-cessful farmer and journalist. As a community member he was well known and respected by his Indian and non-Indian contemporaries. His father's acceptance of Mormonism encouraged him to follow the same path. The LDS faith remained a vital force throughout his life and he believed strongly in its precepts. Though his journalistic style may have been awkward, his historical contribution through it was profound and unparalleled. No other record exists that better illustrates the Northwestern Shoshone world during this period. Ottogary's record stands alone as a powerful witness to Northwestern Shoshone life at a critical juncture.

Editorial Method

Ottogary wrote over 450 letters, and many contain difficult passages, awkward sentences, misspellings, ambiguous meanings, and other problems. The editor has carefully studied each letter to ensure that Ottogary's voice, texts, and subtexts remain intact. Those included in this collection have human interest appeal, relate specific information regarding the Northwestern Shoshone or other Shoshone bands, illustrate Indian-white or Indian-Indian relations, discuss both traditional and transitional lifeways, or provide insight into Willie Ottogary.

The editor's overriding goal has been to present as complete a collection of Ottogary letters as feasible with judicious editing, to maintain consistency and continuity throughout the letters, and to maintain Ottogary's *voice* as reflected through his writing style. Annotations have been limited to significant items, and redundant or obscure passages have been eliminated (and marked with ellipses). Brackets have been used to clarify difficult text. Ottogary's common threads are included, for example, life-cycle events, church, agriculture, weather (when it relates to such topics as agriculture or social activities), comings and goings of Shoshoneans (except shopping and business trips that do not include other significant information). Each letter reproduced in this volume meets the above criteria.

Most letters have been transcribed from microfilm copies of the newspapers in which they appear. The originals no longer exist. Microfilm is an imperfect medium and is sometimes impossible to read. Several important letters have been excluded because of poor reproduction on film. Words or sentences that are unclear or obscured are indicated with the word *indecipherable* in square brackets.

The full title of publishing newspapers and the place and date of publication are shown only with the first letter from that newspaper. Thereafter, this information appears at the end of the letter and is abbreviated in a year-month-day title form. For example, the letter published April 4, 1916 in *The Journal* (Logan, Utah) is identified as 1912-04-16 LJ. To maintain chronological order, dates letters were written govern their placement in this text. For example, 1912-04-04 LJ was written by Ottogary on April 2,1912, while 1912-04-06 LJ was written March 30, 1912. Since the March 30,1912, letter was written first, it appears first in the text. Chapters are also organized by the dates letters were written, so a letter written in December but published the following January will appear in the chapter for the year in which December falls. Column headings, which were inconsistently used in the newspapers, have been included here only at their first appearance or if they are unique. The original letters sometimes did not begin with place names. In those cases, Washakie has been added as the typical locale of the letters.

Sometimes, identical letters were published in different newspapers. Only one has been included here. Letters excluded due to illegibility, duplication, or for other reasons have been identified and explained, for example, "1917-06-22 BEN [Not included, duplicate of 1917-06-22 LJ]." On occasion, information from a deleted letter has been used to clarify the letter included here. For example, 1912-01-30 LJ mentions George P. Lame, while 1912-02-01 BEN calls him Geo. Psam. The data from both was combined and "George P. Sam" was included in the text.

Other alterations made in the text for the purpose of clarity include the following:

* Obviously misspelled words that would be confusing to readers have been silently corrected (for example, "jsut" has been changed to "just," and "ect" to "etc"), except when changing misspelled words would dramatically alter Ottogary's style or voice. Square brackets, [ ], have been used to correct

spelling of words that, in context, show something of Ottogary's writing style (examples are such phonetic spellings as "postpond" [postponed], or "all raddy" [already]). Proper names have been standardized to those used most consistently by Ottogary, preferred spellings of families, or spellings used by living descendants (see the Biographical Register for variant spellings). Also, pronouns and possessives have been silently corrected where appropriate, for example, "there" has been changed to "their."

* If two words should have been separated by a space, the space was added.

* Capitalization errors have been corrected with caution and moderation.

* Abbreviations used by Ottogary appear as published, for example, yr. (year), wk. (week), Geo. (George), Bp. (Bishop), N. (new, see 1914-01-15 BEN), Supt. (Superintendent), doz. (dozen), pres. (president), &c (etc.).

* Ottogary sometimes used *but* and *and* interchangeably. *But* was often used when *and* would have been more appropriate. The correct word was added in brackets [ ] for several occurrences. After this, it is assumed the reader will become accustomed to the nonstandard usage, and therefore, the bracketed word has been omitted.

* Duplicated words such as "home home" (found in 1907-07-13 BEN) have been deleted.

* Erroneous dates have been corrected; e.g., 1911-01-11 BEN, was corrected to 1912-01-11 BEN. The error was probably due to an oversight by the paper's typesetting crew.

* "Winter River Reservation" was changed to reflect the accurate location of the "Wind River Reservation [WY]."

* Grammatical errors, such as agreement in number, have been corrected for clarity, according to current usage.

* Tense agreement corrections have been kept to a minimum.

* Some punctuation has been added or changed for the purpose of clarity.

* Celebrations, e.g., Washington's Birthday, typically followed a set agenda. (The program began at ten o'clock and consisted of select readings, comic speeches, recitations, songs, etc. These were followed by a dinner and a children's dance. Later in the evening a grand ball was held.) Hence, many of the successive references to these kinds of celebrations have been omitted due to space considerations.

* A few sentences have been reconstructed for clarity. Care has been taken to ensure the meaning was not altered.

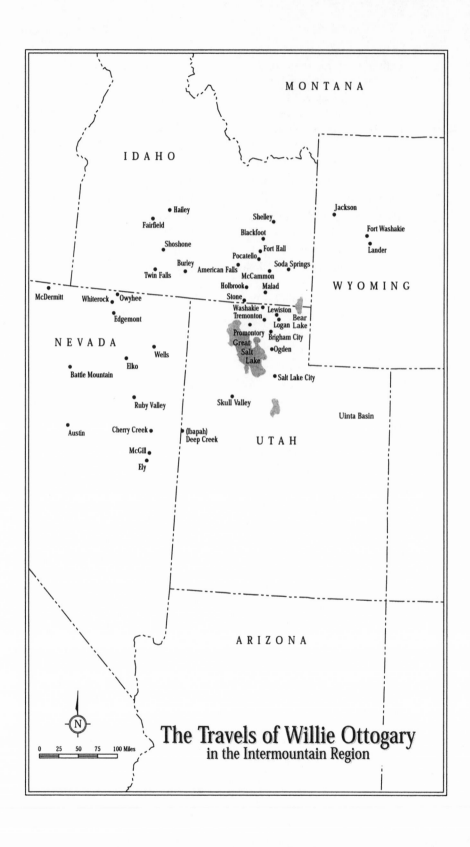

MONTANA

IDAHO

Hailey

Fairfield

Shelley

Blackfoot

Jackson

Fort Washakie

Shoshone

Fort Hall

Lander

Pocatello

Burley

American Falls

Soda Springs

Twin Falls

McCammon

WYOMING

Holbrook

Malad

Stone

McDermitt

Whiterock

Owyhee

Washakie

Tremonton

Lewiston

Bear

Lake

Edgemont

Logan

NEVADA

Wells

Promontory

Great

Salt

Lake

Brigham City

Ogden

Elko

Battle Mountain

Salt Lake City

Ruby Valley

Skull Valley

Uinta Basin

Austin

Cherry Creek

(Ibapah)

Deep Creek

UTAH

McGill

Ely

ARIZONA

N

0   25   50   75   100 Miles

The Travels of Willie Ottogary
in the Intermountain Region

1

"I Will Write a Few Line," 1906–1910

Tremont Times[1]
Tremonton, Box Elder County, Utah, August 23, 1906.
WASHAKIE, UTAH, AUGUST 20, 1906.
   Mr. Sherman,[2]
   Dear Sir.—
   I will write a few line, But I not to much writing for them because I am so busy to write one story.
   Well we have good condition so far. No one sick.
   Our harvesting is over last week, and soon start up threshing probably next week some time.
   Mr. James Joshua and Company was come last week. I hope they will soon start up threshing their grain.
   Two family from Nevada visiting our town last week.
   Mr. James Brown and Peter Haws went out Nevada to visit their friends and relatives.
   But [and][3] Mr. Willie Ottogary and wife were born nice little girl baby [Florence Christina Ottogary b. 14 Aug. 1906] in their place in Elwood, last Tuesday about 12:30 A.M. Her mother is doing very nicely.
   Beet crop are very splendid, this year. I expect there average 15 ton to acres.
   And our second of hay been mowed down last week. It is all get wet and spoiled through this rain.
   Our people are very busy in harvesting the grain.
      Willie Ottogary.[4]
   [1906-08-23 TT]

WASHAKIE, AUGUST 1906   I am write a few words for Times.
   But we bad weather last couple weeks. Cause many damages. Spoil hay out in field, and wheat stacks spoil too. It is start to growing now. We was get our stack clear open up last week and seem to be drying very slowly. We heard machine hum today. It would be long to thresh our wheat. We have two machine up here now starting in same day. I hope we will have a good [harvest] after all. . . .
   Our baseball player want going out Nevada to play ball out there with Indian boys. I hope they have good time out there.
   They start out tomorrow morning, 7 o'clock train.
   Our [People] are doing nicely so far nobody sick. . . . [1906-08-30 TT]

Threshing scene, ca. 1904, in western Box Elder County. *Special Collections &*
Archives, Merrill Library, Utah State University.

WASHAKIE, SEPTEMBER 17, 1906.   Well news from our town. I am sorry didn't write
for the Times about three weeks, but I am try to give the news to-day.

We are all well up here. I was up Washakie Sunday and find all Indians living
alright.[5] No one sick.

Some of them went out west to get some pine nuts. They may come back next
week some time.

Threshing are pretty near through up here. This rain hold it back and one new
machine is break down. I hope they run this week. . . .

One Indian here from Pocatello visiting friend.

The sugar beet crop very splendid this year.

I will tell another story. We been out Nevada country. We take train from
Ogden to Deeth [NV] then we take team from Deeth to Ruby Valley [NV].[6] It take
us travel about one day and a half to get there.

We didn't play ball there, because they think us to much for them, but bluff out
I think. Over two hundred Indians there having good time fandango.[7] We few
Indians out there and they treat us alright. No sick, all come safe only three or four
[remain], they come home soon, before beet digging time. [1906-09-20 TT]

WASHAKIE, OCTOBER 9, 1906.   I will write a few words for Tremont Time tonight.
But we are very busy time after harvest time over and some of us working on sugar

A postcard showing, *left*, Frank Brain from Nevada, who died of smallpox in 1905, and, *right*, Soquitch Timbimboo, uncle of Moroni Timbimboo and son of Chief Sagwitch. *Courtesy Mae Timbimboo Parry.*

Twenge, or Towange, Timbimboo, wife of Soquitch Timbimboo. *Special Collections & Archives, Merrill Library, Utah State University.*

beet around Fielding, Riverside and Garland. Only few Indians are here . . . old age they don't [work] on beet.

There was a Jack Frost been up here about week or two ago sweep everything here. Well everybody getting alright no one sick lately.

I supposed some will be dig beet up here some next Week.

Some Indians from Fort Hall Reservation were here working on sugar beets and also some from Nevada.

Mr. James Brown was in our town two weeks ago.

Well I was so busy could not right [write] for many week. I suppose people thinks I am neglect to write [if] one feel like so excuse me. [1906-10-10 TT]

WASHAKIE, DECEMBER 3, 1905.   I am going to write a few word for Tremont Time. I didn't write a quite while. I suppose am going tell story this. But our people all well up here. No one sick since two little boys died and all people coming back from work. There some loading car to-day with wheat. Mr. C. W. Hall from Portage here buy grain.[8]

Mr. Jacob Bronies was visiting his friend in our town. I expect he going back some time this month from Banna [Bannock] Creek. Our business are good this year. There was about six car loads beets shipped out here and day school is running pretty nicely so far.[9] [1906-12-06 TT]

WASHAKIE, JANUARY 7, 1907.   We are all well living up here to this small town and no one sick. There was a death, a man from Pocatello, Idaho, about two weeks last Friday and nobody sick but Mr. Soquitch Timbimboo is kind of sick.

William and Julia Hootchew. *Courtesy Mae Timbimboo Parry.*

Left to right: Phoebe (infant secured in cradleboard); Twenge, or Towange, Timbimboo (mother of the children); Zu du pa chee (Good Pine Nuts); and Goo seep (Ashes). Soquitch Timbimboo was the father of the children. The couple also had twins. *Courtesy Mae Timbimboo Parry.*

Phoebe Timbimboo, born 1887, daughter of Towange and Soquitch Timbimboo, Washakie, Utah. Phoebe died about 1900. *Courtesy Mae Timbimboo Parry.*

We had big rabbit hunt last Friday and in evening the ball was given by the hunters.[10] We had very enjoyable time I heard we have another hunt next week some time.

Oh, lovely snow, we have had long time. It snowed about one foot and a half.

Our day school start up this morning.

Mr. William Hootchew and wife been up Ross Fork [Fort Hall Reservation], Idaho, returned home last Friday.

I and wife been up to Blackfoot visiting friends and relatives on Christmas, too. We returned home New Year's day. But [And] we had good time up there, too. [1907-01-10 TT]

Washakie Whisperings

WASHAKIE, JANUARY 1907.   I haven't written for several weeks, but will drop you a few lines today.

We are having a good lot of snow this winter. It has been about 18 inches deep, but the warm weather today is settling it quite fast. The people are rejoicing over so much snow this year and having good sleigh rides.

No one sick here since Mr. Wren Soquitch died.

A girl baby was born a few days ago to Moroni and Phoebe Timbimboo, who were married last summer.[11] Mother and baby are doing splendid.

Hay is pretty high this year. It sells for $5.00 a ton. We did not raise good hay like it used to be. It was mixed with June grass.

Some people may think I am not a good correspondent but I want help to make the Times a good paper. [1907-01-31 TT]

Washakie Waftings

WASHAKIE, FEBRUARY 1907.   We have had no sickness here for a time.

Some of the Indians think that spring has come but they are mistaken. The snow all went off last week and the roads are now impassible to travel through with heavy loads because of the mud.

We have had fine weather for two or three days. We had about a foot and a half of snow this year but I hope we may have more later on. . . .

We have had good luck so far this year, nobody sick and our stock is doing nicely.

I think we shall have good crops this year on account of so much wet. [1907-02-14 TT]

WASHAKIE, MARCH 1907.   Well I want to write a very small news. We had cold weather, snow and rain up here. . . . The road is muddy to travel through.

One young lady died here last Thursday and her funeral services were held at their home on Friday morning at 10 A.M. She died of consumption and was ill about two years. The deceased was 18 years old and was born in this town in the year 1889.

Two of our men went down to Garland today. Their names was Mr. Lewis Corsium, and Dick Arritch, and returned home on train No. 31. Also Mrs. Tyboatz went down to Ogden. Her mother was staying there about a month and a half. She might come back home some time next week.

Washakie Indians touring Salt Lake City, Utah, probably while attending the LDS General Conference. *Left to right:* Yeager Timbimboo, tour guide (standing), Yampatch Wongan Timbimboo, Positz Noragan, Towange Timbimboo, Joseph Paniboo (Bumble Bee Eyes), Willie Ottogary, Kip Noragan, Minnie Zundel, Phebe Tyboats, Lucy Z. Alex. *Courtesy Mae Timbimboo Parry.*

Mrs. Pubigee is pretty sick last week. She is little better this morning. They been seen Dr. Francke last Saturday for treatment. . . .

Some of our people was in attendance our Stake conference at Malad last Sunday and Saturday. There was quite many people at conference from the surrounding country. I expect over 600 people were there. [1907-03-28 TT]

Washakie, March 1907.   I write very short story but we are all well up here. The road little bit drier last week, and we have quite a shower last night. This makes mud this morning or today.

Mr. and Mrs. Geo. M. Ward having born pretty little boy baby last Friday morning about 4 o'clock. His mother is doing very nicely.

Some of our people going down to Salt Lake City to conference on April 6th.

Seems to me we could farm if the weather keep up like this, and fall crops are coming fine.

The boys have played baseball with West Portage boys, and beat them last Saturday. I hope they will play again some time this week.

Well, Mrs. Pubigee getting very nicely so far. I hope she gets all right again soon when this weather gets warmer.

Mr. Kippetchew Noragan has been built a nice chicken coop last week some time. [1907-04-04 TT]

Left to right: Ono Johnny, Moroni Timbimboo, and George Peyope, 1898, Ogden, Utah. Note on photo reads: "Ono Johnny is Amy Timbimboo step father very good father to her." *Courtesy Mae Timbimboo Parry.*

WASHAKIE, APRIL 23, 1907.   But I am going write a short story. The Indians are all well up here and they begin start spring work and some of them are hunting wood out in the country some where.[12] We are already putting in our sugar beets. . . . I hope we are going to raise a good crop this year so much wet weather, and quite a shower last night.

Mr. James Brown went out to Nevada again about last week ago, and his son went with him.

Some of our Indian women went down to Ogden last week. . . .

Mrs. Soquitch Timbimboo feels sor[ry] because one of their relatives died up on the Snake River about three weeks ago.

Mr. Owen Davis was seen in Washakie last Sunday on a business trip.

The road is in good condition so far. Some herds of sheep went through our town two or three times this spring now.

Our day school will be out next Friday afternoon, and they will carry out programme. I heard of it. [1907-04-25 TT]

WASHAKIE, MAY 1907.   . . . The people are getting through their spring work already now. . . . We are all well, no one been sick.

Mr. George Peyope went up on the reservation a few days ago to visit his friends and relatives too, and Mr. and Mrs. Soquitch Timbimboo went up to Pocatello this morning to visit their friends.

We had pretty good weather last week and I hope spring is coming. Our people are rejoicing about weather.

Left to right: George Peyope, Ren Hootchew, and Ono Johnny. *Courtesy Mae Timbimboo Parry.*

Mr. James Brown return home from Ogden last week and some more other Indians.

I am so busy I could not write for the Times last week. All my farm [work] done so far. [1907-05-09 TT]

WASHAKIE, MAY 1907   We are all well and our fall crops looking fine. . . . But people are rejoicing about that wet weather we had last week.

Mr. Pubigee and wife been up on Snake River last week and returned last Tuesday.

Mr. Ottogary and son had pleasure trip on Bannock Creek last week to visit relatives and friends. They had very splendid good time up there. . . .

Mr. James McCaskey and his wife visited Mr. Willie Ottogary's place near Elwood town. I hope he will went last part of June. They was up on Nevada.

There are five teams went down to Ogden to-day on business down there.

Our sugar beets are in bad condition on account of so much fleas and eat the tops of beets. I hope we have good crop this year. Our ditch work [cleaning irrigation ditches] will be done some time this week. No one sick so far. [1907-05-30 TT]

Washakie News

WASHAKIE, JUNE 4, 1907.   . . . But our people are rejoicing on the crops and many other things. Some of the men are at work upon the water ditch. They going to have a grand ball up here next Friday night. I hope we have a good old time. Some of the boys are a shearing wool above this town at the mouth of the Canyon. Well, Bishop George M. Ward had some of women thinning his sugar beets.[13] I hope they done this week. No one sick so far. Many of the people are passing through our town every day. [1907-06-06 TT]

WASHAKIE, JUNE 10, 1907.   We all well up here in usual condition. I hope we had good crop this year had so much wet so far. Some Indians are thinning down Garland and east of Tremonton. I hope they are making money. Well seem to me we had bad weather so much wet and mud. But our people are rejoiced over the rain we had last week. Some of the sheep men loading their wool in this station. Mr. James McCaskey and wife are visiting Mr. W. Ottogary place in Elwood. They helped him thin his beets. Mr. McCaskey is from Owyhee, Nevada. His one-year-old boy is sick on account being get wet out in the rain. I hope he will soon over it. They have been see Dr. Francke at Garland to-day. He say he had a little fever. He is doing pretty well today. They want went home last this part month. He was very surprised seeing our country. [1907-06-13 TT]

WASHAKIE, JULY 1907.   Well no much news here today but our stake are going excursion on July 17 to Lagoon [amusement park near Farmington, UT]. It till be tomorrow morning. I hope the people having a good times down there, and also our beet crops are looking very splendid this year. We have watering this week. It seems to me we have good crop again. Our people spent the 4th of July down at Garland and have good time they say. We will celebrate 24 here in our town the arrangements made already.

Mr. Pubigee and wife and also Mr. Ottogary and wife was on sport on Blacksmith Fork canyon three days last week.

Mrs. Kate Pabawena lost her son boy last week some time. He was a year and a half old.

Last Saturday there was wrestling match in Garland between one Indian from our town and the butcher in Garland. They claim he was best man in town, but Indian got the prize. It was witnessed by over 200 people.

I heard the son of chief will be here in our town on 24th to visit his friends and relatives, but he will return home after 24th. His home is upon Wind River Reservation. I hope he will have a good time. [1907-07-18 TT]

WASHAKIE, JULY 29, 1907.   But I am kind very slow on the paper seems to me, and I was so busy last week didn't have time to write one. . . . We had splendid time on 24th of July in our town, and we had a big dinner under big bowery by the Districk school building. Many of our people rejoice over the day. Some of our folks been down Hooper, Utah, to celebrate the 24th down with white people.

Mr. Ed. William was seen in our town last Sunday looking for a header.[14] One of our men promised to come to his place near Malad. Four boys are going up to Samaria [ID] to work. They did not have water enough to raise big crop beet. It seem to me water scarce up here.

We have so many grasshopper here in our field. I don't think we raise second crop lucern [alfalfa hay] on account being so many hoppers. It seems they eating everything up. [1907-08-01 TT]

WASHAKIE, AUGUST 1907.   Well we are getting all right now so far. Our harvesting nearly all done and soon thresh, maybe next week some time.[15] Mr. James Joshua and company have taken their horse power up to Malad blacksmith shop to repair on it. I hope they get it next week some time then start to thresh. Well, our grain crop harvest splendid this year and sugar beet crop good this year. Some hauling second crop hay last week. It seems to me kind light crop on account being so many grasshoppers. Some say they eat everything round there. I hope they are not bad next year.

I am working on a header up Washakie around there. I hope we will get through next week some time. But I am sorry I didn't write for couple weeks. Excuse me. [1907-08-22 TT]

WASHAKIE, SEPTEMBER 1907.   But our threshing is done all last week and we start on our fall crop in.[16] Mr. C. W. Hall and Mr. R. Harris loaded two cars last week with wheat.

Our beets looking very nice so far I hope we have good crop this year.

Mr. George Tospanguitch and James Brown been up Fort Hall Reservation about two weeks ago. Mr. Tospanguitch was return home last week and James Brown is working [for] a man up there, he has not come back yet. . . .

We all well no one sick so far. [1907-09-12 TT]

WASHAKIE, SEPTEMBER 16, 1907.   Our threshing all over. . . .

Some of our women went after some peaches last week, perhaps they might get some all they wanted now. There is about two or three teams went next week.

Some of the boys went down to Toeth [Deeth] Nevada, last week. Some of Indians going have a big time in dance or fandango down there. They see the old times. I hope they have good time while they are out.

There are couple boys from Pocatello in town to visit a few days. . . .

Mr. Lewis Corsium and Newman [Neaman] and Soquitch Timbimboo bought a new drill last week. [1907-09-19 TT]

Willie Ottogary's Washakie News

WASHAKIE, NOVEMBER 19, 1907.   Well all our sugar beets harvest all over last two week ago here. It is pretty big than last year. We are paid for last week. It is cold weather here in our little town.

One old man died week. He was about 60 years of age.

All the Indians are working on sugar beets are return home at last.[17] But some of the Indians are here now from Fort Hall Reservation. They want going home after all paid for their work. Perhaps they may going next week.

One Indian boy in jail for drinking whisky in Garland. His name was Johnny Puape and be from Fort Hall Reservation. He is been release last week and working for W. A. Adams near Sunset school house.

Charlie Broom is in jail for same condition.

Seem to me we had early cold this year. We had freeze night and warm day.

Well, all our people all well, no one sick. . . .

Willie Ottogary,
A Shoshone Indian. [1907-11-21 TT]

WASHAKIE, NOVEMBER 25, 1907.   The people are getting all well so far and fall working all through.

But Mr. Ammon and wife Pubigee went up on Ft. Hall Reservation to visit his
relatives. . . . Indians from Idaho all went back last week. Mr. Frank and Grouse
Creek Jack and their wives camping near Garland factory. He was working on
sugar beets. . . . [1907-11-28 TT]

WASHAKIE, FEBRUARY 1, 1908.   I am going a few stories. But we are very well and two
or three of them was sick in our town, expect they will get well.

Another day they was one man came here from Urmetella [Umatilla], Oregon.
He stayed with Mr. Charlie Broom's family, he expect went back home in spring
some time. . . .

Well was big rabbit hunt about couple weeks ago, South end town have the
prize, in the evening we dance and enjoyed very much.

I and Mr. Ammon Pubigee been down Elwood my place last week, after two
loads of hay, we had on near 3 or 3½ tons or some[where] long there, but come
home all right and safety.

There was 4 Indian from Wells [NV] here yet.

Mrs. and Mr. Nephi Zundel was born twin babies on Christmas night, one was
baby girl and another boy baby, mother and babies are doing all right.

Mr. Charlie Broom digging his well front his house.

Some of the Indians getting out some posts now.

I was been Holbrook, Idaho to on business trip up there. But the people was sick
on measles. We didn't haven't any such disease. [1908-02-06-A TT][18]

WASHAKIE, FEBRUARY 3, 1908.   . . . Mrs. Geo. P. Sam went down on train this
morning.

Mr. James Brown and his company camping out North the town after some
posts, about eight miles north from here.

Sam and wife was born a boy baby last week. But she doing all right and child
too.

Mr. Charlie Broom finished his well last week.

Mr. Bill Moemberg was very sick, his suffer been sick about 3 months, we don't
think he able lived.

Mrs. Woonsook is get well, she was sick. . . . [1908-02-06-B TT]

WASHAKIE, MARCH 10, 1908.   Well I am sorry that write for long time and I am a
few stories. The Indians getting all right so far. . . .

We had spring coming now, the snow all gone the valley.

Some of Indians made beet contract already, they are very anxious raising sugar
beets this year. . . .[19]

Washakie boys play baseball up to Portage last Saturday they got beat, the score
was 6 to 14 in favor of Portage, they want play next Friday afternoon about 2
o'clock. [1908-03-11 TT]

Indian women and children with 101 Ranch Wild West Show. *From* The Journal, *Logan,*
May 7, 1912.

The Journal[20]
Logan City, Utah, Saturday, May 29, 1909
Over in Washakie—Notes From The Journal's Indian Correspondent
WASHAKIE, MAY 20, 1909.   And we are all well, no one sick. There no death took
place, but one child died here about two weeks ago. Some Indians are been down
Tremonton see shows [Wild West type shows] last Tuesday. They went home all
next day. They make friend with the Sioux Indians and Cheyenne Indians too.
    These Indians with a show. After the big show over they have a real good time
about one hour in dancing. They are acquainted with many of our Indians.[21]
    Our crops are looking very splendid after the good shower and our sugar beet
crop didn't come very well.
    But day school stopped for summer.
    We soon start thinning beet pretty soon now.
    The baseball team played up to Malad last week ago.
    The hay pretty scarce here in town.
    We are working on ditch this week and have soon water in.
    Mr. Jim Jack boy baby born last week [Gilbert Jack], but his mother doing all right.
    Mr. George Tospanguitch been up Malad with his folks last week. But he return
home some time ago. [1909-05-29 LJ]

Shoshone encampment on Logan Tabernacle grounds, May 1909. *Special Collections & Archives, Merrill Library, Utah State University.*

Shoshone Indians in Semi-Centennial parade, Logan, Utah, May 1909. *Special Collections & Archives, Merrill Library, Utah State University.*

Yeager Timbimboo, son of Chief Sagwitch. *Special Collections & Archives, Merrill Library, Utah State University.*

Yampatch Timbimboo, wife of Yeager Timbimboo. *Special Collections & Archives, Merrill Library, Utah State University.*

WASHAKIE, JUNE 1909.   Last weeks I was been up through Idaho with brother-in-law [Ammon Pubigee] too. We had fine trip then—been Soda Springs. Some are start thinning beets this week, but soon will all thin. Well, seemed spring late so any thing is very slow growing.

Our day school is stopped for the summer season. Mr. Jim Joshua's wife is get-ting little better; perhaps she might get all right after while.

Some the Indian boys are shearing sheep in Big Canyon. They might soon through with job. Mr. Charlie Broom and Sam Jack with father hauling wood from shearing pen. I hope they making money.

The people all well over here, but Bishop George Ward lost his boy one or two years old, from accidentally taking poison. Wool buyer was here last week, load wool here. There were three carloads wool here last week. Mr. Soquitch and fam-ily are went away from home. They might come back some time this coming week. [1909-06-15 LJ]

From Our Indian Correspondent

WASHAKIE, JULY 12, 1909.   I am going to write to Logan Journal but I am sorrow didn't write quite while and our crops are looking very well perhaps we have splendid good crops. Mr. Yeager Timbimboo lost his boy last week ago he took sick last April. But he had consumption. Some of Indians are been up Pocatello, Idaho on 4th July I am been out Skull valley 4th July But I am very enjoy my trip out there and acquainted some of Islanders out there and few our people too.[22] Mr. Grouse Creek Jack was gone out for Deep Creek and he may return home some time this summer Mr. Charlie Broom was accompany him. Our baseball team go down Hooper tomorrow 23, and played there. But had't played since we played at Logan. [1909-07-27 LJ]

Washakie Notes

WASHAKIE, SEPTEMBER 17, 1909.   Editor Journal: I am going write for short time. But our grain very fine; we was threshing two week ago, but sell all the grain as soon as threshed and load two or three carloads here in our town. But our beet crop is looking very splendid. Some of the Indians been down Brigham City on Peach Day on 15.[23] They was all return home; some of Indians been from Wind River Reservation; they all return home and we have a new motor car through the valley some of our people didn't like this car. and they say it is too small for the people. [1909-09-21 LJ]

Doings at Washakie: Our Indian Correspondent Sends Us The News

WASHAKIE, NOVEMBER 15, 1909.   I am going write to Journal this time. But our beet crop all nearly harvested now and some of them going to 20 tons per acre. But some of the Indians been here a topping sugar beet and we had snow last Saturday night. We good weather today. . . .

Mr. Peter Ottogary was died last week in ripen age, about [probably 9]0 years old perhaps more so. His funeral service held in our meet [meeting] house on Thursday afternoon. . . .

Mr. Nephi Zundel is laid up for ever and other things. Perhaps he may die or not. They send for Doctor to Garland yesterday. But some of others sick too. We buried about 3 or 4 more last month, and hoping we have good weather again. [1909-11-20 LJ]

Washakie Doings

WASHAKIE, JANUARY 19, 1910.   I am going to write Journal today. But they over here are doing all right and we had good time last Friday had grand ball and picnic at night 10 o'clock. We have good sleighing over this away . . . we may have more snow after while. No one sick now they are all good condition. Well, our day school very well. It is very cold in few week ago. Some of people say the weather get warmer after while. I was in Logan last week in business trip and It is very well trip perhaps and I acquainted many people over there to Logan.

I was been in Logan Journal office while I am over and looking back where they printing paper, I am very surprise to see this machine [printing press] I never see one before my life.

But am living on my place at Elwood and have a company with me now. Mr. Soquitch and wife too. There will be another dance here at Washakie on Friday night. [1910-01-22 LJ]

WASHAKIE, FEBRUARY 11, 1910.   Well am going write the Journal. But our people are good condition so far. no sickness among us this winter and much snow: good

Joseph Woonsook (at left) and Lynn Perry at Washakie, Utah, 1910. Joseph was father of Henry, Minnie, and Ivy (or Pojennie). *Courtesy Mae Timbimboo Parry.*

sleighing all winter here. Last month a man name Jas. [James] Brown organized a dramatic troop: they played many town now. But some saying they are good one. I didn't see the show. They call em Sioux Indian Medicine Show. We had very cold weather last week and winter storm too. It is very cold. We had nice dance here this Friday night. I am afraid we going lost our work horse and seem to be we will famine for hay this winter. But bishop Geo. M. Ward lost . . . two horses. We were looking for spring perhaps we may long time spring now. [1910-02-15 LJ]

WASHAKIE, MARCH 5, 1910. We are having real good times, lots snow this winter, splendid sleighing, and our people are good condition, no sickness among us so far. We had our ward conference . . . here our meeting house last Sunday. Our Stake Presidency and his two Counselor with him. But they with us all day Sunday, and talking to us and gave us good instruction and in regard the Gospel. Seem to me snow nearly all gone.

Mr. James Brown and 3 or 4 boys from Plymouth went over to Logan last week ago, but he wasn't get right one boys and took some old men with him. But most his boys stay home. I hope he has a splendid shows if he bring right boys. He was picked these men went over to Logan with [him] and all men disappointed went home. Mr. James Brown he didn't get paid enough, and he entirely stop the show. Some of our people are saying going have a spring, they are rejoicing. [1910-03-08 LJ]

WASHAKIE, SEPTEMBER 19, 1910.   We had very fine crop grain this year we shipped many car load grain this year and all threshing and our fall work nearly done. Some Indians been down Willard City last week having good time. Well, quite lot of Indian been Brigham Peach day, return home yesterday. Old woman laid a rest . . . and another girl died last week too. Mr. Jack Frost has been here last two week ago, take our potatoes vines and other little plants too. Four Indians from Wind River Reservation here visiting a month ago. . . . [1910-09-22 LJ]

"Year 1910. Timus Perdash, Amos Moemberg, Henry Woonsook. Probably in Brigham City, Ut., or S.L.C., Ut." *Courtesy Mae Timbimboo Parry.*

2

"Willie Ottogary Breaks Silence," 1911–1913

"Willie Ottogary Breaks Silence"

WASHAKIE, JANUARY 25, 1911.   Now then I will write a few lines for the Journal. But we all well and happy as ever, and school is very nicely this winter, and boys and girls are learning pretty fast. But they are much [more] number as used to be, about 3 or 4 years ago.

Mr. James Joshua built nice home this fall. . . . We have raise a good crop this summer and expect have it again next summer. But the hay was scarce here. . . . There was been two couples married here lately. Everybody no sick. Weather is been warm this winter, not much snow. Last snow we had fell about 6 inches. It is nearly all gone . . . we had rain last night and snow thaw pretty quick. It is feel like more spring. . . . [1911-01-31 LJ]

WASHAKIE, FEBRUARY 7, 1911.   But we have big storm in our country sometimes last week ago, and the road is badly wash out, and good road is spoil. . . . We much surprise seen such big body of water for long time this time the year.

Our day school running very nicely this year and boy and girl learning very quick. . . .

Mast. Henry Woonsook is sick in bed he is getten well and people are well here. I hope getting spring right away. [1911-02-11 LJ]

Over in Washakie

WASHAKIE, FEBRUARY 25, 1911.   The people are well here in our little village and happy. But one old ladie sick in bed now, and she is doing pretty nicely. We had nice lay of snow here last storm and fell about 7 inches. . . . On Geo. Washington birthday . . . had a nice and jolly time and in evening had banquet.

We didn't have much hay here now. Some of the Indians are poor condition this yr encount [on account] of scarces [scarcity] of hay. Our day school running very nice. . . . [1911-03-02 LJ]

WASHAKIE, FEBRUARY 28, 1911.   We are getting good health this year; no body sick. And we very splendid programme, on George Washington birth which was recitation, songs, select reading and dialogues, etc., in evening we had grand ball, and

41

having real good time. Well, all people are enjoyed themselves, another dance on Friday night too. . . .

Mr. James Brown been down Ogden last week on the business, return home some time last week. Our winter soon over with now. We got much snow but snow nearly all gone by this coming month. Well, think it is little to early spring.

Mr. W. T. Harris and Bert Hall of West Portage put a new gas light in our meeting house. The people think it is all right. It cost us about $135.00, Perhaps no complaint about it. We nice sleighen [sleighing] around here now. [1911-03-07 LJ]

WASHAKIE, APRIL 21, 1911.   Our people are getting all our spring work done, last week some are work out in shearing carroll [corral]. But our spring funny this year, and plenty of storm this yr. And all sugar beet in. I and my cusin, [Charlie] Broom, been out Deep Creek, on last month and acquainted lots of Indian out there. We stayed two weeks and finded good condition only troubled is didn't have any school among them. I expect they have next coming fall, but they held meeting about matter and very pleased to have it, and have picked one man all raddy [already] to teacher there next yr.

They putting all their crops in last month and their land very fertile for any thing; grain, potatoes, and other vegetable, &c. There is about 15 families living out to Deep Creek. I hope [they] have a good crop this yr. But and very enjoyed my trip. That is first time been there.

I return home on 8 April, 1911, from Deep Creek. Our people enjoyed this storm and help fall crop. There was two death here this spring. Their names are George Peyope and Frank Wontook [Frankie Woonsook]. No one sick so far. Mr. Monkey Jack, son Mr. Pin-upe and wife here at Washakie from Fort Hall Reservation.

Mr. Pocatello Washington, Mr. David Halleck, and one man with them on land business. There were been down Ogdan last week ago, return from Ogden last Monday. They from same place these two man, up in Idaho. [1911-04-25 LJ]

The Box Elder News[1]
Brigham City, Box Elder County, Utah, Thursday, May 11, 1911.
Willie Ottegary [sic]

The above half tone [see facing page] is a faithful reproduction of the form and features of Hon. Willie Ottegary, full blooded Shoshone Indian, farmer and newspaper correspondent.[2] Mr. Ottegary was born about 38 years ago, according to his best recollection, in Mantua where his father and mother had pitched their camp. He came from sturdy stock and has lived most of his life at Washakie, where he attended school and acquired a fairly good education. He writes a splendid hand, and speaks the English language fluently. His rhetoric is very good also for the advantages he has had, and his correspondence is always interesting.

Willie has a splendid farm at north Elwood where his people first settled many years ago but makes frequent trips to Washakie to visit his brethren and to get the news. He and Mrs. Ottegary, Willie, Jr. [Chester R. Ottogary], and the baby [Custer E. Ottogary] were in Brigham last Saturday doing some shopping, incidently dropping into this office for a little rest and visit, and while thus engaged, Mr. Ottegary sat down to the desk and prepared the following correspondence.

"Willie Ottegary." *From* Box Elder News, *May 11, 1911.*

WASHAKIE, MAY 5, 1911.   Our spring work all done. But soon start work on ditch. Need water pretty bad now and hope they soon are possible that we have water supply. Our grain crop looking splendid. I hope we will have good harvest this year and don't know when our water be down. All our people are getting well as ever. Haven't much sickness amongst us so far. But baby boy died here last couple of days ago. About 5 days old and buried last Thursday. Mr. Jackson and Mr. Proup [Monkey Jackson and Mr. Pin-upe] and wife is here at Washakie. They came from Pocatello, Idaho. They may return home some time next month. Perhaps they may stay little long. Mr. James Brown went down Ogden last week on business. Our day school soon be open for summer, on 8th this month. I hope the summer is long.

    Willie Ottegary

    News readers will have the pleasure of reading his letters frequently, as Willie has promised to furnish this paper with correspondence right along. [1911-05-11 BEN]

WASHAKIE, MAY 22, 1911.   Well some of our Indians are shearing sheep up in canyon. Quite many of sheepmen are shearing in this country and some hauling wool to the railroad track. But they shipped 2 or 3 carload out last week and some of them have just started shearing.

    I hope they may finish shearing latter part of this month. It seems to be quite a lot business going on here, and also our grain crop looking very promising so far and sugar beet crop, too. We finished our water ditch work.

    Mr. Hyrum [Wongsaw] and wife are returning home from north visiting their relatives and friends up in Idaho, and find everything is all right. . . .

Our country is very dry and needs rain pretty bad. I expect we will have it later on.

Mr. [Yeager] Timbimboo is very sick and may get well; he is been sick for long time, about 6 years, and also Mr. Quarretz [Wongan], and little girl, are pretty sick. She may die. I don't know yet. Perhaps she might get better later on.

Mr. Mose Neaman have little babe last week and mother getting along pretty nicely. [1911-05-25 BEN]

Washakie Whispers

WASHAKIE, JULY 10, 1911.[3] The Indians are getting very nicely so far. Soon harvest is coming here now, until after 24 July. And they going have big celebration here, and they have a program 10 o'clock in meeting house. Mr. Yeager Timbimboo went under Dr. Knife; [per]form operation on him for his bowel trouble. He was long ill, is getting very nicely so far. He down Brigham hospital and return home some time next week. Some of Indian are visiting their friends up to Fort Hall Reservation, and return last week. Well, Mr. Jack Frost was been here last Saturday, but ain't hurt any thing, but hurt little of garden stuff, and Mr. George Comanke going down Mr. Willie Ottogary place while I am away. I am trying a trip up Blacksmith Fork canyon for change, next week.[4] [1911-07-13 LJ]

WASHAKIE, JULY 10, 1911. The Indian are getting very nicely on, no sick here. Soon harvest time coming here now after 24 of July, and they going have a big celebration here and they have a programme 10 o'clock in ward meetinghouse. Mr. Yeager Timbimboo went Dr. Knife from operation on him. He beginning his bowel trouble for long ill he is getting very nicely so far. He is down Brigham hospital and he will return home some time next week. Some of Indians are visiting their friend up to Fort Hall Reservation and return last week. Well Mr. Jack Frost visit here last Saturday didn't hurt anything, but hurt little of garden stuff.

And Mr. Geo. Comanke going down Mr. Willie Ottogary place while I am away.[5] I am trying make a trip up Black Smith Fork Canyon for change next week & etc. [1911-07-13 BEN]

Willie Ottogary's Washakie Letter

WASHAKIE, SEPTEMBER 6, 1911. I now write a few news here going. But we are all well and our harvesting over with so far. Well, Mr. Jim Jack went down Brigham city. He went under Dr. Harding knife. He suffering with appendcis [appendicitis] and perform operation about 31 last month and he is improving all right.

Some of the Indian been down Ogden last week, big circus. Mr. Kippetchew Noragan lost $20 on train while coming back from circus.[6] Some of the Indian from Wyoming reservation visiting here [at] Washakie.

There are two wheat buyers in Washakie and shipped out four carload of wheat last week. Well our threshing done here, except few jobs. We seem to have many travelers through in our town, but some fruit and melon peddler come here very often here.

Mr. Soquitch Timbimboo work on Will Ottogary ranch now.

Mr. Yeager Timbimboo been operation on him last month, but is getting all right.

Well, our people want going to Peach Day in Brigham City. [1911-09-12 LJ]

Washakie (Written by an Indian.)

WASHAKIE, SEPTEMBER 6, 1911.   I was nearly forget to write the news. I wish you will excuse me for being not so long, perhaps may too in future.

Now am write a few news what has gone on here. Our harvesting all over now and threshing nearly all through. . . . [1911-09-14 BEN] [7]

WASHAKIE, OCTOBER 1, 1911.   Well I am going write a few news today. But our fall work is nearly all done and people here soon harvest their sugar beet crops, and hoping we have good harvest our sugar beet. But we have had a four car load of wheat this year.

Well last week ago whole people went down Peach Day having splendid old time and everybody return from Brigham last week.

Our day school is starts up last Monday and it is run very nice, and hoping boys and girls are learning more about read and language.

Mr. Charlie Broom is getting all right, and he can walk around last week and other day received letter from Deep Creek. But stated want him teach school out there. Mr. Charlie Broom went down tomorrow, and hope I will accompany him out here a few days. I hope he will have a good luck with he stay all winter.

Last night our people supprise about good rain we had. I hoping we will have splendid crop next year. [1911-10-05 BEN]

WASHAKIE, OCTOBER 12, 1911.   I am going write a few story from town. Our people are very rejoice when seen that last rain we have had. But it is nice for dry farms. I expect we have a splendid crop next year. But we start our sugar beet crop this week. . . .

Well our threshing all done. Nearly all grain is sell in this town. The grain price higher this year. . . .

The people are start harvest sugar beet around country.

Some of our people working out down around Garland sugar factory. The wages are about $12.00 or $13.00 for acre. Some Indians are from Pocatello is down here working.

Mr. Yeager Timbimboo doing nice. He was been under operating last summer.

Seem to me our baseball team died out this year. Some been down Conference Salt Lake City. All returned home last week.

Well all our people are doing very splendid so far. I was been down Deep Creek last week on business. Well see so many Indians out there and they going have a day school this year. Mr. Charlie Broom is teacher. I expect he will [have] good luck with them this winter.

He is from our town. Well is full blooded Indian. I was very rejoice my trip out there and acquainted many Indians. [1911-10-12 BEN]

1911-11-30 LJ [Not included][8]

WASHAKIE, NOVEMBER 26, 1911.   I am going write a few news, well I take my pencil in hand try too. It is very nice so I did write. It is very nice to have our pen in our hand, But did what I am going to write then working my think box. It is nice thing to have one. But we doing all right, Our sugar beet harvest nearly all done. Some Indians are working in sugar beet field around Garland sugar factory. But some return home last week. Mr. George Tomock lost his 14 year old boy, his death cause [of] the heart trouble. There are few Indian from Fort Hall Reservation, working on sugar beet too, down Garland some just return home. . . . Our day school running very nice this year. Last two weeks ago we have stormy weather. The snow fell about 3 inch. It thaw out pretty quick. The weather get colder.

Mr. Seth Pubigee Divorce his wife last week some time. But he skip the country. He was out Skully Valley country. [1911-11-30 BEN]

WASHAKIE, DECEMBER 17, 1911. Some of our people are return home from working. I hope are doing good this year and some Indians on reservation are return. We had quite snow storm last Saturday and snow fell about 5 inches. Well, one little child died here last week. The little boy father is Thomas Pabawena. The funeral services held at family resident about 10 o'clock some time last week. No more sick neverless and all our people good condition. We grand old time here last Friday. Bishop Ward gave a dance. Today the boys are hunting rabbits. Having good time shooting them.

The hay kind scarce here in our town. All our sugar beet harvest over. Mr. Mose Neaman been hunting deer just return home last Sunday, and two or three more. Didn't kill anything.

Mr. Seth Pubigee been divorce his wife here, about 3 week ago. He went down Skull Valley ever since. He return home last week, but go back on again. Perhaps they may happy again.[9] [1911-12-21 LJ]

WASHAKIE, DECEMBER 18, 1911. The people are all right. But two of them very sick now. One is Dick Arritch he is about 70 years old, and other is about 13 year old girl. I hoping they are getting well later on.

And all Indians from Pocatello return home last week. The boys been hunting rabbits last week and they slaughter quite many of them. Mr. Ammon Pubigee and Sequitah [Soquitch] Timbimboo and myself, are hunting rabbits out Blue Creek [about 14 miles west of Washakie] last week. But some of white mens from Ogden are been out hunt rabbits. Ammon Pubigee son narrow escape, one of the white man shot him with no. 5 shots, and stand about ten rod away from him [one rod equals 16.5 feet]. There is about 12 shots been entered all over his body, one on his cheek one on side his right jaw, 3 on the arm, 4 on right leg, one on his thumb, 3 on right wrist, several fell from him, and found some in overall pocket.[10]

He is get [improving] very nicely, and good as can be.

Well the weather is getting colder here. We had little snow here and people are rejoicing about Xmas is coming and arranged programme for Christmas. We going have a fine time on day.

Hay is pretty scarce here now, I hope we are coming [out] all right. [1911-12-21 BEN]

1911-12-23 LJ [Not included]
1912-01-11 LJ [Not included]

Moroni and Amy Hootchew Timbimboo with their daughter Joana, September 15, 1913, Brigham City, Utah. *Courtesy Mae Timbimboo Parry.*

WASHAKIE, JANUARY 9, 1912.   Well some of the Indians been rabbit hunting last week. They slaughter great many of them in evening had grand Ball. We had quite lot of snow last New Year. Had good time. We had nice programme in morning. There were songs, recitation, select reading, comic speeches, etc., and the most enjoyable time we ever had this year. Last two week ago had two child born. Both was girls. Their parents names are Mr. Moroni Timbimboo [and] Eving [Amy] Timbimboo [dau. Joana, b. 1912], Mr. Jimmy Jack and Agnes Jack [dau. possibly Bessie Jack]. They doing very nicely. No one death since last fall. We had very cold this year. Last Sunday quite snow storm. Laura Quintain from Pocatello been here. All went home. Mr. Preacher Harry [Harry Preacher] from Wells [NV] is been here on New Year visiting his friends and relatives, and Ed. Grand is here too from Pocatello [Ross Fork, ID] and he return home some time with Mr. Harry. Ed Grand is belong to the Christian church, and two boys from Winter [Wind] River Reservation here now. [1912-01-11 BEN]

WASHAKIE, JANUARY 24, 1912.   Our people is good condition this yr. But two woman is sick now. Last week was rabbit hunting. It is very good one like we ever had. The snow nearly all gone so far. But most snow lays out field. Some of our people say going have a spring. I think it is mistake and quite while for spring.

Mr. Frank West gone for Idaho last week.

The hay is scarse here this yr. . . .

Mr. Mose Neaman lost his best horse last week ago.

Some of them digging a well.

No one death so far since last fall.

We had a nice time last Friday night, a grand ball at ward meeting house. But next Friday going have another dance. . . .

Also Mr. George P. Sam been down Brigham for Dr. treatment, and his eyes being so bad. The weather get warmer. [1912-01-30 LJ]

1912-02-01 BEN [Not included]

WASHAKIE, FEBRUARY 27, 1912.   We have a good weather so far and last week three people are sick some of them getting all right. But Mr. Quarretz Wongan & wife been sick for some times ago perhaps getting well soon. The cause of sick is stomach trouble. Mr. Garfield [Pocatello] and Kippoo [Kippetchew Noragan] went home and spend George Washington birthday here with our people, and visit some of their friend & relatives too. Well the people here are having a good time Geo. Washington. We had a very nice program. . . . In evening have a grand Ball and snow all gone here. We are rejoicing for coming spring. I hope we have early spring this yr. Our day school is running very splendid. . . . Mr. Frank West want move up in Idaho some time this spring.

The hay is scarce here now. Some of our people are run out hay. The is worth about $5.00 per ton. [1912-03-02 LJ]

WASHAKIE, MARCH 13, 1912.   Well I am going a few line. . . . Mr. Ammon Pubigee little boy fall of load of hay a week ago.[11] But he is Improving pretty slow. They expect to died and he pull through alright. Perhaps he may trouble for awhile. And he doing all right now. He lit on his back. All our people is supprize about winter is going by. The road through here is impossible to travel. . . . Well we will have another wet weather 2 week more. Some of our [people] wish is spring now are very anxious to start spring work. Mr. James Joshua & wife and I and wife in Logan City to working temple.[12] But we acquainted many people in Logan.

But we see Mr. Samuel Whitney every day,[13] we are please see him because he was talk in our language. I hope we stay in Logan few day more. I been up to college today see what going on up there.[14] I been in Blacksmith shop, carpenter shop, Machine shop, sheep yard, hog yard, cattle yard, and also poultry yard and that is first time been up my life and looking around all over.

I was received letter from cousin Charlie Broom last. He stated in letter "Having a splendid good time out there to Deep Creek." He teach day school out there. There is about 15 familes living out there. [1912-03-14 LJ]

WASHAKIE, MARCH 19, 1912.   The people here are doing pretty very nice this winter here. But we have nice dance here in ward meeting house. The people are here enjoyed when spring time is coming. Some of our men join in Farmer Cash Union. I believed it is pradd [bad?] for them. . . . The road is impossible for travel now. . . . Well nice ward conference here. Our [Stake] President and his counselor were present. President Richeres [Richards] and two counselors was take up time. They enjoyable remark. And also Bp. Geo. M. Ward to Interpured [interpreted] in our

LYRIC THEATRE

Splendid Program for the week end patrons, featuring a splendid western drama

The Sheepman's Escape

A human story portrayed with excellent skill.

Tom Tilling's Baby

A beautiful Vitagraph story of a little bootblack and his little sister Susie. They find a tiny baby, adopt it and it afterwards proves a very lucky find for both.

A scenic picture of

St. John's Newfoundland

A very interesting military picture.

A Question of Seconds

An Edison feature

and a dandy comedy completes an excellent program.

REMEMBER When you visit the Lyric you are in ONE OF THE BEST equipped Picture Theatres in the West. For steadiness, brightness and clearness, our pictures are unexcelled anywhere.

This is a broad statement, but we can back it up.

We use licensed film—The Film of quality—the film that is used in seventy-five per cent of the picture theaters in the United States today. When you visit the Lyric you see the **BEST** always

10 cents   10 cents

Lyric Theatre advertisement. *From* The Journal, *Logan, March 14, 1912.*

language. Of course some of us could understand alright. And day school [running] very nicely this [year]. The hay is pretty scarse here this year. Mr. Seth Pubigee get well now. He was fall of load hay. But he fainted two or three different time. But get over it. He is well is ever. . . . [1912-03-21-A LJ][15]

Willie Ottogary Visits Moving Picture Show

LOGAN, UTAH, MARCH 20, 1912.   Well, Mr. Earl want me a write story.[16] So come over here to Logan city one more [time]. I find the road is impossible to travel, and I want tell about strange story. Me and wife went in moving picture show. Lyric [Theatre], see so many picture.[17] Well, am very surprise to them picture move as nature. The picture move just like human being. . . . My wife say that is funny to see them pictures move. I am very much [pleased] see them Indian picture. Well this is very strange to me. I never see such picture in my life before. When this moving going that make me a loud laugh, and couldn't stop my ugly laugh. I suppose going in [again] some time. But like very much to see them kind show. I don't care for theater, Dramatic and [that] kind show.

Well perhaps may tell you about it again. I meet Mr. Samuel Whitney again yesterday. . . . He is my old friend for long time. That all for this time. [1912-03-21-B LJ]

WASHAKIE, MARCH 25, 1912.   We are start our spring work now, and the people very anxious [to] put in crop now. But no sick amongst us, so far. Well, one woman very

Red Clay, or Frank Timbimboo
Warner, son of Chief Sagwitch.
*Special Collections & Archives, Merrill
Library, Utah State University.*

sick. But her husband want take her down L. D. S. hospital next week to [per]form operation on her. . . . Well she take down today on morning train. . . .

My Bro-in-law, Ammon Pubigee received a letter from his Bro. out Wind River Reservation—he stated they have about 3 or 4 feet snow on Crow Reservation. And there was a big loss of livestock up there. It is very cold up there. . . .

Mr. Frank Warner, Yeager Timbimboo, Soquitch Timbimboo. These are three Bros.[18] They are in Logan a few day, and came over here work in Temple this week. . . . I slip in Journal office today to write the articles. I hope you will glad hear from me again. . . . [1912-03-28 LJ]

Willie Ottogary Visits The B.Y.C.

LOGAN, MARCH 27, 1912.   We are Lamanites visiting B. Y. College yesterday afternoon about 2:30 o'clock. We entered the building first is English Language classroom 12. But find quite many pupils in there. As we visit this room did receive as good a reception as could be accorded a white, little derision, and a small amount of giggle from the pupils. Next room is No. 3. It empty by time we were there; and next No. 4 music room we find it is empty. Next we visit, find the swimming pool, a very beautiful concern. The chapel took our eye in its nice seating capacity. We next went into the mineral department. The specimen in the mineral department was something interesting to gaze upon. Our next visit was the type writing department. The young ladies appeared to be contented at their work. They were even too busy to smile. Next visit is Blacksmith shop, after is gymnasium room to watching basketball game for while and it is very interesting game between 3 and 4 team.

There many people were present. We stayed about [2] hours to look various department. It was very good interesting. . . .

While in Penmanship Prof. Frank W. Warner Timbimboo made a very good talk upon the subject of the writing.[19] [1912-03-30 LJ]

1912-04-04-A BEN [Not included, letter written March 27, 1912][20]

Willie Ottogary Inspects Logan Factories

Logan, March 29, 1912.   I was walking down Cache Valley Creamery factory in company [of] Mr. J. Earl. . . . [The creamery] had about 35 employees or more, shipping one car load per day. It is big business going on there and handling about 40,000 thousand lbs. milk per day. I am surprised see a laboring machine . . . . I never been creamery mill before my life. It was very interesting watching them. I like visit one more next time.

Mr. George W. Skidmore, manager of Union Knitting Mill Co. too invited me come to mill, so I and my wife went down today looking every machine he got in mill, and very interesting to me. I was feel like turn upside down to see diferents of machinery. Well like [go] through one more again perhaps. It is strange to me I like visit every factory in Logan city. If can I wishing your people looking for my letter every day, and I know my letter interesting to your people who read the Logan Journal. Perhaps you may be looking for little next week again. [1912-04-02 LJ]

Willie Ottogary Visits Crystal Theatre

Washakie, March 30, 1912.   I was in Logan last week. Went in a Crystal [Theatre] moving picture show.[21] Mr. Timbimboo and families with me. But we have had very splendid old time while picture are moving. And to see them Indian picture, well I am very surprise to see them picture . . . and see many other picture. We like to see them kind of the show. We got on the laugh quick as moving picture . . . start. Well we haven't seen any nothing like it before. It was very interesting to look at. . . . [1912-04-06 LJ]

1912-04-04-B BEN [Not included, letter written April 2, 1912]

Willie Ottogary Once More at Home

Washakie, April 2, 1912.   We return home from Logan last Saturday morning and find the road was very good condition. . . . Mr. Timbimboo get home same night. . . . [Inserted from 1912-04-04-A BEN: "But as soon get home telephone a child is died, up to Washakie."] It is Mr. Seth Pubigee's child boy. He was born 28 March. He lived about two days old. Then he died about Saturday night. His funeral service held at family res[idence] . . . quite number of them present, and it is good attendance.

Well, Mr. Seth Pubigee and wife went down to the Garland to see the Dr. but didn't feel good after that birth the child. She feel very weak. I hope she get better. This was same parent [of] one who die.

Mr. Quarretz Wongan wife feel little better today. He didn't take her down to the Salt Lake City. Well, she think she will pull through all right in future. Our spring work is visit us now, no one can lay idle.

Mr. Jack Grass Creek [Grouse Creek Jack] and his family are going up there to the Jim John place to work for him,[22] grub sage for his field.[23] There is a small-pox up west Portage, but I heard a four new case last week. . . .

The hay nearly all gone. Some of our people are going down Conference down Salt Lake city. Well, perhaps went down next Friday, April 5, 1912. . . . [1912-04-04 LJ]

WASHAKIE, APRIL 11, 1912.   I would write a story to the Journal. But we are good condition so far. Quite storm we have had here. It is snowing and raining too . . . It very impossible to be working. I think we will have a good weather next week. Nearly all our spring crops [are] in. Some of us just started now. I hope if it good weather we will finish it. The hay is very scarce here in our town. Some of us are out hay the hay price is up and hope we come through all right. Perhaps we may lose some our stock. Mr. Ammon Pubigee and his son Enos Pubigee been down my place for some hay on last Monday.

Some of our people been down Conference. There is Mr. Yeager and wife and Mr. Kippetchew Noragan been down conference. But all return home last Sunday night. I been down conference myself. We are having a splendid good time while we were in city. Sunday noon we was seeing Salt Lake City on the automobile, riding for an hour. We saw many fine houses in city. There is about 5 men 5 women. But women folks are very surprise riding on the car. Mr. Charlie Broom came home last wk. He taught school out Deep Creek Indian children all winter. . . . Well he made good success out among Indians out there. [1912-04-16 LJ]

1912-04-18 BEN [Not included]

WASHAKIE, MAY 16, 1912.   Well can say much now so far. I know we have had a very splendid weather. It more likely summer; everything is turning out very nice. . . .

But one lady [possibly Eliza Wongan, see 1912-05-25 LJ and 1912-06-06 LJ] laid up for long time ever since last year. It is too long she is suffering now. Dr. Rich was examined her last week she cannot be able to live any longer. Doctor did to [didn't do] anything for her. He expect been died some time. Mr. Moody [perhaps Moody Walker from Skull Valley] is here now visiting some of his friends and relatives. He expect return home some time. No more news but Bishop Geo. M. Ward start up a new store here lately. He expect having a good business.[24] [1912-05-23 BEN]

Willie Ottogary, Wife and Family
[The Ottogary family photograph on the facing page accompanied this letter]
ELWOOD, UTAH, MAY 18, 1912.   Mr. England and Earl want me a short scatches [sketches] on my early life,[25] But I set in my seat and try to do it.

But I am sorry to say about my right age, but may guess near as [I] can. I was born in little place above Brigham city on little valleys of mountain, . . . known in our day . . . [as] Mantua, in the 1867, July 20,[26] right in the middle of the valley, and there was much settler [moved] there since. My parents are living on the state every since. But we most time living around Willard City since I was boy about 3 or 4 year. After I [was] 8 years old my parents heard Gospel and converted and baptized by George W. Hill,[27] and join [LDS] church; But later on I been baptized too.

Clockwise from top right: Willie, Chester, Custer, and Nancy West Ottogary. *From* The Journal, *Logan, Utah, May 23, 1912.*

But we lived on Bear River ever since, and after 3 or 4 more year move up to Washakie. Then build school house, soon [as] get it finished, the day school start up among Indian. There is about 50 Indian children going school. I was with them. I been school about 8 year straight. I am raised at Washakie. Well, when I going to school first time, [I] don't know what come next. I don't [have any] interest in em. Before this mission come,[28] my parents been move all time, a hunter [of] games and so on. I think this is nice away to live to be civilize.

But I am think about first time been school: [I] am very sorry for it because I don't know anything. But I am know it is worth something to be edgucated. I am proud of it I can read and write too. That is all I can say today. [1912-05-23 LJ]

WASHAKIE, MAY 1912.   I am going a write a short letter. But we are good condition, and also our day school was let out for coming summer about last Friday. One woman was laid up. Dr. said she had not much chance living because she was suffered so. No one died since last fall. Her name is Eliza Wongan. But she is middle age lady. Well, she might live more. She got 3 children.

Mr. Bishop Geo. M. Ward start up a new store here. The people are very glad to have a store here. He will do good business here.

Our people are greatly surprise looking over their wheat crops. It is looking very promised this year. But Mr. Movddy [Moody] Walker was here now visiting some of his friend and relatives, from Skull Valley. He like this place very much, and return home some time next week. Our boys work in water ditch last week. Perhaps may get through next week. . . . Our hay very scarse here, the price away up. . . . [1912-05-25 LJ]

WASHAKIE, JUNE 3, 1912.   Our wheat crop is looking very promising this yr. . . . We will have much harvest for this yr.

Mrs. Quarretz Wongan was laid to rest in peace [a] week from last Saturday. She left 3 children; one oldest is about 16 years, next oldest 13 yr. and youngest is about 6 yr. old.[29] She was well known in our town. She is about 30 yr of age and her parents join in Church when she about 8 years old. . . . She lived here every since.

Well, I was been Fort Hall last week visiting some my friends and relatives. But acquainted many of the Indians. There is about 1,800 Indian up on that reservation and they have a fine day school there. The Government is looking after the Indians there. They gave them 20 acres land that under the ditch or canal, and about 80 acres for grazing land. There are great many of them didn't like 20 acres. They want 80 acres. But agent didn't have that much. I hope the Indian have that in future. I was been up there on business trip. I may make another trip next week. [1912-06-06 LJ]

WASHAKIE, SEPTEMBER 8, 1912.   . . . Our people good condition. We didn't get that bad storm last week. Bishop Geo. M. Ward was knocked off from stack of hay, not hurt. Some of people went down Garland that big circus Sanger[?]. I was much time write a piece [to] Journal. Then have a little time today set in my chair. It is stormy day. [1912-09-12 LJ]

WASHAKIE, SEPTEMBER 9, 1912.   I am going write a few line. I didn't do anything today, this storming day. But we are getting alright. I was nearly forgot about Box Elder News and didn't write for long time. Am trying to write again in future. M. Lewis Cornsim [Corsium] lost two little girls here lately. One is about 4 years and one was 1 year old. But some the children had a chicken pox last month and get over with now.

Our harvesting grain all done, and threshing is start up last week, and some of our people surprised about the Peach Day coming, and glad hearing something doing on that day and sports.

We load two car load grain last week. Wheat was about 65¢ per bushel. . . .

Some our people surprised at getting big harvest here this year, and some of us had a very poor crop. Our sugar beet didn't much good last year. Some Indian from Wind River Reservation were visiting our town. There were here now. We didn't get any bad storm this year. [1912-09-12 BEN]

WASHAKIE, SEPTEMBER 23, 1912.   We are good condition so far. But some of us are sick with typhoid fever. Mr. Sam Jack and two girls, and also another young man layed up on some [perhaps same] disease.

Some people are in Brigham [City] for fruit and didn't return home yet. There was quite number of been Brigham on the Peaches day, having a good time.

Mr. James Brown, and two or three families away with him on the show business.[30] I expect return home this week. . . .

Our fall crop is nearly all in. . . . Mr. Jack Frost is been here allratty [already] and frozen every thing. . . .

Some of Indians went out to gather some pine nuts, about 80 miles west. I expect may return two weeks or more.

We didn't raise very much sugar beet this year. we are going mowing our hay down pretty soon, and Jack [Frost] was nipped top of leaves. [1912-09-28 LJ]

WASHAKIE, DECEMBER 30, 1912.   I am going write a few line. But we have had nice time on Xmas. We had very nice Christmas tree in school house on Xmas eve, and carried a spendid programme in morning comenced at 10 o'clock and splendid dinner were served at 12 o'clock, by releive society [Relief Society] evening the grand ball have a jolly time.[31]

Mr. James Brown been Ogden on business matter [probably show business], returned home some time ago.

But Mr. Nephi Zundel, our mail carrier, been Ogden city.

Mr. Charlie Broom returned home a week last. He was a school teacher out Deep Creek, Utah, Tooele County. He spend a Xmas here. But his wife want divorce. But they want go back each other. Mr. Broom didn't know [what] he going to too [do], and wrote letter to Indian agent in Salt Lake City.

Our boys had a big Jack rabbit hunt last week ago. There was many bunnies slaughter in that day. We haven't much snow so far, and very cool weather now.

Mr. Bp. Geo. M. Ward start up a small store here. He doing a splendid business here.

Mr. Lewis Corsium son went under Dr. Knife, [per]form operation with appendicitis. He doing very nice, and was down Garland now. . . . He will return home next wk. some time.

Our day school stop for Holiday.

Mr. Mose Neaman returned home week last been out hunting.

Mr. Grouse Creek Jack with his two son went out trapping out west around Promontory. [1913-01-02 LJ]

1913-01-02 BEN [Not included]

Willie Ottogary's New Dish Washer

WASHAKIE, JANUARY 6, 1913.   The people are here all well and we have had very cold weather here right now. The themoteor [thermometer] went down 18 below zero this morning, and we have a very nice dance here on Friday night last. But we will have another one next Friday. . . . Well we had a new dish wash[er] come our home about week ago today. She [daughter, Louise M. Ottogary] was born in December 30, 1912.

But mother of baby doing very splendid, also baby too. I been up West Portage on business. . . .

I am going on mission for two month.[32] I am afraid I could [not] write for long time, then I try to write for Journal if I can, and I expect write again before I leave . . . on mission. Well, Mr. Ward is doing splendid business here.

Our day school is start up again today. Mr. Charlie Broom out for Deep Creek a week last. He was school teacher out there. [1913-01-09 LJ]

Grouse Creek Jack, about 109 years old, 1939. *National Archives, Still Pictures Branch, RG 75, TLA, Box/Folder 28, PO-6.*

1913-01-09 BEN [Not included]

WASHAKIE, JANUARY 14, 1913.   Our people here good condition perhaps some one been sick lately. And Friday night last had having a real good times as dance as joining some white people surrounding our town, and from Portage, and also school teachers from Collinston were here too. But some our boys big Jack Rabbit hunt yesterday. And we slaughter many bunnies.

To Mr. Thomas Pabowana, and Julia Pabowana, has come a new ployboy [plow-boy] come his home week last. His mother doing very nice.

Mr. Yeager Timbimboo made a nice pleasure trip up in Idaho. He was return home week last.

Mr. Joe Baniboo and wife been up to Fort Hall Reservation the matter of busi-ness, and return home Monday last. Well, Mr. [Ray] Diamond has return from Idaho. Next Friday night have another dance here too. I and two companion going labor on mission here through out Malad stake for two month. [1913-01-16 LJ][33]

WASHAKIE, JANUARY 14, 1913.   Our people here good condition. Perhaps some one been sick lately. And grand ball was Friday night last and having real good time. And joining some white people surrounding our little town and some from West Portage and also school teacher man from Collinston were here too, and most rejoyable time we every had.

Blackfoot Indian. Aged 131, Is Oldest Man In the World

"Wah-Hah-Gun-Ta," a Blackfoot Indian. *From* The Journal, *Logan*, *January 16, 1913*.

Yesterday, some of our boys big rabbit hunt, many bunnies were slaughtered.

Mrs. Julia and Thomas Pabawana born boys baby week last. Mother and boys are getting all right.

Mr. Yeager Timbimboo make a nice pleasure trip up in Idaho. He was return home week last.

Mr. Joseph Paniboo and wife been up on reservation the matter of business and return home Monday the last. And also Mr. [Ray] Diamond has return from Idaho. And next Friday night have another grand ball were gave this ward.

I and two accompanys going on labor mission here through our stake for two months. [1913-01-16 BEN]

WASHAKIE, JANUARY 21, 1913.   And we are good condition. No one sick here. Not much snow. But we will have an Old Folks' reunion next Friday night. This is first time ever . . . held here.[34]

I have been my farm Sunday last. Well some hunt bunnies. We slaughtered great many Jack rabbits this year. I think about 2,500 or more. . . .

Our day school running very splendid this year. The hay is very scarce here now. But Mr. Jack and sons out hunting yet.[35]

Well not news just now. And also I got a man with this letter, photo of man.[36] He was a great warrior once when he was young age. And still living . . . and strong as ever. He was 131 years old and oldest man on the earth. And he was kill 3,000 Buffalo, 12,000 deer, 4,000 Elk. 200 Rocky Mountain sheep, 600 moose, 40 lion, 100 bears and many other game.

He was a very great hunter on world. He was been over United States and also in Canada. But he was one of Blackfoot Indian. His name is Wah-ah-gun-to. [1913-01-23 BEN]

WASHAKIE, JANUARY 27, 1913.   The people are here all good condition so far. Everything is quiet here this year.

The Old Folks' Day were held in our school house 10 o'clock Friday and nice program was carried out as follows, which was songs, dialogues, comic speeches, recitations and many others. On the 12 o'clock the dinner was served by the Relief Society and everybody having a real good time. In evening grand ball gave by the old folks. They invited everybody. And real good time which after the dance dismiss.

Miss Allen girl fell from bench and struck her right hip and she was [un]conscious a few minutes. She played for dance. Her violin all smash up, she is sick in bed. . . .

Well, I and two companion labor mission here at Washakie ward. But I am very enjoyed my mission among my own people. . . .

Mr. [Ray] Diamond was return home from Idaho week last. [1913-01-30 BEN]

1913-02-04 LJ [Not included]

WASHAKIE, FEBRUARY 5, 1913.   The people are here good condition this winter. But two girls are sick in bed. I expect they get over it. Some of Indian men are attend Oneida County Union meeting up Malad city other day. They return home yesterday. They say meeting very interesting one. But our day school splendid run.

Well, Bishop Geo. M. Ward doing good business here. I and companion been labor mission here four wk. And am very enjoying my home mission here among people. But our President send us out west among our own tribe. Some Indian living out Deep Creek. They out this place. I expect we start out next Sunday. We labor at place one month out. I expect this will be splendid trip out there.

We haven't much snow this winter. Some of us looking for spring. . . . The hay was scarce were here this town.

Mrs. Joe Moemberg and son went up Idaho last Monday. They received telephone [call] from Pocatello. Her father is nearly dying up there. He was one of Indian chief around Bannock [Creek], and been sick two yr. and being so old. . . .[37] [1913-02-08 LJ]

WASHAKIE, FEBRUARY 1913.   Our town is pretty good condition so far and I been labor mission here at our town for 4 weeks and am very much my mission enjoying among my own people. . . . Sent me out Deep Creek, Utah, about over 200 mile. I like my people join the Church of Jesus Christ of Latter-day Saints. But I been doing great for them among my own tribe. We visit every family in town. Well we have had nice time Friday last at dance.

The our President of stake sent [me] out Deep Creek, Tooele County, Utah. These are some my own tribe again, but am like preach gospel to them. They was non-Mormons and I very glad my mission out [there]. These people here very pleased my labor mission.

Oh I am very sorry the Indian didn't acquainted with much Gospel. I hope they will join the church some time.

Mr. Joseph Paniboo went down to Garland yesterday and Mr. Soquitch Timbimboo return home last Friday But he went back Mr. Willie Ottogary. He was stay another month yet on my ranch while I am going on mission. [1913-02-13 BEN]

IBAPAH, UTAH, FEBRUARY 24, 1913.   I am going tell you we are here among the Indian here at Ibapah [on the Goshute Reservation in Tooele County]. And we are working hard here labors on mission. But we find time here and visit every families in the town, and also visit day school too. I hope we convert some of them. Some of these people are sick with cold, especially children. Most of them well. I acquainted lot of them so far.

I expect return home about 2 weeks more. It is quite cold here now [on] account . . . [it] snowed here last week.

But we visit Skull Valley before we going back. There is a number of our people there so we visit them.

Mr. Frank Eagle was here now, he may return home tomorrow morning.

When we get in Skull Valley, I will write a piece again. The Indian here are good condition yet. Mrs. George Elk girl very low, she said with cold.

The snow fall about foot an half here on the level ground. The day school very perfect running this year. But we stayed with Annie Tonny [Annies Tommy].

There are about 24 children attending school, also learn very fast. [1913-03-06 BEN]

Willie Ottogary Reports Mission

WASHAKIE, APRIL 18, 1913.   I am sorry But didn't write for long time, and I think I will write a story. And I am very good mission away my own people, out west. But we hold three or four different meetings there, and we find 96 people outside the church. We been labor with them about two wks straight, and they want be needed baptized right away. I believe we may going finish our mission. . . . Well, It is very nice trip out there again. We left Deep Creek Indian Ranch on March 3, we got in Skull Valley next day. But start work 4 day of March. But we find 43 people there, and we visit every family in town, and having good time with them.

But we stayed with George Moody. He gave us good bed and meal too. Well, we hold 5 meeting in school house. Our meeting is good attendance, then we came home from there. And we very enjoyed our mission work. After we came home . . . we went up on Idaho to visit some of our friends up there. We made business trip up there, and looking some land up on reservation. I expect we locate up there. I and my companion was see an agent about the land. He was make it right with us. Well, we might [be] going up there again on 3 day of May, and might located head of Bannock Creek.

It is good land up in there. We was acquainted many Bannock & Shoshone up there. They like us fellows, all right. If we located up there and start work.

All our people here good condition, no one sick, no death: But we have had splendid shower last night. It is right time what we want. And all our spring crops put in. Some of our people are going raising sugar beet this year. I hope they will have a fine crop of beets. [1913-04-22 LJ]

Ottogary as a Missionary

WASHAKIE, APRIL 18, 1913.   I am going write a few stories about our mission work. . . . We hold first meeting on Tuesday afternoon, Indian Ranch, Deep Creek, Feb. 13, 1913, about 4:30 o'clock and same day we visit day school, [and] we find 9 boys and 5 girls. The some of the children been sick on account being cold or grip.[38] We find about 13 families in Deep Creek Indian Ranch and we start work Feb. 14, 1913.

We visit every family in town and hold Sunday school at school house about 10 o'clock Sunday morning, Feb. 16. Singing was "My Sabbath Home." Open Sunday school was Elder Ammon Pubigee. But we carried a splendid program.

1. Testimony was made by Prof. Charlie Broom.
2. Tomy Johny [Johny Tommy] gave us good recitation.
3. Cleave McGill reciting a albahet [alphabet].
4. Twiney Toogan recite America first 3 verse.
5. Harry, Clyde and Kenniatra Tomy recite a short piece.
6. Select reading by Gus Toogan.
7. Bessie Benson, Rachel Tomy, Nessia Tomy song from S. S. [Sunday School] hymn book.
8. Speaker was Elder Ammon Pubigee subject was our Sunday School duties, and he also gave us good instruction. Another speaker was Willie Ottogary talking about same subject, and he instructed us and many other things.

And also we held another meeting at hall about 2 o'clock. But Relief Society organized on the Feb. 22 and had a good attendance. . . . We explain the duties of the ladies, and many other thing. And also we held another [meeting] Sunday School Feb. 23. Conduct Sunday School [meeting] by Charlie Broom.

First speaker Brother Elder Willie Ottogary and subject was the Day of Judgement and many other things, etc. Second speaker was Elder Ammon Pubigee. The subject was the Savior Descend from Heaven and visiting Nephites people and Lamanites too, and he gave good instruction. Third speaker was Bond Toogan. . . . Charlie Broom made a very short speech, etc. Singing [after]. Benediction by Antelope Jack.

Deep Creek Feb. 27, little girl [died] the funeral services held at school house about 11 o'clock. The conduct service by Elders Ammon Pubigee and Willie Ottogary. First speaker was Willie Ottogary. He made very splendid talk. And next speaker was Ammon Pubigee and made same testimony.

There was a very cold time [when] we left the town and we was very enjoyed our mission. They treat us alright.

Then we left Deep Creek on Monday March 3 [and] we get [to] Skull Valley.

We reach the town about 2 o'clock and we held meeting same day about 3. We had good attendence, . . . find about 35 members present. The speakers were Elders Ammon Pubigee and W. Ottogary. We talking [about] our mission work. We made good speaks [speeches]. Next speak was David Eagle a short time.

We return home March 12. Then we been up Idaho about week after looking for land. We return 2nd day April, 1913. [1913-04-24 BEN]

WASHAKIE, JUNE 7, 1913.   I am going write a few story. I didn't write for long time am sorry to say. Our people are good condition. Some of the boys are work shear corral up in canyon about ten miles west here.[39] They nearly through by this time. And the crop is looking very [promising] this year.

Some of them went up Fort Hall Reservation get allotment from government. Well, some good land is out there. . . . Our people are good condition, no one sick, no death so far.

Some Indian to celebrate fourth July in S. L. C., Utah. I hope they will have very splendid time. And Mr. Ward still running store here yet. He make good business here. [1913-06-10 LJ]]

WASHAKIE, JUNE 9, 1913.   I am going write a few stories. And we are all well. But no one sick so far. And some our boys been shearing sheep and made a pretty good money. Mr. John Tomock, Mr. Jacob Peyope, Mr. Quarretz Wongan, went up to Montana country. But I didn't, when return home some time next month.

We very splendid crops this year. I hope the grain crop is very promising. The hay are soon ratty [ready] to cut, probably next week some time. Some of our people in sugar beet field. I hoping they are making good money. Around North Garland, Utah, some around Riverside. They are very busy time thinning beets.

One Indian from Fort Hall Reservation been here week last he return home some time ago. I am [not] been writing such long time excuse me, but haven't much time to do it.

Some time ago I been up Fort Hall Reservation looking land and return home two weeks ago. But Government allotment send us back to Washakie. He didn't allotment us [there]. Well, and not sorry for it now. There are 30 Indians went up try to get land up there, so they gave up. Well they not going back anymore. They lazy as baby, didn't any farm work. They got quite [a] lot land. They don't know what going to do.[40]

Oh, am very glad write a few articles for Box Elder News. Good-bye for the Box Elder News reader. [1913-06-12 BEN]

WASHAKIE, JUNE 28, 1913.   The have had very splendid rain here. . . . It is done good our crops. It is worth something I will tell you. But comes little too late. I hope we are harvesting good wheat crop. But some of the crop been damage quite bit. Well all our people are good condition. No one sick so far.

I expect the storm over with. . . .

Malad River Bridge is . . . new iron bridge. Some of our boys are been work on it. I expect they will be finish about 2 or 3 week longer.

Some our boys been work on sugar beet around Garland and Riverside.

All our people rejoice seen such a storm. It is real nice I haven't seen for long time.

Some of our boys been away to shearing sheep up in Idaho. . . .

Mr. Burton was seen here last week, a sheep man and loading his wool. [1913-07-03 BEN]

WASHAKIE, JUNE 30, 1913.   I am to tell stories. Well, our people are good condition so far. Mr. Monkey Jackson was here from Pocatello, Idaho. He is working around here in our town. He may return home some time.

. . . Many hay crop is damaged for rain this yr. It is pretty bad look hay before they hauled it; I tell you a fact. Some of our people didn't like the storm because damaged the hay.

Last week ago the Relief Society [held] social . . . at our meeting house. . . . The luncheon was . . . in meeting house. All our people were enjoyed themself, and evening have a grand ball for . . . everybody.

Our day school was stop . . . last month ago. I expect some our people went down Salt Lake City celebration 4 of July. I hoping have a real good time. And Mr. George Comlank [Comanke] return from Skull Valley. Him and his boy. Our Sunday school is running very splendid so far, and also our meeting: good attendance every Sunday. The meeting house [is] crowed [crowded].

Well, Mrs. Nancy Ottogary going out west to visiting her relation up in Owyhee, Nev. or White Rock, Agency. She may return home some time next month. She don't know. I hoping she will have splendid celebration 4 July out there. She left home Friday morning. June 27. [1913-07-03 LJ]

WASHAKIE, AUGUST 4, 1913.   . . . Week ago we have had fine shower, but it come too late. The people are . . . harvesting their grain now [and] three header busy cutting the grain. Some of the people are went down Ogden on Tuesday last they all disappointed [and] come back home, nothing going on down there. But expect[ed] see Buffalo Bill show. Well, our threshing machine soon start up.

The people are here celebrating 24 of July very splendid this yr. and sport are on . . . and carried programme good condition . . . and dinner served was under big bowery.

Mr. Thomas Pabawena work in bridge gang. . . .

Our second crop hay is very nice than first one. But our first crop hay was all spoil in that rain we had. Mr. Soquitch and [?] been down Mr. Ottogary place putting up his hay. But he been Great Ringling Bro. Circus yesterday 2 Aug. 1913.[41] [1913-08-07 LJ]

WASHAKIE, AUGUST 7, 1913.   We . . . harvesting our grain now. But our crop very good condition and our people are good so far. But we are celebrated 24th of July very splendidly. All kind of sport. Some of our boys are working on railroad for 3 or 4 week.

We have rain here pretty near everyday and hoping may have good weather again.

Our thresher soon start up. All our hay nearly done. Some of the Indians have been down Ogden last Saturday seen great Ringling Bros. Circus.

. . . All our people are rejoice over the grain crops. Some of boys are working steam machine down near Garland. But very few of them didn't like our farms because they have now farm work. [1913-08-14-A BEN]

WASHAKIE, AUGUST 11, 1913.   Everybody is harvesting their grain now, but our four headers are still cutting grain and our threshing machine is not started up yet. One was start first last week.

Mr. Thomas Pabawena went down below to work on bridge near Evan's Station.

Mr. George M. Ward are busy running his binder; the oats coming same time.

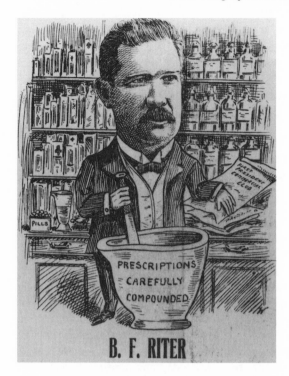

B. F. RITER

Caricature of Benjamin Franklin Riter. *From* The Journal, *Logan, January 22, 1910.*

Mr. Soquitch Timbimboo and wife return home last Saturday from working down Elwood. The little boy of Mr. Timbimboo had appendicitis and he was given Dr. treatment and Dr. say he will get over it. But improving very nice.

Our people are in good condition so far. No more news. [1913-08-14-B BEN]

Our Friend Ottogary Once More

WASHAKIE, AUGUST 11, 1913.   We . . . [busy] harvesting grain crop and looking very promising. But some of the boy working white man steamer thresher down near Garland. Lot of work this county seem to be can[not] get any hand around here. We short hand every day. Mr. Grouse Creek Jack was out hunting now.

We very good condition so far no one sick and some the boy work on railroad now. Well we had nice shower last night.

Mr. Thomas Pabawena down yesterday for working every since two or three month. He is still working on it.

All our Second crop hay is put [up] all ritty [ready]. Our day school hasn't start up yet. We had very nice roads and Bridge put in last three month. It is nice traveling through there. Excuse me Journal readers. But I did[n't] get news quick enough. Because I live quite away from town. I try my best. [1913-08-14 LJ]

WASHAKIE, DECEMBER 11, 1913.   I am going a drop a few word to Journal, But I am kind sorry didn't write a for long time and nearly for got about it until I see Mr. B. Riter in Garland other day . . . so thought I would [write] a letter to the Office. And our people are working in sugar beet fields north Garland. All return home wk last.

Our people are good condition, no one sick, no death so far. Some Indians from Pocatello, from west are working in sugar beet this year. There was three or four Operation happened here in our town this yr. They had appendicitis. Our people are getting same disease as white men. Most young people are sick. There was 11 operation since about 5 year. And our grain crop good this yr.

Mr. Geo. M. Ward still running a store yet. He making a business here. Two weeks ago there was trouble; one boy got away with ladies at night. The boy was arrested but they could not do anything because he was not right age. The court take up the matter can not do anything. And these ladies find [fined] $2.50 each. And court let them go. Our people are having a nice time on Xmas. The Indian are rejoice the Christmas is coming. [1913-12-18 LJ]

Willie Ottogary's Washakie Letter

WASHAKIE, DECEMBER 29, 1913.   I am going write a few line. And we have had pretty nice time on Xmas day. We had nice programme. . . . But big feast in ward meeting house. The house was full, and evening have a grand ball, have a nice old jolly time. Our people are rejoice when the old year gone away.

Mr. Jacob Brownie & his wife was here with us from Ross Fork, Idaho [Fort Hall Reservation]. Then he return next morning. He was very enjoyed and also some [four boys] . . . from Skull Valley was here too. They return home on Friday last.

On Saturday last there was a big rabbit hunt here. They slaughter quite number of bunnies and the boys are nearly hunting every day, and hunting for scalp. The county pay 5¢ a piece for them. We had very cold [weather] here. The snow is 6 or 7 inch deep.

Mr. George P. Sam building a nice home.

Mr. Ammon Pubigee been down Brigham City on matters of business next year. But I kind of sorry I didn't write for long time. It is very nice sleighing . . . plenty of snow. [1914-01-01 LJ]

WASHAKIE, DECEMBER 29, 1913.   I am going to write a few line. But I am sorry didn't write such a long time, . . . try to [do] better next come year. I was pretty near forget all about it, until I call at News office other day. . . .

One boy baby born here two weeks . . . ago. Mr. Heanan [Neaman] wife born boy baby doing very nice. . . .[42]

But our people are rejoiced new year's coming. . . . Our people are all well this year. There was about 12 operation the appendicitis in 5 years. Most of them is young people. . . . [1914-01-01 BEN]

3

"I Am Going Tell Some News,"[1]
1914–1920

WASHAKIE, JANUARY 13, 1914.   Our boys been rabbit hunting every day, They slaughter . . . about 3 or 4,000 thousand rabbit. They was hunting for scalp. They made pretty good money. Well, Mr. George P. Sam nearly done his house. I hope he will have a good home, and Mr. Thomas Tybooty [Thomas Tyboatz] helping him on his house every since before Xmas and N. Year. . . . Mr. Quarretz Wongan sick in bed. He was under Indian Dr. care.[2] He might come through alright. And also Mr. Jim Dioves wife is pretty sick too. He was from Hall Reservation. He may return home some[time] this winter. Miss Terna Pitch is still living she was about 90 years old.[3] She was oldest woman living in our town. One baby girl born last week and she was died here. . . . [And] mother is not well, she get little better now. [1914-01-15 BEN]

Quarretz and Warren Wongan, father and son. Two weeks after this photo was taken, Quarretz died: "Died at hospital in Garland [Utah]. Went by train to hospital by himself." Quarretz's father, James Wongan, and his wife, Lucy Honeva, were grandparents of Moroni Timbimboo. *Courtesy Mae Timbimboo Parry.*

WASHAKIE, JANUARY 13, 1914.   Our people are rejoiced our spring times is coming. . . .
Dr. Gragun from Garland was seen here other day on business. One woman is pretty
sick, having baby birth, and use cholform [chloroform] on her. The baby died. . . .
[mother] was pretty sick. She might come through all right in few days. [Baby] was
buried yesterday afternoon.

They was boys hunting long ears rabbit last week. They slaughter . . . about over
1,000 and some the boys hasn't return home.

Mr. James Joshua lost one of his work horse . . . kicked hind leg and broked. . . .
Our day school very splendid this year. . . . [1914-01-17 LJ]

WASHAKIE, JANUARY 27, 1914.   The people are here rejoice here about winter. We
are good condition this winter. Nearly all snow gone away. Some of our Sunday
School workers been down attend Sunday School convention. There was Supt.
Moroni Timbimboo, Timus Perdash, Henry Wonsook, James Brown, and myself
too. We [had] very enjoyable time. . . .

Last Saturday there was an Indian agent from Salt Lake City, was here at
Washakie, and assist one lady [Philene Hall]. She was sent by Government out
here to examine everyone. . . . She going back Sunday morning soon as she get in
S. L. C. She will report the matter back Washington D. C. Then she will have an
office here at Washakie before long. She going have treatment the eyes. She might
coming back some time next month.[4] [1914-01-29-A LJ]

Willie Ottogary at the Round-up[5]
WASHAKIE, JANUARY 27, 1914.   I visit Utah Agriculture College, accompanied
Bishop K. H. Findall. Then went in museum room. stayed 20 minutes. It is quite
interesting in there to seen many kind quadruped, and various kind fowl, many
insects, so &c.

Next visit was room 177. That was quite interesting too, to see . . . many kind
bone of animals.

But next we went in College chapel to attend meeting [and] hear the lectures.
First on programme was Prof. Louis Boyle from Salt Lake City. The subject was
upon potatoes. . . .

Afternoon session commence 1:30 o'clock sharp. Mr. Bishop A. L. Hyer was
experience on potatoes lecture. He gave on same subject. . . . Next was Dr. George
R. Hill his subject was same, but disease of potatoes. . . . He was from U. A. C.

Mr. Joseph Quinney Jr. treated upon sugar-beet culture. . . .

Well I am very interesting the meeting today. [1914-01-29-B LJ]

Willie Ottogary Reports Roundup
LOGAN, JANUARY 28, 1914.   Meeting. Mr. C. D. Marsh, U. S. Dep. [of Agriculture]
His subject was upon Poisonous plant. . . . Many cattle, sheep, are dying [from]
such plants.

Next speaker was J. W. Hurren from Hyde Park. His topic was upon Irrigation.
. . . And he was explain the yield. . . . His lecture very splendid on this subject.

Also Mr. Hancy was discussion on Irrigation a few minutes.

Next speakers was Pr. [Prof.] W. W. McLaughlin. He was treat upon the Utah First Irrigation after the Pioneer Reach this Utah country. By that time the water has not made then. That was 1830 A.D. [probably means 1850].

Pres. John A. Widtsoe, next speaker.[6] But he was on same track as Mr. McLaughlan, and tell use. How the water their crops so on, many other points. He tell use how much water on acres. He was figured, 5 in., 28 bu, 50—45 bu. so on. You people know more than I can. But our people are never learn to farm in their life.

Mr. Wheelon was discussing the Bear River Valley, before the Great Canal took out, so on. Today this valley splendid water supplier. Raise so much fruit, many kind, chief was apples, peaches, grain, &c.

Meeting January 29.

First speaker was Pro. W. W. McLaughlin on same subject about Irrigation System. . . . Next on program was Mr. W. O. Knudson on cherry industry. He said I find the cherry business are money making. He was mention many kind of cherries which was Windsor, Napoleon, Black Tartarian, Bing, Lambert, Montmorency, & Knudson, & c. He said must select your soil. If want raise cherries. He said it is more money [in] dried cherries. . . .

The next topic was treated by Mr. Hancy about tile drainage. . . .

Mr. Dr. L. Bachlor . . . [discussed] apples, but mention so many. . . . Jonathan, Winesap, rome beauty, Gano, R. I. Greening, Arkansas and McIntosh, &c. And also many kind varieties of Utah fruit, which was, pears, peaches, sweet cherries, sour cherries, & plums and prunes.

In after[noon] session first lecture by Mr. L. Bachlor . . . interesting lecture upon fruit, &c. Next lecture was Mr. Frank Stevephens [Stevens], his subject is about people co-operation in market. How they handle the thing, and purchasing of supplies. What more must be done, and other many work.

Mr. J. H. Barralow [Barlow], his subject was on business. But he told how many men can live in city. How they get their provision by which way, and tell us about co-operation what they done in Great Salt Lake city people. I suppose he was [doing] a great business in S. L. C. and import and export. . . . And he also retreated on how the man live on an acre land in city. How they grow their vegetable and grain, many other. It is very interesting speech upon his subject, &c.

12 o'clock I was been through Green house to look over very beautiful flowers. I seen many kind flowers plant. It is very interesting visit, that place. I am so tired I could [not] write any more. I wish all Journal are great surprized [to] read my letter about farmers round-up. I am stay Logan now. Good by to you all.[1914-01-31 LJ]

LOGAN, JANUARY 30, 1914.   At the opening meeting was Mr. E. B. Hawkins, treated Bee industry. The good profit in raising bee. . . .

Well, next visit Ladies meeting room 29; I was very surprise so many ladies been meeting [in] that [room]. A subject is upon dress good. I believe there was about 3 hundred ladies gathering in meeting that morning. Mrs. J. H. Linford, Mrs. J. A. Widtsoe; the subject was 2 yr girl dress. . . .

Next visit is room 177 where the animal foot exhibit. Dr. H. J. Frederick was lecture upon horses foot; . . . and he mention half doz. kind of shoes. But about one hour spoke in that subject, then turn over to Mr. Wm. Thornley, preparing the horse's foot for the shoe. These was held in the Mechanic Arts building a few minutes. These was great interesting to attend this lecture, so on. Mr. Wm. Thornley lecture . . . in shoeing, demonstration, and fitting shoes, . . . and proper way to nail on.

Next lecture was upon fruit trees by Dr. L. Bachlor. . . .

Jan. 31–14—Meeting held at College chapel. First open was Mr. Peterson the subject was dry farming. He was mention different . . . kind of grain to raise on dry farm, and he tell which kind to sow, and which kind to not sow. Well, he was good lecture on his subject all away through. . . . And also Mr. Pres. J. W. Paxman talking upon dry farming. He said the dry farming crop abundant last year. . . .

Next speaker was Governor Ammon of Colorado, was retreated up on cattle raising. He tell us how raise steers. . . . Kind proper food for an animal, when want put in market, and about weaning calves. . . . Also about the shipment and fatt[en]ing too, &c.

Next was Governor Wm. Spry [of Utah], gave us same as Mr. Ammon did. Welcome address people a few minutes. But he said I set in seat thinking about cattle, sheep and swine. It is good money raising good cattle, sheep and swine. I know barley are good feed for hogs, he said again, and also talk of the pigs. That reason we build a college to help people, that their children be educated in them to learn many things, &c.

Next visit is day Nurse room. Mrs. Samuel Quinney is very busy with children every day. I suppose last Saturday she have assistance a few girls. The children more then any other day. It is lot of fun to see them children play, she got so many plaything for children. Last Saturday I have [company of] Mr. Noragan [Kippetchew]. We to meet in chapel. Then we visit a museum room, horse shoe Mechanic Art building, carpenter shop, electric exhibit, Exhibition of painting, sculpture, design and craft work, and Gymnasium building, and many other I could [not] mention right. He was great surprise been through the college building that was first he ever been through that building.

In evening about 8 o'clock the reception to farmers who visit Logan was given at Commerical room Booster Club of Logan at club room. There is many visitors be present having splendid time. Also the music was played few time. [1914-02-03 LJ]

LOGAN, FEBRUARY 2, 1914.   Meeting held at College chapel open morning session was Mr. B. Eldredge. The years ago there was no dairy. They was a very good dairying today, good market for butter than before. Now is Utah dairying very splendid. . . . Dairy-men are getting more brains than before the yr ago. He said again the dairying a good profit and good business, every where in the state; other states too.

Next Mr. John T. Caine was . . . mention some very best dairy cows in the state which Jersey cow, pure Holstein and many others. . . . Next was treated sick cow. Well, gave cow 2 spoon full of Ginger and apposom [epsom] salt. Then proper food for the cows, this is for milk cows. The feed was rolled barley and bran, which was very best feed for dairy cows.

Two o'clock session. Mr. J. E. Dorman, His subject was upon butter. . . .

Next speaker was Mr. C. M. Lambert. His subject was, related to the factory. The cheese good Produce in whole state. The factory will be better profit. . . .

Tuesday meeting, Feb. 3.—Open meeting was Mr. John T. Caine III. His subject was principles feed of dairy cows. And he mention few of them which is lucern and bran. And he got composition proper food for dairy cows.

Then he mention some proper food for different animal. The alfalfa with corn, bran and timothy and wild hay for dairy cow; short, corn and barley for pigs; alfalfa and oats for work horses, and alfalfa, bran and corn fodder for raising colt or calves.

Next speaker was Mr. David A. Smith. Clean milk delivered in cities. He talk condition of fresh milk a few minutes, the cause of becketeraia [bacteria]. He was mention the right kind of can to [use when] milk[ing] . . . it is good milk bucket to be used. . . . Lecture on same subject by Pross. W. Peterson, U. A. C.

Mr. John Reeve open meeting afternoon session. He was from Hinckley, Utah. His subject was on dairying business, and also Mr. Bailey Nelson from Richmond, Utah, on same subject. Next speaker was Hon. Mr. W. S. Hansen, on the result of Co-operation of the farmers in Box Elder County of Utah, many point of farmer business, &c. He was from Collinston, Utah. [1914-02-07 LJ]]

LOGAN, FEBRUARY 4, 1914.   Meeting held at College Chapel. Prof. John Caine III, the subject was on the swine. . . . It is very profitable raising hogs. . . .

Next speaker was Mr. C. W. Lindsay; . . . he mention proper feed for hogs too. His lecture same as Mr. Caine 3.

Next was Dr. H. J. Frederick his subject was on hog cholera. . . . [Mr.] Murdock. He was a great sheep man in west state. . . . I think the sheep business pretty good profit. . . .

Mr. Wm. Peterson take up . . . road business on the county,—and political business and many other thing. . . . Some the farmer have automobiles some day. . . .

Meeting Feb. 5, 1914, at College chapel. Mr. Prof. John T. Caine 3 was open session in morning. The subject was the beef cattle of west, and also about all United States of the America.

Mr. C. G. Adney subject is on raising beef steer, and he was great cattle man in Box Elder Co. . . . He made good talk up on the cattle business.

Next Mr. C. W. Carlyle upon same subject . . . [and] then he little talk upon hogs raising. He said it is good profit raise pigs. Well, he made very splendid talk upon these subject, &c.

The conjoint meeting held at College chapel, 2 o'clock sharp. The meeting was conduct by Pres. John Widtsoe. . . .

Next speaker was Mr. Ball. He said the great gathering of farmer round up today is very great number. It is more than 7 or 8 yr. ago. There was a great number of people been registered this year. I believe about over 1,000. We had about 1,200 student in our College this year, boys and girls. That is our great mission to teacher boys and girls many things, &c. We not ashame to telling people here today.

Next Mr. E. D. Ball is [in] experiment Station U. A. C. We find that is strong foundation U. A. C. It is secret and wonderful things. But we are larger Utah Arig. College, school in whole United States, &c.

Mr. C. W. Porter talking upon women work is important. I think the importants the girls learn then boys. And well educated girl pretter [better] condition.

Pres. Thomas talk same thing on the . . . work for women. Chief engineer of U.
A. C. talk, take up same subject. Also next speaker was Mr. Lambert, Mr. C. W.
Carlyle, Mr. J. Hamilton, Mr. J. E. Dormus [Dorman]. The stock judging was held at
Pavillion building, about 3:30 P.M. It is splendid one every I know. [1914-02-10 LJ]

LOGAN, FEBRUARY 8, 1914.   Meeting for Feb 6. 14 open morning session by Pro. Mr.
John Caine III Lecture upon the beef cattle. Next speaker was Mr. A. D. Bell. His
subject was butchering cattle and hogs. Showed how the dress beef at the kill. But
he has a kind of moving picture show on kill beef, and dress also hogs. How [to]
hang after dress. How skinning . . . too. The use hammer next is shooting. Right
way to kill and right way to stick the animal too.
    To scald, just put front quarter in barrel first, then next hind quarter. Then next
how cured meat. I will [tell] about cured and salted. Take about 6 lbs. salt, 2 sugar,
2 oz. salt beater [saltpeter or Potassium Nitrate], 5 gal of the water, for the 100 lbs.
pork. Or else you may take wood for smoke. Must select what kind you use. I believe
wild Box Elder tree very good, [make] taste . . . [better] than any other tree. . . .
    2 o'clock meeting. Lecture by the Mr. T. E. Murray The proper method of
killing animal. . . . The proper way condition slaughter yard, [etc.]. . . .
    Feb. 7, 1914. Meeting held at Utah Agr. College. Mr. C. Y. Cannon. Lecture of
the draft horses and business horses. He said about horses are valuable . . . and also
explain about automobile. He [said] the farmer ought have auto on the farm. . . .
    Next speaker was Mr. Carlyle talking about the draft horses and driver. He was
given a pretty good addressing on his subject, and other on the horses. . . . He
from Idaho College. Most his lecture very good and welcome address, &c. . . .
[1914-02-14 LJ]

ELWOOD, JUNE 5, 1914.   I am going write a few stories. But we are good condition. I
heard the Government lawyer or executive lawyer was up to Washakie last month
on his business, investigating the Indian land question. But some of the young
people haven't any land. Then they ask him for land. . . . They want get some land
of their own. Perhaps government might help us. Well, we would like it. Here on
my farm some the boys from Washakie help putting up some hay. . . .
    Mr. L. D. Creel, a special Indian agent, was up Washakie sometime ago. Two
months ago Mr. L. D. Creel and one woman were here to examination our people
eye. But they interfere our eyes get sore worse. We believed she must got medicine
on her finger. Everybody eyes get worse. But she didn't do any good. She said to
come to treated our eyes right away; but she didn't show up. The government sent
her out here.
    Some our people is working around Garland sugar factory. I think good wages,
thinning sugar beet. We have quite storm here. I hope we have a good crop here
this year. The sheep man loading their wool. [1914-06-09 LJ]

Willie Ottogary Writes to Journal
ELWOOD, JULY 12, 1914.   We are very enjoyed to have so much rain. But our spring
grain . . . frozen. They too much damage. So we kind discouraged about it. Our
crop looking very promising also our beet crop too.

85337

Salt Lake City, Utah.
July 25, 1914.

The Commisioner Indian Affiars,
        Wahhington, D. C.
Sir; The Shoshone Indians of Washakie , Box Elder Co.
Utah in council assembled at Washakie Utah , July 24,
1914 decided to write you about our claims under the
Treaty made with the chiefs and head men of the
Shoshone North W estern Bands July 30 1863 at Box Elde
Elder Utah Territory , see Page 850 Kapler Laws and
Treaties and we most respecrfully request that you
investigate this treaty at your very earliest convenie.
nce and reply to our letter as soon as you have done
this .
        We were born and raised on this land and our father
before us were also. We want some of this land around
Garland, Utah.
        We also believe that the money and articles to be
paid as specified in article No.7 of this treaty has not
been paid as agreed.
            Yours very respectfully,

Signed   Mr. Willie Ottogary
          Geo. P. Sam

                    Commitee ·

A letter to the commissioner of Indian affairs by Willie Ottogary, July 25, 1914. *RG 75, 59756-14-Scattered Bands in Utah-311, CCF National Archives.*

There was two death this summer and five accident happen this season.

Well, Mrs. Joseph Woonsook are very sick now. She fell off buggy, hurt her knee and bruised her knee cap about four week ago. Her case was very bad her was swollen offle [awfully] bad. I hope she will get well later on. . . .

Our harvest time is coming now. Our grain start turning yellow. We are much celebration on 4th July at Washakie. . . .

Our young men talking about the land, because they didn't have land, so we talk the matter over and we appoint 3 committee our young people which their name is, Mr. Willie Ottogary, Mr. Geo. P. Sam and Mr. Thomas Pabawena.[7] But we went to Salt Lake City upon the matter to see special Indian agent, Mr. L. D. Creel this matter and about the treaty made in 1863, July 30, which took place in Brigham City.

But I want all people be civilized.[8] I expect the Journal readers must think I am quit writing to the Journal, but I am not give up yet. I trying my very best to write a few line. [1914-07-14 LJ]

Willie Ottogary Heard From Again

ELWOOD, JANUARY '6 [SIC], 1915.   I am going drop a few line; but I am sorry didn't write for long time. I and my people are good condition. Mr. James Brown was died here about 5 o'clock Monday morning, he was well known in our country and also many other country. He is 75 years of age. Some white people known him in this section of the country. He is very good member in the Church of Jesus Christ. He

A handwritten letter to the second assistant commissioner of
Indian affairs by Willie Ottogary, October 23, 1914. CCF
59756-14-Scattered Bands in Utah-311, RG 75, National Archives.

was an Indian interpreter in year 1863 and live alone for many year. His wife been
left about 13 years or more, and one son left behind. Not much property.

Well, his funeral service held at Washakie chapel. . . . Many people are attended his service, and he rest peacebly in Washakie cemetery.

Another old age woman is lyed rest peace. She being 105 year old. Her funeral
service in same [place] on Sunday morning at 10 o'clock A. M. She was relative to
Mr. James Brown. One son live, one granddaughter live mourning her loss; and
also many other friend and relative.

There was about five births in 1914, and two deaths took place in our ward.

We had very nice weather this winter; warm day and night is very cold. The
Indians are here to be get some land from Government in future time. I been working for Indian here on our treaties made in Box Elder Co. in year 1863, July 30.
Well, hope we will get it on next year. I been wrote to Washington, D. C. and I
received [letter], and my last letter stated and promised to pay the treaties. It has
been about 51 years since made with general government. I think we will take this
up with Mr. Harris, second commissioner of Indian affairs, Washington, D. C.
Some my people want one of us went to Washington, D. C., see about the business. I do not know who going back. We will find out later on.

The most of our young boys haven't no land. That reason they to go back
Washington, D. C. talk up the matter.

We have had very good celebration New Year. . . . Well, I hope all the Journal readers must be disappointed on account I being not write for such long time.

Mr. B. Riter wrote me a letter. He was kindalonesome he said in his letter. He wants me to write to Journal again once more. I will do my very best in this. I will say to all Journal readers a Happy New Year all the United States. [1915-01-09 LJ]

WASHAKIE, JANUARY 18, 1915.   I am going write a few stories about our condition. I hope I will do better this coming new year. . . .

Oh, some of our people are deciding get new land. Most of our young haven't got land. I been talking matters with our special agent, Mr. L. D. Creel, Salt Lake City.

Well Mr. James Brown was died. . . . He was well known in our country. And Indian interpreter for many years, and also many other country too. He was about 75 year of age. Once he was raise with white man in his boyhood. His wife been divorce 12 years ago and live alone since she left. . . .

But our day school running very nicely this year.

We had have very nice sleigh this year. The boys been hunting bunnies every week, must be slaughtered quite [a lot] of them this year.

Well been have big council about our treaties in July 30, 1863. I been take this matter with our special agent Mr. L. D. Creel. He say we will government allotted on later on. I like see this come [to] pass. This treaties I mention made a peace with white on northwestern part Utah on Box Elder Country. Our claims bounty [boundary] line west Raft River, north Pornif [Portneuf] Mountains, south middle Salt Lake, East Wasatch mountains so on and I don't know what government says about our treaties. . . .

I am been in town to-day call in Box Elder News office this afternoon and giving some news. Today is the big day. I saw a man from Kansas City to buying some Brigham horses and see quite number of people from north part in the Brigham City to-day. [1915-01-21 BEN]

Willie Ottogary in Washington

WASHINGTON, D. C., FEBRUARY 26, 1915.   I am been in East Country. But and [with] my cousin Annies Tommy. I have been write to you, that tell we are in state Maryland and cross state Colorado, Utah, Kansas, Missouri, Illinois, Indiana, West Virginia and also Maryland. We start from home on 18 February, 1915, and got here on 22 day of Feb. . . .

We meet one of the guide soon as we get off our train and he take to Indian head-quarters, and he took us into Zoogocial [zoological] Park, where they had wild animals and many other thing. I could [not] mention because so many, and also took us in National Museum. It is very large building. It covers about 5 acres ground.

On 25 Feb. 1915, went to the capitol and visit in it, looking through it. Well, it very large building, it covers about 40 acres ground. This large building stand on top the hill. Our next visit was the Capital Laberian [library] we spend about 2 hours reading the book. . . . Other day we was visit Washington port. It was very interesting visit and looking over various kind of ships, and boats, and steamship, we next visit . . . oyster market, where the oyster comes from other country.

Spirit of Unrest Among Red Men of Utah; More Land Is. Demanded.

Believing that under various old treaties with the government that the Indians living on the Washakie reservation in Box Elder county are entitled to much more land than they now have, Willie Ottogary and other Indians from that reservation today consulted local federal officials to see what may be done for the red-men.

Ottogary, who is an educated Indian and has had some experience as a journalist, was sent by the Indians of his tribe to Washington to look up the various treaties and see whether or not the reds are not being deprived of land that is legally theirs. The Indian office there referred him to L. D. Creel, U. S. Indian agent for Utah.

When the delegation called upon Creel today, they were shown the treaties, copies of which are on file, and were told that they had a wrong conception of the matter—that their tribesmen had signed the various treaties which gave much of the land in Box Elder county that they claim to the white men. Ottogary and the others were stubborn, however, and refused to believe Creel. He then advised them to see an attorney that they could trust.

Ottogary replied that there was none the Indians could trust; that the Indians had no friends anywhere among the whites.

After the conference with Creel the delegation spent several hours with. W. W. Ray, United States district attorney. While no trouble is feared with these Indians, there appears to be a general spirit of unrest among all the tribes of Utah, government officials say.

News article reporting one of Willie Ottogary's several visits to Washington, D.C. *From* The Journal, *Logan, Utah, May 6, 1915.*

News article concerning Willie Ottogary's attempts to addresss Washakie Shoshone land issues and Shoshone distrust of Indian agent Creel. *From Salt Lake City (Utah)* Telegram, *April 17, 1915. CCF 59756-14-Scattered Bands in Utah-311, RG 75, National Archives.*

WILLIE OTTOGARY VISITS WASHINGTON

ELWOOD, May 3.—I am going to write short stories what I been known in the past time I have been Washington, D. C. twice this year; but I know so many thing, I could mention so many things, but I been forgot some of them. But I will tell the Journal readers where been, through the different building back and business houses do. I see and through Capitall, White House, Great Post Office building, Congress, House of representative, Senate National Museum, Congressnail Libraries, Pensions Building Zoocail Park, and many others good building. Well and been Haskell Indian school at Kansas on April 9, 1915, where the lot of the Indian boys and girls been school. We been every building in the school. We covered first place laundry, creamery, bakery, kitchen, dinner room, blacksmith, machanic room, engineer room, carpenter room, harness room, mason room, etc. We had very nice trip out their, and very splendid to acquainted many boys and girls to the school. There was about 700 Indian children going to school that place. But went telling all boys up their to Washakie what I have been seen back East. Oh I never see so many people at the East. And also went through big cities back East. I will name some off it, which is St. Louis, Kansas City, Cincinnati, Ohio, Chicago, Council Buff, Omaha City, and Pittburg Pa., and, but I could not mention some small town on the line. Our people at Washakie are good condition so far, no one sick. Mr. Johny Tomock and wife been down to Ogden on little business. Mr. Catch and wife been seen in Garland some ago, last week.

WILLIE OTTOGARY.

26 day of Feb. we visit the Washington Monument and up on the elevator looking around the city. But is grand sight and elevator went a high as 470 ft. The outside this building was 555 ft. off the ground. Our next visit was the Bureau of Engraving and building where the government making all stamps and greenbacks. I believe there is about 4000 emplores [employees] of the whole building. And next visit was the National Museum building, next was Director Medical National building. We were very interesting visit all these buildings see so many we could [not] see before in our lives. And also we acquainted some big town in East . . . Kansas City, St. Louis, Missouri, Cincinnati, Ohio, Grafton, West Virginia and Cormblund [Cumberland], Maryland, and many other towns. We been stayed at the New Capitol Hotel, Philadelphia, 3 Street, N. W. [1915-03-04 BEN]

Willie Ottogary Visits Washington[9]

ELWOOD, MAY 3, 1915. I am going to write short stories. . . . I have been Washington, D. C., twice this year; but I know so many thing, I could [not] mention so many things, but I been forgot some of them. But I will tell the Journal readers where I been, through the different buildings back and business houses do [could mean ditto or too]. I see and through Capitol, White House, Great Post Office building, Congress, House of Representative, Senate, National Museum, Congressnail [Congressional] libraries, Pensions Building, Zoocail [zoological] Park, and many others good building. Well and been Haskell Indian School at Kansas on April 9, 1915, where the lot of the Indian boys and girls been school.

Mamie Perdash Wongan and
Warren Wongan, 1916. *Courtesy
Mae Timbimboo Parry.*

We covered first place laundry, creamery, bakery, kitchen, dinner room, blacksmith, mechanic room, engineer room, carpenter room, harness room, mason
room, etc. We had very nice trip out there, and very splendid to acquainted many
boys and girls to the school. There was about 700, Indian children going to school
that place. But went [want] telling all boys up there to Washakie what I have been
seen back East. Oh I never see so many people as the East. And also went through
big cities back East . . . St. Louis, Kansas City, Cincinnati, Ohio, Chicago, Council
Buff [Bluff], Omaha City, and Pittsburg, Pa., and but I could not mention some
small towns on the line. Our people at Washakie are good condition so far, no one
sick. . . . [1915-05-06 LJ]

WASHAKIE, DECEMBER 20, 1915.   The people here at this town are all good condition. But our day school good running. . . . The school children very good now.
     Mrs. Warren Wongan [Mamie Perdash Wongan] was form operation appen-
dicitis some time ago, a month last. She was hospital in Brigham City. She doing
nicely. She return home week last. And there was about three death took place
this year. There names was Joseph Paniboo, Sig-g-ye-gant Jack and Mr. Seth
Pubigee's little baby girl passed away.
     I want keep right on for yr. 1916. But I was gave any news such long time. I am
going giving news for next year. I will surprise the Journal reader now. . . . I hope
you will very good news from me. It is a wonderful news. The people are giving
good Xmas programme. It is appeared all ready for Christmas. They are happy for
soon Xmas will be here in our little town.

Mr. George P. Sam went down Brigham City for his girl Dr. treatment. She laid up . . . typhoid 2 month. But she is kind worse so he taking her down town. I hope she will recover in future.

Mr. Daniel [?] and wife and family are going up to Bannock Creek last week, for winter.

Our sugar beet are all harvest for last Mo. we had very good grain crop this year.

Mr. Yeager Timbimboo and wife visiting some his relatives up Idaho. He is return home some time last week.

Mr. Dr. F. Shoemaker was here at Washakie some time ago. about 3 week ago. He treating the eyes people here. They claim him very good Dr. They was 40 per-cent operation here on the eyes, the time he was here. And going out Deep Creek. And he appointed one woman from West Portage [Philene Hall] to take treatment the eyes every day. But some splendid good treatment. I hope they all cured in future.

We very cold weather just now. It is winter soon be here. Mr. Grouse Creek Jack and Sam Jack was help [held] up some time a two high away me [probably high-waymen]. They robbed $4.00 and a pair glove . . . they notified police and he could do any thing but notified county sheriff John Zundel. But he went out arrest one them. He was trapping out west somewhere toward Oakley country.[10]

I was meet Mr. B. Riter in his Drug store one day. He want me write pretty long long story and he said about mile long, on account being not write such long time.

Mr. Mose Neaman went over to Logan some time ago last month. [1915-12-23 LJ]

WASHAKIE, JANUARY 26, 1916.   The people are here good condition and some of the boys are big rabbit hunting . . . couple weeks ago. There was quite numbers of bun-nies kill; about somewhere 700 or 800, and there was about 6 or 5 teams out north of our town—about 15 mile morth, around Samaria, Idaho.

Well, there was about 1 foot snow around here in our vicinity. We had very cold weather now. . . .

Mr. Tip Low and family is here now, and living here; he was from Deeth, Nevada. His children went school here with our children and running very splen-did this winter.

Mr. George P. Sam little girl very sick. I hope she may get recover.

There was about 3 death in 1915. Well, hay scarce here in our town, but hay is worth great deal here, and some has got no hay. The people are here not much work done this winter.

Mr. Geo. M. Ward running a little store here, and doing very splendid business.

They was two boys been arrested here to try running couple the girl. But it was not bad case, and they was out night time—but they sent home after they tried their case. It is not serious. They wed here last week ago couple young couple. . . .

Well, I am going write a few stories now. I hope some of the Journal reader have read my artical so far.

Mr. Grouse Creek Jack and Son trapping out west around Oakley country, but they catching very few coyote.

Some of the boys say it is spring is coming. We have had enough snow here in locality. The people think are plenty snow on ground. It is good sledding. [1916-01-29 LJ]

WASHAKIE, JANUARY 26, 1916. The people are here very surprise to see so much snow. There was 2 foot snow on ground some time ago. . . .

Mr. George P. Sam little girl laid up with . . . typhoid for two months and she is pretty sick girl. . . .

Well the hay is very scarce here in town. Some are feed the horse wheat straw all this winter. And hay worth very high. It is high[er] than any other year. The day school is running pretty good.

Mr. Ammon Pubigee has lost 4 head of work horses. The train been run over them going north in night time. He take matter with section foreman. But he isn't hear from R. R. Co. yet.

Mrs. Phealeane [Philene] Hall is take job in treatment eyes here at Washakie people, and they have bad eyes. The Dr. F. Shoemaker has been here and examined the eyes. But he find quite lot of the people here [had] bad eyes. He operated on them many cases. It is improving very quick. Some has good eyes now. This Dr. Shoemaker sent by the Commissioner of the Indian Affairs, Washington, D. C. [1916-02-03 BEN]

WASHAKIE, MAY 19, 1916. The fall wheat crop is very bad catch with Jack Frost, but didn't hurt the spring [crop]; and fruit is gone too. The sugar beet crop doing good so far. Some of the boys been start shearing sheep last week, and their names are Mr. Pubigee, Sam Jack, Lorenzo Hootchew, Tomy Tyboatz, Stanquitch Jack, Jim Jack, Johny Tomock, Charlie Broom, Joseph Monsook [Woonsook], Jack [Jacob] Peyope, and Mr. Mose Neaman, working for William Mason from River Side. On his farm at East Wash.

Mr. Nephi Zundel still running mail business, and Mr. James Brown has not return from his trip of Idaho; he may return right away.

Mr. Soquitch Timbimboo was seen in Tremonton other day going for south and doing little hunting, and also many others too. Mr. Hyrum Wongsaw and wife, Mr. Frank West going over to Cache valley for little hunting. . . .

But Mr. Moroni Timbimboo expect going in poultry business. And start running two incubator. The people cutting the hay on account the frost. We are need rain pretty bad here. It seem this cold weather didn't do any good. I hope we had good weather again. Some of our people lose their horses this winter. . . .

Mr. Tip Low and family is working down Riverside some day ago. I am getting more news later on. [1916-05-23 LJ]

WASHAKIE, JUNE 21, 1916. The people are here good condition, . . . and some of the Indians are working north Garland on sugar beet field. Get through, all some of them went home. Well, we depending good crop this year, and we had nice little storm some time ago.

Mr. Frank West is lost his wife [Satonsip or Teahtonsip West] about last month ago, but she suffered two wk. before she died. Well, he is lone man for while.

The people here talking that frost going lose the grain crop and other thing; well, the frost didn't damage much.

Mr. James Brown and wife and Mrs. Ottogary return home some time ago, last two week ago.

Mr. James Brown back up to Fort Hall Reservation again on Saturday last, and Mr. Stanquitch Jack going with him, going short visit. . . .

We some happy people here now. The men are working pretty hard for their living now, . . . Washakie is . . . locate in year 1880—and the day school running ever since on the place; and still running very splendid run, also many Indian died here ever since. The most of the old people are passed away. We are discrease [decrease] every yr.

We are join Mormonism every since the people settle, and our church running very orderly yet. And some of us getting pretty tired—some dry farm, but want some irrigation land. I hope are going have water right on the Bear River valley land right away. We had about 1320 acres land on Bear River valley. It is all non-irrigation land. We expect going have water right in future. [1916-06-24 LJ]

WASHAKIE, JULY 14, 1916.   The people are here going a big celebration on 24th July. . . . The some people from Fort Hall coming down here help big time. And some from Skull Valley do too. Well, come here yesterday. But have real good time. . . . They is prepared for 24th or pioneer day. And have all kind sports all day long which was foot races, horse races, and many other sports. . . .

We have pretty dry year. The crop isn't so good this year on account being so dry year, the sugar beet pretty poor this year. . . . And frost catch some of the grain.

Some of the Washakie people went to Wyoming to visit some their relatives and friend. I expect return home some time next week. Well, they have good time out there. But Mr. Charlie Perdash and two sons return home some time ago week last.

Mr. Soquitch Timbimboo and wife was seen tremonton last week and doing some shopping and also Mr. George Timock [Tomock] seen Tremonton too. The same Indians are going down to join in celebration down there. Well, this all the news. [1916-07-18 LJ]

WASHAKIE, AUGUST 9, 1916.   . . . Some Indian from Wind River Reservation are visiting here friends and relatives. I hoping have a good time to visit Indians are here, and they busy harvesting their grain now. The wheat crop is not so good this year. These Indians very busy cutting grain, and sugar beet is fall [fail] this year.

Mr. Grouse Creek Jack laid up sick about one month. He is getting little better.

Mr. Yeager Timbimboo and Co. purchase a new McCormick header. . . .

I and Mr. Sacquitch [Soquitch] Timbimboo been over Black Smith Fork Canyon doing little hunting and fishing a few day last week. Return home some time last week.

We have very dry season this year. Mr. James Brown and wife went up Idaho and accompanied Mrs. Willie Ottogary. And they has not return home yet. I expect be home this week. . . . [1916-08-15 BEN]

WASHAKIE, AUGUST 16, 1916.   The people are here doing fine and harvest nearly all done by this time and some of them start thresh now. Mr. Charley Smith with steam thresher pulled in here threshing all our grain. The grain crop not much good this [year] on account being so dry and also the sugar beet crop too. . . .

Mr. George Tanguitch [Tospanguitch] been in Gentile Valley at the hot spring having been good hot bath; but he is kind sick.

Mr. James Brown has not been return yet from Idaho, and made a long visit. Nobody sick now. But Mr. Grouse Creek Jack sick. He is getting pretty good now. . . .

Mr. Thomas Pabawena is not return from Wyoming visit. He may return next month.

Some the boys been down Tremonton on Sunday and enjoyed themself in town. The water is very scarce this year.

Some of Indian have land down near Tremonton and leasing out to the white man and some of them run they own self. I hoping them make some money. . . .

Mr. Henry Hootchew made a quick trip up Idaho with some white man in auto. But he looking for some one owns the land down near Tremonton, and didn't find anything.

Mrs. Willie Ottogary has not return from Idaho trip. She expect be down 20th . . . this month. But going up on her health and sick-bed when she went up, and now is improving and well as ever. I hope she made good visit to her relatives and friends up in Idaho.

The people enjoyed to harvest their grain and nearly over with. . . . [1916-08-22 LJ]

WASHAKIE, SEPTEMBER 11, 1916.   The people are progressing right along and our school hasn't start yet. It is soon. But our threshing is done for this year and sold our grain [and got] good price this year, the sugar beet crop is not so good this year. . . . The people are here rejoice hear the Brigham City Peach Day is coming. And some of them want join the crowd. I hoping they are splendid time down there. Mr. Soquitch Timbimboo and wife return home from Hyrum and gather some wild fruit.

Mr. George Comanke was hurt through [thrown] out from wagon near the West Portage and is layed up now and hurt pretty bad and one wheel run over him across his stomach. He was going to Portage then his wagon hit little hole and jump, then he slip his foot hold and fell under the wagon between his horses.

Well sir I was meet Mr. F. F. Whitt from Lewiston, Utah in the Mr. Everet Hardware Store on 24th last month. But he talking with me and he find I am one of the responded [correspondents for] the Journal. He want me advertise his twin boys, he said to me I have twin boys 21 year in 2 day of Sept. 1916. . . . And certely [certainly] supporter to President Mr. Windrow [Woodrow] Wilson. . . ."
[1916-09-12 LJ]

WASHAKIE, OCTOBER 5, 1916.   The people are rejoicing here. We have had very spendid storm here in our vicinity.

Well, there was a quite crowd went down Peach Day. . . . Our people very surprise to see the air plan[e]. They never see one like it before. It is very strange—to them man going up in air with his air machine.

Postcard of Henry Hootchew and Amos Moemberg in Western outfits. Note on back reads: "Picture was took in Salt Lake in Aug 19-1916. . . . Henry Hootchew, Amos Morbang." *Courtesy Mae Timbimboo Parry.*

Some of them been out west around Cassia County, Idaho, and all return home last week, but gather some pine nuts and gather quite number of bushel. Mr. William [?] and wife just return from west, and gathering pine nuts, and some Indians is in Tremonton town and doing some shopping.

Mr. Charlie Broom, Enos Pubigee, Amos Moemberg and wife are going work . . . soon ground get dryer. We had about 3 day rain and soak in ground about 3 foot . . . but it is impossible to work. All the farmer ready to digs and commence raining and stop everything.

Some boys are out working Pocatello Valley. They pitching on steam thresher.[12] I believe about 20 boys out helping white men out there. I hoping get through this week.

We don't have Indian fair this year on account our agent been call off his term. We might for next yr. I am telling people go have an Indian fair. . . .[13]

Well Indian land on Bear River Valley all lease out this fall and some Indians are business to leasing again and some of them to move down on farm, I hope next spring. . . . [1916-10-10 L]]

WASHAKIE, OCTOBER 18, 1916.   . . . The people are working take their crop out the ground, we will make little money working on sugar beets. They topping sugar beets for 14 or 13 dollars per acre and three Indians come from Fort Hall Reservation were here with them down valley, and there was very few Indians is here now. Most of them work on sugar beets. The sugar beets poor this year.

Indian women stitching. Caption at top reads, "Each of these
Indian women were awarded prizes." *CCF 10366-14-Scattered
Bands in Utah-047, RG 75, National Archives.*

There was hay very scarce this year. . . . Some Indians move down on lower farm
for next year, and work their own farm, and some been release [re-leased] again, 4
or 5 year.[14]

Our day school run very poor; the children are down Garland. Well, some of
them return 2 weeks yet.

We had very poor wheat crop this year.

Mr. John Green from Fort Hall Reservation visiting some of his old friend. And
also Mr. Johny Ond-baby, is come here last 2 day ago. I been still working [for] my
people now. I write letter to Indian office, Washington D. C., on special business
as follows:

Tremonton, Utah, Oct. 17.—Mr. J. H. Doutch [Dortch], Washington D. C.
friend.

Mr. Mc-Conihe was here about Oct. 1915 and made council with [us] at
Washakie. But asked us . . . where are you want land, we said around Garland on
Bear River valley. We . . . said to him you look and see page 850 Kappler laws
and treaties, you will find our treaty there.

This Moroni Ward telling untruth statements. These Indians having no land
allotted, and all [our] children we desire should not move. We been forever
[here] all our lives. Because this our native land we desire this Moroni Ward

Outside of an Indian fair venue. Caption reads, "Indians passing in and out as they were called to receive their prizes." *CCF 59756-14-Scattered Bands in Utah-047, RG 75, National Archives.*

should move out. . . . Also this Moroni Ward misleading Indians outside the country claims by Pocatello from himself and his people is bounded on the west by Raft river and on the east by Portneuf Mountains.

From you, Willie Ottogary and Geo. P. Sam.

[After inserting his and Sam's letter to the Indian office, Ottogary returns to his regular subject matter:]

We have pretty bad weather this year. Indians here are never anything from Government. They need pretty bad too. Well, we might have it later on. But everyone the Journal readers open the eyes about these matters. I see the people are not seen our treaties made in Brigham City in year 1863 July 30—So I take matter to commissioner year from last June 15, 1915 we will receive it later on soon. [1916-10-21 LJ]

1916-11-10 BEN [Not included]

WASHAKIE, OCTOBER 19, 1916.   Our people are working in sugar beets down near Garland factory for white mens. But is bad weather for it. The people are worrying [how] get their crop out the ground. They will making a little money working on sugar beet. Some Indians from Fort Hall reservation coming down work too.

Mr. Grouse Creek Jack is sick in bed, and hoping he will get better later on.

School is not so good, the children take away from school [for farm work]. But some get through topping [beets] . . . then go to school.

Nobody died here now yet. There is about one or two death this year.

And some Indian boys working on threshing machine up in Pocatello Valley. [1916-10-20 BEN]

WASHAKIE, NOVEMBER 6, 1916.   . . . Mr. Bannock Frank and wife is here also work in sugar beets. Mr. Grouse Creek Jack is still sick now, but he get little improved. Mr. Moroni Timbimboo and Warren Wongan is working sugar factory. We have had quite storm here; last night snowed some and cold here.

There was quite lot of sugar beet in ground yet down around Garland city. They are very anxious to harvest their beet crop. There was about 4 inch snow on ground yet.

Mrs. Willie Ottogary is run away from home and divorce about a month ago. She won't come back home any more. She will be no more wife to Mr. Willie Ottogary. She refused our home and going away, and went up to Fort Hall Reservation, Idaho. I am trying to take her back home, but she refused me. . . .[15]

I been up Idaho last week am acquainted many Indians up around there. We had very nice time while . . . up there me and [my] two boys. We come down on automobile all way from Pocatello, Idaho.

Our day school not so good this year, on account children been away school. We had pretty bad storm here. But we will have a nice weather later on. [1916-11-11 LJ]

WASHAKIE, DECEMBER 4, 1916.   I and my boys been down Brigham City on special business. . . . Some of the Indians are waiting get warmer. But we have had nice good day today. The frost out the ground. Now is the time to get sugar beets out the ground.

I hope we fine weather for some days. Most of the Indians went home last week. They may going down tomorrow morning.

Mr. Bannock Frank and wife went home some time ago. They live up on Fort Hall Reservation, last week and more anothers.

Mr. Moroni Timbimboo still working in sugar factory. He pitch his tent near the city jail. But his father Yeager Timbimboo went home yesterday. . . .

Mr. Thomas Tyboatz is born baby boy last week. Then took sick and died. The funeral service will be held at meeting home on Monday.

I was been over to Logan City on Thanksgiving day business. There was football contest on that day. I was watching the game. It is interesting one. But I never seen one all my life, this first go into. It surprise me watching the game. I think it is too rough play and wild. I don't be one of the players because too rough plays.

But Mr. Grouse Creek Jack getting better now he can getting around now. He was nearly lost his life. He laid [up] for six months before he get out the bed &c. [1916-12-08 BEN]

ELWOOD, JANUARY 17, 1917.   The people are in very good condition and some had measles, and new cases are come in. Some will be all over with soon. No deaths here since last fall.

Willie, Custer, and Chester Ottogary seated in a car with what appear to be Sunday clothes and work aprons, ca. 1916. *Courtesy Clyde S. Ottogary.*

Back row, left to right: Warren Wongan, Moroni Timbimboo, and Amy Hootchew Timbimboo. *Front row, left to right:* Joan Timbimboo, Yeager Timbimboo, Hazel Timbimboo, Yampatch Wongan Timbimboo, and Mary Timbimboo. Taken at Malad, Idaho, 1918. *Courtesy Mae Timbimboo Parry.*

Elwood grade school class, ca. 1917. Miss Shepherd, teacher. Chester Ottogary, *center, front row* (with arm around Dorothy Christensen); Custer Ottogary, *far right, back row* (partially in shadow next to teacher); Owen Rasmussen, *far right, second row. Courtesy Owen Y. Rasmussen.*

We are short hay this year. I believe the people are going lose their horses this winter on account being short of hay. They can't afford to buy on account the hay price so high. The cost is about $20 ton around here, and nearly everywhere the county.

We have had crop wheat and some could[n't] make even living; also our people run short everything. Don't know what we going to do this winter.

Mr. George Moody is stayed at Willie Ottogary place on special business. He is been for two weeks or more, and he was up Idaho last month talking up land matters with our agent Mr. Miller. He expect going up there again for this week to see him again on same business. His home is in Skull Valley, and he will return home some time next month.

Mr. E. [Albert] Saylor from Seattle, Washington try to propriated [appropriate] the Indian land here and Bear River Valley. But we talk with him on this matter. . . . Then we stop him from doing it. . . . Nobody . . . want him any more because he is not right.[16]

I was reading Logan Journal this morning about rabid coyote. The piece the county commissioners putting in paper to muzzle dogs. I will say . . . I looking . . . [at] that the muzzle [and it] wouldn't stop . . . rabid coyote for biting. . . . I think county commissioner made great mistake on that subject. . . .

But we had foot and half snow . . . also we had very cold weather in few day here.

Our day school is not running yet on account the people had much disease here in our little town. [1917-01-18 LJ]

GARLAND, UTAH, MARCH 20, 1917.   Mr. B. F. Riter, General Manager Riter Bros. Drug Company, was in Garland today, and also Mr. Cole, the local manager, was present. He is represent many pretty good business in county, and branch houses. [There] is one in Garland, Utah and many other are in Logan, Utah, Smithfield, Utah, Franklin, Idaho, Preston, Idaho, and one in Bear Lake County which is in Montpelier, Idaho. They sell some articles which is writing book and stationery, cold cream good for chappy hands or face, Rexall medicine and various kinds [of] hair tonic, and writing pens, tooth brush, shave razor, dolls, balls, soap, chewing gum, candy, cigar, hot water bags, olive oil, cotton, perfume, liquid perfume and Dr. Medicine and also selling good fish. But selling some patent medicine too. They making a very splendid business, and every houses is full of pretty medicine, and they treat people right. [1917-03-23 LJ]

WASHAKIE, MARCH 29, 1917.   . . . The people are poor condition this winter. Their horses are dying account the hay been scarce. Well sir, some have no horses left now. . . . The winter is so long. We didn't see such winter for long time. I don't know what we going to do in farming. Some have no hay, some have no horses. The people are very anxious for spring.

Some of the Indians are selling their land down on Bear River Valley, but some are holding land yet.

We have about foot snow on level ground yet. The snow is thawing pretty fast now. We like the spring coming. Soon seeding time is here. . . .

They was order one car of hay some time ago, the hay is not come yet. It might reach [here] this week; and some Indians went Ogden sometime ago last month, but they haven't return home. . . .

Well, sir, our day school begin some time ago. And school was stop last fall account the people been working beet field and take children with [them]. . . .

Mr. George Moody been here on special business here couple days ago. But return home yesterday.

I am going out to Skull Valley on special business. I might return home 5 or 6 April. I heard some kind of trouble out there now but want me to come settle up.[17]

The hay is pretty scarce around Garland or Tremonton now . . . and selling for $30 per ton . . . now. [1917-03-30 LJ]

TREMONTON, UTAH, JUNE 18, 1917.   Well, I am write once more for the news. And I was put near [the colloquialism pertnear] forgot about to write news of the paper and I tell we are the Indians are good condition. So far some of the Indian boys been shearing sheep up to Big Canyon for white man and some are working on sugar beet. Indians raise not much of crop this year.

Well sir I looking for the money that President United States promised to pay the Indian way treaties stated in year 1863. . . . We begging this money over three years now, but we have [not] received it yet. And there was about $20,000 supposed to paid Indians are on the Utah and I understand the our Indians on war path the white people said to me other day. But I didn't away see anything happened right now and I see my people are not on war path because I know that no trouble all among Indians. I think the white men are mistaken about this matter.

"Will Ottergary" and Annies Tommy, about the time of the Shoshone-Goshute draft resistance movement, 1917. *Courtesy of Church of Jesus Christ of Latter-day Saints Historical Department.*

But white men are believe what coming in their mind every little thing what people say. This is not right, because this not that away. I know my people been friend to white every since the treaties made with President United States.

I will this day tell [that] my people are not on war path because our forefathers made peace with President United States many years ago. We are very proud about this matter and many others. We want help our country and our soldiers too. The Indians are on this country are blind in mind and eye. I will tell white people are mistaken today because they edjuciation knowing everything our people not knowing anything today, because not learn White people always [ways]. I am sorry I do not write for long time. [1917-06-22 LJ]

1917-06-22 BEN [Not included, duplicate of 1917-06-22 LJ]

Willie Comes Again Alright
Journals Famous Correspondent is "Awoke up" by Local Walt Mason
WASHAKIE, NOVEMBER 23, 1917.   Well I am been sleeping for long time but I did awoke up right now. I think be awoke after this. There is about 10,000 people missed me for such long time. I will do better for next year to come. And also my people are good condition so far. There was a quite number from west or Nevada Indian are here topping sugar [beets] around Garland but they are going up Fort Hall Reservation now for winter. There is some Indians still working in beet field. I expect got through in short time now, Most of the Nevada Indians are poor have no home, no land. There about four deaths all this summer. Mr. George Tomock and Miss

Indian Maggie was on that rail wreck about last month or so.[18] They are getting alright down Brigham City. Our wheat crops is not good this year. . . . We may have better crop next year. Some of the Indians are moving away from our little town. Well I did [didn't have] much News to tell this year I been home all time. But I am kind negelect my duties. I will try it again and open my mind on this business.[19]

Nearly all fall work is over now. Mr. George Tospanguitch is in Tremonton other day doing some chopping [shopping]. Mr. Catch Quipitch is getting very nicely he was went operation . . . on appendicitis in the Dr. Merrill Hospital, Tremonton. Mr. Moody to going his farm a few days be right back in few days. Well he is got his family at Garland. [1917-11-24 LJ]

WASHAKIE, JANUARY 23, 1918.   Well, the people are here all right and some of them under the weather. Our day school running nicely this winter.

Mr. Tip Low little boy is sick in bed. He is very low. The Doctor said to him can be live no longer. . . .

We had plenty of snow and had good sleighing all this time.

Some of the Indian are moved out our town last fall. . . . They was big rabbit hunt some time ago but not much Bunny were killed. Seem to [me] the Bunnies are pretty well clean up this time. . . .

We had such nice winter this year. Some of the boys work on railroad. And doing a work on road. But they keep up the war. The Indian might to go hungry. We don't raise much crop last year. We did [didn't] work enough on the farm. The hay kind scarce here. [1918-01-25 LJ]

Willie Ottogary Is With Us Again
TREMONTON, MARCH 18, 1918.   I am going tell some news. We are been good year. I hope we had good crop this year. And the some Indian been down Brigham City all last week. The Indian get through with their land [cases]. They probate estate [of those] who been dead many years ago. And the heir are terdimement [possibly determined] on their estate. I am been attending the court all last week to helping some on it. I am glad so they have fix it up. I been Deep Creek country about a week ago, and return from west some time ago. Some Indians from Fort Hall to have interest some estate down here also. Some of the Indian are sick here now. We are rejoicing when the spring time is come. . . .

Miss Moroni Timbimboo is down Brigham City hospital and her little girl laid up with amomonia [pneumonia]. She been sick for couple week or more. And she is little better.

Well, soon our spring work be here. They get through probate last week. Mr. [Albert] Saylor is land buyer with Indian down all last week. [1918-03-19 LJ]

1918-03-19 BEN [Not included, duplicate of 1918-03-19 LJ]

TREMONTON, MAY 30, 1918.   The people are rejoice on the splendid rain we had for such long time. The crops are looking pretty good now. . . . Some the boys and mens and women are start thinning sugar beet down around Garland now. Mr. George Comanke was died here some time ago. The cause death was pneumonia and pardishia stroke. There was a quite lot sickness among us this spring. Master Stephen Peyope is died about two week ago, he was laid up for 4 month. He had a consumption. But we had about 3 death in two month. Well some of the children are sick now . . . cold weather we had and it cause a sickness. When warm weather open up there no more sick. All our spring working is done some time ago. I hope we had good splendid crop this year to win the war.[20] Nearly all old people are soon gone. There are very few living yet. Mrs. Pa-da-Zya and daughter and her son been down here on land matter on the first part the month and return later on. The land on Bear River valley is on sale. Soon a[re] about through in the district court. Some white people are around Garland to bit [bid] on the land. Mr. Albert Saylor is trying buy Indian [land] around here but he was working on it now. I am to sorry about Indian selling land on Bear River valley and selling pretty cheap. Mr. Tip Low is laid under the weather. He may get over it in few days. [1918-06-01 LJ]

WASHAKIE, JANUARY 22, 1919.   Well Sir. I am trying a few stories in our little town. But, two our boys have a little trouble last Saturday night. But the trouble is not settle yet, they was quarreling about something. Their name is George P. Sam and Jim Wagon. The Jim is got gun and trying shoot George P. Sam and he made mistake shot wrong feller his name is Stanquitch Jack this young man jump on Jim Wagon took a gun away from his hand after his be shot on shell. And George P. Sam went to Brigham [City] and complaint against Jim Wagon. And attempt to arrest him. But notified County Sheriff. But he did [not do] anything on that trouble. This was happened Garland, Utah. I and George P. Sam and two boys near escape. When we going to Washakie on my Ford car. And the road is so bad while going down hill and the car slipped on one side and upset. She roll over once and straddle a barb wire fence. But we are lucky . . . bunch no one hurt in accident, and smash all windshell and tops too. We all good sound after that. That was happened on Tuesday Jan 21, 1919. . . . Our day school is running very good this year. . . .

The ineflence [influenza] is over with now, no body died. Seem to me influenza not hard on our people.[21] [1919-01-24 LJ]

TREMONTON, FEBRUARY 24, 1919.   I am going write a short stories. But our people are all well and Flu is all over with us now. Nobody died this winter. We have a snow storm last Saturday night and snow fall about 5 inch. . . . Well don't much celebrated on the George Washington birthday. On Saturday evening we a dance in the big hall. Everybody enjoyed ourselves.

Mr. George Moody been here week ago last. He was going to visit his daughter. But they moved up to Idaho. He didn't stay very long. He was from Skull Valley, Utah.

There was about four new babies born . . . and doing very splendid.

The People are rejoicing when spring time is coming. . . .

The hay is very scarce here in our town. And they are buying some hay out the town. And hay price coming down now. About $10.00 to $12.00 per ton now. Mr. Charlie Perdash is brought some hay from Garland last week on the Mr. A. J. Grover place and all hauled away. . . . [1919-02-26 LJ]

WASHAKIE, MARCH 6, 1919.   The snow is nearly all gone. But we have snow storm last night and fall about foot and half—last night and is still snowing this morning.

Mr. Mose Neaman was laid up week last and he fell down from coal house at West Portage and sprain his back-bone and he get all right now. But he could [not] move around for three or four day. Now he is . . . well as ever. Well, will have a spring time now. No one sick. Mr. Tom Elk is gaving a dance on Friday night. I hope our people have a joyous [time]. Our day school running splendid this year. . . .

Well Mrs. Thomas Tyboatz from Garland up here now and her grandson was sick. But he is getting better now, and be [getting] Doctor's treatment. Everybody is alright. . . .

Mr. Timus Perdash and Jacob Peyope went down Ogden last week to buying some ammunition and return next morning. . . .

Mr. George P. Sam is purchase a new team two week ago. He buy from Bishop George M. Ward, here in our town.

Mrs. George Elk was down Garland week ago Friday for medicine treatment, and she was sick some time ago and she is getting all right now. [1919-03-13 LJ]

WASHAKIE, MAY 13, 1919.   I am going write a stories about condition we had here at Washakie. But Mrs. Ammon Pubigee was died here about a month [Willie's sister, Eliza Patzonah Ottogary Pubigee, died 31 March 1919].[22] She was middle age woman and faithful worker in church and she was [have] trouble in bowel about thirty years ago. She left three sons and five grandchildren. Well she was friend to everybody.

Master Henry Woonsook run away with Tip Low girl. The girl is about 14 or 15 years of age. Last time heard back [they] in Kemmerer, Wyoming. And Mr. Moroni Timpimboo went after him and didn't . . . hear from him since he left out. The might change some other place.[23]

There was quite lot of the Indians been down Ogden on big celebration [Decoration Day]. Some of the Boy and man and woman join in parade. Their names are Jim Joshua, Seth Pubigee, George Tospanguitch, Willie Neaman, Mose Neaman, Elias Pubigee, Johnny and June Neaman, Herbert Pabewena, Katie Neaman, Susie Highyou, Minnie Woonsook, Tiny Jack Pajanna [Pojenny] Pubigee, Phebe A. Neaman and included with children. Also some more others went. They return home from Ogden yesterday.

Mr. Charlie Broom and wife return home from Idaho last Sunday.

And all our spring work is done. Mr. Hyrum Wongsaw made a business trip in Salt Lake City about three weeks ago. It was about his land.

Miss Cohn Zundel laid up with cold and under Doctor treatment. She is little improved now. I hope she will get over it.

The grain looking well here in our locality. [1919-05-15 LJ]

WASHAKIE, MAY 28, 1919.   . . . Our people are doing pretty well and no one sick right now. Some of are working in the beet field . . . around Garland and near sugar factory. . . .

The weather is very dry. . . .

I and my brother-in-law [Ammon Pubigee] been up Idaho country. I will name some town where been which was Burley, Shoshone, Fairfield and Hailey and more

A five-generation photo, ca. 1917. *Clockwise from front left:* Anzi Chee, or Susan Purdawat ("Survivor of 1863 massacre. Jumped into Bear River with her baby. Wounded in breast. Baby drowned in river."); Ivy (or Pojennie) Woonsook Eagle/Pubigee; Lena Wagon; and Mary Woonsook. The baby in the middle is Eddie, or Eddy, Wagon. The generations, from oldest to youngest, are Anzi Chee, Mary, Ivy, Lena, Eddie. *Courtesy Mae Timbimboo Parry.*

other town in Idaho. We had very fine trip in Idaho. We was return home last Sunday.

Well sir, some of our boys shearing sheep. . . . for white man. I expect they will get through this week or later on. [1919-06-04 LJ]

WASHAKIE, JUNE 25, 1919.   The people are getting alright. But our weather is too warm and drying everything around here.

And Mr. George P. Sam . . . buried his daughter week last, and she was sick quite awhile and she was operation perform last month. But she has appendicitis and then she only six or seven day live.[24]

Well sir some Indian are went up to Camas Prairie, Idaho [a spot for gathering camas bulbs since prehistoric times] and has not return yet. They may return some time next week. The boys went up to Fort Hall Reservation for going to see the Sun Dance this week. Monet [many?] the Indian went home that was working in sugar field. But some went out fishing and do little hunt too.

The some Indian went Wyoming country to visit some relatives there.

Mr. Thomas Pabawena and his brother working in sugar beet field yet up . . . near Fielding. . . .

Well Mr. Hyrum Wongsaw and wife went to Idaho sometime ago. Mr. Henry Woonsook return and was run away with Tip Low daughter. He was been down Uintah country. Well no one is sick so far.

And Mr. Nephi Zundel, Jacob Peyope went down Salt Lake City to attend the wild west show and return home now. They having a splendid good time.[1919-06-26 LJ]

Advertisement for a Wild West Show at Utah State Fair
Grounds. *From* Salt Lake Tribune, *June 20, 1919.*

WASHAKIE, JULY 2, 1919.   . . . I am going telling some stories. But last week been up
to Blacksmith Fork Canyon on hunt and fishing. But we are very enjoyed time up
there and accompanied my little boys that time. We had bad luck coming home.
And we had blowout up in canyon two miles from Hardware Ranch and was going
there on rim [of] . . . the wheel. And we come down from the canyon on afternoon
next day. We hardly get in Hyrum City [when] we had old tire puncture on the
road. Then we got fixed by Hyrum and also other blowout near the Logan river. So
I went up town and took one wheel off and left the car on road. Then we go home
at last. I am going for Indian Reservation today out Nevada. But I will drop another news when return from Nevada. [1919-07-05 LJ]

WASHAKIE, JULY 19, 1919.   There was a very dry out Nevada. . . . Indian having a
splendid a good time on Fourth July out Owyhee, Nevada, having a horses races,
foot races and many others sports. I have seen some Indian boys played on instru-
ment and they have their own Indian band which was called Owyhee Indian band
and played many good pieces on 4 day of July and we acquainted many Indian out
Reservation and also the Indian agent. We went in his office to see him. We went
through Snowville [UT], Strell [?], Abrin [Arbon ID], Burley [ID], Twin Falls [ID],
Bliss [ID], Glenns Ferry [ID], Mountain Home [ID], Brone Vally [Bruneau valley
ID], Riddle Creek [ID], then up to [Owyhee] Indian Reservation. I find the country

Rose Parago Sam (b. October 13, 1906), daughter of George Parago Sam and Pompy Worritch Perdash. Rose died June 17, 1919. *Courtesy Mae Timbimboo Parry.*

"Henry Hootchew and Elice [Alice] Low 1919, (father Tippi, mother, Susie) from Elko area." Other notes attached to this photo read, "Alice Low the one Willie said ran away with Henry Woonsook"; and "Alice Low heard the owl calling their father's name—He died the same night." *Courtesy Mae Timbimboo Parry.*

was very dry and hay is scarce out through such places. Some saying the hay is scarce this year they going [lose] their cattle. The water supplies is scarce. Then went to White Rock [NV], Edgemont [NV], Deep Creek [NV], Elko [NV], Wells [NV], Cobre [NV], Montello [NV], Lucin [UT], Park Valley [UT], Kelton [UT], Promontory [UT] and Tremonton, Utah. We are very splendid good trip out there. This all news by this time. [1919-07-25 LJ]

WASHAKIE, JULY 22, 1919. I was been up to Pocatello last week to see the Sun Dance. They let it out before I was get up there. I was about half day late. But I never seen a Sun Dance all my life. I was kind discourage and [went] home. I was going see the Sun Dance. Some of Washakie boys join the Sun Dance up to Pocatello last week. They say have splendid time. Mr. Joe Trim was visiting Brigham City last week on special business on Thursday, July 17, 1919. He return on next day and visit my farm near Tremonton, Utah [on] way home. The [Indians] is harvesting grain now, very busy every day, and hope get through some time this coming week, and soon start threshing. The grain crop was not so good on account the dry weather. There is very small grain raised at Washakie this year.

Mrs. Rose Arrtanip [Arranip] is died on Tuesday last. She is about one hundred years old, and second old woman living; one more woman yet, she will be about 110 years old now. . . .

Mr. George P. Sam and wife and George Tospanguitch they return home from Pocatello last week and stopped at Tremonton and went on morning train.

I acquainted one Indian and wife and children in Tremonton last week [they] act in moving picture show. He was from South Dakota and he went home. He was stay a two night in Tremonton. [1919-07-26 LJ]

WASHAKIE, NOVEMBER 6, 1919. I was coming home for one week and been Wind River Reservation, Wyoming. We find it very cold just now. I was accompanied Mr. Moddy [probably George Moody, see Biographical Register] and his wife. We have been gone for three week. And return home about one week next coming Thursday. We was acquainted many friends of ours and had very splendid trip. Well sir we [had] important business. One week on the road going over and one week coming from South Pass City. Mrs. Moddy [Moody] take a train from Rock Springs and take about one day came home out there. Well Mr. Moddy [Moody] was sick now in bed since we return home. We find all Indian all well here.

Some Indians from Fort Hall are been working in sugar beet field. But some went back home. The Washakie [people] are working in the sugar beet crop and around Garland factory. But some may return home next week sometime.

Mr. Preacher Harvey [Harry Preacher of Wells, NV] and his two sons went over to Cache valley to topping beet over there, and accompanied his son-in-law.[25] I expect he will [go] up to Fort Hall Reservation again.

I was been down Uintah Basin last month and acquainted some of Uintah [Ute] Indians. But acquainted with chief Mr. James Atwin and Redcap and Happy Jack, Charlie Mack, Wash Indian, Piah-nanp [Piah-namp] Charley and also Grant and Mr. Redfoot. And many others Indians boys and girls. [1919-11-10 LJ]

WASHAKIE, DECEMBER 26, 1919.   The people are having a splendid old time on Xmas. They having Xmas tree in meeting house and also have carried on programme in morning. It is a real good time. And had a big dinner in the hall and dinner over, the children dance. And evening old folks have dance too. All enjoyed on the Christmas day.

We have very cold weather here now. The snow is six inch. . . . Some of us lost horses on account the hay being scarce. But some been buying [hay] down Tremonton. We good condition for nobody sick yet. No once died just now. Mrs. Moroni [Amy] Timbimboo was to Tremonton last Tuesday doing some Xmas shopping and her sister.

Mr. Catch Quipitch was down to Tremonton looking for his missing one year old colt.

Annie Hootchew purchase some deer hide and Elk down Salt Lake City some time ago. Mr. George Moody was left here last month for Idaho and with his family. To go winter over there and he was from Skull Valley country and he act off chief over his people. But he may return his home in the spring. Well, he is very good man. He is grandson of the Mr. Taba. This Mr. Taba was a great warrior in the early day and he was one of protect the emigrants. But he is the man made a peace treaties with the President of the United States. This was done in Tooele [UT] in 1863. And also more other chiefs. Well then this Moody took his place, and control his people. But he has no schooling or not educated in his life. He was born in West Great [Salt] Lake About sixty year ago. [1920-01-02 LJ]

WASHAKIE, FEBRUARY 12, 1920.   I am nearly forgot to writing articles until this nice morning. Well, am been up to Washakie Monday last. The people are well and few is sick with bad cold. But one baby girl died about two week ago. Her parents . . . Mr. Mose Neaman and Katie Neaman. . . . Some people very poor, can be able their cloths and food. The hay is very scarce here in town just now. But some our people are been council about our condition. Then send telephone down Salt Lake City for our new agent. . . . He said you people ask for some grain. So I made a arrangement . . . when the grain harvest time. So the [he] agreed to do that. They was sign the name for that. But very few didn't agree and I hope coming alright. I expect the grain soon be here.

The snow is all gone here and people are rejoicing when spring time is come. Most the hay we have got bought from Sandvattes Bros. in Tremonton. The hay price went up. They is holding for $30.00 per ton around here.

Mr. Seth Pubigee down Brigham City on special business. Well Mr. Joe Woonsook been down Brigham City on same business. Soon our spring work coming now. We have got fine weather so far and Mr. Ammon Pubigee been down Tremonton on Monday on special business and accompanied Master Jurce Neaman [probably June Neaman, see 1922-05-12 BEN] too. [1920-02-16 LJ]

WASHAKIE, FEBRUARY 23, 1920.   . . . Our day school running nicely. And some of the people are had flue. But didn't died so many. But there is only two death this winter. Both children about . . . one year of age. All sick people are good now.

We had snow storm last night. It fell about 2 inch. . . . Well, we are looking for . . . spring just now. Mr. Yeager Timbimboo and son are working for Jap [Japanese] man. . . . [named] Fred Nickdore.[26] Just south of the Garland town about one mile.

Mr. Joseph Woonsook went down Brigham City on the special business and Mr. Seth Pubigee is interpreted for him. The commission[er] is been here in our town . . . 17 Feb. 20. He come from Washington, D. C. and he want to see the Indians. But he had chance happen to see them and talk with Bishop George M. Ward. He . . . is not long enough to see him. I suppose we need some help from government. We haven't seen our agent yet. But we heard an agent been our little town some time ago.

There is some Indians visiting Brigham City some time ago on the land business. But some of our boys trying to get land here. . . . [When] the commissioner come here we are going see him and get some land. . . . Many haven't got no land. Our people lose some stock this winter on account being too dry summer the hay price is very high. About $30.00 dollars per ton. [1920-02-26 LJ]

WASHAKIE, MAY 28, 1920.   I am going write articles this lovely morning. But I am been laid up with smallpox now and I am get little better now. . . . There was two death with smallpox here at Washakie. Their names was Mr. Charlie Broom and Sig-go-tooch Arritch. . . . She is about 70 years of age . . . also three families been quarantine for 4 weeks now. Mr. Charlie Broom was about 56 years of age, and he is well known man around here in our country.

Mr. Ammon Pubigee and with two sons been down Salt Lake City other day on special business, and they purchase . . . second hand Ford car. They buy the car for $400.00. . . .

Mr. Nephi Zundel was in town other day and looking for little boose.

Nearly our spring work is over now. . . . our grain crop is looking very promising. Everything is blooming now. [1920-05-29 LJ]

WASHAKIE, OCTOBER 18, 1920.   . . . We are good condition for this fall. We lost our best man here at Washakie. He died down Ogden D. Hospital. His name was Mr. James Joshua. And he is one of the 2 Asst. Bishop, about 3 or 4 year. He was a good Latter-day Saint. His funeral service held at Washakie school house. The President of the Malad Stake were present and his two Counselors. . . . [Mr. Joshua] only left his wife and no children. Well some Indians working sugar beet field around Garland. There is about 40 or 50 Indians from Nevada and also working beet field. . . .

Mr. Yeager [Timbimboo] and wife been down Brigham City first day of the last week on business. And Mr. Johny Tomock came down from Idaho reservation last week on the business. Mr. Johny Goods from Idaho reservation was in the Brigham City on the business and other Indians [the business may have been land concerns]. . . . Well, no more big news this time. It will be on next letter. . . . [1920-10-20 LJ]

WASHAKIE, OCTOBER 19, 1920.   I was return home two weeks ago. But visiting some my people and relations out Nevada country. But acquainted some Indians out

James Joshua and his wife, Hitope Joshua, on their way to Ft. Washakie, Wyoming, to serve an LDS mission. *Courtesy Mae Timbimboo Parry.*

there. We very good trip. We to Elko, Ruby Valley, Cherry Creek, McGill, Ely, Deep Creek, Skull Valley, St. John and Salt Lake City. . . . There is many Indians in those places. We stop at Mr. George Mose at Bill Shorty ranch 4 days and to Ely and seen some Indian there. . . . We visit Indians . . . at Deep Creek and see some my acquaintances there and some . . . work out for the white man. Mr. Ell [Al] Steel and Morgan and Samie was my old pals and glad to [see] them and many others were there. Well am at home now, and very good condition. Miss Louise Ottogary down with bad cold. She is little better now. We had snow storm last night. But nobody work in sugar beet field yet. It is very wet to work in. I hope we going a fine weather after this bad storm. . . . [1920-10-23 LJ]

WASHAKIE, NOVEMBER 12, 1920.   The people are here all good condition. But some them working in sugar beet. . . . Mr. Moroni Timbimboo is moving town to Garland. His mother-in-law purchase a house lot down Garland and he moving in it house. There is about more than 40 Indians from Nevada are working sugar beet now. . . . Mr. Corsium boy is very sick now. And he was in medicine treatment. I hope he may not sick any longer. And he was very bad. And he is not able getting around much yet. . . .

But our fall working is all done right now. . . .

Miss Louise Ottogary is under the weather and she was very ill last month. She is very well now yet. [1920-11-13 LJ]

WASHAKIE, DECEMBER 2, 1920.   . . . Some of the [Nevada] Indians are return home all last week. They like this country best. I hope some of them are going moving here some time next year. Well we held some kind conversation with the [?] over our treaties made at Brigham City, Utah in year 1863. And quite lot of the Indians want come this country. Some . . . are coming home from Garland. Sugar beets are getting through now. Mr. Jim Yorup and family are still here working in beet. They making pretty good money in beets. And also some from Fort Hall went home last week. The weather is very cold now. Some our beet growers not get through with their beets. Perhaps may get through next week. . . .

Mr. Harry [Johnny] George and his wife and children are return on Monday last. These people from Ely, Nevada. And some of them are still working in beet. . . .

And also Johnny Mickey from Fort Hall Reservation been here last week and was visiting his daughter at Washakie. . . . [1920-12-04 LJ]]

WASHAKIE, DECEMBER 22, 1920.   . . . We have about three or four inches fall snows here now. The weather are very cold here now.

Mr. Kippetchew to Logan to buy some Xmas shopping other day. Some of the boys have big hunt out . . . west. . . .

Well Mr. Lewis Corsium are living at Garland on account his boy beeyin sick all summer. But is pretty bad yet. All Nevada Indians are return home by this time. I think they may coming back next year. Mr. George P. Sam visiting some of the Indian up [Washakie] too. Well our day school running pretty nice now. And the Indian have going consil [council] one these day. But talking about our treaties made at Brigham City in the year 1863, July 30. But some of the land down Garland is on sale. But the Government holding this land back to the Indians on later on. We are all Indians are going sent 2 act chief to Washington City, D. C. in month of March. Well that is for all. [1920-12-24 LJ]]

4

"I Will Start on My Stories,"[1] 1921–1922

WASHAKIE, JANUARY 7, 1921. The people at Washakie are good condition. But some of the boys was big rabbit hunt out there to Blue Creek before the Christmas time. . . . Mr. Lewis Corsium lost his son before Xmas time. He was died at Garland and under care such long time. He was buried 27 day of December in Washakie cemetery. Our people didn't celebrate on the Christmas time on account the boy been passed away. Mr. Johnny [?] and are staying Washakie. He lives in Wind River Reservation on Wyoming country. And has got no money. No go back home. He may stay until next spring. But all Indian from Nevada went home long time ago. Mr. George P. Sam has not return yet. He went 2 day before Xmas. And he was in special business to attendent to. Our people are poor in land and money too. We

Shoshone rabbit hunters, ca. 1920. *Courtesy Earl D. and Beverly Crum.*

are asking President about our condition. Well must have our legal rights from Government. . . . I tell you want send one good chief and interpreter too with. We was going more other thing. Our people need help here on Utah. [1921-01-10 LJ]

WASHAKIE, JANUARY 20, 1921.   Well, we are been holding a council last Monday night, the business was to the land also about our treaties here in the years 1863 made in Brigham City, Utah. But was not fulfill, etc. We want get Government look after that thing. And also our father[s] had some land took up about forty year ago. These was a homestead land. Then [indecipherable] land is bad condition. About three year [indecipherable] the was probate. But the Indian have not money for probate matter. The court was forced Indians pay up the probating. Some white men are buying land from our people. I see they didn't paying enough money. They was cheating Indian. Some the land for $60.00 to $100 dollars for acres. These only half the land worth. Some land is valuable. I will telling one reason. Our people are uncitizen. They are not paying tax because they can sell land. We want took up these matter with the New President [Warren G. Harding] U. S. We are going send one man to Washington D. C. to settle up this. We are donating some money that count.

We send one man out Nevada today on same business. His name is George P. Sam. Mr. Dick Arritch is very sick. He was laid up for last three days. And we very wet weather. . . . and snow nearly all gone.

Mr. Nephi Zundel went up to Idaho this morning to spend a few day up there. Our people are good condition. Well going a party next Friday night at people meeting house. Our day school is running good this year. And Mr. Catch Quipitch [Toyahdook] is going up Fort Hall Reservation on Tuesday last and he going important business.[2] [1921-01-22 LJ]

WASHAKIE, FEBRUARY 1, 1921.   The weather not pretty bad here this winter. But snow is about two inches here now. We have a enjoyable time last Friday night which we have a dance. . . . Mr. Seth Pubigee and his brother going Idaho Reservation last Sunday night on business. He may stay two weeks or more, I don't know yet. And also Johny England is accompanied these two brother. Well Mr. George P. Sam is return home from Nevada on his business trip. And not much business is around here now. But our people is very poor this time and [don't] have much provision. . . . Last Friday night after the dance two woman a trouble they was jealous. This wife of Mr. Enos Pubigee. But he divorce his wife last summer then married another girl, his former wife try to whip other wife and some of people watch them and two the boy a separated before hurting each other. [1921-02-03 LJ]

WASHAKIE, FEBRUARY 3, 1921.   . . . Mr. Lewis Corsium and wife are moved away after his son died. He went up on Fort Hall Reservation and not heard from him yet. . . . The hay is very scarce are here around. But the hay price is very low this year. Also have no sickness among us so far. Mr. Harry Johnny George was here last fall and working in sugar beets and his company too. And received his letter yesterday and stated in letter all the Indians out Nevada are getting all right. Mr. Jacob Peyope been down Garland flour mill and getting grist [flour or meal].

And some the Nevada Indians like Utah best. And they don't like Nevada any-more. Well all people like them all right. [1921-02-08 LJ]

WASHAKIE, FEBRUARY 8, 1921.   Well we have stormy weather and had a good lay snow on ground yet and good sleighing now. Our people here very good. Mr. Seth and his brother has return from Idaho trip. They said the Indian up on Fort Hall Reservation are good condition. We are going grant [grand] party next Friday night. We will have a big council over our land matter. My people want me make a big trip to Washington, D. C. But it is too hard for me taking up some big men back there. I am going try my best I can for my people. And I been study pretty hard on this matter. I know take a good man can do this kind of business. But I was not so big man for the business. Well I got letter from friend Reporter Mr. Louis Mann, from North Yakima, Washington. He said me my friend I am at home again. I come home from my trip to state legislature to Olympia about my fishing rights and hunting rights and may be in few days from now on I shall make that long trip to the capital city, Washington, D. C. about citizenship our Indians are too ignorant to be a white men when that law does not compel no one to citizen-ship. Well we are no foreigners like white are and what is the use want to be white men and on that matter my people going to send me. We want to remain Indians as long as we can pay no taxes.[3]

Mr. Harry Stoney from Logan City was in Tremonton and selling baseball suits for coming summer. But he sell suit for Tremonton baseball team. He was call Garland some other place around this section country. He went on after train to Salt Lake City. . . . He expect be around again properly three or fourth month again. [1921-02-11 LJ]

Willie Ottogary in Washington
Journal's Indian Writer is in Washington in Company with
Others of His Race, Advocating Some Rights of the Red Man.

WASHINGTON, D.C., MARCH 19, 1921.   I am going write a little articles this lovely morning. I am coming Washington City and was very surprise see so many Indians from different tribes of the nation. But pretty well acquainted with them. And seen an inauguration day on 4th day of the March. There is a big crowd of the people was here. Well and listen what other Indians say about our Indian right and more other thing. We seen Congress[man] M. H. Welling, Senate Reed Smoot and more other men, I cannot remember it all. We was seen President Harding 8 day of March and shake hand with him. We was in that bunch too. We was very glad that day. This Indians delegated for their people. Some of them went home last week. I surprise some Latter-day Saints here at Washington City, D. C. I been Sunday School with them and very glad when found some I know from our own county. First Sunday I came here met Mr. Welling, Mr. Smoot, Mr. Spry, Mr. Horsely too, and . . . others. . . .[4]

I been to New York 8 day of March and had very splendid good trip. And I been to Brooklyn and that town too. We seen all big building in this city. We been up to Capitol, Senate building, Library building, Congressmen building and more other buildings I can mention it. . . . [1921-03-22 LJ]

"William Otagary," photo by Gill,
1921, National Anthropological
Archives, *Smithsonian Institution*.

Willie Ottogary in Washington

Willie Ottogary, famous Indian correspondent to the News, is now in Washington,
D. C., on some matters pertaining to the title to Indian lands in this county. Before
he started on his journey, Willie came into the News sanctum and secured a supply
of stationery, part of which he promised to use in writing a news letter on his experiences. The first letter came this week and we are sure our readers will be interested
in following our famous dark skinned journalist in some of the experiences he has had
at the nation's capital and in other cities in the east.—Editor [News].

WASHINGTON, D.C., MARCH 20, 1921.   I am here at Washington, D. C. I been all
big buildings in the city. But I been seen Pres. Harding and get hands shake with
two different time and we are very glad to seen. And I Sunday School with the
Latter Day Saints at this town and acquainted some new members of the Church.
I have been two Sunday and their night sacrament meeting too. . . . I have been
seen about 20 different tribes of the Indians from part on the country. . . .

I expect we may return home some time next week. But we been here long
enough. But we did hardly get through land business. Last week been to New York
and Brooklyn City. But I stay just one day. But went down to see liberty of statue
on steam ships. Spent about one hour and half looking around there and return
same day and I was walking over the great suspension bridge in world. I been surprise see this bridge. Well and many other I have been. Well I am staying Master
Mr. Wm. Stueler place now for few days he was a good Mormon boy he just join
L. D. S. Church. He treated me very fine. I have been Mt. Vernon some time ago

about 2 week ago to locate President George Washington grave. I had a company Mr. Hon. C. H. Bates. [BEN 1921-03-25]

TREMONTON, APRIL 25, 1921.   I am return home just now. But I may going off in short time, at my home. And I have a great experience while I am on my long trip for East. Well while am back in Oklahoma and acquainted many of my own people down Oklahoma country. The Indians are well off, some of them. We been down about three weeks staying. And there was about fifteen Indians of nation, all in Oklahoma state. The Government been building houses for them and paying some money every six month. Indians down Lawton have a good condition and they are the United States Government ward. They have got some good land, some of them raise cotton, corn and wheat. We find some our relation down to Lawton and Cach[e], Oklahoma. Well we have been four different places in Oklahoma. The Indians are down there join the church. Some join Baptist church, Metecah [possibly Methodist] church, some other church. But many others none the member the church.

Well the weather getting warm now. Their grain field looking pretty good. And they been planting some corn just now. I have seen many timber country through Oklahoma. And they doing not much spring work now. There was five Indian went to Washington, D. C. while we was there. We been on train about three night and four day coming from Lawton, Oklahoma. It is very expensive ride on train. It is cost about $500.00 going back and all expense. Well are getting pretty good so far. [1921-04-27 LJ]

WASHAKIE, MAY 15, 1921.   . . . [I] return from west or Nevada last week and attending my business. And going out again. Well am been away from home about 2 month. But I was acquainted some whites and Indians. I hope we going have our land matter straight out. The Indians enjoyed to land around Garland. But I want not going a back any more unless our land attorney want me to come see him on this land claim. I have been a big council among my Shoshone Indians band out Nevada or Idaho and Washakie people too. The people are get through with their spring work and the grain in ground now. We going have another council meet soon. I am been work hard just now. I want get this our land claim through Congress this summer if I work it right. Well and people well satisfied when this passed through the court U. S.

Mr. Elias Pubigee is in the Tremonton hospital now. Has been operation on appendicitis. He is get well now. He is going return next Tuesday and his wife visiting him last week ago. . . .

I have received 3 letter from honor Mr. B. Riter from Logan while he on train write to me. And he made a big medicine business out California and his return last week. Well our day school is stopped now for summer vacation and boys and girls are happy now school stop. [1921-05-18 LJ]

WASHAKIE, SEPTEMBER 1, 1921.   I will start on my stories. But we are good condition and Indian boys are going down Ogden to join in Great Wild West show commence on 5, 6, 7 and 8 day of the month. There is about 25 of them went down day before yesterday. Well, are bring some horses. We are gather all our good horses here at

Washakie town and some of the boys has not going. They want going end this week. But some of the boys going ride buck horses. Well the Indian agent was here yesterday and some prospect here. Week last I [and] two the boys start for Austin, Nevada. The Ford car was over turn and smash two right hand wheel and none of us get hurt and we buy second hand wheel and been as far as Skull Valley. It is about 80 miles from Salt Lake City straight out west. We seen some of the Indians there and are good condition and all their threshing done.

There was two death is happened the this summer and some of them moved to Deep Creek, Utah. But our threshing is done. Our old machine is get old so they not run it. This company trying to get new outfit. They order one about two week ago. It has not come yet. We looking for it every day now. We had very splendid crop here this year. The grain is about 80 cent per bushel now. We hope we start thresh next week. And we will been through next month.

I am still looking for Indian business yet. But I want beat the Government that on our treaties and claim here on northern part Utah. And we hire the attorney at Washington, D. C., on this our land claim. And he is going fight with Government. And that gave us some good location or allotment by the Government. Well, I visiting all Indians out Nevada and more places telling them we going have a land for our own. We want our Indian have a good farmers all we get through.

We have three death this summer. Mr. Joseph Woonsook is laid up with consumption and get little better he went down Ogden yesterday and Dr. treatment.

Mr. Moroni Timbimboo been Fort Hall, Idaho, looking for land lease from Indian. He going moved right away and start work Indian land.[5] [1921-09-05 LJ]

WASHAKIE. OCTOBER 8, 1921. The people are . . . working in sugar beets around Garland and Fielding and the other places. Well some of Indians from Nevada are here working sugar beets now. But some might coming in two. And the some from Fort Hall Indians are here too and also working in sugar beet too. Our grain crop is not good on account we had late frost. . . . Our day school are running now. Some of them still in fall work now. Most of them get through. Mr. Moroni Timbimboo been down Fort Hall looking for land lease up there. He expect to move up Idaho next spring. . . .

Mr. William Hootchew and wife is down from Fort Hall too and he may return some time this fall. Well sir, the people are here like to working sugar beets. The men is working on threshing machine a while this year. . . . [1921-10-10 LJ]

WASHAKIE, OCTOBER 17, 1921. . . . Some of our boys were out deer hunting out Black Pine. It is about 60 miles out West here and they has not return home yet. The Indians from west [Nevada] are here topping beet and some from Idaho reservation. And our fall work is all done just now. We have not hear from our Lawyer yet . . . from Washington, D. C. on our old treaties. That claim by our chief and warriors. We are awaiting hear from him. But our men did agree on this our treaty. All young men are work for it. It cost us about $1,000.00 ever since we start work on it. I hope we are going win this case. Well haven't had any one sick just now. Mr. Jimmy Chicken is here now. He was from Idaho, and sick in bed for long time. He may not live any longer.

We are not start dig our sugar beets yet up here to Washakie. Our day school running now. All our threshing through all last two or three weeks ago. The grain was about 85 [cents] per bushel and now is about 65 per bushel. And Mr. Dan Parry is bought a Indian land up here to Washakie. He raised $2,000 bushel wheat this year. The Indian from Fort Hall Reservation taking their land. The agent didn't treat right and he stole something from Indians so they have big council over that. [1921-10-31 LJ]]

WASHAKIE, OCTOBER 24, 1921.   We had very stormy last night. It is little snow up on mountain top. It is very wet today and looking like we going have some more yet. Some are still working in sugar beet field yet around Garland. We had good rain last night and settle all dust.

Mr. Sam Panquitch and his family was down here working beet too. He may return some time next week. But was from Fort Hall Reservation and more others with him. And all our fall work is done . . . . Mr. Ammon Pubigee was been down Ogden last week and buying some small bead and going send bead to his friend Mr. Red Fingernail down Surry, Utah.[6]

Our people are good condition yet. . . . Nearly all sugar beet is getting through by this time. There is about 10 Indians from Nevada is also working in sugar beets too.

Mr. Stanquitch Jack is ran away with Mr. Tomy Tyboatz wife along in summer time. And he come to near Tremonton topping sugar beets. Mr. Tomy Tyboatz heard his [wife] is down Tremonton work in beet then he come down from Idaho on train and he try take his wife home up in Idaho and both of them jump on him and nearly kill him and she like a new man best, she don't want home. There was another couple is fighting on same way, these Indian from Nevada. [1921-10-24 LJ]]

WASHAKIE. DECEMBER 6, 1921.   . . . Some of the mens are big rabbit hunt now out to Promontory or Roserell [Rozel].[7] They has not return home yet. I believe at 6 wagon went out on last Tuesday. And Mr. George Moody is come up other day on important business. His home was in Skull Valley, Utah. But he is visiting his wife relation out in the Uintah Reservation. He may stay all winter over there. Well he said some them Ute Indian made a big council on land matter. He want going a back in few days. We had a very cold snap other day, everthing has frozen hard. Mr. George P. Sam is not so well. He was had condition all summer long. He just little bit better.

Some Nevada Indian are here at Washakie yet, because they cannot going home. They expect be here all this winter. Mr. Mose Neaman been over Cache Valley. He was return week ago. And his three sons with them and some more Indian boys is with. They all return. And they is join that big rabbit hunt. . . . There is 20 pupil are attending school here Washakie. . . . [1921-12-08 LJ]]

WASHAKIE. DECEMBER 27, 1921.   The people are good condition so far. And a Christmas celebration on Monday. The programme was carried out for the New Year celeberation on Monday. We have had very good programme. . . . Everybody turn out and had very splendid dinner and evening was a grand ball. We have a joy time in dance. The snows is about one foot one-half deep here. But we had a rain and settle the snow. . . . Mr. Moroni Timbimboo went up on reservation before Christmas. He look some business up there. The boys been big rabbit hunt sometime ago. They . . . kill about 10,000 bunnies in side one week. They expect another great rabbit hunt on after New Years. . . . Well all our people are very poor this year and hard time get money just now. We had [not] much hay now. Some may buy here through the winter. [1921-12-30 LJ]

Washakie. January 5, 1922.   The people are good condition. We have a storm weather. . . . and the is about six inch snow now. But we had enjoyed time on New Year's Day. . . . Well everybody was enjoyed. Mr. Seth Pubigee was lose his little boy. He was about eight months old. His funeral held at ward meeting house . . . he died on New Year's Day. Mr. Moroni Timbimboo return on his business Idaho and he also visit some his relatives. Mr. George Moody return home some time ago. Well the boys are not decided when that another big rabbit hunt come off, might they out again some this month. Mr. Henry Woonsook has twin little baby boys and they was born before Christmas time. They is doing pretty good so far. Mr. Jim White is still here at Washakie. He was from White Rock, Nevada. But he is going winter here. Some are saying going have a hard winter this year. But not much cold here now. We have heap cold weather after this. The hay is very scarce now. Some of our people are very poor this year and not much wheat crop, and crop is fail. [1922-01-06 LJ]

Washakie. January 30, 1922.   The people are here are good condition now and some of them under the weather. We had snowstorm last Friday night. . . . The Mr. Jim Chicken was pretty sick and he nearly dying last summer and he still living. He is acting Indian chief for himself. He was raised here this country and born here. But he have had little . . . schooling here at Washakie and in the boyhood. I expect he was about 50 years of age man [when he died, see 1922-02-18 LJ]. I expect he is buried at Washakie cemetery. He was live up on Fort Hall Reservation all his life. But he moved out Washakie over 30 year ago. But has some relation living in this little Indian town. Mr. Dick Arritch was living here now and he was coming from Wind River Reservation and he was join in Latter-day Saint church forty year ago. And he buried his wife here at Washakie cemetery. . . . Some of the older people say [winter] is over now and they say the spring is nearly open. I expect they was made a mistake. . . . Well our stock are very poor on account we had very cold weather. So far our day school very nicely. We had nice time last Friday and had dance. But every come out he a jolly good time both old and young. [1922-02-04 LJ]

Washakie. February 14, 1922.   The people are very good condition so far now. We have had a very cold weather here on last week and Mr. Jimmy Chicken is past away . . . last part of the last month ago. But was sick for long time. Well sir, he was not member of the church. And he used to be a member of the church about 30 years ago. And he move away from this town then he was a out the church since that time. Well he living up on Idaho and he was received a government allotment up there and his son. He haven't any children left behind or wife. Mr. Jacob

Peyope was taking care of him while he was sick. But he made a will to Mr. Jacob Peyope before he died. We had about two foot snows here right now. It is very good sleighing now. The hay is very scarce here right now. The price is a $15.00 per ton. Some of us buy hay up to West Portage. . . . One man and wife is visiting Miss Hightop Joshua and one other relation from Wind River Reservation. He may stay two week or more I don't know yet. [1922-02-18 LJ]

WASHAKIE. FEBRUARY 23, 1922.   The people are good condition. The Indian and wife has not return their home yet. The snow nearly gone. Our older people said to have a early spring this year. And Mr. George P. Sam is sick. He been sick for several year. It is kind bright disease.[8] Well sometime he get well as sometime get worse. . . . Well one middleage woman is sick a week ago and she was under the weather. She is get all right. . . . I been visiting some my relative up here. It is doing pretty good in the church works. It seem to me we are the Indian not progressing in the ways of the white people. It is pretty hard for us to [do] it. And we are not trying to learn much each year comes. I can see how is that. And some of the young people are trying progressing. I was been in Washington, D. C. to see our Indian commissioner about our legal right and our treaties and many other business. But I hire me a attorney back Washington, D. C. He will fight our cause in the coming March. I expect we will hear from him in future. I don't know what I may do, or rather come back [to Washington D.C.] or not. I will know in future. My two [boys] been up Washakie visiting some of their friends and relation too. They hasn't return home yet. They went up on Thursday last. Well I may go getting more news later on. [1922-02-25 LJ]

WASHAKIE, MARCH 3, 1922.   The people are doing fine this winter. Well some of them been very poor didn't have any money so far. We must come through the winter yet. About last storm we have had a few day ago. It was very fearce storm we ever had. The train was blockade up Malad city and rail covered up with snow so train late going down other two mornings. And every cut [passage or ravine] were fill up snow and the section gang working very hard. The snow is about 3 feet. . . . Wind River Indian and wife is return home some time ago last weeks. He was going visiting more relatives up in Idaho. . . . They celebration Washington birth day on Friday last. . . . But every body turn out pretty. . . . Every body come to dance that night and good old jolly time both young and old. . . . We stake Quarterly Conference up the Malad city. Some of the our people attended the Conference and the conference were a very good one. All the people are belonging to L. D. S. Church. Some of our people splendid worker in the Gospel, and most the old people are good worker, and quite lot of them went through the [Logan] Temple and also doing some [temple] working done.

Our little town used had lots people here before some of them moved away up in the Idaho Reservation. I see they haven't any Government allotment yet they been up there for 5 or 6 yr. now. [1922-03-11 LJ]

WASHAKIE, MARCH 6, 1922.   . . . Friday last was a sparrow hunt dance which is the town split up two and the South and North part. Well they counting their birds in that evening. And side their birds which come to be 118 and 108. But south side is winner of the town and the lose side pay for music.⁹ We had pretty nice time. . . . The big crowd turn out. Mr. Amos Moemberg little boy is fall down on smooth ice broke his little leg. He is getting pretty good. Mr. George P. Sam and wife and Bishop Catch Toyahdook and wife was fishing up hit spring.¹⁰ It is about 7 miles from here straight north. They mostly catching Corps [probably carp] and more other fish. . . . Well I and one boy was visiting week last taking some news up to Washakie. I am make my home near Tremonton district. Bear River Valley Stake had a Quarterly Conference held at Garland stake building the Saturday and Sunday the people are good turn out attending Conference every ward were present. We had two visiters from Salt Lake City. Which was Mr. George A. Smith [LDS Apostle] and one I could [not] mention his name. They made splendid remarks. Mrs. Timus Perdash been up Fort Hall Reservation. She went up about two month ago, and she return home week last. She was visiting some the relatives up Idaho. That Wyoming Indian went home about two week ago. He was accompanied his wife. They want stay up to Idaho Reservation about 2 month or more with their relation before return home.

Mr. Jim White is still living here at Washakie. And he stay with his friend Mr. Henry Woonsook all winter long. Well his [wife?] want him come home right away. He home is on Owyhee Nevada Reservation. It is about 300 miles from here, just straight West. [1922-03-18-A LJ]

WASHAKIE, MARCH 13, 1922. . . . The snowing and blowing last Friday night, weather is very cold. We hard time this yr, the hays was scarce this year. Well, Mr. Thomas Pabewana was Tremonton last week accompany his boy. But doing some shopping. Mr. Ammon Pubigee buy some hay up to West Portage some time ago. Well, Mr. Jim White is still here now. Mrs. Geor. P. Sam is sick, she is under the weather. The boys are good this year and also the girls in the school.

Mr. Tom Elk, Mose Neaman was fishing other day catch very few fish. It is too cold to fishing now, and fish not bit very good. They say the fishing poor this year. But will enclosed with this a piece from newspaper what has Senator Bittman [probably Key Pittman] said to the Indians this country and claim by old chief and warriors.¹¹ [1922-03-18-B LJ]

WASHAKIE, MARCH 20, 1922. The people are good condition, no one died now. . . . The weather getting a warm. And the snow nearly gone now. But the Relief Society has big celebrate last Friday. We have a nice programme before noon. . . . The programme was rendered as usual. Which was select readings, song and comic speeches, & etc. After all get through . . . the big dinner was serve by the Relief Society in the ward meeting house. And in evening was Grande Ball given by Relief Society. They have a very good time in the dance. Mrs. George P. Sam is ill and she is getting better now. She was under the weather. And the people are pretty anxious getting spring. Some our people getting poor they could[n't] buy a loaf bread for their family. I hope soon spring open, then had a plenty work for them now on.

Well sir, I have been working for my people on these old treaties by signed by our chief and warrior. It is pretty hard matter for me. . . . We read in paper this business been taken up by Senate McKey Pitman [Key Pittman] from the Nevada. He said in the paper we ought to be ashame and taken away Indians legal rights away from them. We're the foreigners from other country. And getting away Indian's water, mineral, forest and also hunting right away from them. I hope we getting it a back again some day or future time. But all over United State the Indians are been to Washington, D. C., begging for these our legal right. And I was on the same business last winter to delegate for my people around Utah and Nevada. I think it is cost us about $3,000 to [go] Washington, D. C. I will surprise some my people and also white people when these land matter come through. Well I am working pretty hard up on this old treaties [made] about sixty year ago. [1922-03-25 LJ]

WASHAKIE, MARCH 27, 1922.   The most of the people are have flue this winter. But it is over nearly yet. This year seem to me is very light. And are doing good this winter. Well Mr. Jim Wagon's little boy died here last week. He died with flue. That is only death here with flue. And also Master June Neaman is very sick now. He is under the weather or flue. We are the rejoicing when this spring time is come. The snow is nearly gone now. The road is pretty bad condition now. Our hay and stuff is nearly gone so far. The Government is purchase about 1000 lbs. flour here at [probably means for] Washakie Indians. The agent is here at Washakie about two week ago. He was in the sand [land] business or some other matter. Well not understand what he come here for and he took some business with our white man Bishop. I like see him when he comes here. But he is kind some crook work on our people some away rather [way or other]. We want know his business. He didn't care for our people. That is all I know about him. I thought his business come here and talking with the Indians. And make everybody understand his especial business is. We are under his jurisdiction now or his is our agent. . . .

We are very poor this year. And we have no money cannot buy a flour just now. . . . The Malad river is over flowing just now and water keep raising every day and we got still more snow up on mountain yet. Well sir I will gave you Journal reader a short story about Mr. Frank Harris in Logan.

I was visiting Logan city on Tuesday a week ago. That day I went in Mr. Harris Music store. I talking with Mrs. Harris, and Will, the clerk, and Miss Budge. There is Mr. Frank Harris come in store. He was gave me a real nice selection on violin. He is supprize me. A piece he plays and Indian war song. I thought he could play Indian song. That was "Pet Me" [a song title] etc. I see all people I acquainted with that day. I met Mr. Lofthouse from Paradise. We eat dinner together. [1922-04-01 LJ]

WASHAKIE, APRIL 3, 1922.   The people are good condition this year. But one boy is very ill just now. He been sick week or 10 days. He name is June Neaman. . . .

Some the people are going down Salt Lake City Conference. The weather is warmer right now and people are rejoice the spring is coming.

Mr. Enos Pubigee has arrived new baby boy latter part week last. His mother is not so well. She is sick just now.

One Indian come from Wyoming Reservation, visiting his relation at this little Indian town. I hope he may stay two week or more. . . .

The Senator, Key Pittman try to the work on this Indian matter. And he said on this old treaties, he want government make it [right] with Indians. [1922-04-04 BEN]

WASHAKIE, APRIL 3, 1922.   . . . Snows are already gone now. But the road is impossible to the travel. The hay is scarce now. The hay is worth about $5.00 to $6.00 per ton. . . . and the fall crop is coming up fine so far. But I was visiting up there [Washakie] latter last week spend two or three day and find Master June Neaman is very ill with a flue. His grandparent is not expect any longer. He had it pretty bad. I thought he may live longer. He was in bed for two week now. But the some boys been getting out cedar post now. They selling for 20 cents piece. . . . Some of the Indians went down big annual conference. Mr. Kippetchew Noragan and wife and Mr. Catch Toyahdook and wife and going down Salt Lake City and they was representing for Washakie Ward. And they recite 4 article in faith in their native language in the Salt Lake City Tabernacle and our Bishop Mr. G. M. Ward is going down too.[12] Mr. Thomas Pabawena and Mr. George Tospanguitch are going Salt Lake City and driving team down. They start last Thursday. And also he is accompanied Master Jim John Neaman. . . . One Indian from Wyoming Reservation visit Mr. Warren Wongan last week. He is still up there yet. . . . Mr. Jim Wongan little boy died on Tuesday last. His funeral service at Joe Woonsook resident on the Thursday last. [1922-04-08 LJ]

WASHAKIE, APRIL 17, 1922.   . . . The weather is been so cold and the fall crops not even start to grow on account the weather been so cold. . . . The ground is too wet to be worked. Well I expect we will be late getting our spring crop put in. . . . We had a good time last Friday night as in dance. There was few attend to come dance. Mr. George M. Ward and wife is return home from conference on the Monday last. All the others has return too. Mr. Kippetchew and Catch Toyahdook and their wives are return from conference. These was represent from Washakie and the Indians as the members of the Church of Jesus Christ of Latter-day Saints and they was recite the first Article of the Faith and their own language, and also wear their custom [or costume, meaning traditional Shoshone dress] on the Sunday night in the Salt Lake Tabernacle.[13] Well they done pretty good. Master June Neaman still very ill yet. Miss Ida Zundel is sick, very sick now. She was took sick week from the day after tomorrow. Miss Petersen our school teacher is down on Saturday morning train to visit her parents at Ben Rose [probably Penrose], Utah. Well our day school run good. There is about 14 children been attending here at Washakie. Mr. George P. Sam, Thomas Pabawena, Seth Pubigee these three brethern is been as act teachers and some family in the night to explaining the Gospel among us this winter.[14] And they doing splendid works. . . . [1922-04-22 LJ]

WASHAKIE. APRIL 24, 1922.   . . . Weather is turn warmer just now. And the spring work is come. I expect the grain crop is looking pretty good now. . . . Well, some of the men getting out some post [cedar posts] and price is pretty low. Mr. William Thornton is buying some their post. And some been hauled their is to the Garland. . . . Hay is about $10.00 or $11.00 per ton right now. Mr. Yeager Timbimboo and son been purchase six ton hay from Mr. John Wells from East

Left to right: Hyrum Wongsaw, Tom Alex (or Elk), Moroni Timbimboo (with face partially obscured), Yeager Timbimboo, George M. Ward (bishop), and Ketch Toyahdook. The last three were members of the Washakie LDS ward bishopric. *Courtesy Mae Timbimboo Parry.*

Portage. And some of us been buying from him. He has got about 100 ton to sell for last week. Mr. Thomas Neaman been buy from John Wells too Thursday last. Wyoming reservation boy is still at Mr. Warren Wongan place. He may return home in 2 month or more. And there was another reservation Indian here now. And he stay with Joe Woonsook place. He is staying all this winter. He was from Nevada reservation. His father want him come back home soon as possible. He like Washakie people. Mr. Ammon Pubigee is been down Tremonton town last Saturday and getting some grist on flour and he companied his two sons. And Master June Neaman is still sick. He had been sick over three weeks. Dr. Jensen was come up to see him. He said he had Penmona [pneumonia] and his heart is out order and that is trouble. . . . Well, Mr. George P. Sam is getting pretty bad now just now. [1922-04-29 LJ]

WASHAKIE, APRIL 27, 1922.   I was visiting Logan City yesterday and looking for the some business. The people of the Logan is doing much business. While I was in city and enquire J. A. Crockett City Mayor Office. He gave me a new programme [upcoming projects] was made this coming summer. Well the first is Logan Island Sewer. . . . gravel the road to the Fifth North Street . . . new water sprinkler apparatus . . . new electric light plant . . . [also] water system . . . building a big garage near the Fire Department . . . for the take caring of our automobiles in the summer. I was visiting Mr. George Skidmore, manager of the Union Knitting Works Company in the Logan

City. But he showed me the various machinery and doing knitting work. And I guess about twenty or more employees are getting busy as bee. He showed me every department in his big new building. I meet Mr. Sam Whitney on inturben [interurban] car going to Logan.[15] He was a great friend the Indians in his early life. He can talk in Indian language as well as any other Indians. But he is cripple pretty bad. That was first time I have been seen him for 13 years. [1922-05-06 LJ]

WASHAKIE, MAY 1922.   The people are here in good condition yet we have had pretty good weather and the Malad river overflowing the bank just now. We are pretty busy get our spring crop put in. Well, nearly getting thru with our work and people are here rejoicing when spring is open. We had very bad storm here yesterday and today all day long and the road . . . muddy again. Our fall crop looking very splendid. I expect we had very good harvest this coming year.

No one been sick just now. But Master June Neaman died down Deweyville on Saturday last. About 8 o'clock in the morning and having medicine treatment Dr. Mrs. Buecannon [Buchanan] he died in her home. It was on the 29 day of April. He was born at Washakie on the 16 day of June, 1906.[16] But his mother died about 14 years ago. Then he was raised with his grand-parents ever since about two years old. But his father still living at Washakie. The old grandparents are feeling pretty bad about him. And they was missing him every days their lives. Well funeral service held at Washakie ward meeting house on Saturday afternoon . . . and buried at Washakie cemetery. . . . There was his white friend attend his funeral service the from West Portage. Some of our boy's been down Tremonton on the Saturday last to see a big May celebration down there. [1922-05-12 BEN]

1922-05-13 LJ [Not included, duplicate of 1922-05-12 BEN]

WASHAKIE, MAY 13, 1922.   The people are doing fine and dandy. The are getting all crops in now. . . . Some of our people are going down the Garland . . . the white people are having a big . . . track meet for students for northern part Box Elder County. . . . Well all the school are vacation for coming summer. The Mr. Dick Arritch and Mose Neaman are went down to Brigham City again yesterday on the importants business. And Mr. Thomas Pabawena is accompanied. . . . And he was especial interpreter. . . . Mr. Moroni and Yeager Timbimboo and Mr. Henry Woonsook and taken these folks in his Ford car. And attended on business trip. Well Mr. George P. Sam is bad condition now attact with Bright Disease and he expect getting better some time in future. . . . Mr. Willie Neaman was a purchase a old second hand Ford car from Mr. Ralph Stayner some ago. . . . [1922-05-20 LJ]

1922-05-23 BEN [Not included, duplicate of 1922-05-27 LJ]

WASHAKIE. MAY 19, 1922.   The boys are like hear from Washington, D. C. about our land business. But we are not hear from lawyer just now. Mr. Ammon Pubigee are went down to Brigham City on other day on importants business. Well we are all good condition so far. Mr. Jim Wagon and Jim White is working Mr. L. Grover east Garland. He made a contract with Mr. Grover about a couple weeks ago. And he start works on it now. He expect stay his place all this fall until sugar beet all harvest time. Our people are not start thinning sugar beets yet. They may start pretty soon. The come Indians are hunting some sheep wool out country. But all our spring work is getting all through by this time. Mr. Seth Pubigee, Mr. George P. Sam and Mr. Henry Woonsook is company too. The wild bird was flying over our little village last Monday last and heading for north. Our people are surprise to see this big bird flying up in air. But our people didn't know about this before. It seem to [them] a very quiar [queer] to see such a big human bird [airplane]. Mr. Warren Wongan been down Tremonton yesterday to see Mr. Dan Parry. He was working for him all winter along. But made arrangement so he can quit soon as possible. Well sir no sick just now. Our fall crop is looking pretty good. [1922-05-27 LJ]

WASHAKIE, MAY 30, 1922. . . . Our spring crops are all through and . . . we need water pretty bad just now. Well Mr. George P. Sam purchase about 200 baby chicks. He expect to start on poultry business. But he just received on last Saturday night. That is first one Indian to going in poultry business. And there is two or more try do some business now. Some of our boys been up to Malad city, Idaho to attend . . . May festel [festival] day on May 27. And having very splendid old good time. They having some sports and have a foot race, high jump, vault jump, bee hive girl race, peanut race, and Scout boys ball game, etc. I was been up too accompanied my boys and splendid old jolly good time. Well all our people are rejoice when summer time is here. Mr. Mose, Mr. Thomas Pabawena, Mr. Neaman are went up on reservation and on especial business and so on. They may return sometime this week. Mr. Yeager Timbimboo is running Mrs. Hightop Joshua farm this coming year. She was widow of James Joshua who was died here on a year ago. Her got a splendid farm on south part the Washakie town. Master Dave Barry went home sometime ago week last. He may stop at Fort Hall Reservation to see his own relation there. Been about one month here. Well his home is at Wind River Reservation. . . . [1922-06-03 LJ]

Washakie Items

WASHAKIE, JUNE 1922. The people are good condition now. Some people are been celebration the Decoration Day [now called Memorial Day] and the grain is not looking well on account of the dry weather and we need rain pretty bad. . . . The couple Hess boys been renting some Indian land at south part of Washakie. They summer follow [fallow] the land prepared to next year. They lease the land for 4 or 5 years longer now.

Mr. George P. Sam is doing fine on the chicken business. But he may have good luck, he done no [doesn't know] the business just now.

Mr. Willie Neaman and wife going down to Garland town on Sunday last and accompanied his two brothers in his Ford car.

Well Mr. Harry Steed and Dan Parry had trouble over the land. In the first place Mr. Steed bought an Indian land south part our little town, and he sold some to Mr. Parry, it is about 80 acres. But Mr. Harry Steed has not been paid all of it now to the Indian owner. These Indian live up Fort Hall Reservation. Mr. Moroni Timbimboo, is been down to Garland attending stake conference and he was accompany Mr. Warren Wongan and Henry Woonsook and they also attended stake conference. [1922-06-06 BEN]

1922-06-10 LJ [Not included, duplicate of 1922-06-06 BEN]

LOGAN, JUNE 6, 1922.   The Elk [B.P.O.E.] big celebrating is going today. But Main
Street is decorated with the red, white, and blue, or with American flag. The committee of Elk big celebration is pretty well attended today from different section of
State of Utah. And there is about over 1 thousand Elk people are here today, in
the city which is Salt Lake City, Ogden, Provo, Eureka and more other little
towns. I met Mr. Hon. Harry S. Joseph in the city and he was with Elk today.[17]
    The Provo band is given a very good selection on the Tabernacle Square on
11 o'clock sharp. And Logan citizens people are very enjoyed. . . .
    And big parade start . . . First is Logan City Fire Department. The Provo
Band came next . . . Logan military band . . . [and] training camp from Fort
Douglas Utah. And also many automobiles are represented the various business
department. . . . The Elk people are very welcome visiting in Logan city that different places . . . A Parade . . . is very splendid one. [1922-06-13 BEN]

WASHAKIE, JUNE 26, 1922.   The people are good condition just now. But some of the
Indians are going up to Fort Hall Reservation some time week last to see a big Sun
Dance on the Portneuf bottoms and the commence at latter part this month and
they have in the three good solid days. They may return before 4 July. They are not
been very long up there. Week last Mr. Elias Pubigee little baby died . . . and buried
at Washakie cemetery.
    Mr. Ammon Pubigee and his son was down Tremonton last Thursday . . . after
baby casket. Mr. Thomas and Jim Pabawena wives and children been down
Honeyville is thinning sugar beets and return home on Thursday last.
    I have been out Promontory . . . looking for the work and not have find work
and went down Brigham and Mantua too, and I was visiting my birthplace. I was
accompanied Mr. Stanquitch Jack and his wife too and also my little boys. But had
very splendid trip out country.
    Well we are doing good on our trip and just return home last week ago.
    Mr. Stanquitch Jack wife was visiting her daughter at Washakie just now. . . .
    Well Mr. George P. Sam is doing very fine with his poultry business just now
and he may have a very splendid business.
    The weather is very warm just now, and wheat crop is looking very bad on
account the weather, and everything is very dry down here now. [1922-06-30 BEN]

1922-07-01 LJ [Not included, duplicate of 1922-06-30 BEN]
1922-07-08 LJ [Not included, duplicate of 1922-07-11 BEN]

WASHAKIE, JULY 6, 1922.   The people . . . at Washakie all are went up to West
Portage celebrate there. . . . Baseball game and foot races and picking contest and
other sports and baseball between Thatcher and West Portage. The score was 12
to 16 in favor of Portage. . . . Some Indians went to Nevada for spend 4th July out
there. Their names is Mr. Tom Elk and family he was gone for two weeks just now
and also Mr. Mose Neaman, Mr. Thomas Pabawena and Jim Pabawena and wife.
The west Indians are having a big Sun Dance. . . . near the Deeth, Nevada. Well
sir, I hope they having very splendid good time. Mr. Mose Neaman purchase a new

automobile before went out Nevada and he bought on time and he gave mortgage his crops. . . . Well Mrs. Stanquitch Jack is very ill. And she was taken down to Tremonton Hospital here two days ago and under the Doctor treatment. . . .

I was visiting Logan City yesterday on some business and the seen allbody is very good. Well sir, and made good trip over there. Mr. Elias Pubigee and wife was accompany me. Mr. Henry Woonsook been down Tremonton other day and doing some business. The crop is not so good this year the weather be warm. We need rain pretty bad. The hay is very scarce this year and our hay crop is poor so far. . . . Well all summer plowing is all done here. Mr. Jim Wagon is down Fielding town working in sugar beets. And he made a contract Mr. Claud Grover's beets this season. [1922-07-11 BEN]

1922-07-15 LJ [Not included, duplicate of 1922-07-18 BEN]

WASHAKIE, JULY 10, 1922.   They are not celebrate on 24 July. . . . But our amuese-um [amusement] committee is going made a trip up Idaho in Fairfield, Idaho . . . expect return before 24. Well some of the boys been down to Tremonton attended that big . . . stock show Saturday last. And some from West Portage people were to Tremonton to see the big time too. Mr. Stanquitch Jack is in Tremonton just now. But his wife was under Dr. Treatment and she is in Hospital at Tremonton she is improvement fine. But she confined [from] a baby birth in hospital she doing splendid just now. . . .

Mr. Jim Wagon and wife still working in sugar beet up to Fielding and he has very splendid worker in beet field. Mr. Enos Pubigee and wife been to South-Elwood and buying some cherries for the winter, and his father is with him too, he return same day.[18]

Mr. Warren Wongan is been down Tremonton and buying some cherries for winter. But he was driving team.

Well, all people are here good condition now. Mr. Neaman, Willie Neaman and two Pabawena boys were accompanied and they was stailed [stalled or stayed] out west and have no money to take them home. They may come home after 24 July.

I was in Logan City some time ago week on the important business. I been visiting . . . Riter Bros. Drug Co., and seen Mr. B. F. Riter in his office and also seen Mr. Wm. Curel the great express man in city. But driving his Ford tract [tractor or truck] out street and doing some delivering.

The weather is very warm just now, the grain crop is very dry. We need rain pretty bad here now. . . . [1922-07-18 BEN]

1922-07-22 LJ [Not included, duplicate of 1922-07-25 BEN]

WASHAKIE, JULY 19, 1922.   The crops are soon harvesting. . . . maybe next week probably. Some of our Indians went on Idaho Reservation here two day ago and visiting some their relatives and acquaintance. . . . We are not celebrate here in our town this year seem to me kind dead here no celebrate. We was kind haven't any money and could doing anything this year.

Our wheat crop not so good this year on account being not rain this year. We have got all dry farmers . . . here around Washakie only we got very small amount of water supply. They are much water in our ditch. Well sometime we have a rain it amount anything because too late in season.

Mr. Tom Elk has not return on his trip out Nevada yet, and also Mr. [Mose] Neaman and sons and Mr. Thomas Pabawena and his brother and wife are not return from Nevada yet, but they may return home some time this month.

Mr. Henry [Woonsook] and Stanquitch Jack are went down town other day and buying some fruit down to Deweyville, Utah. And he went up to Idaho yesterday and visit some Indians up there.

Mr. Enos Pubigee went up Idaho about last week on his automobile. But wrote letter to Mr. Henry Woonsook and telling him he broke his car up on the Reservation. So his brothers and father went up there and help him fix it up, so he can come back home. . . .

Well Mr. Jacob Peyope, and wife and childrens are return home from Fairfield, Idaho some time last week. [1922-07-25 BEN]

1922-08-05 LJ [Not included, duplicate of 1922-08-08 BEN]

WASHAKIE, AUGUST 3, 1922.   We are start harvesting our grain crop just now. And our crop not good. . . . We didn't have any rain, but had rain other day, didn't amount anything. There was about 3 header going on. We didn't have any sugar beet this year. And we got [not] enough water that so we didn't raise it. But some of us didn't have grain. Most the young fellows have [not] any wheat this year.

Well, sir, everybody has return by this time from different trips. Mr. Mose Neaman and his company are return home from his Nevada trip, and all the boys too. And all boys been from Idaho are return too. Mr. Ammon Pubigee and one his son are been down Tremonton and getting his header extra.

Mr. Soquitch Timbimboo and his brother Mr. Yeager Timbimboo been up Hardware Ranch some time ago on hunt and fishing trip. They are return home some ago.

Mr. Tom Elk has return home his Nevada trip, and all his family too.

Well, Mrs. Stanquitch Jack return home from hospital Tremonton about couple week ago and her baby doing fine.

Mr. Jim White return home for Nevada some time ago last week. We expect he will able return by this time. He was stay all winter along.

The people been buying fruit down Brigham and Tremonton for the winter.

Mr. Seth Pubigee and family are made a splendid trip up Blacksmith Fork Canyon and for fishing.

Mr. Jim Wagon and wife are working in sugar beets at Fielding and he may stay at Fielding all this coming fall. . . .

Our mail carrier is still on business his name is Mr. Diamond. [1922-08-08 BEN]

WASHAKIE, AUGUST 12, 1922.   We have had splendid nice little rain. That was not much wet. That is to stop from our heading grain. And it was come too late in season in year. The was about 2 combine harvester are going on. This was belong to 2 white men. They buy Indian [land] in Washakie. The people are good condition here now. Only one baby died here last Saturday. And she was buried on

Sunday afternoon. And she was died after her birth. The baby belong to Mr. Jacob Peyope . . . well known in our town. And also Mr. Stanquitch Jack baby died some time ago. And buried in Washakie cemetery. Mr. George Elk was hunting some wild cherries town below, and he came back on same day. . . .

Well some of our people are rejoicing when our fall is coming. Mr. George P. Sam and his grandson are went out Star Valley country [WY]. And he may return home some time next week. And he is hunting some deer skin. Well and making some gloves and his wife is splendid hand for gloves and made a fancy gloves all kinds. Well Mr. Thomas Pabawena are still out west yet now. He may come home some time next month. [1922-08-12 LJ]

1922-08-15 BEN [Not included, duplicate of 1922-08-12 LJ]

WASHAKIE, AUGUST 19, 1922.   Our harvest is over now. And waiting threshing machine come. Well all our grain kind of fail, on account being too hot this year. But had some rain here lately, and didn't amount anything. And soon . . . our threshing done. There was no sugar beet raise here in town. . . . Mr. Kippetchew Noragan and wife is been to circus yesterday. Well Mr. George P. Sam is return home on his long trip in Idaho, and he also going to circus over to Logan. Mr. Ammon Pubigee is repairing his old horsepower threshing machine and company Mr. Tom Elk, they may start soon get all repair done. Probably first next week. Well, our weather pretty warm so far. . . . Mr. Seth Pubigee is been down Brigham City on special business and he made Beach [Peach] contract with Thomas Bros. south the Brigham. [1922-08-19 LJ]

1922-08-22 BEN [Not included, duplicate of 1922-08-19 LJ]
1922-08-26 LJ [Not included, duplicate of 1922-09-01 BEN]

WASHAKIE, AUGUST 23, 1922.   We are start threshing now. Our wheat turn out poor this year on account being so dry. Mr. Any Shuty from Plymouth [UT] is pull his steamer thresher in our town start thresh on Mr. Ammon Pubigee on the lower part the town. I suppose he may get all job around here. His grain going about 10 [¢?] per bushel acres. I expect they will be two thresher in our town and thresh for our people. And wheat buyers paying only 75¢ per bushel today and it drop about 5 1/2¢ today. It was about 80¢ last week. All heading done just now. We had quite rain storm here other night and yesterday too. . . .

Mr. Thomas Pabawena is return his trip Nevada some last week. . . .

Mr. Ammon Pubigee want go up Fort Hall Reservation pretty soon, and to see his sick cousin and he was received letter from his he be wanted soon as possible. Well he may next Friday to go visit him.

Mr. Stanquitch Jack is still at Washakie yet.

Mr. George Elk is come home last night and he is hunting wild berries. . . .[19]

Mr. James Pabawena is out west yet he may return some time next month.

Mr. Willie Neaman is still out Nevada and he got automobile. But he has got no money to come home with. He wrote to his father stated he has got money just now. He say can come home now.

Mr. Frank Bannock is visiting his wife relation here. And went down below and looking around country. He was from Fort Hall Reservation. [1922-09-01 BEN]

1922-09-02 LJ [Not included, duplicate of 1922-09-05 BEN]

WASHAKIE, AUGUST 31, 1922.   . . . [Some] of the Indian went up big round up [Wild West Show] to Preston, Idaho. . . .

The threshing is nearly done here now. Well the grain did not turn out very good this year and our fall is start now. And [they] are not seeded the ground yet. Well and some of their grain down Tremonton. The grain worth about 10¢ per bushel here now. There was about two buyers are here now.

Mr. Soquitch and wife went over to Richmond [UT] and hunting some wild berries. He out yesterday. . . .

Mr. Casper Anderson is threshing for Mr. Harry Steed. He was from Elwood, Utah. And he may get thru threshing tomorrow some time. Well he return to his home after all done here. Mr. William Hootchew and wife are visiting his daughter here in our little town. And also Mr. Grouse Creek Jack is visiting his son here. And these from Idaho. Well and they are all good condition. One family from White Rock Indian Reservation is visiting here our town some time last week and he went home already. Mr. Mose Neaman and family went to big round up last night and his brother-in-law is accompanied him too. [1922-09-05 BEN]

1922-09-05 LJ [Not included, duplicate of 1922-09-08 BEN]

WASHAKIE, SEPTEMBER 4, 1922.   The threshing all done here. Now, but our grain is turn out pretty poor. Well some of our Indians are went over to Preston, Idaho, the big round up there. The has not return home yet. Well there was about 20 or more Indians from Fort Hall Reservation I expect there was about 20 Indians from here in that big round up. They have about 5 from Washakie fellow and about 15 from Fort Hall Indians joined the big parade . . . each morning. And also have a regular Indians War Dance in the city Park in afternoon, somewhere about between 4 or 5 o'clock, and some squaw races, too. Indians relay race for 1 1/2 mile on their own ponies. Some of the Fort Hall boys riding a buck contest too. All our people was having there good time in that round up. Well and the return on Sunday last. . . . All our very good condition just now.[1922-09-08 BEN]

1922-09-16 LJ [Not included, duplicate of 1922-09-19 BEN]

News Items from Washakie

WASHAKIE, SEPTEMBER 14, 1922.   . . . We are very busy getting our fall crop put in now. Well some of the Indians been over to Preston, Ida. the wild west show and they all return home about two weeks ago, and they having a pretty good time. The white man watermelon and peaches peddlers are around here in our little town nearly every day. The threshing is all done last week and the grain is all sold around here now. We are getting about 75¢ per bushel here now. Some of our late grain has not thresh yet. Mr. George P. Sam is looking for thresher yesterday. He has got some late grain. Well sir we haven't any sick amongst us. . . . Mr. Grouse Creek Jack and his son Mr. Stanquitch Jack went out west and hunting some wild pine nuts and his son-in-law is accompanied him too. They may return home some time about two week later. Mr. Bannock Frank is still in our town yet and he was visiting his relation. But he from Fort Hall Reservation and return home about week or more. Mr. Ammon Pubigee and John John [probably 13 yr-old Jim John Neaman] been hunting some chicken [grouse] out west hills on Monday last. And they can [not] find any chicken. Mr. Enos Pubigee want going up on Idaho and to visit his wife folks in few day. . . . and he may stay about week. . . . Mr. Julius Youpe and family are visiting Mr. Mose Neaman place now and he is from Idaho. [1922-09-19 BEN]

WASHAKIE, SEPTEMBER 1922.   . . . Our people are going down Brigham City for Peach day today. And nearly whole town going down yesterday. I hope they having good time down there. Mr. Warren Wongan and Nephi Perdash been down Brigham City on Monday last and getting some Peaches for the winter fruit. Mr. Enos Pubigee and wife been down south Elwood and getting some peaches and on Mr. W. Ottogary place. Mr. Julius Youpe and wife been visit our town some time ago. And he was been on Wind River Reservation Wyoming and visiting his relation out there. But he is return home on his long trip. Mr. George P. Sam went down Brigham City yesterday and accompanied his wife. . . . Well Mr. Soquitch and wife has not return home yet from Paradise [UT] and hunting some wild cherries. He may return some next week. Well Mr. Bannock Frank still in our town yet. And he was from Idaho Reservation. [1922-09-23 LJ]

WASHAKIE, SEPTEMBER 25, 1922.   Some of our just return from big Peaches Day. And they buying some fruit . . . to put up for Winter. Some are stay for picking some Peach just now. . . . [and] some of them stay for drying peaches. Mr. George Jackson & wife are here visiting some his relation here at our town. Well he was from Wind River Reservation. He was coming Mchurlie [Charlie] Perdash place. Mr. George P. Sam trade on the Buick car at the Tremonton today. Well he will taken his 4 horses and one cow and cow heifer about one year old. I expect he made a good trade. And also he gave a [one] set harness. He will bring his car home tomorrow sometime. Mr. George Innock [Tomock] is return home today from Brigham City. Some our are been surprise to [see] the airplane flying over the city. Our people are never seen an airplane before. . . . I will be going on long trip out Nevada. We are start on next Saturday yet. Well are going have some kind of talk out there to Battle Mountain. We stay about week or ten days. Mr. William Hootchew is been down below. And dry some peaches just now. And he was with all his folks. [1922-09-28 LJ]

ELKO, NEVADA, SEPTEMBER 25, 1922.   I am reaching here yesterday about 2:00 o'clock here at Elko But I find the Indians are good condition. And some of Indians went down to Battle Mountain yesterday on train. They are going have a real Indian Fandango Dance. I am going down on [train] No. 19. and accompany me Chief Harry Dixon. Well going to here [hear] big talk down there Battle Mountain. We will have a talk about our Land claim here on Nevada State and Utah State we have been organized friendship about 2 year ago. We are act chief of this Indian

Back row, left to right, Ammon Pubigee, Ketch Toyahdook, Harry D. Tootiaina. *Front row,* Aaron Pubigee, Nellie Tootiaina. *Courtesy Mae Timbimboo Parry*

tribe was Mr. Harry Dixon. Well he will take charge, his own tribe. But these will be our last council at Battle Mountain. The Rodeo is over last Monday. And all Indians are gone for different places. I may stay out here about week or ten day I don't like this country very good. Just now it is very dry country out here around Elko. I have a been acquainted quite lot of the Indians here now. [1922-09-30 LJ]

BATTLE MOUNTAIN, NEVADA, SEPTEMBER 28, 1922.   The Indians are here big gathering. . . . Today they had a big council over to begin to appointed as Indians chief [from] places in Nevada country. I have been acquainted with them. But we are going to return on Thursday. And Mr. Seth Pubigee and Mr. Nephi Zundel out with me. Some from Austin, Elko, Winnaeeuma [Winnemucca], etc. The appointed one chief from Austin, two from Elko, and two from Battle Mountain. Their names are Harry Dixon, Dick Hall, Jim Seuch [Leach], and Dick Indian. Well they all Indian accept these chief.[20] The weather is cold here now and they going to have another [meeting] tomorrow. Mr. Capt. Bill Hall is from Beowawe, but his wife is with him. All Indian having a good time at big Fandango Dance near Battle Mountain rail road station. There were lots Indians boys been drinking heavy. Well and they have three men as appointed as police as long is big time is over. [1922-10-03 BEN]

Washakie Indian Letter

WASHAKIE, OCTOBER 1922.   Well all our fall is pretty well done just now. But we are good condition and I was return home from my western trip today.[21] I have been acquainted lot of Indian just now.

There is about over five hundred people are attend there regular celebrate at the Battle Mountain on the 2 day of September. Well we have appointed 7 at chief from different part the country of Nevada.

These are going control his own people. Last Tuesday we coming from in Salt Lake City from Nevada. We find some Indians from White Rock Reservation.

They was been playing on war dance every night. Start about 8 o'clock. We having a splendid good old time. [1922-10-06 BEN]

1922-10-07 LJ [Not included, duplicate of 1922-10-03 BEN]

WASHAKIE, OCTOBER 14, 1922.

Our people are good condition and they been working on the sugar beet down north the sugar factory most of them are work out for the white men. Our day [school] is running just now. But Miss Rassmussen from Bear River City [UT] is teaching school this year. Mr. Moroni Timbimboo and his wife been down to Salt Lake City conference week last. . . .

One boy baby died here last ago. He was taken him down to Ogden to have Dr. treatment and he died down there. His funeral service held at ward meeting house. . . .

Mr. George P. Sam is on hunt east the Logan mountain. But he stop off at the Logan city. But some one is stole his pinto horse. But he notified police. And they wire all over Cache Valley. And they find him all right. Well he got . . . horse back then he went right on his hunt to East Logan. Also Mr. Mose Neaman lost his little baby boy some time ago. The weather is getting to cool just now. Mr. Henry Woonsook is went down buying some fruit. . . . Well have very good rain last night. But these was good for fall grain. [1922-10-21 LJ]

WASHAKIE, OCTOBER 28, 1922.   The people are good condition, no one sick so far. Most of them are topping sugar beet down there to around Garland. But they are earning some money for coming winter. There was not much people is here now. Our day school is not running yet, it might be later on. But teacher went home . . . couple days ago. The agent was here at our little town some time ago last week ago. He want take the school children up to Fort Hall Industrial school. But our Bishop won't let him take a children because we want our day school here our town yet. . . .

Mr. George [Jackson] and wife is visiting Mr. Charlie Perdash place from the Wyoming reservation. But he is work on sugar beet near the Garland factory. Well he may all winter at Washakie. And also one more from same place and wife here now.

Mr. Charlie Perdash is on his deer hunt on East . . . he has not return yet. Mr. George P. Sam is on Elk hunt on East the Logan mountain, he was return home week last. He has [not] kill anything. But our boys want out deer [hunt?] pretty soon now.

Mr. Moroni Timbimboo is moved to Idaho. But he want Government allotment up Fort Hall Reservation, or rent some land up there. [1922-11-04-A LJ]

WASHAKIE, NOVEMBER 1, 1922.   . . . There was no hay in our town this year. Well the our people didn't [know] what they going to for feed this coming winter. We haven't got any money two to buy hay with. And some of them are working in sugar beet just now. And some are getting through just lately and went home. Mr. Thomas Pabawena and company is work in Mr. Charlie Hess 3 mile west from Tremonton and 1 mile south. But his sugar beet is pretty dirty, and they quit the job and move off on Monday. But he going on another job near the Honeyville, and North Honeyville flour mill. Mr. Ammon Pubigee and his two son with Mr. Thomas Pabawena and topping beet with him. Mr. George P. Sam was been Logan Temple and administering his poor health. I been over to Logan city with George and I have seen all I acquainted over there. [1922-11-04-B LJ]

WASHAKIE, NOVEMBER 10, 1922.   . . . [George] P. Sam are doing pretty . . . [good raising] chicken this year. He was [indecipherable] [bought second] hand Buick car some time ago last week. Well he has not learn yet to run his car. . . . Mr. Enos Pubigee and wife been up to Washakie on Monday night. Well he may return soon as get through the beet and his company. Mrs. Annie Hootchew been down Brigham on Monday . . . doing business. And also Miss Susie Highyou is staying down to Brigham City just now and doing some buck tanning for white man.

We found a our treaty on page 850 of Haper [Kappler] book, and the stated that our people should hunt anytime in season. These is away that reads. The article seven of the Treaties year in 1863. Department of the Interior, officer of the Indian affair, Washington, D. C.

My friend, American Indian of the United State. These regular game warden of the United States Indian Deputy. But to kill a deer any time they want to. Because this all kind game to belonged to North Western Shoshone tribe and is hereby permitted to hunt in deer in the accordance with the Laws of the Government hereby acknowledged. But the right hunt on the Public Domain, and to fish any of the stream there of must be exercised in accordance with the Laws of the state of Utah, or Nevada and Idaho and Wyoming, as was determined by the United States Government Laws of the United States to the Indians. I case against any of white men to kill deer any other of these game. This, Indian game not kill by any of white people their [they're?] be arrested so on. This game and be permitted to hunt duck, geese, or sage hens. And all this game belonged to United States Indians and this game accordance by the laws of the Indians. And whatever the white men to kill a deer why to pay in advance: whatever it worth any of this game pay for it Indians. Why be on arrested so on with limits may be declared by commissioner, all other omniverous and insectiverous the protected except Indian game. Indian commissioner Indian affair and these forest not untaked by white mens. The forest what it belonged to Indians and any other counties reserves do not cutting by the white people any of these forest. And any of these white men against to Indian on the forest why be arrested so on. Any white men responsible why be arrested so on.

Very respectfully,
Acting E. W. Merit,
Commissioner.[22]
Willie Ottogary. [1922-11-14 BEN]

WASHAKIE, NOVEMBER 16, 1922.   The are poor condition just now. But we are not much money now. The hay have got any this year. Well some of our people has return home and all done with sugar beet. Some of them are not through yet. . . . We had rain all night last night and cool now. And [those] been out hunt has not return yet. Mr. Thomas Pabawena is not through his job yet, and company. . . . Mr. Ammon Pubigee been up to Washakie week last. But he return on Monday. Mr. George P. Sam are doing pretty good for his chicken this year. . . . Mr. Moroni Timbimboo move to Idaho for last month. We didn't hear from him yet. I expect he may good condition now.

Mr. Enos Pubigee and wife been up to Washakie on Monday night. Well he may return soon as get through the beet. And his company. . . . One Indian [Mr. Danyhay] visit at my place at South Elwood from Idaho Reservation. But he gone home about two week ago. Him and his wife. He may return any time now. He expect to send his girl in Elwood school, and quick is return from Idaho.[23] [1922-11-18 LJ]

WASHAKIE, NOVEMBER 20, 1922. . . . We are having very cold weather right now. The people are not so good just now. Master Wilford Peyope is very ill . . . been sick for nearly 2 month. His parents are working on sugar beet at the Riverside. He is getting little better now. . . . Mr. Mose Neaman been down Brigham City on special business [possibly land related] week last. Mr. Thomas Pabawena is in the Deweyville District working in sugar beets and company by Mr. Ammon Pubigee and Enos Pubigee. They was soon getting through. . . . [1922-11-25 LJ]

WASHAKIE, DECEMBER 2, 1922. The people are good condition just now. But they get through with now. And they all return home last week. Well some of the Indians been down Garland for two month keep busy on the sugar beet. Mr. Moroni Timbimboo went to Fort Hall Reservation and never heard from him yet. But move his family up there. . . . Mr. Danyhay been up him home Fort Hall Reservation and companied his wife and return at South Elwood. The place Mr. Willie Ottogary and he expect stay all winter there. But he send his 12 year old girl at Elwood school.

I went over two Logan last week and see all my old acquainted over there. But no bad news from Logan city so far and return home last week ago.[24] But all my friends are very rejoice to see me over there. I was very thankful for them. [1922-12-02 LJ]

WASHAKIE, DECEMBER 9, 1922. The people are . . . not make any money just now. . . . The hay was very scarce right now. Well some of us try buy some hay over to West Portage. But the hay was scarce over there. And people are holding their hay for $8.00 Dollars per ton just now. Mr. Yeager Timbimboo and wife went up to Idaho yesterday. . . . Well sir our day school is running now there is about 12 children went to school just now.

Mr. Moroni Timbimboo is been here our town last week. He was move up to Idaho about month ago. [1922-12-09 LJ]

WASHAKIE, DECEMBER 12, 1922. We are now pretty good condition but the weather is getting colder just now. Last Wednesday night real snow storm, and about 6 inches they . . . say winter begin now. . . . [The] hay price . . . $8.00 and $6.00 per ton but we have got no money. . . . Mr. Soquitch Timbimboo buy one cow from Bishop Wa[rd].

He pay for cow about $35.00. Mr. Moroni Timbimboo is join Baptist Church since he move to Idaho Reservation but left this our church and join other church.[25] Well Mr. Danyhay is going wintered at South Elwood on Mr. Willie Ottogary place. His little girl going school down Elwood school. Mr. Tom Elk and Jacob Peyope are out trapping now. They haven't return yet. Mr. Yeager Timbimboo and wife went to Idaho Reservation and moving his son furniture and other stuff. He may return some time next week. Well sir Mr. George P. Sam been over to Logan and getting his horse, About early in fall some one stole it. [1922-12-15 BEN]

1922-12-16 LJ [Not included, duplicate of 1922-12-15 BEN]
1922-12-26 BEN [Not included, *indecipherable*]

WASHAKIE, DECEMBER 21, 1922.   We are having a lot snow up here. The last snow fall about 1 ft ½ inch, and it is good sleighing now. A weather is getting colder now. And our boys went out rabbit hunting pretty soon maybe after Xmas. But they figuring go out to Salt Well, and many other places out west. Everybody is good condition thus far. . . . Our day school is running good condition. There was about 20 to 21 children in the school. Well Miss Vida Ward are Teaching the school here now. Mr. Kippetchew Noragan is been down Salt Lake City some time ago and buying some deer hide. Mr. George P. Sam is very well just now. But he had a Bright's disease. The hay very scarse here around our little Indian town. I have been over to Logan on the special business. But I found every thing splendid condition. But I was glad to see my old acquaintance over there. Mr. Yeager Timbimboo has not return from Idaho yet, he may return sometime. But go up visit his son on Fort Hall Reservation. Well people are rejoice when Christmas soon be here. When the old Santy Clause chinking with reindeer and sleigh [with] some toys. That make Children happy, so on. [1922-12-30-A LJ]

WASHAKIE, DECEMBER 27, 1922.   The people are here been Xmas celebration and some been up to Idaho and visiting relation there. Some of the Indian from Reservation, Idaho, here spend Christmas here. And also visiting some relatives here too, and some been return home on Tuesday last. We have very good Christmas programme here. . . . Well sir this was very splendid . . . one we ever had for long time. Mr. Kippetchew Noragan and wife been up Idaho Reservation week last and return before the Christmas Day, and the was see a dead man. He was relation to his wife.

Mr. Eddy Drinks been here our town some time ago. . . . But he return home day after Xmas he visiting Mr. Catch Toyahdook place and more others relation. Mr. Warbonnet and wife was here visiting some his relation here. Well he may return home some time next week. Well Mr. Danyhay been here our little town on Christmas Day. And spend with us. He went home on Tuesday last. [1922-12-30-B LJ]

5

"We Expect Get Some Land from Our Big White Pop in Future Time,"[1] 1923–1924

WASHAKIE, JANUARY 4, 1923. . . . We had a very nice New Year's programme. . . . After the programme was close have children dance in the ward meeting house. And evening was a grand ball for the old folks, and the very body is enjoyed. But our days school is running very nice.

Well sir, Mr. Yeager Timbimboo and his wife went up Idaho on the New Year day, and they going visit one of their relation up to Idaho Reservation, and he expect to visit his son up there, and more . . . relatives. . . .

Mr. War Bonnet is return home last week with his wife, up to Idaho Reservation.

Mr. Kippetchew Noragan and wife is return home from Idaho Reservation some time last week ago. . . . one his relatives died. He name was Elno Pocatello. He lives out west Pocatello about 12 miles from the city.

We had good lay of snow just now, and it is good sleighing everywhere here.

Well, all our people a getting pretty poor this year, and hay pretty scarce here around our little town, and hay is about 12 dollars per ton here. We can't get any hay now. [1923-01-06 LJ]

WASHAKIE, JANUARY 13, 1923. We have been good winter no one sick just now. The snow is nearly gone, last we some rain and nearly thaw all snow here. Well some of our people think is spring time is near. . . . I expect we going lose our horses. And it is mighty hard on our horses when we have [not] got any hay. But we are very poor and haven't any money this year to buy hay with. It is very hard to find hay. . . . Our grain crop is fail last summer. Our day school is running very nice. There is about 20 or more pupils attend school this year. It is good when thing for children. . . .

Mr. Jacob Peyope is out country doing some trapping for coyotes. Mr. Danyhay and wife went down Ogden city and trying sell some gloves and there own made gloves. But he making pretty pair gloves today. [1923-01-13 LJ]

1923-01-20 LJ [Not included, duplicate of 1923-01-23 BEN]

WASHAKIE, JANUARY 18, 1923. . . . Some of us are under the weather, and they are coming through last week. Our boy go to be a big rabbit today and they going to have a grand ball tonight. . . . The lose side be a paying for music and winner side

125

not be pay and get free dance ticket. They are to choose a south and north side against each other for shooting contest today. Well I hope are go have enjoyable time. Nobody sick just now our school is nice condition. . . . Mr. Jacob Peyope is return home from his trapping business. We haven't got much snow here just now the sleighing is very poor and snow is nearly gone here. Some of our people say they going have a lots snow in next month. The is so warm here just now. Some of say the spring begin now. Also Mr. Kippetchew Noragan and wife return home about 2 weeks ago and visiting some of their relation up Fort Hall Reservation and more others Indians up there. [1923-01-23 BEN]

1923-02-03 LJ [Not included, duplicate of 1923-02-06 BEN]

WASHAKIE, FEBRUARY 1, 1923.   The people are poor condition this year. But our wheat is fair [inserted from 1923-02-03 LJ: " . . . our wheat crop is fail."]. . . . We had a regular snow storm here, it is last three day, and snow fall about 1 foot. . . . We have good sleighing just now, but the snow was nearly gone here about 3 week ago. Well the people are have got any hay now. I expect some of us lost horse. Because they have no money to buy hay with. The hay is very scarce here in our vicinity. We have such good weather for long time We think the spring time is coming. Our people are made a great mistake. But other day the weather is change and turn too cold now. Mr. Yeager Timbimboo and wife are return from Idaho reservation, and visiting his son Mr. Moroni Timbimboo. He was move up there last fall. Well sir more other his relatives or friends up there. . . . [1923-02-06 BEN]

WASHAKIE, FEBRUARY 10, 1923.   Mr. Amos Moemberg lost . . . one of his horse while out shooting rabbits. This was happen about week or 10 days ago. They return home . . . and had a very good trip out there. Mr. Soquitch Timbimboo is been down to Garland yesterday and doing some shopping. He went down on morning train, and return home on the evening train on same day. . . . Our agent is issued some 200 lbs. flour, and 1 sack sugar and sack beans, and was distrubit [distribute] among our people some time ago last week. . . .

Mr. Yeager Timbimboo and wife was return from Idaho reservation about a week ago. Last week we have a splendid good jolly time at dance. On next Friday night another good time again. [1923-02-10 LJ]

WASHAKIE, FEBRUARY 14, 1923.   Our weather are getting is meloate [possibly mellowed] just now. . . . We have had a very enjoyable time last Friday night. The Relief Society gave a Grand Ball in the ward meeting house. They are pretty bad condition and having no hay this winter. But their crop is fail last summer. But some of our people are rejoiceing about spring is coming near. They was been working in sugar beet field last fall down to near Garland factory. But seem to me we winter pretty good no one starve yet. Mr. Charlie purchase some hay from A. R. Grover from Garland and about 5 ton. George Indian from Winter [probably Wind River] Reservation is visiting here in our town some time ago. Will was collect money on his father [e]state down to near Tremonton. It is right straight East from this town. But was purchase some hay for Charlie Perdash. He is relation to this man. Other day is some [possibly his son] is hauling home hay. The price was about $12.00 per ton down around Garland. The Garland is straight South from here. But he was return about three week ago. No one sick just now. Down near Tremonton on my place have a two family living this winter. Mr. Danyhay . . . living down my place and his family is doing fine. But his 13 years girl went school in Elwood this winter and she doing fine in school. And one old lady sick. . . . I expect she about 100 years old. When in early days she seen great herd of Buffalo in this part of the country. [1923-02-17 LJ]

WASHAKIE, FEBRUARY 23, 1923.   The people here good condition. . . . The hay price is very high. We have had snow here are good lot off it. And sleighing here just now. But snow about 6 or 7 inch on the level the ground. The weather is getter colder just now. Well there was a big celebrate here in our little [town] today. Everything pretty splendid here no one sick and the stock in fair condition. Well our day school running very nicely this year. There is about 10 or 12 children attending this year. Our mail service is change last week. The time is 6 P.M. used to be at 7 A.M. But it is better for mail carrier. And he is old man.[2] There was not so many people is here now it is numbered about 50 with concloud [including?] children. . . . Mr. Yeager and Henry Woonsook been down Garland yesterday and purchase some hay from Mr. A. R. Grossen. Today we had a big time. . . . In the morning we . . . nice programme. . . . [1923-02-24 LJ]

WASHAKIE, MARCH 3, 1923.   Say Mr. England could you send me a $6.00 Dollars right way. I need pretty bad now buy some hay for horses and nearly starve, oblige.[3]
      The weather is change just now, and getting warmer. The snow is thawing pretty fast. But the Sleighing is fine around here just now in our vicinity. Our people been celebrating George Washington birthday last week. . . . In the evening we have a old fashion white men dance and everybody a very nice time. Well we have a big dinner in the ward meeting house . . . served by the Relief Society. This was the honor of the first President of our country.
      I was a pretty close call last Saturday afternoon on East of the Tremonton on county road and fell off from spring wagon and nearly broken my neck. I was 3 or 4 minutes [un]conscious before I knowing anything. We been Tremonton while we return home from town this was happen. . . . Two week ago Malad Stake conference was held at Malad City, Idaho. There is about 10 or more been attended the conference and they said had a splendid meeting. I heard report they made on the Tithing Fair. Our little town is leading ward of the Malad Stake in the Tithing Fairs and also we had about 100 percent on the Tithing record. That was showed a fine credit for our people here just now.[4] The farmers hold their hay for $10.00 per ton just now. But we have no lose our stock yet. We haven't much snow this year. The first snow we had about 6 inches on the level and last time we had about 5 ½ on the level. But not much cold this year has been before. [1923-03-03 LJ]

WASHAKIE, MARCH 8, 1923.   The people are very poor this yr. Last summer small crop of wheat, not much money. . . . Last Monday we had a snow storm and the weather was very cold. . . . I hope we will have a warm weather after this time. But some of the our people not ready for spring. Our day school are going very nicely this year. Our mail service was hance [change] last month, and taken mail on afternoon train instead of the morning train. The hay is very scarse around here just now. . . . The farmer been holding the price pretty well up and also and hay is pretty well gone. . . . Mr. James Pabawena has not return from his Nevada trip yet and also his two brothers is out there. We haven't heard from him for long time. They might return next summer. Well and visiting his own kin out Nevada Country. I have been kind of sickness since been fell off from wagon about two week ago. Mr. Danyhay and family doing fine here. He is from Idaho reservation. His girl is going school at Elwood school. Well is doing very nicely so far. Mr. George Moody was been here in last fall in Brigham City attend on land business. He was going down to Uintah Country in the month of September and visiting his two daughters down that country. But was the Chief of the [unclear, looks like Goshot—Goshute] Tribe. [1923-03-10 LJ]

WASHAKIE, MARCH 14, 1923.   My people are pretty well just now. . . . Some of the people are lost their horses now on account having no hay. . . . . Some of our boys been buying some hay from Mr. Johny Wells from East Portage. He was selling his hay for $10 or $8 per ton about two week ago. They been buying hay for all winter.

There was two white men in our town today. And doing some horse trading one of them name Mr. Frank Parson. But he is well known horse trader in this part country. He live in Malad City, Idaho. But he made several trade here ever since he comes. . . .

Mr. Dick Arritch was visiting our town about a week ago he moved from here last fall. . . . Mr. George P. Sam went down to Tremonton this morning and to buy some hay on Mr. Dean Hows place on the east of Malad River and cross bridge from Tremonton town. I was been up Washakie town other day. . . . [1923-03-17 LJ]

WASHAKIE, MARCH 30, 1923.   . . . We are getting ready for spring works. But is kind too wet yet. And our fall crop looking very splendid just now. Well sir we are very anxious start our spring works. . . . Some of our boys getting out some cedar post and make their living just now. But some of people going to Malad city to attended their Priesthood meeting. . . . Our day school are running very nice this year. There was about 18 boys and girls attended school here in our little town. . . . Mr. Bile [Bill] William are down Tremonton and doing some business there. He may return home on next wk sometime. But he was from Skull Valley. Mr. Moroni Timbimboo and wife and family are still in our town yet. He may return up Idaho later on. His two little [children] are attended school down Garland just now. The was stayed with Grandma there.

Mr. George P. Sam went down Tremonton and getting some his hay. . . . Mr. George Tospangquitch was been down below and doing some business he return home other day too. But he was narrow escape and he fell off the spring wagon. His horses start run and [he] fell under the wheel and two wheel run over him. He is cripple. . . . [1923-04-02 LJ]

WASHAKIE, APRIL 7, 1923.   . . . I was visiting our town last week and find every is very nicely, and snow is gone just now. . . . I hope we will have a splendid wheat crop this year. Some of want going on Idaho for work. Agent on Idaho want some hands and teamster work on the canal up around Blackfoot. I expect they will have . . . made some money. Mr. Moroni and wife is still here now. But he going up again yet and he left his thing[s] up there. . . . We having a big celebrated on next Friday. And going a big dinner and in evening have a Grand Ball.

Mr. Nephi Perdash born a big nice boy baby last week sometime and they doing nicely so far and also Mr. Danyhay born a boy a week ago and doing splendid. Well Mr. Bell [Bill] Williams and wife was down Tremonton and doing some business there also he was visiting Soquitch Timbimboo place here. He was from Skull Valley. But he return home on Monday last. He may come back up here again in the summer time. Mr. Joe Woonsook is sick all winter. But he getting little better just now. Mr. Kippetchew Noragan wife pretty sick. She been down Deweyville see Dr. Misses Peucanon [Buchanan] other day. But she got kidney trouble. [1923-04-07 LJ]

WASHAKIE, APRIL 10, 1923.   Our people are very good just now. And Mrs. Kippetchew Noragan is on sick list. But is getting no better yet. Our fall wheat looking very promising so far. And our spring work is soon start. I expect we are going have a nice wheat crops this year. . . . Mr. Jacob Peyope is expect going to Wyoming to shearing sheep. But he may going next week some time. Mr. Hyrum Wongsaw is been down Tremonton other day and motoring down there. Mr. Jim Wagon is made a contract sugar beet for Mr. Will Adams for coming summer. . . . He expect made some money this year. Our people going have a big celebrate on last Friday. But they had postponed for next Friday and going have a big dinner in the ward chapel. And in evening going have a big white men dance. I hope are lively a good time. Well Miss Louise Ottogary was attack by the appendicitis about last week. Mr. Dr. O. D. Luke was examine her she had a appendicitis. She was about 11 year old girl. A little daughter Mr. Willie Ottogary and for corresponded papers. . . . [1923-04-14 LJ]

WASHAKIE, APRIL 19, 1923.   . . . Our spring work is start just now. But most of us have not got land for their own. But they getting some on share [sharecropping]. . . . We been good time last week. We have had a big dinner in the ward chapel and in the evening had a white people dance. But a everybody enjoyed and good turn out and they are not much people were here in our little Indian town. Some been a moved away from this place. . . . Mr. Seth Pubigee and his father is been down to Brigham City yesterday and looking for some Indian land business. He return home yesterday. But he was the appointed looking after some land business for his own people.[5] He is well known in our town. Our agent been sent some flour here last week ago. I expect about 40 lbs. hundred flour [could mean 40 one hundred pound bags] and about 2 hundred lbs. sugar, 2 hundred [lbs.] Beans. We all divided up among our people here. We asked our agent for seed wheat on later on and some hay for our horses. Our weather are getting very warm so far. Mrs. Willie Neamuir [Neaman] is on the sick list. She been down Deweyville to see Dr. down there. She was very sick woman. I hope she may get well. Mrs. Shippack coming home from below and stay down all winter down there. She came home yesterday. [1923-04-21 LJ]

WASHAKIE, APRIL 25, 1923.   We are soon get through with [putting] spring crop in, and our people are rejoice when spring is here just now. Our boys want to get work up on

Idaho reservation, and some of them figuring going up for work on big canal up around Blackfoot. But I hope they will made some money. Well people are very poor this winter and the money is scarce here just now. Mr. Geo. Tospangquitch was through of [thrown off] spring wagon and making him sick for while. We are good condition so far. . . . Our fall crop is looking splendid. I expect we going have a heavy wheat crop this summer. . . . Mr. Frank Parson horse trader this section of the country. But he was well known of our people here. Some of our people are lose horse the spring. And our people are been poor this year. Some of our boys getting . . . some cedar post. But Mrs. Danyhay boy baby is doing nice and he was about month old, his mother is doing splendid, and all the family is well and good condition. Mr. Jim Wagon is made a sugar beet contract down to east Garland factory. Miss Louise Ottogary is attacking with appendicitis a last week, she is improving very nice. She is under Dr. care. I expect she may get alright in few days. Well sir there was much news for this time. I hope all the News reader was great interested in the in Indian reporter or by Mr. Willie Ottogary. I am try to get very nice letter every week the month. I hope this will reach the Newspaper subscribe. But I am very much surprise some people and many town and city as well. This is about all this time. [1923-04-28 LJ]

WASHAKIE, MAY 3, 1923.   Our people rejoice over the wheat crop. It looking very well and they rejoicing our fall crop are all looking very promising. . . . Mr. George P. Sam was bought a 6 passenger Buick last fall but he is not run it yet for this spring. he may run it later on. The boys are not going to Fort Hall yet and they are going later on, probably next week. I have been over to Logan City yesterday on the especial business over there. But I seen all my old acquainted there. Also Mr. Bill Curel is doing fine on his express business so far. Well he was a very good man. I know him for 4 years. Mr. Danyhay and wife mother went over with me to Logan and they doing some shopping. We have had a fine summer weather here now. Mr. Jim Wongsaw is down in the east Garland. He may stay all summer. His wife and working in sugar beet field. But our people are good condition so far no one died. Our day school very nicely this year. Miss Vida Ward was our school teacher in our town. But the children are good condition in school and they are learning fast too. [1923-05-05 LJ]

WASHAKIE, MAY 12, 1923.   . . . Last Saturday some the boys been down to Tremonton to some big time. It was May festele [festival] day 5th day of this month. But was coming home same day. Well our agent was been buying for our people and also some seed wheat to plant this spring. Last Friday was dance in ward meeting house, the was a big crowd was there. There was quite lot of white men and women folks was attended to. Mr. Elk Hale and wife was been up there to visit the dance here in our town. Well sir everybody was enjoyed. Mr. Ammon Pubigee and his 3 sons been down to Brigham City yesterday to an importance business. . . . Mr. Timus Perdash been down to Deweyville to see his sister's little boy. He was under the Dr. care last Friday, and he was about 6 month old. But he is getting little bit better. . . . [Mary] Moemberg was her one leg badly cut up with her tic [disk] harrow on the Saturday and she was taken to Tremonton hospital. And Dr. Luke and Dr. Black was dressed her wound. She was working out field and her foot caught on the ground and the cut the one leg. [1923-05-12 LJ]

Mr. and Mrs. Grouse Creek Jack, 1938. *Courtesy Mae Timbimboo Parry.*

WASHAKIE, MAY 15, 1923.   . . . Our agent is visit here in our town yesterday and he is talking some of our people and some matters of business. All our wheat crop looking very splendid and they are rejoicing over the crop. . . . Our school children are rejoicing over the school vacation for the summer. . . . Mrs. Johny Jack wife is to Deweyville. . . . Her little boy is very sick. Mr. Willie Neaman is went up Idaho sometime ago. But he was looking for job. Some of the boys been clean water ditch last week and get through and ready for water just now. Everybody is well in our town. No one die here now. But weather is little bit change just now and it is cold here now. . . . [1923-05-19 LJ]

WASHAKIE, MAY 26, 1923.   . . . Our day school is running very good. But our children is rejoice when school closed for summer vacation. . . . Miss [Mary] Moemberg is taken down to Deweyville to have Dr. treatment, her leg been cut up with Disk harrow. She working out on farm, her leg caught on the ground and drag her few distance. She was cripple up pretty bad. She was improving fine. . . . Mr. Grouse Creek Jack is visit out town now a few day ago. And he was from Idaho country. He may return home some time next week. But he was accompanied his loving wife. And also Mr. Wm. Hootchew visiting our town too. [1923-05-26 LJ]

WASHAKIE, MAY 30, 1923.   . . . We have a very nice rainstorm today. But our wheat crop looking very good. I hope we splendid harvest when grain getting ripe. Our people is not much doing today on account the storm. Well some of our people is working in sugar beet field just now. But they start work last week ago . . . near the Garland factory. Our people very rejoice over this rain we had.

Oh, it is wonderful rain we had for long time. It make everybody feel happy around our vicinity. Enos Pubigee and John Johny was motoring down Tremonton last Sunday. He return in the evening. Mr. Danyhay and family return home for last two weeks ago. His home on the Idaho Reservation. But his 12-year-old girl went school at Elwood school all winter along. She was learning good. He expect may return again for next school start. [1923-06-02 LJ]

WASHAKIE, JUNE 13, 1923.   . . . Our wheat crop is looking splendid. I expect we . . . have a real nice harvest this year. Some of our people are working in sugar beet field just now, around down Garland or near sugar factory. Some of them getting through about this time. Mr. Geo. P. Sam is working in the sugar beet field up on Idaho and his family. Mr. Thomas Pabawena and his 3 brothers working down near around Madison beet dump. . . . Mr. Willie Neaman went up Idaho about two week ago. He expect may return home some time next month. . . . Mr. George Elk was been down below some time ago. Well some of our people are working in sugar field up around West Portage. Mr. Jim Wagon still working for Mr. Will Adams in the East Garland. Some of our want going down Nevada. On the special business, about latter part this month. [1923-06-16 LJ]

WASHAKIE, JUNE 20, 1923.   The people are good just now, no died or sick. . . . Our people are working in sugar beets field just now. But some of them are finishing and come home. Some of them working near Garland factory. Some was down near Deweyville. Well sir, I hope they may get through all in side this next week. . . . It is wonderful rain we had for long time. I expect we had very good harvesting this year. Mr. Soquitch and wife been down to Mantua on little hunt down there. He was return home yesterday. But was rejoice over his little hunt trip he had. That was on the East Brigham City. But on Sunday last I was down to Mantua and visiting my birthplace. I was return home on Monday last. We doing little hunting trip. But we had our Ford car trouble over there while we were down that place. . . . Mr. Geo. P. Sam and Thomas Pabawena was going to Nevada country on the important business. I am going accompany with them. We are going start on 30 day of this month. But we are going to Battle Mountain to meeting some big chief Shoshone out there. I hope we are going have a real good time out there. . . . Mr. Willie Neaman went up Idaho some time a going last month and has not return home yet. He went up there for work. [1923-06-23 LJ]

WASHAKIE, JUNE 28, 1923.   . . . The grain is looking poor before that heavy rain come. But they looking very good. And I expect we have very splendid harvesting this yr. Well sir the people are good condition so far. There is one death took a place here lately. The baby boy was died here some time ago about 2 weeks. But he was the boy to Mr. John Johny. And some of our people are working in sugar beet field yet. Our sugar beet here looking pretty good. Every body was rejoice over the splendid rain we had. The weather is getting pretty warm so far. We are going have a big celebration on the 4 July. The program was made at last Sunday and going all kind sport. Our musiun [amusement] committee is prepared for the big program for 4 July. Mr. George and Thomas Pabawena is start out on Monday next for the west. I hope

they may have a good trip out Nevada. But western Indians going have a big celebration on the 4 July. They want some of our leading men coming out among them.
I expect there is about 3 men going out to Battle Mountain that is the place going
have it. Mr. Enos Pubigee is going up Idaho Reservation to see a big Sun Dance up
there. And he want to going White Rock Indian Reservation too. On before the
4th inst. Mr. Willie Neaman was not return home yet. He was looking for job. Mr.
Thomas with his 3 brothers thinning beet for Mr. George Steed, he was from
Plymouth [UT]. But he own a place near Fielding dump. [1923-06-30 LJ]

BATTLE MOUNTAIN, JULY 4, 1923.   I am out to west country now. But I see many
Indians out here. They are good condition. But they are homeless Indians all over
this section of the country. They was very few of them were home just now. These
day the Indians are very quiet here no celebration big day 4 July. Some of these
Indians are going to Austin and join big celebration. It is about 90 miles south
from here. The weather is hot today. These Indians are not farmer for their own
name.

They are carried out different place for white men farm. And working for white
men as near as I can guess. About 200 soul are living here at Battle Mountain just
now. It is dryest place around here. I was coming here on big Indian business and
among Shoshones. We was coming out here last week, and my boys was accompanied with me. And also Mr. Harry Dixon coming down with us yesterday. He was
act of chief of these Indians around these country.

But we met Mr. Jim Leach this morning. He was another chief to his tribe. And
we have little council meeting here this morning. Every body was well satisfied at
business. We are going back to Elko tomorrow. Mr. George P. Sam is coming out
there to Battle Mountain today. He was coming on train. [1923-07-07 LJ]

OWYHEE, NEVADA, JULY 9, 1923.   I am among Western Shoshone Indians today and
find these Indians very poor this year. They was good celebrating 4th July on the
Owyhee River and they are good condition just now. But business is pretty poor
this year. . . . I am with my two boys here. But the Indians are poor condition.
There was church work among these Indians. It is two years ago. There is about of
them join the church since the start church. There is about 30 or concluds [includ-
ing] children and women. These Indians are rejoice when they join the Baptist
[Presbyterian] Church. Mr. George Washington and three more Indians went to
Nez Perces Indians Reservation, Oregon, about two weeks ago. But they may
return home some time this coming week. And accompanied the church minister
on the special matter of the church work. He was join church about year ago.

Some the boy's running horses today just now. Well sir. Some been Mountain
Home on 4th July and join big celebration up there. And also Owyhee Indian
Silver Band been to Mountain Home, Idaho, 4th July and return home last
Monday and having real good old time while they was out there.

Mountain Home is about 130 miles from here on Oregon Short Line. There was
about 600 Indians living on Owyhee Reservation. They seen cutting meadow hay.
They hay crop looking fine. Better than last year. There was few grain raised here.
The grain crop . . . looking bad on account the squirrel so many, and didn't have

enough water supplies. I believe the land is so poor. And also the weather is very hot. Some of the school boys coming home from Carson City. . . . [1923-07-14 LJ]

OWYHEE, JULY 28, 1923.   These reservation is good for cattle raising. But there about over 2000 Indians living here on this reservation now. Well sir all Indians are good condition so far. Some of them start put up their winter hay for the cattle. And the hay is pretty scarce this year. There was a very small crop lucern [alfalfa] hay raise here. But the water supplies is very poor.

They try to raise some wheat and [it] start burning up. The water is scarce and river nearly drying up weeks ago. They been running wild horses and branding the spring colts. There was a good hunting and fishing on reservation and weather are very warmer. But water is dried up. In evening night is cold.

The Indians are here poor condition. Some say their hay very poor they may lose their cattle this winter, and the meadow hay very poor stand, and some not worth cutting, and they start haying just now. And also the water is scarce here. Last Sunday they are gathering some cattle and branding spring calves. These Indians have about over 200 head cattle on reservation. Some of them have no cattle. The Owyhee Reservation is about 15 miles square. But this is not farming land. Most this land fit for cattle raising. They raise very few grain, and the grain looking very poor condition on account the water scarce and the grey squirrel so numerous this year. They was been used poison on it, and didn't catch so many with poison. The agent is handling a poison for the Indians on this reservation. Some Indians didn't like him, because he is cheat Indians pretty bad on the trade and keep his cattle on this reservation and he didn't pay enough. He paying half price on the rending [renting]. Mr. George Washington is return home from Oregon week last. These Indians have good horses. Some the school boys from Carson [City] is still here. These Indians have a regular Indians Silver Band for their own. They return from Mountain Home for last week.

Mr. Charles McCackey said they was band concert for President Harding at Mountain Home station and they marching up into the city park, and they played two or three times there. These Indians have a good Indian band and also good Indian base ball team. [1923-07-28 LJ]

OWYHEE, AUGUST 4, 1923.   The Indians are good condition just now. But I am still here yet. I expect will be here about 2 week more. All Indians are busy on their hay field just now, some of the working out the reservation. Some of them nearly through with the hay. Some of them thinking lose their cattle this winter on account the hay is pretty scarce just now. Well some of the hay isn't worth cutting. They have a hot days and very cold nights. The grain is burning up so far. . . . This reservation is looking very poor condition in line of vegetation. Soil is gravel condition, cannot raise any kind of grain. One thing is the squirrel is so numerous.

This section of the country mostly raise cattle. This reservation looking wild all into sage brush for miles. There is very few white men live on this reservation. [1923-08-04 LJ]

OWYHEE, AUGUST 11, 1923.   We are still out here among Western Shoshone Indians. The Indians are very good condition out here. Well, sir, we may still stay with the Indians about two week more before going back on to Utah. The weather is began to cold just now. The elevation this country about 7000 thousand above sea level and the Indians are through their hay just now.

The wages is about $3.00 per day. There was a Baptist [Presbyterian] Church among the Indians. I was visit the Sunday school last Sunday. I find there was about 4 teachers, about 10 women, 25 or more children and also some white children attended Sunday School. Mr. Swab, an Indian, going have summer vacation about two week out Winnemucca country. This is Baptist [Presbyterian] minister on Owyhee mission.

Seem to me the Indians not like the church. They was trying to convert some of the Indians. These Indians raising good cattle that is Shorthorn and Hereford. Some of them trying to raise some good tipe [type] cattle. There was a very good hunting and good fishing out here on the reservation. Some these Indians pretty well off in cattle business. These country are good for raising stocks [livestock]. The Indian boys have a game base ball every Sunday afternoon. [1923-08-11 LJ]

OWYHEE, AUGUST 14, 1923.   I am still with Western Shoshone Indians just now. But everybody is pretty busy put up hay, nearly every through their hay. But they out working for white men. That is outside Reservation. Some Indian work for Spanish ranch, that is about 15 miles from here. But they paying about $3.00 per day. And another ranch is north about 20 mile from here. All Indians nearly gone on the Reservation. They working out side the [boundary] line. They have about three day school here on the reservation. Some time ago one Indian man got hurt and his wrist bone and he was taken to Mountain Home a Doctor treatment. And he was return home yesterday. But he has not get better now. Two little Indian boys stolen a woman silk dress and police was after them and under arrested, and they is in jail. One Indian family visiting on reservation. But had visit his son. But he was on his way home yesterday morning. He real home in Austin, Nevada. He expect going move on this reservation next year. It is pretty good hunt and fishing on the Reservation. But all wheat crop is fail there will no grain raise on this place. It is poor country for grain. The hay crop is very poor. They afraid going lose their cattle on account shortage the hay. The Utah is best country for grain and some other crop too. But here on reservation trying raise all kind of stuff it is poor climate, and water is scarce. [1923-08-18 LJ]

OWYHEE, SEPTEMBER 1, 1923.   I am going Elko now. But the Indians are on reservation is good condition just now. Well some them working for white men around reservation. Some them getting out some winter wood for agent. Well sir I am leaving for Utah on 18 Sept. 1923, there was about two girls are very sick. And one Indian woman is taken for Elko Hospital last week she is very sick just now. . . . Well sir the Indians Agent think they going sell some cattle in fall on account the hay been scarce. The agent order to examine school children on 29 and they taken to Carson City Indian Boarding school. One white man went taken school children to Elko Station. The weather is getting cold now And there a very good hunting and fishing just now. I expect we stag[e] a big roado [rodeo] and big fair at Elko. Some Indian are going to Elko on 12-13-14 Sept. and also the Indians Silver Band are good too.

The Indians going have a big Fandango at Elko. [1923-09-08 LJ]

SUN DANCE
and
FANDANGO

Wells, Nevada, Fair Week

5 Big Days 5

Sun Dance Will be Given Under the Direction of Johnnie Thompson

Fandango Will be Under the Direction of Joe Temoke

The Biggest Attraction of the Fair

DON'T FAIL TO TAKE THIS IN ABOVE ALL OTHER AMUSEMENTS

Advertisement for a Sun Dance and fandango to be hosted by Western Shoshone in Wells, Nevada. *From Nevada State Herald, July 27, 1923.*

ELKO, SEPTEMBER 7, 1923.   The Indians are in good condition. All Indians are working for white men ranch around this vicinity. But they working hayfield and many other things. There is about over one hundred souls live in Elko. Mrs. Hanks was taken to Carson City Hospital yesterday. She was here doing operation, while back about in June with tumor in stomach. But she getting worse here every day. And her mother was companied her. I hope she may not live any longer. But she was suffer just now. We came up last night here at Wells, Nevada to see big white men fair here now is on. It start 6, 7, 8, Sept. and they have a big horse races too. But the Indians having a Sun Dance here too. The dancer about 7 of them. But Indians are charge about 50¢ for adult and 25¢ for children. Probably will last until next Saturday. I believed there is some Indian from Smokey, Ruby Valley, Deeth and Austin, etc. But all Indians are going down Elko county fair on 12, 13, 14, 15 Sept. I was seen some my old acquaints. I have seen Mr. Tonnywhom he is especial Indian interpreter for long time. We going back to Elko when this fair over. [1923-09-15 LJ]]

ELKO, SEPTEMBER 13, 1923.   . . . One Indian is died. She sent to Carson City Hospital about one week ago yesterday. Mr. Harry Dixon was received telegram from Carson City Hospital. She died yesterday afternoon. Her Husband want to ship her body here Elko. But they not arrange her funeral yet. And there was about 3 hundred people are here now. But they have a dance here. I expect is about over 40 from Owyhee, 15 from Deeth, 10 from Wells 20 from Austin, 30 from Ruby Valley and more other places country and also with their chiefs. The Indians boys is drinking pretty heavy. But some of them under arrest by White man police. . . .

Owyhee Indians Silver Band is playing for Rodeo here just now. There was a big gathering Indians here just now.

Some of the Indians are working out around this vicinity. All Indians are not good fixed. These Indians are homeless. Mr. Carsen is expect to issued some provision for the Indians people. He is running the fair ground. [1923-09-22 LJ]

WASHAKIE, SEPTEMBER 29, 1923.   The people out Nevada is very good condition. And the different part country was at Elko. To attended big Rodeo. I expect is numbered about 400 hundred Indians were there. But some from Owyhee, Austin, Battle Mountain, Ely, Wells, and also Ruby Valley. And having a big fandango going on and Sun Dance in two night there. Well sir. Mrs. Johny Hank was died about two week ago. And she left her husband and one boy behind. She is buried at the Elko cemetery. On the north side the town. The two Indian men still in county jail for drinking moonshine. They gaving 30 days in jail and hard labor. One man from Austin, Nev. We return home Friday last. And I find my people here at Washakie are splendid condition. Nobody sick just now. The threshing are all done here. We raised quite lot grain here this summer. And all fall work is nearly through by this time. Mr. Nephi Zundel been down to Nevada. And also Timus Perdash made a trip Nevada too. He was return home week last. Mr. John Brown is visiting our little town last week. He is going to stay all winter here. But he was from Wyoming Reservation and all his family too. Mr. Thomas Pabawena has not return from his Nevada trip yet. He may come home about 1 next month. We had a real rain storm today here. It is doing good for the winter crops. Mr. Henry Woonsook went up Idaho on Monday last and he was working Jap and try some Indians for beet topper. [1923-09-29 LJ]

Willie Ottogary Writes from Washakie to Journal

WASHAKIE, OCTOBER 6, 1923.   The people are going for work just now. But some of them stay home now. Most of them out for working. They went down to Garland and Riverside, to work in sugar beets. Mr. Harry Dixon is coming from Nevada here other day, and more other Indians too. There was more others too, Well sir we have had regular rain storm, all last weeks and this week too. . . . Mr. Nephi Zundel is return his Nevada trip, also he have nearly all done for fall work just now. Mr. Timus Perdash is return from his Nevada trip a week. Mr. Ammon Pubigee and Soquitch Timbimboo been down to Elwood to help cut wheat for Mr. Willie Ottogary. . . . and return home other day. Well . . . more are coming out from Nevada country. Mr. Dick Hall and his wife and more others are coming on train later on. They will be getting here some time this week. Mr. Moroni Timbimboo was been on the Wyoming Reservation. He was accompanied his wife and mother aunt. They was all from our little town and they return home week last. Mr. Henry Woonsook made a business trip Idaho Reservation some time ago. Mr. War Bonnet was looking for his wife here last week ago. But said his was ran away from home. And she been here in our town. She [s]tay about 6 or 7 days here and went back, but she went back on the Idaho Reservation. [1923-10-06 LJ]

WASHAKIE, OCTOBER 11, 1923.   The Indian are working in sugar beet field just now around north sugar factory. There is a very few folk home now. Some Indians are coming from Nevada is here now. Mr. Harry Dixon and family is here work in sugar beet for Utah and Idaho Sugar Co. Down to south from Deweyville, Utah, and also Mr. Dick Hall and family is here too. He is from Carlin, Nevada. Mr. Jack Ramsey and family here work in beet too. He is from Idaho Reservation. But everybody could not work on account the storm is pretty bad. . . . Mr. John Brown and family is working for Mr. John Oiler, East Garland. He was from Wind River Reservation, Wyoming. He expect stay here all winter long. Mr. [Enos] Sam Pubigee come home from his Montana trip week last. [1923-10-13 LJ]

WASHAKIE, OCTOBER 18, 1923.   Our people are nearly all working out in sugar field. . . . And all our fall work is done just now. There was some Indians from Nevada still work in sugar beet field now and also from Idaho too. We had about 3 weeks storm here now. The weather is getting cold just now. Mr. Jack Frost is been here . . . and taking . . . garden stuff last week and start winter here and it very cold and freezing now. Mr. Seth Pubigee and wife been down to Brigham City on special business on 16 Oct. Mr. Harry Dixon been here on Sunday last on the important business, and several more other accompanied him. He is Indian Chief of Nevada and also Mr. Dick Hall is here now and working sugar beet field. Mr. Elias Pubigee is work for Mr. George M. Ward here down near Plymouth station. But his little baby girl is sick and he went down yesterday to see Mrs. Dr. Peaugannow [Buchanan] at Deweyville. [1923-10-20 LJ]

WASHAKIE, OCTOBER 23, 1923.   Our people are working out in sugar beet field just now. We had very bad storm weather on last Monday night. The snow we seen first time this year other morning about 1 inch snow.

Mr. Thomas Pabawena and one his brother came home from Nevada trip and there [they're] working in sugar beet now. And more others from west, and also Mr. Johny Pabawena his family is come with him.

One baby girl died here last Friday morning. She was baby to Mr. Elias Pubigee. The funeral service held at ward meeting house Sunday last. . . . [1923-10-27 LJ]

WASHAKIE, NOVEMBER 2, 1923.   The people are here good condition just now, and all work is done now. The Indians are from Nevada. Is still here now work in sugar beet field and also from Wyoming Indians still here now. Most the Indians out working now. Mr. Mose Neaman is sick now for three day. He been Dr. yesterday. But today is little better. Well sir he was nearly dying in days ago. Mr. Harry Dixon is working for sugar Co. . . . Miss Susie Perwhat is very sick. She is about 70 [or 90] year old. And she was getting little better just now. Mr. Timus Perdash went down to Deeth to his sweetheart down there about two week ago. He has not return from Nevada yet. [1923-11-03 LJ]

WASHAKIE, NOVEMBER 16, 1923.   Our people are good condition now. Well sir the weather is very cold. There is very few sugar beets raised here this summer, and they harvest their beet crops just now, and they nearly done. Probably get through next week. Some our people come home from their works now. But some white men get through down near Garland. There was some Indians were here from different parts of states. They are still work in sugar beet field yet. Mr. Seth Pubigee and his company been up Malad City on big carnival doing up there. They was taking parts on old time stage held up [hold-up] he stay about three day up there.[6] He return his works on Tuesday last from Malad City. Well Mr. Enos Pubigee is keep busy to working up his Mine on the East Mountain of our town. Mr. Hyrum Wongsaw is return home from his work last week. There was about six or seven boys from Idaho and they return home. [1923-11-17 LJ]

WASHAKIE, DECEMBER 8, 1923.   . . . Nearly everybody come from their sugar beet work. The weather is very cold now. This is lasting about two days. We pretty bad storm here now. The hay is kind scarce in our town, but the grain crop pretty this year, better than any other so far. The people different part of country are return . . . two weeks ago. Some from Wyoming and Idaho, Nevada country too. Mr. Dick Hall and his company return home last week. He was from Carlin, Nevada. Mr. John Brown went home for two weeks ago, and also Jack Ramsey return home from his Idaho Reservation and his one family. He topping beets East Garland. Mr. Thomas Pabawena and Jim John [Neaman] been Idaho week last. And return home other day and doing some matters of business. Well sir Mr. Moroni Timbimboo was been down Garland buying some his winter potatoes and also doing some shopping too. Mr. Ammon Pubigee and Willie Ottogary been out promontory week and doing some prospect, they stop at Mr. George Marsh and picking a Thanksgiving turkey.[7] This white man got lot turkeys on his place. . . . Mr. Harry J. Dixon was seen in Tremonton yesterday and today and attending some important matter business. And also Mr. Geo. P. Sam been down to Tremonton and doing matter of business too. The winter going be easy this year. . . . Our day school is going fine now. . . . about 16 children went to school in our little town. The school teacher was Daughter of Bishop George M. Ward [probably Vida Ward], here in our ward. . . . Mr. Thomas Pabawena and more fellows been down Ogden and spending Thanksgiving down there, and return next morning. Mr. Harry Dixon and company been down Ogden too and doing some Thanksgiving shopping. But he was from Elko Nevada. He expect he will remain here all winter long, and his wife was sick just now. He expect to going up on the Idaho Reservation to her, have a Dr. treatment for awhile. He will return her from Idaho, when she is no more sick. Mr. Ammon Pubigee with his two sons, been Brigham City business on Monday last. Mr. George P. Sam and Thomas Pabawena was down Tremonton and doing some important business yesterday. . . . Mr. Dick Hall and company return home before Thanksgiving. His home in Carlin, Nevada. Nearly everybody from different part of country is gone. There is very few left yet. [1923-12-08 LJ]

WASHAKIE, DECEMBER 24, 1923.   Our people are prepared for the Christmas is coming now. But makes everybody heart rejoice now. And they are looking for old Santa Clause once more. . . . Well our people are very good condition now. Nobody sick now. And Mr. Geo. P. Sam was been down to Salt Lake City about couple a weeks ago and buying some deer hide, and also Miss Emma Brain and Miss Posspia was been down Salt Lake on same business. They was return two weeks ago. Mr. Harry J. Dixon went on Idaho reservation two weeks to live but he may return in spring with all his family. His home is in Elko, Nevada. . . . Mr. Warren [Wongan] was selling some Christmas trees on last week ago. Mr. Soquitch Timbimboo and wife been down to Tremonton about last week and doing some Christmas shopping. . . . Mr. Thomas Pabawena with his three brothers working sugar beet pile down to Fielding station and working Mr. Dom Ingshing. He was paying for 30¢ per ton. Mr. Mose Neaman is hauling beet from same pile now. . . . The weather is very colder here just now. We haven't got no snow at all. [1923-12-24 LJ]]

Oneida County Enterprise[8]
Malad, Idaho, Thursday, January 10, 1924.
Washakie Indian Letter
By Willie Ottogary.

WASHAKIE, JANUARY 3, 1924.   The people are splendid celebrate on the New Year. They had a nice programme . . . had a big dinner was served in ward meeting house . . . and everybody was fill with some nice food. Afternoon 2 o'clock the children was start dance in hall. But our people are turn out splendid and . . . also the old and young was a Grand Ball in evening and everybody is enjoyed themself very splendid time. They had very cold weather on News Year's Day. Some our people say the winter is start just now. Well had a rain last week ago. They are poor condition on hay business this year. The hay is very scarce around here now. . . . Mr. Kippetchew Noragan and wife been down Salt Lake City on Christmas Day and also Mr. Yeager Timbimboo been down Salt Lake City and more other Indians too. Mr. Moroni Timbimboo and Mr. Jacob Peyope are hunting and trapping at Snowville country yesterday. . . . [1924-01-10 OCE]

WASHAKIE, JANUARY 10, 1924.   Our people are doing pretty good this year. Nobody sick just now. Of course some them under the weather and getting over with this. Mr. George Tospanguitch was been over to Cache Valley and motoring around there. Mr. Thomas Pabawena and his three brothers has return home last week from the Fielding Station where he was working on sugar beet pile. They get through on New Year Day . . . all his company too. Mr. Catch Toyahdook and wife was return too. Mr. Mose Neaman and wife, his two sons, was return home. He was working same pile. . . . Mr. Moroni Timbimboo and Mr. Jacob Peyope has return from the hunting trip out there Snowville. Some our people think we going have a long winter this year. The hay was very scarce here in our town just now. . . . [1924-01-12 LJ]]

1924-01-17 OCE [Not included, duplicate of 1924-01-12 LJ]]

WASHAKIE, JANUARY 19, 1924.   . . . Winter is very cold this year. The snow is about 4 or 5 inch . . . and hay is pretty scarce around here just now. The hay going up high about $8 or $10.00 just now. . . . Mr. James Pabawena with his two brothers winter at Fielding Station on Mr. George Steed place. Mr. Dock Bird is here now, he was been on the German war. But he was the men go on front and went through the German trenches.[9] He is the brave Indian boy on the state of Nevada. But he say he didn't want going back anymore. Because he not paid in full by the government. [1924-01-19 LJ]

WASHAKIE, JANUARY 30, 1924. . . . We have a dance last Friday night. Everybody enjoyed in dance. It is kind of Leap Year dance. Weather is getting warm here just now and thaw some snow on road but still has a good slaying [sleighing] yet. Mr. Enos Pubigee was doing very nicely. His brother was taking him home on Saturday last. He was been 5 days for the hospital. . . . And also Mr. Henry Woonsook been down Deweyville to see Mrs. Dr. Beucannon [Buchanan]. But his little boy was sick now. Mr. James Pabawena was sick last week ago. He is around again. . . . Some our people say we go have a short winter. Our little Indian girl Miss Smiling Sun she be going to drive some dogs up in Idaho at Malad where there be going to have lost [lots] fun with race dogs. I guess pretty warm make snow go off pretty quick. Well sir, we all us Indian boy going for see races when Indian girl beat them Idaho boys up there. [1924-02-21 OCE]

WASHAKIE, FEBRUARY 8, 1924. . . . The weather were kind of warmer and some the is thaw out. But we had very good sleighing yet. It is not hard winter we ever had before this year. Well, our say it gone [going] be a early spring. The hay is pretty scarce around here. And hay price is about $10.00 or $12.00 per ton right now. We haven't much hay a raised around last summer. But the water is pretty scarce around here in summer time. We have got about 4 inch snow here right. Mrs. Johny Pabawena was visiting here our town with two girls. Mr. Johny Pabawena is wintering at Fielding station. He is looking for spring working now. . . . Mrs. Youcup Moemberg been down Salt Lake City and purchase buying deer hide and Elk hide some time ago, last two weeks ago, and she is accompanied her grandaughter.[10] She is starting making a regular buckskin gloves. If any body want a glove call her, and she is living about one mile from Washakie town. Some our people been up Malad City and attended Priesthood meeting on last Saturday. We had a dance last Friday night, and everybody having a real good old time. But everybody is turn out. Well sir the programme was read for 22 Feb. after meeting was closed.[11] I hope we going have a celebrate Washington birthday. Mr. George P. Sam been up Malad city to attending a regular monthly Priesthood meeting, and Mr. Tom Elk and Mr. George Tospanguitch also . . . on the same meeting. Mr. Thomas Pabawena been down Garland on some matters of business and accompany by Mr. Nephi Zundel and return same day, with his Ford car. [1924-02-09 LJ]

WASHAKIE, FEBRUARY 23, 1924. . . . Snow is all gone . . . feel like more spring and our people are rejoiced when spring is near. Well sir Mr. George P. Sam bring his automobile car home last week. But he was been up Malad week ago last week to attend regular stake priesthood meeting. When return home he missed grade [and] run into a ditch. The front axe [axle] is pretty well bent up and he call carge [garage] man to fix his car for em. So they take up Malad to get fix. Mr. Ammon [Pubigee] and son been down Salt Lake City on special business. He return home last week. Mrs. Rachel [possibly Rachel Perdash] been down Salt Lake City to buy some deer hide. Our haven't got much hay now. . . . But we had very nice winter.

Not much snow. The cold weather we had month of January. This winter no death to speak of. The our is pretty poor, no money tall [at all]. Mr. Enos Pubigee is well as ever and he was operation here about 4 week ago. Mr. Ben Ponco is still here in our town. His home is at Pocatello, Idaho. He may return home in spring. And also Master Ben Indian still here. His home in Wyoming or Wind River Reservation. Our day school very splendid this winter. There is about 10 boys, 14 girls, are going school in our town. Mr. John Johny is purchase an old Ford car last fall. But he was running around with it and run out oil and burned the engine out. He cannot run any more. [1924-02-23 LJ]

WASHAKIE, FEBRUARY 1924. . . . It is feel like spring weather and our spring work nearly here before long. Our people say they going have short winter this year. The people are been up Malad city. The stake is held conference up there. . . . Mr. George P. Sam . . . get [car] fixed for him and brought it back home last week. . . . There was big Indians land going be sold by Fort Hall agent up by Fort Hall Reservation on 23 of February 1924. Now is time to buy good land on Idaho if any want to buy good land.[12] Mrs. Rachel Indian [possibly Rachel Perdash] been down Salt Lake city to buy some deer hide. [1924-02-28 OCE]

1924-03-04 LJ [Not included, duplicate of 1924-03-06 OCE]

WASHAKIE, FEBRUARY 27, 1924. The weather is fairly condition this winter here. Soon the warm weather comes. We had a fine celebrate on George Washington . . . and everybody had enjoyed a good time. About two week ago the flue is visited our little town, but no death report now. The people are getting over the flue just now. But some of them are laid up with it. They soon alright. We have not heard from Fort Hall Indians they celebrate Washington. We expect hear from when they return home. Mrs. John Pabawena been up Washakie to celebrate Great White Father birthday, and with her children. Yesterday we had a snow storm. The snow is all gone now. Soon are spring work is begin. Some our start contract beet now. There is some are men are raise sugar beet. Some of our boys going visit relation out Wyoming this coming summer. [1924-03-06 OCE]

WASHAKIE, MARCH 5, 1924. The people are here good condition again, all get through with flue. But nearly every family had it. Well, the spring is here now. We are rejoice over the spring is here this early. The weather is get warm just now. We soon start farm again. Our fall crop looking pretty good now. The hay is pretty scarce around here now. Most of our people haven't got land their own name, so we expect get some land from our big white pop in future time.[13] Well sir, we would like getting some more land some away rather [some way or another]. For the young people around our vicinity. But there was a big council meeting when the chiefs coming home from Washington, D. C. They went on the especial on land business. We might hear from them later on. And been out for three weeks and they might came by this time now. The Indians are not knowing about the Government made a agreement with President of the United States in the beginning. The reading in the treaty of the 1863. And stated the Government should

Rachel Perdash. *Special Collections & Archives, Merrill Library, Utah State University.*

paying Indians so much each year. Well we haven't pay for yet. What has made agreement with our chief and warrior in this section country. But our people was looking for this payments. I was understand in the treaty when my people coming country of yours we must play your game and so on. It seem to me the government done some crook work among our American Indians so on.[14]

Well sir, our people been very poor condition in our days. . . .

Mr. Doet [Doc or Dock] Bird is sick last week ago. But is ex-soldier for German War. He stay here our town all winter long, but he is discourage about his soldier[ing]. But the government did not doing his promising to him.

Mr. Moroni Timbimboo was attend Stake Conference down Garland last Sunday.

Mr. Enos Pubigee is splendid condition after been operate sometime ago last 2 month.

Mrs. Moroni Timbimboo has been ill. She lost her child. The baby come before time and died. And buried last week ago in the Washakie cemetery.

Master Chester Ottogary and his brother, Master Custer Ottogary is visiting our town here on the last Saturday and went home on Sunday afternoon. They live near Tremonton in Elwood district, and also Mr. Willie Ottogary, paper reporter, is visiting Washakie town too, in end of the last week. [1924-03-08 LJ]

WASHAKIE, MARCH 15, 1924.   We had very stormy weather last Monday . . . lasted about few minutes. And had a little snow. And all gone by time now. Nearly our spring work start. We going raise some sugar beet here this year. And the weather is start for warm just now. . . . We going have a big celebrate Relief Society day on

Saturday and the program was arranged all ready. Mr. Dock Bird stepmother was died up Fort Hall Reservation about two week ago. But he is still here. But he was being sick couple weeks ago and he well as ever. Mr. Ammon Pubigee went going up Idaho on important matter. But he expect going lease some land up there he may move up in coming spring and for some of relation's land. . . . Mr. John Pabawena and wife and children were visiting our town last Friday. Went back home last Saturday. And he making his home at Fielding Station all winter long. He expect going up big celebrate on Saturday. Last Friday night we have a white men dance. Everybody is enjoyed and real good time too. Mr. Ben Ponco and still our town yet, his home is up Idaho Reservation. And also one boy from Wyoming Reservation too. Well sir they may going home in next spring. [1924-03-15 LJ]

WASHAKIE, MARCH 1924.   . . . We got thru with flue we have had nearly all winter long. Well sir, some of them had it about the last week ago but they have some other decease [disease]. There was no death this winter. . . . I expect we are going to have nice [spring] after this cold weather we are having here. Mr. Ammon Pubigee has been up Idaho country and he is going to lease some land up there. He expect going move in next month start up there but he arrangement made with his cousin. He may stay up there all summer long. He have seen some Indians about land matter and also he visiting some his own relations up there. He return home last week ago. We had pretty good celebrate a Relief Society Day last Saturday and had nice program . . . and after have a big dinner in ward meeting house. The was a big number were present. But everybody enjoyed such a big dinner we had. In the evening the Grand Ball was gave by the relief Society in ward meeting house. They have good real good time. . . . Mr. John Pabawena and wife and children been up Washakie to celebrate big day last week and return on Sunday home. . . . [1924-04-03 OCE]

1924-04-05 LJ [Not included, duplicate of 1924-04-10 OCE]

WASHAKIE, APRIL 1924.   The people here are good condition yet. . . . It snow about one foot here and on the ground yet for three four day and start thaw. The weather . . . very cold here.

Seem we can't get spring here and seem me the winter is not be gone yet. We are been surprise see so much snow this time the year. Well today is good day we ever had for one week so far. I hope have good weather after this time. We was very anxious to put our spring crop in. I expect some people were going to Salt Lake City conference. Well sir, Mr. Mose Neaman was purchase a second hand Ford car about last week ago. But he is been down Tremonton last Monday and accompany his brother-in-law and trying his car and also Mr. Thomas Pabawena and Seth Pubigee motoring down Garland on last Monday and take his car back on to Mr. A. Grover. But this man is sell car to Mr. Thomas Pabawena but he didn't last fall give bill of sale him so he ask Mr. Grover to give bill of sale and he want get license number for car. And also Mr. Timus Perdash want buy new Ford car this year and looking for one last Monday down Garland. Mr. David Pabawena, Doc Bird, John Pabawena also been down Tremonton and doing some shopping on last Monday.

We had very nice dance last Friday night and everybody was enjoyed. They was a big crowd were there. Mr. Hyrum Wongsaw is up again. He was sick some about two weeks. Some our people want going up on Idaho reservation, want some work there. There is lots work up there this spring on road and canal and more other things. Nearly all our old people are gone by this time. The old people can tell about weather and pretty close now we can tell about weather soon. [1924-04-10 OCE]

WASHAKIE, APRIL 11, 1924.   . . . The spring time is here and the weather getting very warmer just now. We start on our spring work now. Some of them are going raise sugar beet this year. And they made some contract about couple weeks ago. Our fall crop are looking very good so far. But I expect we may have a fine crop this coming year. Some our people are been down Salt Lake City and attended [semi-] annual Conference down there and all return last Sunday. And some of them return on Monday last. Mr. Bishop George M. Ward and wife been down Salt Lake City conference. But he was going down with his son, Master John M. Ward and he sent to mission in the Eastern [States] Mission. But he is going out after Salt Lake City big Mormon conference. They held farewell party at West Portage meeting house . . . last week. Mr. Mose Neaman was return on Sunday last. But his mother was been hurt down Salt Lake City and had a broken leg. She was slip on the wet pavement, and fall on hard paved. And she went down [on] electric car and Miss Susie Highyou was accompanied her. She was at the hospital, Salt Lake City. But she quite old, probably about 100 year of old. Mr. Yeager Timbimboo and Mr. Moroni Timbimboo and wife was coming back from conference on last Monday. Mr. Ammon Pubigee wasn't move up Idaho pretty soon and he going lease land from friend up there. But he let his son Mr. Enos Pubigee running his farm while he was up there to work Idaho land. Mr. John Johny was a purchase a second hand Ford roaster [roadster]. Some time ago. And he was down to Garland and motoring down there. Mr. Seth Pubigee and wife was been down Tremonton last Tuesday and doing some shopping. But he want going down so as to get fix his Ford car. He going down in side of three day or more. Our day school running very nicely this year. But there was about 20 boys and girls are going school here in our town. Mr. Elias Pubigee is purchase second Ford car some time ago last week. [1924-04-14 LJ]

WASHAKIE, APRIL 26, 1924.   It is getting warm just now. But our spring is nearby us, and last week there was a sugar beet man coming in our town and making a contract beet. I expect there was about 6 men want raise sugar beet this coming summer. But water is pretty scarce in the summer time. The people are here very good condition. Nobody is sick now. Well sir and the hay is very scarce just now. Last Friday we had dance here in the ward hall.[15] And everybody have a real good time here. And I and my boys visiting Washakie last Friday and Saturday. I find everybody is good condition. Mr. George P. Sam is out hunting. Mr. Ammon Pubigee going up Idaho in a few days now. He is going lease some land up there and . . . expect to stay up all summer. . . . Mr. John Pabawena and family been up here at Washakie last Friday and went home on Saturday last night. They went to move picture show. . . . Mr. Nephi Zundel been down Garland last

Friday and he was looking something to drink. Our fall crop looking pretty good. Mr. Thomas Pabawena looking for [beet] thining contract down to near Garland. [1924-04-26 LJ]]

WASHAKIE, MAY 3, 1924.   The people are enjoyable time on the last Friday night. The amusement committee was giving a dance, and everybody was enjoyed. There was no sickness reported just now. Our men are keeping busy put in spring crop. They may get through this week. But our fall crop looking pretty good this far. I hope we may raise a good crop again this coming summer. Some of our boys made a contract with some white man down near Garland for thinning sugar beets. . . . Some time ago sugar beet man been up here too and made sugar contract. . . . Bishop Geo. M. Ward . . . raise most sugar beet in our town. And there was about 50 acres beets raise in this place. Most of our land was dry farm. . . . Mr. George P. Sam is returned his hunting trip for last week. Mr. John Pabawena and wife been down Ogden last a week ago. And he return last Wednesday. But his little boy is living down in East Garland. But his boy getting pretty well. Mr. Charley Indian's girl is very low she has been sick two weeks ago but he may lose her or not yet. Mr. John Johny bought second car ford about three weeks ago. But is running round with her now. The weather is pretty warm just now. And our spring work is nearly done. Our people will rejoice the summer is here. But everybody is getting pretty good condition so far. Mr. John Pabawena little baby boy died down east Garland. One the Sunday afternoon about 3 P.M. They went down Tremonton and get a casket for the boy. There is some his relation went down sunday morning to see him, but he died after noon and they take remain up to Washakie. To going buried him up Washakie Cemetery. . . . I was visiting Washakie Saturday and find everybody in good condition. But Washakie boys going get a baseball team this summer. And one white man is trying to get our boys to rig up team and he furnish all things so the boys can have a ball and bats and mittens too. Our boys play with West Portage boys and the score was about 11 to 12 in favor of Portage boys. Our boy meet a good practice so they can play ball team. Well I expect to go a good ball team to see. Mr. Jacob and Thomas Pabawena is shearing sheep for Mr. Adams all last week ago. Mr. Nephi Perdash down Garland to see Doc but his wife is sick now and he went home. [1924-05-03 LJ]]

WASHAKIE, MAY 17, 1924.   Our people are good condition just now. But we have a dry weather here. Our boys are not through their ditch work yet. They may get done in few days, all our men ditch. They want get out this week. Some our people been up Malad City attending Stake Conference up there and return home last Saturday. We need a good rain up here everything getting very dry. Our fall is looking good so far. Our school children are mighty glad when the school is for them to go no more sometime. Mr. Soquitch Timbimboo wife is sick. She been sick about two weeks. . . . Mr. Enos Pubigee is taken her to Dr. down Tremonton. She is getting little better just now. . . . Mr. Warren Wongan is been down Garland to see Dr. and his wife is sick. And he went upon ditch work afternoon on Monday. . . . BIG SALE AT RITER BRO's DRUG. The big sale at the Riter Bro's Drugs start on 14, 15, 16, 17 day May. . . big 1c sale. Everythings pretty fine sale on that. Now is time to buy something in drug store. Come early to buy, whole lot stuff going on sale cheap. But

I could not mention all the stuff. . . . Well sir, [come] and buy something. This big sale last in four day. I want you Journal readers can tell your friends and neighbors to buy lot stuff in the Riter Bros Rexall Drug Store now . . . and save money. The Riter Bros will be kindly waiting on you. They are making this spring sale an anniversary of the great company and it is through our connection with the same that makes it possible to offer you two articles for the price of one, plus the one cent. Buy one at the same price and get the second for 1c is the descriptive slogan of this unique sale.[16] [1924-05-17 LJ]

WASHAKIE, MAY 24, 1924.   . . . Some of the men working on water ditch now up around by Samaria Lake.[17] They are going to finish a few days. But we need some good rain here. Our dry farm getting pretty dry now. . . . And the weather is getting too warm. Our sugar beet crop not going very good. Some places is fine. We are much out sugar beet crop here right now. Our agent is been here in our little town. He want our baseball team come up Fort Hall to play some boys in school. He said he will give us a bed and some to eat and also and pay some our expense too. This was on the 31 day of May. The Fort Hall Indians School track meet on 31 at the school. I hope our boys going up there play ball. Mrs. Soquitch Timbimboo is very sick. They been down Tremonton to see Dr. Mr. Luke. But she is getting little bit better. Mr. Enos Pubigee and wife been down Tremonton and accompanied her on the last Monday. Mr. John Pabawena and Thomas Pabawena are working Mr. Jeff Rods, east Garland and shearing his sheep. . . . Mr. Warren Wongan is been down Deweyville to Miss Dr. Beconnan [Buchanan]. His boy is sick. He is getting better now. Our school chldren is going down Garland next Friday and they take a part in the program. I expect some of us may going down to see a big time. . . . Some of us people been attendence [Stake] conference up the Malad City. Mr. Dick Arritch been down Garland others and motoring down there. Some of our men asking Bishop about our playground. And Mr. George W. [M.] Ward gave us a 4 acres ground by the roadside on the country road. It been working and leveled it already now. The boys been practicing ball now on the new baseball diamond. Some of them are proud of it. This was for long time. We going have a baseball team this summer. Well sir it is real nice to have a playground for our little town. [1924-05-24 LJ]

WASHAKIE, MAY 31, 1924.   The weather is getting too warm. The fall crop looking dry. But we need a rain pretty bad here in visinity. The other day looking little bit like rain and gave up and springle [sprinkle] little bit here. They [plants] didn't do pritty good. Some of them up and didn't come and they going replant some place. We have a water in ditch now so we water some of the ground. Some of our people have been go to Malad city to see May carnavol [carnival]. They have horses race and bucking contest too and do all kind sports. There was about over thousand people is there witness to the sport. Some from Salt Lake City, Ogden, Pocatello, and round this section of country. Mr. Mose Neaman and his son mister Jim Neaman, . . . up by Idaho and getting his son up there and helping to thinning sugar beet north of Garland. Mr. Jim Pabawena is take his horse up Malad City but he change his mind and didn't put him up on track. I am and the boys been up Malad see big time last Saturday. I return home on Sunday night but we are very much enjoyed the horse races they had up there. Mr. Stanquitch Jack is visiting our little town on the Sunday. He going down on the Wednesday to attend the court in Brigham City. And is wife estate. She died ago about seven year. Her father he had land here south of the town. And he had wife and three child living now. She was of the Heir. . . . Mr. Charley Indian's girl died on the Sunday 10 o'clock. She buried here Washakie cemetery on the last Monday. She about 17. She not married. She born out Deeth, Nevada. Her parent coming out here Utah seven year ago. Mr. Tom Elk is went up Idaho for looking work. Master Ben Ponco was rode bucking horse on last Saturday up Malad City. Master Ben Sactlar [Saintclair] was rode buck horse too. He was from Wyoming reservation. Well sir, Mr. Moroni Timbimboo was been down Tremonton and Mr. Warren Wongan too see Tremonton and Malad playing the ball on Sunday afternoon. And also Mr. Jim John Neaman and Mr. Jim Pabawena watching the game too. [1924-06-05 OCE]

WASHAKIE, JUNE 9, 1924.   The sugar [beet] crop is start thinning now. But some very poor and they was replanting and thinning be later. Most our people are going down Garland for thinning beet and they will be done about three weeks or more yet. We need a rain right now pretty bad the fall crop looking pretty dry and the want a rain. But we didn't much of it last week ago. Well Mr. Ammon Pubigee change his mind not begin going up Idaho reservation. He may going this fall, and he was summer plowing his dry land farm but all his boys work in sugar beet. Mr. James Wagon and wife return back from Idaho reservation about a month ago then he is thinning sugar beet down west part of the Tremonton. Mr. Mose Neaman and his gang thinning for the Jap down the north the Garland factory. Well sir all our people are work out [of town]. Two Indian boys from White Rock Reservation were here at Garland sugar factory. They was looking for some work. Well some of our people [work or grow] their own sugar beet. Mr. Moroni Timbimboo been down Tremonton to getting sharpening his cultivator shovel. . . . Mr. Geo. Elk been down Bear River City for looking work. . . . The weather is getting pretty warmer here just now. . . . Mr. B. Riter was visiting his drug store on last Sunday and he is [owner of] greater Rexall drug store in the country. He return . . . home Sunday evening. Some our people are visiting cemetery on the 30th of the May and decorating grave. Well sir and haven't got much time to going out. They was too busy to go out. [1924-06-12 OCE]

1924-06-14 LJ [Not included, duplicate of 1924-06-19 OCE]

WASHAKIE, JUNE 1924.   . . . Our fall crop is not look very promise on account we had [not] much rain. Last week had a little rain up here but it is cooling the air and didn't amount anything. If we rain two or three time now our wheat crop is good. Everything looking affle [awfully] dry around. The sugar beet not much good this year it being so dry. But most our people working in sugar field just now. Some of them return from Farmington now. Some working on their own sugar beet. There was about 50 acre sugar beet in our little town. Well sir, I hope we be going have good a sugar beet crop this year. Some of Indians from Idaho visiting our town here about middle part last week and return home this week. . . . Mr. Tom Elk has not return home from Idaho. But his family went down Farmington and has not return home now. They thinning sugar beet yet. They may return home next week. Mr. Thomas Pabawena has return from Farmington about last week ago with all his gang. And also Mr. John Pabawena and his family is return. Mr. Thomas [Pabawena] with his three brother have been down Tremonton on the last Monday and try to buy . . . second hand Ford car. Mr. Paul Heize going [sell] this cars for them and very lowest price. Each one cost about a little better that $200.00 dollars. They expect make trip Nevada about after this month. Mr. George M. Ward Bishop of Washakie Ward was down Tremonton on the business. To about his car. But his new car was burn up some time about ten days or week ago. But buy car from the Mr. Heize and Windezeler [Nindezeller in 1924-06-14 LJ] Motor Co. . . . Most our people are working sugar field just now. There was about three Indians is working Mr. S. Marble down there Deweyville. They stay all summer. They do not know yet. They have been about three week now. Mr. Harry Dixon is still up Idaho reservation yet. He expect coming back in July 4th. [1924-06-19 OCE]

1924-07-03 OCE [Not included, duplicate of 1924-07-05 LJ]

WASHAKIE, JULY 5, 1924.   Our people are feeling pretty bad [about] wheat crop in fall. We have had a cold snap here and nearly take all wheat crop around up this valleys and the no wheat to speak of. Mr. Jack Frost is visit in the county and taking every wheat crop. Well I don't know what we going to do now. The dry land farmer are kind disappointed so far. The wheat field is desting [dusting or desiccating] other day it is gone. It might some place all right. The weather is pretty warm here now. Mr. Catch Toyahdook and wife went up Idaho reservation some time ago last week. But may return week more. But is taking his niece. She live in up there west Pocatello. . . . Mr. Nephi Perdash and wife made hunting trip and come back home other day. Mr. Jim Wagon and his company went down Brigham City. Try get job a picking some berries. . . . Mr. Henry Woonsook and Elias Pubigee and Nephi Zundel motoring down tremonton last Saturday night. Mr. Jim John Neaman and Emmeline Pabawena was married about month ago. They was married in the Indian old way. . . . Mr. Soquitch and wife visiting Mr. W. Ottogary place down South Elwood in the few days. [Inserted from 1924-07-03 OCE: "Our people going have a celebrate 4 July here. I hope we going a real old good time here. And everybody come home from working. Mr. George Tospanguitch is going out hunting trip a short time. But he may return home before the 4 July."] Mr. Ammon Pubigee has been up Idaho about last week ago. He expect going up next two weeks . . . to . . . put up hay for his cousin. Well sir everything is good condition. Some men put some hay just up. Mrs. Esther Proncho [Broncho] is coming home for a while, or short time she up Idaho reservation. And she married one of the Jim Brown son about last summer. Mr. Ben Saut Clar [Saintclair] went home last week ago. But he stay all winter here in our town. Mr. George Christensen fire insured [insurance] man is going visit Logan some time next month. He living in Tremonton, but he want doing some business over there. And he want me to put in the paper. He was well known businessman in the Tremonton.[18] [1924-07-05 LJ]

WASHAKIE, JULY 24, 1924.   Our people are went over there to Logan. To going have a big Celebrate over Logan City. Some of them stay home just now. And they are going to harvest the grain after come home from Logan. The about 8 family going over to Logan, and join celebrate. But one boy is kill[ed] here our town. On the last Friday about 11 o'clock in the morning. But his father went to Nevada about fourth day before he [died]. The boy was about 5 year old. His brothers went after him last Saturday, and over took him to Wells, Nevada and they return Monday after. The Funeral service were at Washakie meeting house about 1:30 o'clock. Well I hope that they have a real good old time over to the Logan. There was about 4 families from Fort Hall were here at Logan. We was coming over yesterday some of them join big parade. Tomorrow 10 o'clock. The son of the old Erimo [Arimo] was here from reservation and his brother and son[,] Eugene Arimo. He is best roper and rider too, and also Mr. Billy and wife is here from Fort Hall Reservation. I am here in Logan to take a write up.[19] We come over from home yesterday afternoon. But and find everybody in good condition here at Logan today. We going stay all this week. They bring some good horses, to with them. I am going more news in the next few days. Well goodbye all Journal Reader. [1924-07-26 LJ]

WASHAKIE, AUGUST 14, 1924.   Our grain harvesting is nearly all over with. But thing is threshing time. But grain buyer is here at town now. He buy it and loads here at Washakie [railroad] switch. I was visiting Washakie today and find every-body is very good condition just now since that little [boy] kill. Mr. Ammon Pubigee is still cutting grain today and he cutting for Mr. Mose Neaman. The agent was down today and with eye Dr. But he is going down Brigham City today and on especial business. But he was our agent and Fort Hall too. He just stayed long enough to get dinner at Mr. Bishop George M. Ward. Some the women folks is gathering some wild cherries for the winter use. Mr. Soquitch Timbimboo and wife and more other women going over to Paradise on the same job. There was lot berries over there. Mr. Moroni Timbimboo is start peddle some fruit last week. He been up Fort Hall Reservation some ago last week. Mr. Wayne Warner and family has visiting our town and his relation here too. Mr. James Pabawena and three brother went to Nevada some ago couple week ago. They are going [back] in month Sept. Then all work is done by that time. Mr. Ammon Pubigee want going up there Idaho Reservation after get all grain cut. and with some his boys, and going up there on the hay. . . . Mr. Seth Pubigee and family been down Mr. Willie Ottogary place down to Elwood, and they gather some berries down there and return yesterday, etc. [1924-08-16 LJ]

WASHAKIE, AUGUST 21, 1924.   The harvest is all done now. But the harvesting is not very heavy this year on account being late frost we had here in the month of May. It nearly [destroy] all the wheat crop. They was waiting for threshers now. They sell their grain right at the [railroad] station here. The sugar beet crop is not so good this year. The people are working out now. But very few at home just now. Some going out Nevada, Idaho, and others places. They return home again in the next [while] . . . and start on the topping beet. The weather is getting colder here just now. Our fall work soon start. Mr. Casper Andersen from Elwood is threshing south end of our farm. And our farmer want him thresh their grain. But he went home yesterday. I hope he will threshing all grain is around here. . . . Some women folks are coming from Paradise. They were gathering some wild cherries. Mr. Soquitch Timbimboo has not return yet and he will in few days. Mr. Ammon Pubigee and two boys figuring going up Idaho reservation to getting hay job, soon he getting threshing done. Mr. Tom Elk is went out Nevada for some work out there. He will stay about two month before he coming back home again. Soon our day school start here on the 8 Sept. The childrens are getting prepare now.

Mr. James Pabawena and his one brother went out Nevada for some work. They expect return home in next month. They been gone for about three weeks ago. Mr. George P. Sam didn't want going out Nevada. He said he haven't got much time. Mr. Moroni Timbimboo still on the job, and peddle some fruit just now. Mr. Timus Perdash, Nephi Zundel and Henry Woonsook motoring down Ogden, and his two sons and wives too. . . . Also Mr. Wm. Donner been visit our town about middle last week. He is our agent. He office at Ross Fork, Idaho. But he coming down once while in month.[20] [1924-08-23 LJ]]

WASHAKIE, SEPTEMBER 18, 1924.   The things are pretty quiet around here now. And the weather getting pretty cold now. The fall is soon start here now. Our people are not much wheat crop this year. But some of our out hunting some pine nuts out west now. They was gone for last week some time ago, and some of them gone out today. The sugar beet crop is fail this year, they going about 1 ton to the acres. But water is very short too. Soon our fall work is done here. Nearly every body getting busy get fall crop in. I was coming from Nevada on the Sunday afternoon. We had very good trip out Nevada. We visiting some of our own relation and acquainted more other Indians. We have been as far as Battle Mountain. It is about three hundred and 40 miles on one way, and 680 miles on the both ways. The Indians are good condition. We meet some different places of the country of the Indians, the Nevada.

Last Saturday Mr. Hyrum Wongsaw nearly escape of his life. But Mr. Joe Hara team run away with him and hit his buggy hind-wheel and smash and knocked him on the ground. He is not hurt. He was stop at Mr. J. K. Haws to buy some watermelon.

I have been visiting Malad on Monday last. And I seen some people I aquainted there. But I was taking old folk up. The Malad Stake was Old Folks Day on 9 day of Sept. 1924. This was their annual Old Folks Day held at new tabernacle. They had very nice program commence at twelve thirty. After the program over a nice big luncheon was served down basement of the tabernacle. There was about 150 guest and different parts of the Stake present. And also the fair start yesterday and some of our boys going up there to see wonderful fair. Mr. Jack Johny is seen up Malad City with family. He going out getting some pine nuts. Mr Ammon Pubigee went to Idaho about two week ago and he going there for work. I expect he may come home on next month. Mr. Henry Wonsook wife and baby run away from home a week ago. She was interrest [perhaps under arrest] by Fort Hall Indians Police. And Mr. Henry Woonsook went up last week and getting his wife and baby. They has not return home yet. He may return home this coming week.

Mr. Yeager Timbimboo is going out Raft River to hunt some pine nuts, and more other Indians women. [1924-09-20 LJ]]

WASHAKIE, SEPTEMBER 22, 1924.   Our people are poor condition. But our wheat crop and sugar crop are pretty poor this year. Some of them not even cut their wheat, and the hay is pretty scarce too this year. There is pretty few went down Peach Day. Mr. Kippetchew Noragan is went down Peach Day. And also Mrs. Cohn Zundel and family been down Peach Day too, and some our boys went up American Falls [ID] other day to see a big Rodeo. Mr. Enos Pubigee and Chester Ottogary went up Idaho to see a big horses races. They may return latter part this week. Mr. Pubigee had a races up there. But he going have a race. And also his brother Mr. Elias Pubigee and Nephi Perdash got race horses up there too. Mr. Hyrum Wongsaw narrow escape he on Tuesday after. But his team scared [by] an automobile and run away and knocked him off the white top buggy. Nearly broke his neck and he was unconuse [unconscious] for few minutes. This was happened at Mount Spring about 3 mile southeast of the Washakie.[21] But he is sick in bed now, and he is [im]proving nicely now. Mr. Yeager Timbimboo and wife gone out Raft River to hunting some pine nuts, and also Mr. Joe Woonsook and family is out there on same business. They may return home in few day. They was gone for week now.[22] [1924-09-27-A LJ]

WASHAKIE, SEPTEMBER 25, 1924.   . . . Our boys coming back from Idaho just a last Saturday. But [some] of them remain in Reservation and doing some work up there. Well Mr. Ammon Pubigee is still up there and doing some work for his cousin. . . . He was put up some hay for him. Mr. Nephi Zundel still up there. And he expect be down some time next week. Mr. Elias Pubigee is coming home with his race horses a few days ago. Mr. Jim Wagon and Timus Perdash is still up there too. Nearly everybody is home now. But our fall start get busy every days now. Mr. George Tospanguitch is return home from Idaho Reservation and he was visiting his own relatives. Mr. George Tomock was return home last Friday night. He was gathering some pine nuts out toward Snowville or Black Pine. Mr. Yeager Timbimboo is still out Black Pine yet and hunting some pine nuts. He may return home some time in few days. And also his son and wife went out west to too. Mr. Joe Woonsook was still out there too. There not many people at home yet. Mr. Soquitch and wife is been down to Elwood and buys some fruit. But is return middle part last week. . . . Our people are not much been down to Brigham City Sept. 17, 1924 [Peach Day]. I want going visit a Washakie once more before this coming [?]. Mr. Enos Pubigee is return home last Saturday. But he having a good old time. Not much sugar beet to speak of. This was very poor year this summer. Some of our people say they going have a early winter and the hard winter. The oldest Indian say our people can judge [weather]. But the older Indians can. [1924-09-27-B LJ]

WIND RIVER, WYOMING, SEPTEMBER 29, 1924.   I am among Eastern Shoshone now. But I find the Indians are very good condition. There was a good big crop hay raised here this summer. Their stock won't get starve this coming winter. These Indians are [raising] some cattle and some haven't got much. Well sir they have not through with thresh some grain has not cut yet. But the season is very short.

The elevation is 7860. They could not raise a fruit here. But some white men raise apples, plums, strawberries, etc. But could not raise peaches, apricot. I expect am going around and more acquainted with these Indians here. About mile East from Agency. The game is plenty on the Reservation for the Indians to used. I am find some my own relation here. But and mighty glad. Well sir I am just coming in from Lander [WY] this morning on the mails [on mail train]. It is about 15 miles North West from Lander. Some the Indians are gethering some winters wood some selling wood to the agent, and some others [to] business houses. They have a good warm water resort here. It is about one half mile from big school. The was about over 2000 thousand Indians on this reservation, and there was some Arapahoes Indians living away down about 30 mile east from here and on the same River [Wind River]. All Journal readers could hear from me again when I return home. I am going stay a few day here on this Reservation. [1924-10-18-A LJ]

WASHAKIE, OCTOBER 8, 1924.   I was found my people are good condition when I return from Wyoming back home on the Monday. The weather is very cold out Wyoming. There was about 6 inch snow on the top the mountain. But we find very rough road through big Piney country. But was going out for prospecting out Wyoming. They found great many oil and coal in the Indians Reservation out big Wind River. And many other places of the country. We find there was a very good fishing and hunting out Wyoming. We expect may going out again in next summer again. There was a plenty work on the reservation. . . . Our people working sugar beet field now. Some of them starting topping now. Some has not start yet. Mr. Seth Pubigee is working for Mr. Bishop George M. Ward put in some grain for him. He going get through in one day or three day. Then he is going work in sugar beet with his gang. But he going work Jap north the Fielding station about 1 mile and half. All Indians are return home from West and gathering some pine nuts out around Black Pine. They fetch some pine nuts home. Nearly everybody out work in sugar beets yet. . . . [1924-10-18-B LJ]

WASHAKIE, OCTOBER 23–24, 1924.   . . . Most of [people] working out sugar beet field now. Last week Mr. David Pabawena little baby boy died down to Fielding Station. They was taken up here to buried him. And his mother died after his birth, from blood poison. She was quite young woman . . . about 25 years of age. She was born out Nevada. They moved out here about two year ago this fall. There is nothing new to tell about. The weather is getting pretty cold just now. Our people are looking for a long winter this year. Some of our want move up Idaho reservation for the winter time. But they haven't got hay here. Mr. Ammon Pubigee is still up the Idaho I hope they may stay all winter up there. Mr. Thomas Pabawena is coming home from Idaho about last week ago. And also Mr. Willie Neaman and wife is return home for his trip Nevada. Mr. Tom Elk still working out Nevada now. He expect coming about next month. Mr. Seth Pubigee want going up Idaho to work for agent up there. After all sugar beet done around Garland. Mr. Jacob Peyope and Nephi Perdash went out hunting deer. They was return other day. Mr. Catch Toyahdook and Joe Woonsook out hunting too, they has not return home yet. Mr. Enos Pubigee baby born on week last. . . . [1924-11-08 LJ]

Willie Attends the One Cent Sale

LOGAN, NOVEMBER 4, 1924.   The Riter Bros. Rexall Drug Store a big One Cents Sale start on today. But everybody is want anything come as you can. Then you can get what you want a reasonable price. In the line of the articles is anything you need in house hole [household] use, or other proposed. They will treat you right. They will fairly with you. But this a great big sale for forty year, every had before. I want every Journal reader telling your neighbors to come see the big sale. But never missed it. Be sure bring your friends or some your relation too. I have been in the store today examine the articles. It is all good stuff. I want all people in Cash [Cache] Valley rush out and buy the store out, before new year coming. Well, I am in town for some business. [1924-12-04 LJ]]

WASHAKIE, NOVEMBER 24, 1924.   The people are pretty poor this year. The crop is fail and the hay is scarce. Some of us wish move to Idaho Reservation for the winter. So they can have some hay for their stock. Mr. Mose Neaman is taken his horses up there for last month. He may going up there about next month. Mrs. Kippetchew Noragan motoring over to Logan last week. . . . Mrs. Cohn Zundel and family been up Idaho Reservation and visiting her granddaughter up there. She was return home last week. Mr. Catch Toyahdook return his hunting trip out to Black Pine, about last week. Mr. Seth Pubigee and Mr. Thomas Pabawena want going out and doing some trapping. Mr. Ammon Pubigee still up there to Idaho and he is work for the agent. But he want his son come up there, and he got some hay. But he want sell it and figuring buy [or sell] some hay down to the Fielding or some other place.[23] The hay is worth $12.00 to $7.00 per ton. I and boys been up there Fort Hall Reservation last week on the especial business and acquainted with some Indians up there and also seen some my relation. We return home last Monday. Now is time buy good land. If anybody want buy good place. There is about 1000 acres Indians land sale up around north Pocatello, Idaho. The land worth about $50.00 or $30.00 per acre. It is good water right. This is agent sale. These land is all under water.[24]

The weather is getting very cold here now. Mr. Peter Bird is here now. But his wife died last February. He is making his home Idaho. He want going home in few day. But staying with his sister here. [1924-11-29 LJ]]

WASHAKIE, DECEMBER 3, 1924.   The weather get very colder here every day now. But the winter so nearer. Our fall crop coming fine now. I hope we going have a big crop next year. And crop is so fail. And expect our going hungry this winter and some has not even buy hay for the stock. And they figuring going move to Idaho for winter. Mr. Ammon Pubigee still up to Idaho. But he expect return home on the next month. Mr. Enos Pubigee and his brother, Mr. Elias Pubigee went up Idaho reservation. But they got some hay up there. They was going to sell the hay. They buy [or sell] hay down Garland someplace. Well, they has not return yet. . . . Mr. John Dick and his family was return home their works. Mr. Mose Neaman and two sons motoring down Tremonton other day. Mr. Thomas Pabawena and Mr. Seth Pubigee went out trapping in few days ago. Mr. Nephi Perdash is been down Tremonton yesterday. But doing some Thanksgiving shopping. . . . Mr. John Pabawena and family return home from his sugar beet work about two week ago. Mr. Henry Woonsook has not return from Idaho yet. He went up month of Sept. But he is working for agent at Fort Hall. [1924-12-06 LJ]

WASHAKIE, DECEMBER 24, 1924.   Our people are poor condition for this winter. We don't expect Santa Clause will stop our little town on account the people being so poor. He might going next town. And we had have a pretty bad weather, a real snow storm and blizzard too. It is lasted about five days here and cold weather too. The thermometer say about 22 below zero here. This was coldest weather we ever had here by this time year before. O expect there will be a good sleighing here for this winter. The snow is about one ft. and half a level the ground. Mr. Mose Neaman and family went to Logan last two weeks ago. When he will spent Christmas over there. And also Mr. Kippetchew Noragan went down to Salt Lake City to spend Christmas down there and doing some business too. Mr. Ammon Pubigee and his two sons return home from Idaho about a week ago. They expect to move up there until next spring. They was already job up there to saw mill. He was working for the agent. Mr. Henry Woonsook and family still up Idaho Reservation. He going all winter up there and he is working for agent too. Mr. Jim Wagon was went down Tremonton with Ford car last Tuesday. And stall he could not going home. Because his engine refuse to start and left his car at Texco [Texaco] garage and return home on the evening train. But he was doing some Christmas shopping. . . . [1924-12-27 LJ]

WASHAKIE, DECEMBER 31, 1924.   The people are here very good condition just now. But the weather we having here pretty cold this year. Yesterday we a another snow storm too. It last about all day yesterday. We have had a good sleighing . . . about two foot snow here. The hay is scarce . . . it is about $12.00 per ton here now. The hay going to be $15.00 per ton here in spring. But it is no work here just now. Some not even buy hay their horses. Mr. Kippetchew Noragan return home from Salt Lake City other day. He was spent Christmas down there. Mr. Mose Neaman has not return from Logan yet. He went over to Logan week before Christmas. But he spent Christmas over there. . . . I expect they have a good Christmas celebrate and people are here happy when New Year coming just now. But we hope will have a nice early spring weather soon. [1925-01-03 LJ]

6

"You People May Read My Writing
Long as I Work,"[1] 1925–1926

WASHAKIE, JANUARY 7, 1925. The weather getting warmer here . . . [but] the snow good enough good sleighing for this winter. This will be a last about two month or more. I expect we have a good crop of wheat next year. But the lot more snow up on the mountainside yet. We haven't got much hay for our stock this winter. We might lost some of our stock. . . . Some of us not got money to buy hay with because our crop is fail last year. The people is very poor this winter. Well some our people say the spring in the next two month. Our people spent very splendid Christmas here. They have good Christmas program. . . . They spent News Year Day just same way. In the before noon have program in the ward meeting house. And in afternoon children dance. In evening have for the grown people dance. But every body enjoyed themselves. Good old jolly time. And also luncheon were served for each home in the ward. Mr. Ammon Pubigee was return for three week and with his two son. He going back up again toward spring. He got job already now. . . . Mr. Mose Neaman and family return from Logan city. . . . He spent Christmas over there. Mr. Geo P. Sam been down Tremonton and doing some New Year's shopping. . . . Mr. Jim Wagon left his Ford car down Tremonton about two week ago. But he hasn't go after him yet. [1925-01-17-A LJ]

WASHAKIE, JANUARY 14, 1925. The people are fairly condition now. But no one die this winter. . . . Some our people are afraid going lose the stock. No hay around in our town. The hay is pretty high price this winter. Some of our people say going have a long winter this winter. But there is most big part winter is gone here now. Nearly everybody is home now. Miss Neatze Moemberg and daughter been down to Salt Lake City to buying some deer hide. They return home after New Year's day. . . . Mr. Amos Moemberg and family return from Idaho. He is taking care his father-in-law land. He was died there about year ago. Mr. Ammon Pubigee want going up Idaho again in open spring he got him job next spring up there to agency Mr. Valentine. . . . Mr. Riey Johny [Jim] is still in our town yet. He was come there before the Thanksgiving Day. But he stayed with Mr. George P. Sam all winter. And there is nothing doing here now. No work all we have had very nice sleighing just now. There was a big rabbits hunting about two weeks ago, down West of Garland. Nearly all the boy been out hunt. They slaughter quite lot of bunnies. Mr. Warren Wongan hunt coyote nearly everyday. He hasn't catch any yet. Our day school very nicely. [1925-01-17-B LJ]

WASHAKIE, JANUARY 22, 1925.   The weather are getting warmer here now. Some our people say spring start now. Well can [not] tell now until next month. . . . The is very quited [quiet] here now. No work for this winter. I hope there will be will a plenty job in spring. But some our people afraid going lose their horses this winter. And short for hay. Our people are pretty poor this winter now. Everybody is have a good health now, no one died here in our town. Mr. Jim John Neaman got married last summer. He is living with his father now. Master Chester Ottogary is graduate from district school last year. Now he is going to the Bear River High School this winter. He like it pretty good. Of cause [course] the government paying his school. He will learn something in the school that will his own benefit. But he was first Indian boy graduate from district school on the Box Elder County. We are the very small tribes of band Shoshone Indian here at Washakie. The our little town named by [for] our Chief Washakie of the Wyoming. . . . On last Friday we have a dance. And everybody have a good enjoyable time. This dance given by Relief Society in the ward chapel. [1925-01-24 LJ]

WASHAKIE, JANUARY 29, 1925.   . . . Mr. Tom Elk little boy died fore part week and buried about last Tuesday. The funeral service held at ward meeting house. Bishop [counselor] Mr. Yeager Timpimboo was take charge the funeral service.[2] These was only one death this winter. Mr. Catch Toyahdook was been up Idaho Reservation some time ago forepart last week and return home last Sunday. He was visiting his own brother up there. But he was sick in bed. But he seen many his old acquaintence there too. And also Mr. Joe Woonsook is been up there to Fort Hall, Idaho, and visiting his son and family up there. He was return home some time last week ago. His son went up there last fall for some work. But he is working for agent.

There was candy party here on the last Thursday night at the ward meeting house, and everybody have a real enjoyable old time. There will be another dance next Friday night. I hope we will have another good old time again. We haven't much hay for our horses yet. The hay is pretty scarce around our town just now. And people are rejoicing when spring time is near. We expect going have a good crop of everything next summer. I received letter from friend Mr. Harry Dixon other day and he say everybody is doing well out Nevada this winter. But his wife was left him, after the Thanksgiving. Now he stay all alone his home, etc. [1925-02-02 LJ]

WASHAKIE, FEBRUARY 5, 1925.   . . . Weather is getting pretty warm now. The snow thaw pretty fast. Here we have had pretty nice weather here in few day this week. I expect we going have good weather after this time. There is only one death this winter and one birth too in the year 1925. Some our people are pretty anxious getting spring because they having [not] much hay for their stock. They expect going lose some the animals. . . . Mr. [Tom] Elk was trapping this winter the north West Portage. But he ran a bunch of deer and he kill some deer. And he was under arrested by Game Warden Mr. Grover. But he telephone down Brigham City. Mr. [B. C.] Hall came here and got him. And he went down on morning train on the last Thursday on the 29 January and with his two brothers and have hearing same day. But they got the treaties of the Law United States for the Indians. And Mr. B. C. Call read the treaties to the court. The was read the Indians can hunt any time

Handwritten letter to E. B. Meritt, commissioner of Indian affairs, by Willie Ottogary, February 2, 1925. CCF 8760-1925-115, RG 75, National Archives.

the year. Because the game is belong to the American Indians. But this treaties was made in year 1863 July the 30, in Brigham City between the white and Indians. And signed by the chief and warriors too. Then judge say the was pretty hard to beat. And the turn him loose. It is didn't cost him anything.[3] They went home next day. I and Mr. Ammon Pubigee on the Friday on 30 January. But they came home. But [we] went up Washakie to see them. And also on last Monday I and Mr. Thomas Pabewena on the same business. Mr. Joseph Woonsook was visiting his son up Idaho Reservation. He was gone for last fall. And he was working for the Agent. Some our men been up Malad City to attend regular Stake Priesthood meeting. Last Friday night we have a dance. Everybody enjoying a splendid old time. [1925-02-07 LJ]

WASHAKIE, FEBRUARY 12, 1925. . . . Some of us pretty poor. They could not buy anything on account the crop being so poor last year. Some of think going lose their stock. . . . The hay price is about $12 or $13 per ton. There was about one death this winter. The weather is getting warmer so far. The snow is nearly gone here. But sleighing kind pretty poor just now. Last Friday night a Relief Society gave a dance in the ward meeting house. And everybody was real a jolly good old time. . . . Last Saturday night we have a kind of council meeting at the Mr. George Tomock residence. And every men be present this meeting. It was quite interesting meeting we ever held. The meeting was take charge by act represenative, Mr. Willie Ottogary and also by Mr. Thomas Pabawena. Mr. George P. Sam was sick last week. He was under the weather. But he is getting up and around again. Mr. Riey Jim still in town yet. He expect return in the spring. His home was out Nevada. Mr. George Tospanguitch motoring down Fielding station last Saturday with his granddaughter Miss Kazza [possibly Etheline (b. 1916) or Lucille (b. 1923)] Pabawena. She is daughter of Mr. Thomas Pabawena. Mr. Tom Elk still trapping now. And also Mr. Jacob Peyope was a trapper too. There is sad news reach Mrs. Kippetchew Noragan [Positze Noragan] home week ago, from Washakie, Wyoming. Her uncle was died about two weeks ago. But some our people to visit her home and comfort her. And he was well known all over this country. He making his home on the Wyoming Reservation. [1925-02-17 LJ]

WASHAKIE, FEBRUARY 18, 1925.   . . . I made a business trip up there [Washakie] last week. And find our people are bad condition. Some haven't got any money to buy foodstuff with. Not even buy a setting hen.[4] We was asking our agent from Fort Hall need help in line of food and hay. I received a letter last week. He stated in his letter. There is no Government [help] at all. But I send his letter with my letter to President Calvin C. Coolidge. But this kind [of] disappointed us saying toward about our Government. We expect to hear from our President in next three weeks or more. We write a letter to our agent again in the few days ago. I expect hear from our agent in the few days. Well having a very nice weather here. Our people rejoicing, they say spring is here now. Mr. George P. Sam is still sick. But he [has] Bright's Disease. But had it for 10 year. Some time get well, some time get worse. Seem to me he never get over this disease. Mr. Riey Jim still living our town yet. He expect be here when spring open. . . . Mr. James Pabawena and Dave Pabawena business trip down Elwood. Mr. Willie Ottogary place. And they return last Monday night. Indian movements at Glacier park. [Ottogary inserts an article dealing with Blackfeet Indians and Glacier Park:]

> Washington, D. C., February 9, 1925.
> —An Indian tepee village is maintained at the Gateway of Glacier National Park, Montana for the edification of America's tourists in commemoration of the fact that the Blackfeet Indians ceded to the United States Government these 1,500 square miles of Rocky Mountain country which Congress set aside as Glacier Park in 1910. This territory was famed as the greatest hunting grounds of all American Indians.
> [1925-02-21 LJ]

WASHAKIE, MARCH 4, 1925.   . . . The spring is here now. Makes our people happing [happy]. We are soon our spring work is here now. . . . Hay is pretty scarce around here now. We don't know what we going to about hay. I expect our people are going lose the stocks. We are pretty poor condition this winter has be for many year, on account all fall crop is fail last summer. I hope we are going have a good crop this coming summer. The fall crop is looking pretty good now. The snow is all gone just [now] and drying pretty fast. Mr. Bishop George M. Ward two work horses was kill by train other day. They probably weigh about 1300 lb. each. And make him angry. And make complaint against railroad Co. This is a valuable team he had on this farm. Mr. Moroni Timbimboo trying start plowing his ground other day and he is figuring going put in some grain for his uncle [Soquitch]. Mr. Willie

Neaman was motoring down Tremonton other day. And also Mr. Jim Wagon was been down Tremonton and getting his Ford car. But left down Tremonton couple weeks. . . . Last Friday night having a dance here in ward chapel. And everybody enjoyed themself. Mr. Seth Pubigee and Jack Johnny was motoring down to Fielding and other places too. Mrs. Susie Charlie and two woman and motoring down below some time ago early part of this week. And also was visiting Mr. Willie Ottogary place too. [1925-03-10 LJ]

WASHAKIE, MARCH 12, 1925.   The people are here good condition now. But we spring time here now. . . . Everything pretty quiet just now. There is only two death this winter here and nobody is sick now. The hay is pretty scarce . . . [and] price is high . . . about $12 dollars just now. And the few farmers has got hay around our vicinity. But hold their price high. We are nearly run out hay now. We was begged our agent to helping us on the hay matters. But he didn't help us. Seem to me this our agent don't care for Indians people. We asked him two time about him. Last Friday night we had a dance here in the ward meeting house and everybody having very good time. . . And also the Relief Society . . . annual party given at the ward meeting house about 3 P.M. o'clock. The programme was a real good every had before. And in evening the dance was given the Relief Society and everybody was having real good jolly time. They have a good music. The railroad agent come down from West Portage here play for the dance. But the sorry news come to Mr. Tom Elk home last Monday from his stepdaughter, Mr. Jim Broncho died at his home down to Portneuf Bottoms, Idaho Reservation. He was well known around the country. And he was man about 80 year of age. But he is big cattle ranch West Pocatello. He has many relation throughout the country. But he got some relation living in our town. . . . [1925-03-17 LJ]

1925-03-21 LJ [Not included, mostly duplicate of 1925-03-27 Box Elder Journal]

Box Elder Journal[5]
Brigham City, Utah, March 27th, 1925.
"Indian Letter"

WASHAKIE, MARCH 25, 1925.   The people are very good condition, there's nobody was sick so far. There was only two death this winter and everybody have good health just now. The spring is here now but our spring works begin to start now. Well, there was a sad news coming from west on last Monday at my place in Elwood on last week. The death of our relation. He living in Owyhee, Nevada, he is about 75 years of age. Most of his relatives living in Idaho Reservation and also his sister died there two week before him. He was soldiers scout in the early days and he join the Methodist church about six or seven years ago, he was good member of that church. He left his good wife and stepsons behind him. . . .[6] Mr. Moroni Timbimboo and with Mr. Socquitch Timbimboo been down Tremonton and buying some alfalfa seed. I was made arrangement with Mr. Will R. Holmes, Editor Manager, all who can read Box Elder Journal going read my article in that paper now on. The hay is pretty scarce now. But some our men getting some hay from Mr. George M. Ward, he was selling some hay for $12.00 per ton now but he is

only man got some hay in our vicinity, you may excuse me such poor hand writing. [1925-03-27 BEJ]

WASHAKIE, MARCH 25, 1925.   . . . All our people are rejoicing when spring is here.
But some our people are want going up Idaho Reservation after next month to
work. Mr. Ammon Pubigee was left here for Idaho some time ago. Mr. Seth
Pubigee and family move up Idaho. He expect going work up there. But he may
stay all spring up there. And also Mr. Elias Pubigee and wife moved up there with
his father too. But their father is lease Indian land up there. So this two his sons
going help him on the land he leased from his relation up there. There was some
of our people been up Malad City, Idaho. The Relief Society has big annual doing
up here. They return home last week. Mr. George P. Sam was up around again. But
he was sick a week. . . . Mrs. George Tomock went down Salt Lake City some time
ago. They has not return home yet. And also Miss Susie Highyou is accompanied
Mrs. George Tomock too. Mr. James Pabawena, with his two brothers been working for Mr. George M. Ward down one mile west Plymouth. They finish their work
last Friday night. They was doing some fencing down there on the Mr. Jensen farm.
Mr. Jim John [Neaman] was proud daddy. The baby boy was born his home on the
Sunday March 15. The mother of the new boy took sick on Sunday last. And she
was taken down Deweyville for Dr. treatment. But she was feeling pretty good last
Monday. I was made a business trip down Brigham first part week. But and get
another job. I am going be correspondent for the Box Elder Journal now.[7] I was
made arrangement with Mr. Will R. Holmes, Editor manager. All who can read
Box Elder Journal going read my article in that paper now on. . . . [1925-03-28 LJ]

WASHAKIE, APRIL 7, 1925.   . . . Most of us get through their spring crops in now. And
our fall crop is looking pretty promising. I hope we going have a real good crop this
year, and our people are rejoicing over our new crop. Our day school is running
pretty good this year. But I was visiting on last Sunday and find everybody is doing
good. But Mrs. Jim John Neaman is very sick just now, and she improving nicely.
But she had a flue. Mr. Joe Woonsook went up Idaho Reservation about last week
and his wife went up there about two week ago.
    There was two Indian boys from Wells, Nevada, staying at Mr. Tom Elk home
now. Their home is in Wells, Nevada. Our boys was organized the baseball team
here last week. They are going have a practice game with West Portage boys next
Saturday. . . . Warren Wongan little boy was burned his hands about week. He
went down Deweyville last week for Dr. treatment. . . . Mr. George M. Ward just
returned home last night. He and his wife been down attended . . . Conference
down Salt Lake City. None of our people been conference for this spring. . . .
[1925-04-14 BEJ]

WASHAKIE, APRIL 8, 1925.   . . . Our people are getting busy right now put in crops.
Well sir, our fall crop looking pretty promising this coming year. We expect going
have a real good harvest this year. The hay pretty scarce now. The was only two
death this winter. Mr. Ammon Pubigee and his two sons went up Idaho
Reservation about two week ago. They went up there for the working. One of his

[relation] is going run his farm while he is working there. He expect be up there all summer along. Mr. Joe Woonsook went up Idaho about one week ago. He is looking for work up there. He may stay up there in couple week or more. Mr. Warren Wongan little boy was badly burned about his hands. But he is getting improved pretty slow. And he was take his boy down Deweyville last week to take under Dr. treatment. . . . Mrs. George P. Sam been down Salt Lake City about week and buy some deer hide. Mr. John Pabawena and Dave Pabawena been down to Fielding other [day] on the important business. I have received sad news from Owyhee, Nevada some time ago last week. The is some our relation died out that country. I went over to Logan City and find everybody is doing [fine] over there. I have seen some my old acquaintance there. They are doing fine and dandy so far. I went in Riter Bro. Drug store to see Mr. B. Riter and Mr. B. Curel and more others too. But everything pretty quiet around Logan just now. [1925-04-11 LJ]

WASHAKIE, APRIL 15, 1925. . . . The people are very good condition, nobody sick just now. There is only two death this winter. Mr. Yeager was took [sick] on the Saturday last. He is getting better now. Mr. Jim Wagon and wife is motoring down Brigham City about last week. And also Mr. Dick Arritch accompanied Mr. Jim Wagon. . . . Kippetchew Noragan was motoring down Ogden about last week ago. Mr. Warren Wongan and wife and another woman is motoring over there to Cache Valley. And they was return home last part of the last week. Mr. Soquitch Timbimboo was motoring down Brigham City about last week. Mr. Timus Perdash and Mr. Nephi Perdash and wife been up Malad City for part last week. And also Mr. John Pabawena and family motoring Fielding last part of the last week. There was a very sad news come over our town. That one Indian was kill by two Indians. They was drinking some whiskey at Pocatello City. He was suddenly kill and is cut his throats and also cut around his body too. He was kill on the little Pocatello Creek. It is about 1½ miles north the Pocatello. There is one Indian Police and white man Police. They search [for] him many hours and at last found him among pinch sagebrush. They made arrest one Indian already and haven't found another yet. They might find him later on yet.[8] [1925-04-18 LJ]

WASHAKIE, APRIL 22, 1925. We having pretty wet weather here just now. And we had 3 or 4 days rainstorm . . . here. Our crop looking pretty good now. All our spring crop put in already just now. But our people are rejoicing over the nice rain having had now. . . .

Mr. Joe Woonsook and wife return home from Idaho reservation last week. He was visiting his son up there and also visit some his relation and friend. . . .

Our boys played Baseball with West Portage boys the [score] was about 4 to 5 in favor of West Portage.

Bishop Geor. M. Ward was gave out notice on Sunday there will be Quarterly Conference held at Malad City Stake building next Saturday and Sunday, and commence 10 o'clock Saturday morning. I expect some our people are going up there for the conference.[1925-04-25 LJ]

1925-04-28 BEJ [Not included, duplicate of 1925-04-25 LJ]

WASHAKIE, APRIL 30, 1925.   The summer soon be here now. Our people rejoice when summer is coming. But our crop is fine and dandy. I expect we going have a good harvest this year. All our spring crop is put in already. Most our people are been conference up to Malad City about last week ago. Some our boys been up Broad Canyon and shear sheep for man from Salt Lake City. . . .

Mr. Timus Perdash went to Ogden yesterday and on matter of business.

Mr. George Tospanguitch motoring over to Cache Valley about week.

Mr. Ammon Pubigee wrote to his son, Mr. Enos Pubigee. He say in his letter doing fine up there. But he is lease his cousin farm up in the east of Fort Hall and also one of his sons helping him too. . . .

Mrs. Mose Neaman was motoring down Tremonton about last week ago and more other women.

There was about seven men going raise sugar beet this [year] our town. They made contract about three weeks ago. The sugar beet was fail last year. I expect the sugar beet good harvest this coming year.

Some our want going Wyoming to visit some their relations and friends out there.

Mr. Enos Pubigee . . . expect enter horse race next fall over to Logan. But he was asking about the Logan Fair in Sept. He is got a Buckskin Nelly. She is real race mare. She outrun anything around here. She was run against fast horse in the state last fall over to Logan Fair. She going entered [this] fall too. [1925-05-02 LJ]

1925-05-08 BEJ [Not included; much of the information is covered in 1925-05-09 LJ.]

WASHAKIE, MAY 7, 1925.   The crop is looking pretty good this time. But we expect going have a good harvest this year, and our men are cleaning water ditch now pre-pare for water. All spring crop is put in already. Well some our people want going up Malad City. It is kind of social going to be held at Malad City. Our boys organ-ize a base ball team here some time ago last week ago. They played with West Portage boys, our boys they [Portage] beat them twice already. They was going have a ball suit in later on. They wrote letter to our agent and asked him going help us to buy ball suit for our boys. Mr. George Sam was going up there Idaho Reservation and to home next week some time. . . . Mr. Jacob Peyope went to Wyoming to shear sheep. He has not return yet. [1925-05-09 LJ]

WASHAKIE, MAY 13, 1925.   The crop looking pretty good. And we had a nice little shower here on last Monday. And it is help everything and rain all day long. Our boys been organized baseball team here . . . [and] I expect they played all summer long. Mr. George P. Sam was return home from Idaho Reservation last week. He is visiting some his relation and friends too, and many more others. Mr. Willie Neaman and Master Herbert Pabawena was sent to Idaho, and looking for some work. They has not return home yet. Mr. Tom Elk and family went up Idaho and going visit their daughter up to Idaho Reservation. He expect may return home next week some time. Mr. Enos Pubigee and wife [and] I was motored over to Penrose, Utah. We return other day. Mr. George Tospanguitch is return home from Idaho, and he is visit some his relation and many friends. Mr. Inarich and wife was visit our town here yesterday. They went home same day. There were at near Blackfoot, Idaho. Some our people are went to Tremonton May Festible [Festival] Day on May 9, 1925. Some went up Malad City too. Mr. Soquitch Timbimboo went down Tremonton doing some business. Mr. Jim Wagon and Joe Woonsook was motored down Brigham City about last week ago. The county want to be appointed some an Indian game warden. These will be a good thing and they will doing these duties this summer, etc. [1925-05-16 LJ]

WASHAKIE, MAY 19, 1925.   . . . Our school is have a summer vacation now, and make a little children so happy. I expect we going have a new school house erected for the next coming school. Our agent is going start a building right away. Our boys want going up Idaho Fort Hall school when school stop. But the manager of our boys baseball team is write a letter to Supt. school. He want our boys coming up there to play ball. But he is going let us know pretty soon. I hope they will have a good time. . . . Mr. Enos Pubigee went to Garland High School to see some school doings. But Mr. Soquitch and family and Mr. Enos Pubigee went motored over to Penrose and doing some shooting [hunting]. They may return home in a few days. Mr. Tom Elk has not return home from Idaho. He may return this week. I and my boy been down to Brigham City last week and doing some business down there. Mr. Willie Neaman and Herbert Pabawena has not return from Idaho yet. Mr. John Pabawena and wife been down Garland and Fielding and looking for [beet] thinning job. [1925-05-22 BEJ]

WASHAKIE, MAY 21, 1925.   The people are rejoice over the crops. It is looking fine now. We expect going have a good harvest this year. Everything look good now. Our agent just a locate where to the school house be. We going have a new school house be built this summer. Get ready for next school start in September [see 1926-10-23 LJ]. Our [boys] want go up Fort Hall School to play ball when the school close for summer. The Supt. school wrote letter to our baseball manager some time ago but he want our boys coming up there to play ball. Then he will let us know again in the few days. Our boy is pretty anxious going up there. Mr. Jacob Peyope has not return from Wyoming yet. He has been shearing sheep out there. Mr. Tom Elk and went up Idaho to visit some his relation and friends. And he was accompanied with his whole family. . . . Mr. George Tospanguitch was return his Idaho trip about last Sunday. . . . [1925-05-23 LJ]

WASHAKIE, MAY 29, 1925.   . . . Perhaps we may have a good harvest this year and also the sugar beet look pretty good now this year. The beet start thin now yet. Some of our people are thinning beet some white men down north of Riverside now. Well sir, everything looking pretty good conditions. . . . Some our want go Fort Washakie, Wyoming, this summer, to visit some of their relations and friends. I expect going about next month. Mr. Tom Elk and family return from Idaho Reservation about last week ago. They was visiting their daughter up there. Mr. George P. Sam is looking for some job down Garland other day. And he want thin beet. . . . Mr. Jacob Peyope has not return home from Wyoming yet. He was gone about last month. He will return next month yet. [1925-06-02 LJ]

A New School For Washakie

Supt. Skidmore got word yesterday from the Federal officials that money will be available after July 1 for the erection of a new Indian school, the same to provide for a place for the teachers to live. The government proposes that, if possible, the Superintendent should employ a man and a woman for this school. The man would put in all his time and the woman half time. She would spend half time on sewing, handwork, and the like, and the other half in household duties. The Superintendent is now in search for the right type of couple that will be suitable for this position.

News article concerning plans for construction of a new school at Washakie. *From* Box Elder News, *May 4, 1926.*

WASHAKIE, JUNE 3, 1925.   The people are rejoice over the rain storm we have today. The crop is looking pretty good now. I expect we are going have a good harvest this year. Everything splendid now. The sugar beet crop is good condition this year. Mr. Jacob Peyope just come home from Wyoming last week. But he was gone for month and he was shearing sheep out there. Mr. George P. Sam made a business trip down Tremonton other day. . . . Mr. Jim Wagon and Riey Jim went over to Cache Valley [Lewiston] to looking for sugar beet thinning job. They will be over there about two weeks. Mr. Soquitch Timbimboo and family went down Tremonton. But he was going stay on my place while I going up Idaho trip. Mr. William Donner the Indian agent want our boys coming up Fort Hall to play ball on the 5 June. They going have a big time that. This was a field day for Industrial Indian School. They want our baseball team come up there to play ball. Our ball team manager was received word from Supt. school last week. Some our people working for white men down near Garland factory. They was thinning beet. [1925-06-06 LJ]

1925-06-09 BEJ [Not included, duplicate of 1925-06-06 LJ]

WASHAKIE, JUNE 11, 1925.   Our people are keep busy thinning sugar beet for some white. And also thinning their own beet. The sugar beet crop looking pretty good this year. I expect we have a good harvest this year. Our ball player been up Fort Hall Idaho to play ball with Fort Hall baseball team about last Friday, June 5, 1925. The score was 10 to 5 in the favor of the Fort Hall team. There was big field day

for the school. They have nice program . . . [and] play ball before noon, and afternoon all kind sports. There was a large crowd at school that day. Some of them taking [their] children home. All Indian are happy when the school ended for the
summer. Mr. Mose Neaman and I was been up Fort Hall with our boys. We return
home last Saturday night. . . . Mr. Tom Elk [and] Nephi Perdash is shearing sheep
up to Broad Canyon now. Mr. Jim [Wagon] and Mr. Riey Jim over to Lewiston a
thinning beet for some white men. [1925-06-13 LJ]

WASHAKIE, JUNE 16, 1925.   The people are keep busy thinning their sugar beet just
now. But the beet splendid crop this year. Some our people are thinning beet for
white man down near around North Garland and also around Fielding too. Our
fall crop wheat is looking very promising this year. We made a little hunting trip
down east Brigham City up to Mantua on the Sunday last. . . . Some our [people]
want going out Wind River Reservation to [see] some of their relations and friends,
on the next month more. Mr. Soquitch Timbimboo still down Elwood on my farm
and with his wife too. [1925-06-23 BEJ]

WASHAKIE, JUNE 17, 1925.   Some our farmer raise sugar beet this year. It was looking pretty good crop this year. And also wheat crop is good. We had a nice shower here last Sunday night. And some of them working in the beet field for white
men. And some thin their sugar beet now. Nearly all thinning through . . . now. I
expect we are going have a good harvest this year. The people are rejoice over the
rain we had this spring. Mr. Ammon Pubigee now return home from Idaho
Reservation with his son, Mr. Elias Pubigee. One of his son still up Idaho. Mr.
Mose Neaman motoring down Garland other day. . . . Mrs. Neatze Moemberg and
two little boys hit by automobile nearly kill them. She is knock off the buggy and
her head was cut two or three places. She was unconscious for the hour. The [boys]
wasn't hurt, and also knock one of the horse, and nearly kill him too. This done
by the last week ago. She is getting nicely now. Mr. Soquitch Timbimboo still
down Mr. Willie Ottogary farm down to Elwood, Utah. He will be there until he
going Wyoming. Mr. Nephi Zundel was been down Tremonton some time ago last
week ago. I get letter from my cousin, Mr. James Pingree. He say in his letter there
going a big celebrate on that fourth July and going a big feast too, and horse races,
and more sports. I expect we time get there to see the big time. We are going leave
for Wyoming on the 19 or 20. . . . Some of our people want going to Wyoming and
visit some their relation and friends too. [1925-06-20 LJ]

WASHAKIE, JUNE 24, 1925.   . . . The sugar beets is splendid crop this year. The was
been so good has been for long time. And also the wheat crop is looking good too.
Our agent want school house built before the next school start. They soon start on
the building now. . . . Mr. Enos Pubigee and wife and his brother was visit my place
at Elwood on the last Sunday. Mr. Soquitch and family and I and my [boys] doing
little hunting over to Mantua about last Sunday. Mr. Tom Elk is finish shearing,
then he want going Idaho for some work. I expect all The Journal readers will hearing from me again out Wyoming for next week sometime. I expect to leave for
Wyoming for next Friday. We are going remain in Fort Washakie until September

or more. I could not tell now. Mr. Dick Arritch is still work up Idaho Reservation now. He may coming down next week and he visiting some his relation. Mr. Mose Neaman was motoring down Tremonton for part of last week. Mrs. Neatze Moemberg well again. She was hit by automobile down near Tremonton some time ago. Mr. Moroni Timbimboo and family went to Fort Washakie to visit some his relation out there. [1925-06-29 LJ]

Willie Ottogary Writes to The Journal From Washakie

FORT WASHAKIE, WYOMING, JUNE 30, 1925.   The Indians are very good condition now. But we just got here yesterday and haven't got much news now. I will give more news next week. Some Indians coming here from different Reservation some from Idaho, Uintah, Oklahoma and more other I could mention. These Indians just cutting their hay now. The hay crop kind pretty slow this year or else the hay is later than Utah. Some of the Indian boys going ride on the four July at Lander and at Fort Washakie too. And the Arapahoe Indians going celebrate down to Arapahoe too on same days. I expect they have a big time everywhere the part section the country. Mr. Jim Wagon and his wife is here now. His home at Washakie, Utah. He may stay here about month or two. I expect will be more acquainted with Indians here. Well going have a horse races here at Fort Washakie. Some the boys been practice ride here all time now on and prepare for 4 July. I hope we will have a gooding [good time]. There a good hunting and good fishing on Indians reservation here. [1925-07-06 LJ]

Willie Ottogary Writes From Ft. Washakie, Wyo.

FORT WASHAKIE, JULY 6, 1925.   These Shoshone Indians are good condition. But they been celebrating Pioneer day [Fourth of July] for two day. And do same over to Lander too. But been rain on the Thursday night so they didn't celebrate. . . . But they have a big dinner afternoon the last Thursday. And everybody is there. But they get pretty time here at Fort Washakie and also they have an Indians dance about three night. They didn't cut their hay yet. They going cut their hay after this week and thing cost pretty high. The four is about $3.40 per hundred here. Everythings are pretty good this year. The grain and hay crop is good. The hay worth about $6.00 Dollars per ton here now. One Indian man died here two days ago. There was about 600 Indians are here on reservation here now. Yesterday some Indian boys ride a bucking horse and some races too. There was a good hunting and good fishing too here on the reservation now. We celebrate over to Lander last Saturday and we celebrate at Fort Washakie yesterday. [1925-07-11 LJ]

FORT WASHAKIE, JULY 9, 1925.   The Shoshone are been celebrating 4th July. But rain stop a big time. They celebrate about two day, they start on the 3 and 4 July. But the was rain on last Thursday and the road was pretty wet and muddy so they post pond [postponed] to 4 and 5, to celebrate annually Pioneer Day. We have acquainted many of Shoshone Indians, are here and also on Thursday, have a big feast and everybody was full up with some good stuff to eat, and also some Indians are help celebrate [for or with] some white men, at Lander, Wyoming. . . . And Arapahoe Indians is celebrate down there own town. It is about 30 miles east from here. These here Indians have horses, buck contest, and squaw race and more other sport. They are having a War dance and Wolf dance. Some Indians from Fort Hall Reservation here too, and from Olk [Oklahoma] Reservation here too. Nearly everyday have rain here and the grain and hay crops is looking pretty good. Today they have a celebrate because they have so much rain here. The weather is get cold here now. But all Indians well. One Indian died other night, and with heart trouble. [1925-07-14 BEJ]

FORT WASHAKIE, JULY 13, 1925. . . . Seem to me the hay crop is pretty late here. And haven't any hay and also have no stock too. Mr. Disquime is man got some horn stock. But he was lost some of his stock about year ago now. The amusement committee to gave order all his people must get through by 24 July so they going have a Sun Dance. But he said all [that] wish to be dancer get ready by that time. I was inquire the Mr. R. P. Hass gave me the information. So he gave some. He stated the grain crop and hay crop is splendid has been for 15 years and these Indians is rejoice about it now. I hope they are going splendid harvest. Miss Minnie Horn from Fort Hall reservation and Master Yamp-sia-tick has wedding for 5 days ago. They are making their home on this reservation. Some Bannock Indians and some Shoshone from Idaho here now. They soon going return home. Mr. Pah-wea and wife is return home about 3 days ago. He home is at Genry, Oklahoma. But he was visiting some his own relation and friend too. Some the Cheyenne Indians chief and more other is arrived here at 5 days ago. They may stay for the Sun Dance and they going Fort Hall Reservation after Sun Dance. Mr. Annies Tommy and family and his brother Mr. Peter McGill and family is here and they spent four July with these Indians too. They may return home after Sun Dance. Their home at Fort Hall, Idaho. [1925-07-18 LJ]

FORT WASHAKIE, JULY 14, 1925. These Indians has been cutting their hay now. They are going have a Sun Dance soon get through with hay. Mr. R. P. Hass, agent, is gave information the condition of the grain crop. He was stated their was a splendid. He here on the Reservation for the [last] 15 year. They Indians all been take care of their crop, then the such good crop and the hay crop good, too. They just put up the hay now. The hay price is now about $6.00 a ton. Some Indians hauling their hay to the Lander, for six dollars per ton. The Shoshone Indians good celebrate 3 and 4 July, here this year. But some been Lander to celebrate 4th and there was a splendid celebration down there. Miss Minnie Horn from Fort Hall Reservation, she was wed to Master Yamp-sia-Tick. He live here. They make their home here now on. The weather is pretty dry just now. [1925-07-17 BEJ]

FORT WASHAKIE, JULY 21, 1925. The Shoshone Indians are doing pretty good condition now. Some of the Indians buying some new wagon from agent. I expect they are going paid for wagon for 4 year. Everything doing fine here now. The weather getting too warm now. The . . . Shoshone a Sun Dance after their second crop hay. There will be a big gathering here Indians by that time. I expect every part of the country. I have been here about couple days and among the mountains and didn't find anything. We been up to the Lake up in the Rock[y?] Mountain. We could hardly get through the timbers. There was a trail through the timbers. There was a trail through among rock. We followed that trail when we came home last night, and also doing some fishing too. Everybody is ready for the Sun Dance here now. I expect go stay here about another month. But we doing some working here. I will give more news next week. Don't discourage this time Journal readers. [1925-07-25 LJ]

FORT WASHAKIE, JULY 28, 1925.   The Shoshone just through Sun Dance yesterday before noon. There was three diffrent tribes to join in the Sun Dance; one Ute Indian, 2 Bannock Indians, 57 Shoshone Indian boys in Sun Dance, and white people are see Sun Dance clear from New York and from Chicago. And there many white people witness to the Sun Dance. Mr. Oliver Hower was white man. He belong to St. Micheuts [Michaels] Mission or Supt. that Church . . . uttered prayer to the Sun Dance dancers. Here the word he said, ["]Almighty and ever-lasting God[.] Thou art our Father and we are all thy children. We come to thee at the close of this day knowing that thou art ever present and with us. We thank thee for thy blessing bestowed on our father and our father's fathers in time past. We hunger and thirst to know thee better and want to be filled with a desire to know and do thy Holy will. Grant to us, our father the fulfillment of every worthy desire. Bless and strength us in our affliction, make us strong and unselfish in our service to each other. Speed the day when our fellowship may be as inclusive as is thy love for us. And now father we pray thy special blessing upon these thy Indian children who are having part in this ancient tribal ceremony, and help us white people to be ever conscious of thy loving presence[.] Visit with thy healing spirit our diseased eyes, open our deaf ears, feed thy hungry and may we run the race of life and not be weary. These blessings we ask in thy Holy name. Amen.["]

All the Shoshone acpection [accepting] this man prayer. But these Indians are not through with their first crop hay yet. The wheat crop soon harvest time. The elevation is about 679. The weather is very warm and night is cold. All Indians are return home yesterday. There some Arapahoe Indians are been here to see the Sun Dance. They all return yesterday. But have a big dinner afternoon. Every[one] is enjoyed good jolly time. Mr. Annies Tommy and Mr. Pete McGill and family is going return to Fort Hall about next two week. Mr. Willy Indians and brother, son, are going remain here for winter. I expect Mr. Jim Wagon and family is remain here all winter long. [1925-08-01 LJ]

FORT WASHAKIE, JULY 28, 1925.   I am among Shoshone Indians now and finding everybody doing good now. But they haven't get through with their first crop yet. They may get through next week. They crop is good this year. I am acquainted many Indians and Arapahoe too. The grain crop soon start harvest. The weather getting warm and night get colder. . . . There was a splendid hunting and fishing on this reservation now. They just got through with Sun Dance. They have about 60 boys join in dance about three different tribe of Indians. Some Idaho Indians return last week and some still here yet. The Sun Dance start on 25th. July and lasted [until] 27. The man named Mr. Oliver Hower from Ethete, Wyoming. Supt. St. Micheuts [Michael's] Mission visit on the Sunday . . . July 26, 1925. He was cor-day [cordially] invided [invited] to pray to the Indian people and also some white.

In the evening in same day about 9 o'clock he come to the Sun Dance. He was pray for the Indians and everybody enjoyed his prayer both white and Indians. Mr. Harry George from Nevada is here. But he is doing prospecting in the mountain. There is good propect this country yet. Mr. Annies Tommy and Mr. McGill and family are soon return for Idaho Reservation, probably next two weeks. We are going to remain about another month here yet. [1925-08-04 BEJ]

FORT WASHAKIE, AUGUST 4, 1925. The Shoshone Indians are good condition. But some of them just got through with first hay. The grain nearly harvesting time now. They cut some early wheat and oats now. Some come here for the Sun Dance, but they come here too late. Some Shoshone Indians going to Fort Hall Reservation about Saturday; they going stay over there for all winter. And also Bannock Indians all went back just now. The weather is warm daytime and cold night time. We are visiting Mr. Nampy-dooah place here today before he going to Idaho Reservation. He expect going Idaho in the few [days]. On the train. But receive word from his uncle, Big Elk. But he want him come to see him before he died. And he received [word] three different time from him. He expect gone for a week. . . . Mr. Pete McGill be here all winter long here and two more Indians and families too be wintered here at Fort Washakie. In the next month there will be a wild Buffalo hunter [hunt] up around the Yellowstone park and it was open for every around here for the Shoshone. I guess is about 150 miles from here. There was a very good prospect up around mountain. The not much mines around this Reservation. [1925-08-10 LJ]

FORT WASHAKIE, AUGUST 11, 1925. These Shoshone Indians are doing fine. The season are pretty short, and frost be soon will be here next month . . . weather is getting little colder. On the Reservation is good hunting in fall the year, plenty of wild game here, and also good prospect up the mountains. There is some gold miner be found by Indians around among the Rocky Mountain region. We been visit two lakes which is pretty good fishing in that lake. Last week we visit Big lake and Dawgers lake ever known in the early days. The lake is about 3 miles length, and wide is about ½ mile. The Indians start cutting grain here now. . . . I expect we may return for Utah 20 day of August 1925. But fall be here soon. Mr. Peter Pingree is taken Mr. Nampy-dooah to the station Rock Springs a last week. He going to Fort Hall, Idaho, going visit his uncle, Mr. Big Elk, and he nearly dying. He may week or ten days or more. There was two death here all summer. Mr. Harry George still here and working for Mr. Roberts and Bisbuist [Baptist] minister on the Wind River. . . . [1925-08-15 LJ]

FORT WASHAKIE, AUGUST 18, 1925. The Shoshone Indians . . . start cutting grain last week and they very good harvest. I expect going about 40 bushel to the acres. And also nearly second crop hay ready to cut, and the weather is getting colder now. The season is pretty short here. They raise some vegetables here. But they can raise good watermelon and squash like they raise over on the Utah. There is very few fruit raise this country. But the season is too short. Mr. Chickey is still here now. But he was ready to going home on last Sunday. But broke his rear axle on his car last Saturday now he cannot go home for while. His home at Fort Hall, Idaho. Mr. Nampy-dooah

Willie Ottogary Writes From Ft. Washakie, Wyo.

FORT WASHAKIE, Wyo., Aug. 25.—The Shoshone Indians are doing good condition. The weather is good now, and colder at night. The harvesting grain is nearly done now. But the second crop hay is ready to cut. The season is pretty short, and the soon have a snow fly here about next month, and the colder weather soon be here now. The season is pretty short here. These Indians soon cut second hay now. They only cut two crop hay here. The hay is worth about $6.00 per ton now any where. We just come from Bull lake last night on our fishing trip up their. We have a real good time here. We acquainted with many Indians here. We are very glad to see so many Indians here. These Indians have a dance on last Sunday night. They having a good time. Mr. Nampy-dooah has been gone for two weeks now. He can come home any time. Mr. Harry George is still here now. But he expect going home some time next week some time. Mr. Shonshone Bob is coming visit his daughter here now. His home at White Rock, Utah. and also some Oklohoma Indians visiting here now. We are start for Utah next month or 1st Sept. All you Journal readers can hear me again. Come to Utah.

Willie Ottogary

WILLIE OTTOGARY.

Example of newspaper printing of one of Willie Ottogary's letters from Ft. Washakie, Wyoming. *From* The Journal, *Logan, Utah, August 29, 1925.*

has not return home yet. He went to Idaho about two weeks ago, on the important business. Now he return home any time this week. Mr. Shoshone Bob is coming visit his daughter here at Wind River. His home at White Rock Reservation, Utah. Mr. Big Elk is died at his home near Fort Hall Reservation. He is well known all over the country. But he is one of the Shoshone Chief. Mr. To-de-neda was kill by lightning here about week ago, and there is about more other Indians boys with him. They knock unconscious in they few hour. They doing nicely now. Mr. Jim Wagon and family still here now. But has have any money to go back on. He may remain here all winter long. [1925-08-22 LJ]

FORT WASHAKIE, AUGUST 25, 1925. . . . Soon have a snow fly here about next month, and the colder weather soon be here now. . . . These Indians soon cut second hay now. They only cut two crop hay here.[9] The hay is worth about $6.00 per ton now anywhere. We just come from Bull Lake last night on our fishing trip up there. We have a real good time here. We acquainted with many Indians here. We are very glad to see so many Indians here. These Indians have a dance on last Sunday night. They having a good time. . . . Mr. Harry George is still here now. But he expect going home some time next week. . . . Mr. Shoshone Bob is coming visit his daughter here now. His home at White Rock, Utah, and also some

Oklahoma Indians visiting here now. We are start for Utah next month or 1st Sept. All you Journal readers can hear me again. Come to Utah. [1925-08-29 LJ]

FORT WASHAKIE, AUGUST 31, 1925.   The Shoshone Indians are doing good now. The harvesting is nearly all done here now and they ready to get threshing now. . . . Some these Indians raised good crop hay, grain and vegetable. This country is good for raise stock. They have a plenty of the water this year. There was about 4 different Indian tribes been visiting Shoshone Indians here during this summer. Some of them went home already and some of them still here. . . . Mr. Jim Wagon is still here. But he been whip his wife last Saturday and try to divorce her. And took all his three children away from her. And he begged her go home with him yesterday. So he took her, and also Mr. Roger Wagon is divorce his wife too on same time. . . . Mr. Nampy-dooah has not return home from Idaho Reservation yet. He been gone for three week on the special business. Mr. Na-do-yo-kar and wife are waiting for him now. But he is one of his own relation. His home is at Cache, Oklahoma, and also Mr. Pawee [Pawnee?] and wife is here too. I expect we soon going on the Utah. This is last letter [from] Wyoming. All journal reader will read a Utah letter next week. [1925-09-05 LJ]

MALAD CITY, IDAHO, SEPTEMBER 10, 1925.   We come home from Wyoming last Monday night, Washakie. But we are at Malad City now. Some of our people are here at Malad to attend county fair. They start yesterday, and the horse Races start this afternoon today, and 12 race horses ship in from Pocatello Idaho, last night. Some our people are here now to see the races, and some went to Brigham City to Peach Day. We come through Jacksonhole [WY]. It is pretty rough country, and we crossed two mountains some places are pretty steep hill to climbs. Mr. Catch Toyahdook and wife made a business trip up Fort Hall Idaho last Monday. Mr. Geo. P. Sam and his wife are here at Malad to see big fair, and Mr. Warren Wongan been up Fort Hall too. Mr. Enos Pubigee is here with his Buckskin Nelly race mare here at Malad City try to match her for race. This is first time we ever been this fair. [1925-09-12 LJ]

WASHAKIE, SEPTEMBER 15, 1925.   These people are doing fine and dandy now. Well, I just return from Wyoming and the harvesting all over and ready for threshing and some already thresh.

The sugar beet crop is pretty good this year. Some our people been up Malad City to attend Oneida County Fair. It is good fair they ever had this year. Mrs. Jane S. Compton [from Compton's Photo Studio, Brigham City] was visiting Washakie last week and take some information old custom Indians, and take up the generol-ogy [genealogy]. . . . And also Miss Jennie Compton accompany . . . her. Mr. Catch Toyahdook is going down Farmington to buy some fruit. [1925-09-18 BEJ]

WASHAKIE, SEPTEMBER 16, 1925.   I was return from Wyoming about a week ago. But I find every body is fine and dandy. The grain and hay, sugar beet crop is splendid. The harvesting is all over now. The threshing is nearly done. These people are very good condition now. There was Mrs. Jane S. Compton from Brigham City visiting our town here last week with her girl Miss Jeanie Compton. But she was take up old costume [customs] away of Indian which was the old dance they have, War dance, Grass dance, Wolf dance, and Bear dance, etc., and also she take up a kind of old [information] about Mr. Frank W. Warner. The Indian by [boy] which was sold to Mr. Warner folk in the Willard in 1864. He was raise with well. He has a two half brothers living in our little town now. One of them is 1st Counselor [to] Bishop in the ward [Yeager Timbimboo. The other is Soquitch Timbimboo]. Mr. Thomas Pabawena been out Nevada some time ago last month. He was return home about two week ago. Mr. Tom Elk still work up Idaho Reservation now, but his little girl return home . . . to go school. He may return home this month. Mr. Catch Toyahdook and wife visiting his brother and some of his relation up Idaho Reservation last week ago. I and Mr. Ammon Pubigee went up Idaho Reservation on important business. [1925-09-19 LJ]

WASHAKIE, SEPTEMBER 23, 1925. . . . I find our people having a splendid a good crop—grain and sugar beet too. The threshing nearly through now. I and Mr. Ammon Pubigee made a business trip up Fort Hall reservation last week and also attend the county fair at Blackfoot, Idaho. The Eastern Shoshone Indian are doing good this year, have a good crop grain and hay, etc. I was return from Wyoming a week ago last Sunday. I was visiting some my relation Idaho and find not many as about 25 year ago. It is great loss since I was been there. I expect there is small families living over there now. We was coming through Bannock Creek Valley and find some our relation there. There is very small families living that place. They having a good crop this year. Well we return home about last Sunday or some time. Mr. Tom Elk and wife still working up there now. Mr. Catch Toyahdook been down to Farmington buying some fruit. Mr. George Tospanguitch was struck by automobile some time ago. But he is doing pretty good now. But he was motoring down Ogden that. This happened North Ogden. . . . Mrs. Hightop Joshua and Rachel Perdash was return home from Cache Valley last week. They motoring over there. Mr. Nephi Perdash been up to Blackfoot to seen a county fair. He return about week ago. Mr. Seth Pubigee and wife still up Idaho reservation yet. He working with his friend up there. I went over to Logan to see county fair. But they have so much rain and call it off for next year. While I was over to Logan and miss my old pal Mr. B. F. Riter, and feel sorry about him [Riter died while Ottogary was in Wyoming]. But I seen all my old acquaintants there. And everybody is doing good over there. Goodbye Journal readers. You people may read my writing long as I work for [Journal]. [1925-09-26 LJ]

WASHAKIE, SEPTEMBER 29, 1925. The crop pretty good this year and also sugar beet crop is good too. We have not through our threshing yet, most wheat haven't thresh. . . . Mr. George P. Sam is getting first prize on his oats raised at our little town here. Mr. George Mose are visiting at the home of Mr. George Tomock. He expect be here couple weeks or more. . . . Mr. Elias Pubigee is doing very nicely now. But got hurt on Roman [style] Race down Tremonton while they had a fair and he fall over two horses. He sprain one of his foot. . . . [1925-10-06 BEJ]

Box Elder County Fair, 1923. *Special Collections & Archives, Merrill Library, Utah State University.*

WASHAKIE, OCTOBER 1, 1925. . . . Some our people are been down Tremonton attended big Box Elder County Fair. . . . Everybody return home just now. The crop is splendid this year, and also sugar beet crop is good too. The wheat near-ly all thresh now. The most is grain is thresh now. Mr. George P. Sam get first Prize down to fair at Tremonton on his oats is raised here in our town. Mr. George Mose is visiting his father-in-law's place, Mr. George Tomock here in our town. He be here about couple week or more. Mr. Soquitch Timbimboo and wife just return home from Cache Valley on last Sunday. He was motoring about two week or more. Mr. Seth Pubigee just return Idaho reservation early this morning and more with three boys. He come for the Box Elder County Fair at Tremonton. Mr. War Bonnet is visiting our little [town] here last week, with his whole fam-ily. Some of our horses win the races down to Tremonton on this big Box Elder Fair. . . . [1925-10-03 LJ]]

WASHAKIE, OCTOBER 13, 1925. . . . There is some Indians working in sugar beet field down near Garland factory. And some . . . of them taken order to dig there sugar beet. But most of the wheat haven't thresh yet. They expect to thresh soon as can and our fall crop put in already just now. Mr. Tom Elk and family return home other day. He expect going back Idaho in the few days and rent one of the Indians farm up there.

   Mr. George Mose is still here, and he was helping his father-in-law in the sugar beet field. Mr. Harry J. Dixon with his crew is working for Jap about 4 mile east of Tremonton. Mr. Enos Pubigee and I made a business trip up Idaho Reservation last week ago. Mr. Bishop George M. Ward been down Salt Lake annual conference

Seth Eagle, or Pubigee, and his wife, Iva, or Ivy Pojennie, Woonsook Eagle. *Courtesy Mae Timbimboo Parry.*

too. Mr. Elias Pubigee doing pretty good with his sprain ankle about two week ago. We have a very stormy day on Sunday and Monday last. I and Mr. Enos Pubigee motoring over to McCammon, Idaho on the last Sunday, and return same night, too. Mr. Johnny Jack's [Johny Dick in 1925-10-17 LJ] little baby girl die about on last Sunday morning and buried here at Washakie cemetery last Monday before-noon. [1925-10-16 BEJ]

1925-10-17 LJ [Not included, mostly duplicate of 1925-10-16 BEJ]

WASHAKIE, OCTOBER 20, 1925.   These Indians are doing splendid. They have a real good crops wheat here and the sugar beet is splendid crop too. They was start har-vesting the beet crop about last week ago. The beet pretty good this year. The wheat near all thresh. But there is very small grain haven't thresh yet. They expect the thresher their grain this week. . . . Mr. George Mose is still here and with his family. They working a sugar beet field too. Their home is Ruby Valley, Nevada. And also Mr. Harry J. Dixon is working a sugar beet field too, and more others. Their home at Elko, Nevada. Captain Mr. Harry J. Dixon wanted some kind meet-ing down to near Riverside, Utah. But he want send some paper to our lawyer at Washington, D. C. These lawyers working on our claim here on the state of Utah. Mr. Dick Arritch was looking for some job beet topping. There was several Indians from Fort Hall Reservation here and they also working sugar beet, too. [Inserted from 1925-10-17 LJ: "We have a regular rain storm here last week and its help our fall crop."] [1925-10-23 BEJ]

WASHAKIE, OCTOBER 20, 1925.   The people are here splendid crop wheat this year
and also have a splendid crop sugar beet too. They start their harvest sugar beet
about week. . . . Mr. Tom Elk and family were return home some time ago last week
ago. But he is work for the Moroni Timbimboo. . . . Mr. Harry J. Dixon, chief of
Nevada, is here. But he want to hold some kind of the meeting near Belmont
[Belmont or Riverside], Utah, on the next Monday night. He want send paper to
our Lawyer. Mr. C. [Charles] H. Merillat, Washington. These Lawyer working on
our claim. The Lawyer live at Washington, D. C.[10] [1925-10-24 LJ]

WASHAKIE, NOVEMBER 3, 1925.   The weather getting cold now. We had nearly get
threshing now. And all our sugar beets all harvest, and done last. The crop was
splendid this year. But we had a storm . . . [and] snowing all last night. It is about
two inches snow lay on [ground] this early morning, and is still snow now. Some
of our men and women is still working in sugar beets field down there to around
north Garland factory. Well they was pretty anxious get through with beets. Mr.
Annies Tommy going through our town on the Brigham and Malad Stage yesterday to Brigham City on the important business matter. Mr. Jim Wagon just come
from Wyoming about last week ago. And he purchase our old Ford car last week.
Then he went down Garland to topping sugar beets. . . . Mr. Brownie Mose and
with his boy still he help Mr. James Pabawena field in sugar beet. He home out
Ruby Valley, Nevada. He expect going stay next month. . . . [1925-11-06 BEJ]

WASHAKIE, NOVEMBER 7, 1925.   The weather is getting cold . . . now. The sugar beet
crop nearly through here now. The weather is getting pretty wet weather now. We
have about 3 or 4 inch snow here last Monday and the snow all gone. The road is
impossible to travel through. They may get their sugar beet [done] this week. I
hope the weather get pretty good again now on. Mr. Annies Tommy went on a
business trip down Brigham City on Monday last. He return home this morning.
He's at Fort Hall, Idaho. Mr. Geo. P. Sam went down Honeyville other day and
doing some business there. . . . There was some Indians from Nevada is still here
topping sugar beet. . . . Mr. Harry J. Dixon is still down near Tremonton working
in sugar beet. He expect to return home as getting through beet. His home at Elko,
Nevada. . . . [1925-11-07 LJ]

WASHAKIE, NOVEMBER 18, 1925.   The weather is getting very cold and the winter
soon be here. The sugar beet is [nearly] all done. But they pile here in our [town]
to get ready for [railroad] car. I expect the about 2,000 ton beet raise here this summer. I don't know how [much] there is now. Our fall work is all done about three
week ago. Mr. Harry J. Dixon and his company return last Tuesday. But he want to
stop in Salt Lake City in the few day. And all his company too. And want next
stop at Deep Creek Indian Reservation. . . . Mr. Nephi Perdash with his father is
motoring last Saturday. Mr. Dick Arritch was motoring down Garland last Sunday.
Some of our Indians still working down Garland but they may be finish there soon.
None of our boys took part in big Elk hunt yet. [1925-11-21 LJ]

WASHAKIE, NOVEMBER 25, 1925.   . . . Soon the winter is here now. Some of our people are still working sugar beet down to north Garland factory now. The sugar beet

Shoshone woman with turkey. *RG 75, TLA, Box/Folder 28, PO-8, Still Pictures Branch, National Archives.*

nearly through with their beet here now. There was about 6 cars load ship out our town about last. I expect there is about half the sugar beet done here now. I guess they through by next week. They have a good crop of sugar beet ever had for long time. They went about 15 ton per acres. Mr. Comrath with his two brothers went home last two week ago. Their home is at Fort Hall Reservation. Mr. Brownie Mose with his boy return last week. Their home is Ruby Valley, Nevada. . . . Mr. Ammon Pubigee is motoring down Fielding Station last Saturday and taking his son home from working. Mr. Jack Ramsey and wife is still working on the sugar beet. His home at Fort Hall, Idaho. He may return next ten days. . . . Mr. Enos Pubigee was purchase an old second hand sulkey plow from Utah Farm Implements Co. about last week. . . .[11] [1925-11-28 LJ]

WASHAKIE, DECEMBER 9, 1925.   . . . Well sir, all our sugar beet done here about week ago. There was about 12 carload ship out our little town. Some our people are return home from Garland and sugar beet all done now. One young man was died down Garland Hospital last Friday night. His remain was brought here from funeral. A Mr. Amos Moemberg he was well known up Idaho and Utah. But has some relations living up there too. Some of them coming down for his funeral. The funeral service held at Washakie ward meeting house about 2 o'clock last Monday. He [buried] here at Washakie Cemetery. But his relation went home on last Tuesday, up to Idaho and he was well known all over the country, and he left his wife and three children behind. He has mother and sister too. . . . Mr. Amos [Ammon or Enos] Pubigee, I and with my two boys been over to Penrose, Utah, and picking some Christmas Turkey about last week. [1925-12-12 LJ]

WASHAKIE, DECEMBER 23, 1925. We have storm weather other day here and didn't amount anything, no snow here yet. All our people are coming home from their work now. We having a fairly winter weather now. It is warm weather now. . . . No snow now. People are rejoicing over the Christmas is coming. Well going have a Christmas program on Christmas day, which is song, comic speech, select reading and dialogs [i]n our own tongue etc. I hope we a real good old time. Mr. Enos Pubigee and his brother Mr. Elias Pubigee been down Ogden and purchase an old second hand Ford car about last week. And also Mr. Joseph Woonsook and with son Mr. Henry Woonsook been down Salt Lake City buying some deer hide. Mr. Moroni Timbimboo is getting around and was bit by a rabby [rabid] dog here in our town and they kill a dog last. Mrs. Amos Moemberg [Mary] was down Tremonton last week and doing some Xmas shopping. I and boys was busy getting some Christmas tree out for Tremonton and Garland people. Mr. Tom Elk and Mr. Jacob Peyope hasn't return from Idaho yet. They was on the big rabbit hunt. They expect return before Xmas time. . . . Mr. Seth Pubigee was return home from Idaho Reservation last Saturday. Mr. George Mose and with his mother-in-law was motoring down Salt Lake City about week ago. [1925-12-28 LJ]

Willie Ottogary Writes from Fort Hall Reservation, Idaho

FORT HALL, IDAHO, DECEMBER 30, 1925. I am up here to Fort Hall, Idaho. We come up last Saturday. I expect be here [until] next Thursday. These Indians having a big gathering for Christmas day, and different Indians dances which was a Warm dance, War dance, and also Grass dance, etc.[12] There was so many gathering here about 5 miles west of Fort Hall School 5½ miles northwest of Pocatello city. We seen so many our old acquaintance here this section the country and also seen our own relation and friends. And weather is getting little bit cold here now. No snow here just now, in the night the heavy foggy. These Indians say there will be no snow this winter. There was a another gathering here before the New Year's Day, and they doing some [same] kind dance. Some of Washakie boys were here now, to see a big time they having. And also Mr. Catch Toyahdook is here to visit his brother, Mr. Sam, and more his relatives too. These Indians are some farming work. And crop is very splendid this summer. There was about three death last month ago. Mr. Dr. John Dan is sick in bed here about last fall and he is still sick and he is improving pretty slowly now. I and Mr. Tonhee and boys been shooting jack rabbits yesterday a crossed Snake River out toward Sterling, Idaho. [1926-01-02 LJ]

WASHAKIE, JANUARY 7, 1926. The weather pretty good this winter. The night is cold now. We haven't any snow here just now. It is feel like spring time. . . . Some of our boys been up Idaho on the big rabbit hunting. They all return last night. We have a nice programme on New Year's Day which is Comic Talk, Select reading, Songs, etc. Mr. George Mose still here with his father-in-law here. Mr. Soquitch Timbimboo is up around again. But he was laid up with a mucial Phumisum [probably muscular rheumatism, see 1926-04-10 LJ]. About three or more month in the bed. Mr. Kippetchew Noragan and wife went to Logan City before New Year day. But he hasn't return home yet. Master Herbert Pabawena went up Idaho last week. He is going stay up there rest of the winter. The Indians are up Idaho, still having a Warm dancing. . . . Mr. Catch Toyahdook was been up Idaho about last two week ago and he visit his folk and relatives there. [1926-01-11 LJ]

WASHAKIE, JANUARY 13, 1926.   . . . Our boys going big rabbit hunting next Thursday, and they going have a dance and Friday night. They . . . choose a side on this big hunt and the lose side going pay for the music. . . . I hope we going have a real old good time by doing this. We have a dandy weather this year. We have no snow now—every body feeling good that. The was not much sickness this year. Our day school running this year. The was about 25 children going school here in our little town. It is was a good school. The boys and girls learning fast now, and have a good teacher. . . . Mr. Catch [Toyahdook] having a car trouble here other day he could not start his Ford car. Then he take it down Garland to going fix up again. He expect some matter of the engine. . . . Mr. Jim Wagon is motoring down Tremonton yesterday. Mr. Enos Pubigee been down on my ranch yesterday. But he is fixing his back spring his Ford car and he broke it other day. Mr. George Mose is sent home for his saddle and saddle come on the express last week, and he is breaking some horses now. Miss Susie Highyou was received a bad news from Nevada and cousin died out Elko, Nevada. His name is Mr. Tomy Whaney. But he was born here on the Utah and raised here and school here for several year. But he was about 40 year of age, and well known a section of the country. Mr. Tom Elk still trapping here and he was a great trapping in our town. But he catch several coyote and some skunks, etc. Mr. Moroni Timbimboo was been out Calton [Corinne or Clarkston], Utah, some time . . . ago, and doing little hunting out there, and also Mr. Warren Wongan was accompanied him. Mr. Soquitch Timbimboo is getting a profect [perfect] well just now. [1926-01-16 LJ]

WASHAKIE, JANUARY 20, 1926.   The weather as has been change since last Monday. It is cold weather now. But we have about one foot snow here now, and it is good sleighing yet. This first time snow we seen here in community. Well sir, we had a splendid good old time here last Friday night and everybody was turn good. We all in join us dance. But the lose side pay for the music and they going have another big rabbit hunt next week. Mr. Moroni Timbimboo and wife was visiting his brother-in-law up to Fort Hall Reservation, Idaho, and return home last a week ago, and also he was visit his cousin Mr. Warren [Wayne] Warner up to Tehee [Tyhee], Idaho. . . .[13] Mr. Enos Pubigee was take his wife to Dr. treatment down Deweyville station last Saturday night. She is getting pretty good now. . . . Mr. Moroni Timbimboo and wife and also Miss Towange Timbimboo [wife of Soquitch Timbimboo] was been down Garland and doing some shopping last Friday before noon. Mr. [Ray] Diamond still mail carrier for our town. He been on the job for 6 year now. Mr. Warren Wongan was been over to Logan temple and seal to his wife, and also Mr. Moroni Timbimboo take him over to Logan on his Ford truck. And they was return in the same day. This the last part of last week. Mrs. Sear Poncho was down to Miss Dr. Prue-Cannon [Buchanan] at Deweyville under the medicine treatment just. She was improving pretty slow. Her home is up to Fort Hall Reservation, Idaho. She stay her grandma place here. Mr. Henry Woonsook little baby girl is pretty sick, she might not live for several days. Master Herbert Pabawena was motoring up to Idaho and he was nearly starving when he came home, and he hasn't taste food for several day and he run out money and he glad

when he came home, and he is about 17 year of age. There was a few old folks living our little town yet. [1926-01-23 LJ]

WASHAKIE, JANUARY 27, 1926.   Our people are rejoice soon spring time is come. We
have a snow about 9 inch and the weather pretty cold just now. We have much
sickness here now. Some of our people had a influenza now. Some of them getting
over the flue. There was a baby girl sick now. She was daughter of the Mr. Henry
Woonsook and they was expect not live no longer. She been sick for one month.
Last Saturday and Sunday there was a Quarterly Stake Conference held at Malad
City. Some of our people attended Conference up there both times. We haven't
any meeting here last Sunday on account the Stake Conference. I expect some visitors from Salt Lake City was there. They have a real good Conference. Mrs. Sear
Poncho was return home about two week. She was very sick the time she come
here. But her health was proved while she under Dr. Treatment. She was first class
condition after get through with treatment. I expect she going surprise her husband. He know her health pretty bad condition before she left home. Last Friday
night we have a white man dance. But we have a real jolly time the evening, and
everybody enjoyed themselves. . . . Mr. Moroni Timbimboo and wife has been
down Garland on some matter of business. Mr. Jim Wagon was motoring down
Tremonton and accompanied Mr. Bishop Catch Toyahdook other day. Mr. Enos
Pubigee and with Chester Ottogary was motoring down Tremonton first part of last
week. Mr. Geo. Mose was been up Malad City last Saturday. Some or our boys want
going down Brigham City to see big boxing contest. Master Chester Ottogary was
on the programme. To going [boxing] match one of the Brigham City lad tonight.
In the Brigham City on the January 27, 1926. I expect am going down tonight see
the big boxing down Brigham City, Utah. [1926-01-30 LJ]

WASHAKIE, FEBRUARY 2, 1926.   The weather getting warmer here just now. But snow
commence thaw. And some of our people are sick. Mr. Henry Woonsook little baby
died here last week. And funeral service held at ward Chapel on the last Thursday,
January 28, 10 o'clock. Mr. Bishop Yeager Timbimboo was down Brigham City to
attend court, and also Mr. Joe Woonsook. Mr. Kippetchew Noragan on the same
business. . . . Some our boys been hunting Jack rabbits last week—they slaughter few
of them. Miss Amos Moemberg was a proud parents as baby boy born some time last
week.[14] I was a business trip over to Logan City on last Thursday. While over in city
I get in touch with Mr. Charlie Harris the geniel [genial] Harris Music Co. expert,
and Harris was knowing some the great warriors and the chief of the Shoshone
tribes in this [land] in the early days when the Indians was running wild. And after
made a peace treaties the Indians had made a good friend for every body. They don't
have fight since in the year 1863. Well sir, Mr. Charlie Harris make me a present
nice little Edison Phonograph.[15] But he like our people. And he say was one time
Indians himself &c. Mr. George Mose still living here now, he expect return home
next summer. Mr. Enos Pubigee and Master Chester R. Ottogary motoring down
Tremonton on the last Friday. But have a nice dance here on the Friday night. But
everybody enjoyed very much I expect going have a another one soon. Mr. Bishop
George M. Ward, on the court about last Saturday and he accompany with

"Kickapoo Dan" Ottogary (above)
full-blooded Washakie Indian, will be
one of the headline attractions at the
Legion boxing program to be held
next Wednesday, (bargain and bar-
becue day.) He meets the Bear River
slugger, Jackie Andrews.

Chester Ottogary in boxing pose.
From Box Elder News, *December 10,
1926.*

Charles M. Harris, owner of Harris
Music Company, Logan. *From Noble
Warrum, ed.*, Utah Since Statehood,
Historical and Biographical,
*Chicago-Salt Lake: The S. J. Clark
Publishing Company, 1919; Special
Collections & Archives, Merrill
Library, Utah State University.*

Mr. Ebraham [Abraham] Hall from West Portage on real land matter. Mr. Soquitch Timbimboo is feeling very splendid just now. He been laid up Phrumice [probably muscular rheumatism] for three month and is well as ever now. And I was received a letter from Harry J. Dixon yesterday. But he received letter from our attorney at Washington D. C. on the matter our claim. But he want us people have a big council meeting right away. I expect we going to attended that now, etc. I am going up Washakie now. [1926-02-06 LJ]

WASHAKIE, FEBRUARY 11, 1926. . . . The snow nearly all gone by this time, and we had little rain storm last night here. Our is rejoice when spring time is coming near. There was only two death here this winter. Well I was made a business trip down Salt Lake City last Monday and return last night. And also Master Chester R. Ottogary was accompanied me. Mr. Kippetchew Noragan went down Ogden last Monday and return same day. He come up on the evening train and doing some business. . . . [This] winter seem me to almost like fall weather so far. Mr. Soquitch Timbimboo is well as ever. But he was laid up with a mucial Phreumtism [muscular rheumatism] for 4 month and he is getting first class condition now. Our day school running pretty good this year. Miss Hogson teachering our school this year. Well sir, I and sons coming over on the 16 this month again to see Jim Rose [Ross]. [1926-02-13 LJ]

Willie Ottogary Tells Story about His Boy's Fistic Bouts[16]

WASHAKIE, FEBRUARY 17, 1926.   The weather change here yesterday. And we had storm weather here. Start snowing last Monday night and still snowing Tuesday all day along. And snow about 5 or 6 inch, here now. We was down Salt Lake City last Monday. But my boy (Kickapoo Dan) [Chester's boxing name], C. R. Ottogary was fight on Monday night with Young Loader from Bingham Canyon and Kickapoo Dan knock out him out in second round. But came up to Logan City last night and Kick Dan was going fight with Jimmy Ross at Logan, and Chester R. Ottogary big thumb sprain pretty bad. But we bring his brother, Master Custer Ottogary for substituted, or took, his place. Well he was pretty good. I expect this boy was surprise the Logan people to boxing with clever boxer, Master Jimmy Ross. Well sir this my boy never been ring before, this is first time he in ring. He knock out Master Ross in second round. I expect he will box again here some time. But he is only 16 year old boy. Some our boys kind disappointed they was going see that fight. And the so stormy could not go. The road is impossible to travel through. All our people are very good condition. [1926-02-17 LJ]

WASHAKIE, FEBRUARY 24, 1926. . . . Mr. Enos Pubigee and Master Chester R. Ottogary motoring down Tremonton latter part of the last week. . . . Mr. Seth Pubigee was motoring down Tremonton for part of last week and accompany his brother-in-law Mr. Henry Woonsook. Mr. Kippetchew Noragan going down Brigham City this morning and on the important business down there. Mrs. Sear Poncho was died here on the last Thursday. But she was buried on last Sunday. Her funeral service held at ward meeting house . . . and her little boy baby was died here last Saturday about 4 o'clock, and they have a funeral service same time. Mr. Sear Poncho her husband and with his mother was came down from Idaho

Brigham City-Malad
Stage Line
SCHEDULE

Effective Sept. 20th, 1925
INTER-STATE BUSINESS ONLY

Leave Read Down		Arrive Read Up
10:30 A. M.	Malad City	3:55 P. M.
10:40 A. M.	Cherry Creek	3:45 P. M.
10:45 A. M.	Henderson	3:40 P. M.
10:50 A. M.	Woodruff	3:35 P. M.
11:00 A. M.	Portage	3:25 P. M.
11:10 A. M.	Washakie	3:15 P. M.
11:25 A. M.	Plymouth	3:00 P. M.
11:35 A. M.	Fielding	2:50 P. M.
11:40 A. M.	Riverside	2:45 P. M.
Arrive	Garland	Leave
11:50 A. M.		2:35 P. M.
Leave		Arrive
11:55 A. M.		2:30 P. M.
Arrive	Tremonton	Leave
12:00 A. M.		2:25 P. M.
Leave		Arrive
12:05 A. M.		2:20 P. M.
12:15 A. M.	Bear River City	2:00 P. M.
12:35 A. M.	Corinne	1:50 P. M.
Arrive		Leave
12:50 P. M.	Brigham City	1:35 P. M.

NOTE—We make connections with W. I. C. Coaches at Brigham Citiy for Ogden Salt Lake and Logan. We also meet coaches from Salt Lake, Ogden and Logan on return trip.

Advertisement: "Brigham City-Malad Stage Line Schedule," from *Oneida County Enterprise*, October 29, 1925.

Reservation and attended her funeral. They return home on the Sunday. And also Mr. Mule Pocatello was accompany him too and more other two women. Master Fosy Peyope is here now. I expect he going stay with his parents now. We have had a dance on the George Washington Birthday and also had a nice programme. . . . Mr. George Mose and family is stay here for the winter. His children went school here all winter along. Some of our people had a flue and most of them getting over with now. Today we have another snow stormy weather here now. . . . It is bad muddy road now. It is impossible to travel through. [1926-02-27 LJ]

WASHAKIE, MARCH 3, 1926.   The people are here good condition . . . but some of us under the weather and our people had a flue now. But they getting pretty good just now. I expect soon our spring is here. But our people are rejoice is here. The hay is scarce here now. The hay price is about $6.00 to $7.00 per ton around our vicinity. There was only 4 deaths this winter. Last Saturday some of men were up to Malad City to attend Union Priesthood Meeting held at Malad City. Well sir, Mr. Tom Elk still trapping just now, and also Mr. Jacob Peyope is trapper in town too. . . . I was been down Salt Lake City about last Monday to see a big fight that night. But my two boys was on the programme. These boys was fight against three colored boys. But the fight was last 3 minutes. But this was pretty fast going in the ring. The lots of peoples witness this three colored boys knock out. The boys was pretty good condition after getting through fighting with three smokeys.[17] This Kickapoo Dan knock out two colored while the General Custer Ottogary fighting the other one. But these two last one knock out the same time. And also these two boys go match again in Salt Lake City next Monday night on the 8th March, and the also a new boy coming in for the boxing contest. His names Mr. Enos Pubigee, and he never been in ring before. Well any body want see this new boy while coming down Salt Lake City next Monday night. I am the manager of these boys. If you read about them you wish you could see them. These boys training at home, and they boxing every Saturday afternoon up to Washakie. Master Chester Ottogary or Kickapoo Dan want at Brigham City 3 week again. These my boys made a pretty good [boxing] records so far, etc. [1926-03-06 LJ]

WASHAKIE, MARCH 10, 1926. . . . The boys was trying getting up Basket Ball team now. Why last night our play with West Portage boys. And they got beat. I hope our boys getting a good if had enough practice. . . . Mr. Soquitch Timbimboo and wife been down Deweyville and have seen Dr. down there. But his wife is sick. . . . I was been down Salt Lake City on the Monday, March 8, 1926. Two my boys been on the boxering contest. Master Chester Ottogary was fight with the Bob Young, colored boy in Salt Lake City, in about 4 round. And his brother, Master Custer Ottogary was fighting with Pete Nordoff, Salt Lake City, in the four around bout. And also Mr. Enos Pubigee was boxing with Mr. John Soaker and all the three boys win [with knockouts] the fight in Salt Lake City last Monday night. I am here at Logan just now on matter of business. I am going back on the 8 o'clock car [train] tonight. [1926-03-13 LJ]

WASHAKIE, MARCH 17, 1926. . . . Spring is here now, and we start our spring work is now. But some of us going plant some sugar beet this year. I expect they was start contract now. And we are poor condition in the line of foodstuff. And we short- age on the hay this spring. The hay price is about $6.00 to $7.00 per ton around our vicinity now. Our agent want a build new school here in our little town. It soon start work on it. Well it will be good one. . . .[18] Mr. Seth Pubigee and Chester R. Ottogary motoring down Elwood last Sunday. . . . Master Chester Ottogary got his left ear hurt last Friday night down Brigham City in the boxing contest. But he is under Dr. treatment just now. But his ear getting pretty good now. He will laid off for couple week and he will fight again. Master Custer Ottogary and Mr. Henry Woonsook in the fight programme down Salt Lake City last Monday night. But we lose one fight. Mr. Henry Woonsook was knock out in the second arounds [round]. Master Custer E. Ottogary is knock out his men in the first round. But he good condition after his men out. There was a pretty fast fighting these two boys between Master Custer E. Ottogary and Jack Kelley from Salt Lake City. And we was return home yesterday noon. I expect our boys going fight in the Logan about 30 this month. But my boys need lots training going some this fight. It is hard for the boys to fight. [1926-03-20 LJ]

WASHAKIE, MARCH 24, 1926.   Our people is getting busy putting in spring grain now. There is only 3 death this winter and no one sick just now. But they are very good condition so far. The weather getting warm here now. Our day school is doing pretty [good] now. There was about more than twenty children going school here our little town. Well sir, we had have a fine weather this winter. The hay pretty scarce around here . . . price is about $7.00 per ton. Mr. George [?] was on the sick list last week. But he getting improvement very slowly, and he was weak health. I and Pabawena brothers has been down Ogden last week on the matter of the business. It is land business. We return home last week. Mr. George Elk was accompany too. . . . Mrs. George P. Sam was been down Ogden on some business. Mr. Jim John Neaman trying to gather some boys to play base ball team here in our town. But he suppose to be a team manager. Well, Mr. George Mose is still living here our town. His home out Nevada. Well he may return next summer. But his children going school here just now. My boys are coming over to Logan next Tuesday, March 30, 1926. Mr. J. C. Allen and family is visiting my place on last Sunday and he want boys come over to Logan [for boxing match]. But we all arrangement to willing going Logan boxing and also Master Ed. Wagon on the program too. This will be a curtain riser. One kid from Tremonton to box him. His name was Don Luke. He is . . . Mr. Dr. Luke boy in Tremonton, etc. [1926-03-27 LJ]

WASHAKIE, MARCH 31, 1926.   We have a storm weather here all day yesterday. But and snow about 4 inch here this morning. The people are good condition, and no one sick just now. Some of our people are been over to Logan yesterday to see the fighting there and return home last night. Our boys have boxing over there lose two fight and one winner. There is quite big crowd to witness the fight. Our boys show last night. But Kickapoo Dan is hurt his ear again. But he want lay off again and three week more again. He was lose his game [bout] last night on account his ear. Mr. George P. Sam been over to Logan to see a fight. Also Mr. Ammon Pubigee accompany Mr. George P. Sam. Mr. Catch Toyahdook tawe [take] his minner [minor] boy over to Logan Ed. Wagon on the same business.[19]

Our fall crop wheat looking pretty good so far. We nearly through with our spring work just now. . . . Mr. Jim Wagon is working for Mr. John Oiler East Garland. Mrs. George P. Sam was motoring down Ogden last week ago. Mr. Jim Peyope and wife was a proud parent and new born baby girl about two week ago. I expect some our people want going Conference in Salt Lake City this coming Saturday. . . . I try getting more news next [time]. I was read in Telegram an Indian from Washakie to fight down Salt Lake City last Monday night. This Indian not belong to Washakie. I expect he come from some other country. But he only fake boy. I never know this name, Chief Gonzales. I expect he was one Mexican boy. [1926-04-03 LJ]

WASHAKIE, APRIL 7, 1926.   The people are here good condition since last death. We have had stormy weather here about 4 or 5 days here just now. And it is real nice rain we had and there was a plenty of moisture in the ground now. But good for our fall crop, and looking good after this nice rain we had. I expect we going have a good crop this year. But we had all dry farm. But very few got irrigate land here. And our day school is good this year. . . . Some our people going down to Salt Lake City attend the big Conference. Mr. George M. Ward and wife went down on Sunday

Women at an LDS General Conference, probably in fall 1925: "S. L. City conference. Emmeline P. Neaman, Nellie Pabawena, Lucy Alex, Positze Noragan, Margaret Neaman, Lena Wagon." *Courtesy Mae Timbimboo Parry.*

Left to right: Kippie Noragan, Eddie Wagon, Mose Neaman, Everett Neaman, James Pabawena, Linford Neaman, John Pabawena, Jim Wagon, and Dave Pabawena, at an LDS General Conference, probably in fall 1925. *Courtesy Mae Timbimboo Parry.*

morning for Conference and also his two counselors to the Conference. Mr. James Pabawena and his two brothers went down Salt Lake City to attend conference, and also with their wives too. Mr. Soquitch Timbimboo is well as ever. He been sick all winter long with a musceler phmetisum [muscular rheumatism]. We going have a fight with some white boys down Tremonton on the 13 of these month. It is all ready fixed up now. Well I guess we going stop fight after this one. [1926-04-10 LJ]

WASHAKIE, APRIL 14, 1926.   The weather is getting warmer just now. But the cold passed away, and the summer is coming and wheat crop is looking pretty fine now. We will have a good crop this year, and our spring work is nearly done. The sugar beet hasn't planed [planted] yet. They getting ready the ground for sugar beet just now. There three boys from Idaho Reservation visiting at Mr. George P. Sam place . . . last week. But they went home on last Saturday. And These boys was related to Mr. George P. Sam. Mr. Catch Toyahdook and wife went over to Logan doing some temple working. . . . Mr. T. Elk expect going up to Idaho Res. for work. I and boys been down Salt Lake City on the same business. But the boys on the program last Monday and all boys win Battle Royal with negro boys and also master Kickapoo Dan knock out Mr. Battling Barbar in the second round. The boys going have a boxing with some farm boys at Tremonton tomorrow night about 8:30. I expect our win again. We coming from Salt Lake City yesterday, and having a good time. Well I expect will go out Nevada on 20 this month, and some other boys important business out there. [1926-04-17 LJ]

WASHAKIE, APRIL 29, 1926.   The summer soon be here. And our people are rejoicing over the everything good here. But our wheat crop looking very splendid this spring. I expect going have a good crop here this year. Our sugar beet all ready just now. Our boys been organized a Baseball team this coming year. They played with West Portage boys and they going play again next Friday. Their big doing. Mr. Hyrum Wongsaw was motoring down Tremonton about last week. But Mr. Seth Pubigee and Chester Ottogary was motoring up Idaho Reservation last week and return home last Friday. Mr. Chief Gonzales is an Indian, home at down New Mexico. But he stay with Mr. Henry Woonsook place. And he was a fighter and he looking for fight all the time. Well sir, I am coming home from Nevada about last Sunday. And everything looking pretty. We visit Twin Falls, Burley, Idaho, and the grain crop looking very splendid up Twin Falls country and also around Burley country too. We left off at Wells, Nevada, and coming through the Contract [?], Rosein [Boise?], Idaho, Twin Falls, Burley, American Falls, Pocatello, Idaho, and Malad City, Idaho, and then home. I expect may going out again some time next month. We find everything splendid out there. Some them Shoshones working for ranch man. These Indian out Nevada is homeless Indian. They haven't got any land for their own name. They ask government need help and they was very bad condition just now. Their numbered at about over thousand Western Shoshone out there to Nevada, just roming [roaming] around the country, etc. [1926-05-01 LJ]

WASHAKIE, MAY 5, 1926.   Our people are getting first class condition. But we had a splendid nice rain yesterday and today. Some of our boys are start shear sheep now.

The spring is pretty going fast and soon spring is nearly gone by. The grain crop is looking pretty good now. But our spring crop is come good now. . . . Our boys been playing [baseball?] with Plymouth boys. Our boys win game. Last Friday have big program up to West Portage. The day programme was a boxing contest and game ball. And we have a good old time up there. And some our people went up to Malad City to attend stake quarterly conference up there. About two days. Start Saturday morning about 10 o'clock and Sunday too. . . . There was two Bannock boys visiting last week and return home a Fort Hall Reservation. . . . Mr. Tom Elk and family too moved up Idaho Reservation last week ago. He going work up there. And he is leasing some land from one Indian on the Reservation. He expect remain there all summer. . . . My boys been boxing Monday night. But they was boxing with Steele brothers. I expect these boys were even boxing so far. Mr. Custer Ottogary was boxing older brother. Chester Ottogary was boxing younger brother. Both young brother was K. O. both side. But they show good boxing so far. Well this was last time boxing for the season. But we are return home yesterday afternoon. Mr. Soquitch and family coming down my farm down Elwood, Utah yesterday and stay for while this week. And he may return for next week or more. . . . I expect our boys may go Salt Lake City to play baseball some time this summer. We are going arrange that . . . We had good baseball team this year. We had about four inch rain here last night and it is very splendid rain we had for long time now. [1926-05-08 LJ]

WASHAKIE, MAY 13, 1926. . . . The crop is looking pretty good this spring. Our school soon summer vacation, this week is last school for the last year school. Well the children are rejoicing when quit school. The people have no sick here just now. The crop is good for this year. Some of our people been shear sheep for Mr. Charlie Peterson down near the east Tremonton. And also some went up to Idaho to shear sheep. They be gone week or ten days. Mr. Moroni Timbimboo is the boss for shear gang. Well, Mr. Thomas Pabawena is boss another gang. Mr. Soquitch Timbimboo and [wife] stay Mr. Willie Ottogary place down near Tremonton now, and he been up to Washakie last Sunday, and return on the place last Monday. But he expect motoring down. My boys are going fight over to Lewiston, Idaho, on the 3 of the next month. But they haven't fight since last fight down Salt Lake City. I expect quit for the summer time. . . . Mr. Catch Toyahdook been work in Logan Temple about week ago. . . . Mr. Seth Pubigee and family stay at my little place down near or East Tremonton now. I expect stay all this week. He expect to going up to Idaho next week. . . . [1926-05-15 LJ]

WASHAKIE, MAY 19, 1926. The crop is looking pretty good this year. But our sugar beet crop look good too. I expect we will have good year. Well sir, it looking pretty good everywhere this valley. Some our boys been Idaho for working to shear sheep. But they all return home last week. And they made a pretty good money. Now they clean the water ditch and they get through this week. We have very nice race track just east side of the Malad River. They been working on it for three days and they are go try out their horse or training horses for coming fair day this year. We have some good horses here now and going have a big race here some day. This race track is half mile around. It is good for our town. Well sir it is benefit for our little town. Our boys going play ball with Garland team next Saturday afternoon, I expect have a nice game. I expect our going the game. Well sir our boys have sure play good game every time when play. We will have a real baseball team this year. Well sir if our boys stick together. They been organized a team about last month. . . . Mr. Jim Wagon was looking for work . . . and return yesterday. Mr. Nephi Zundel been down Tremonton and also working down Tremonton again yesterday. Mr. Seth Pubigee is return home from my place last Sunday. But he stay at my place for several days ago, and with his family. [1926-05-22 LJ]

WASHAKIE, MAY 26, 1926. The summer time is soon here, and weather is getting pretty warm just now. Most our grain crop is looking pretty splendid so far. But our spring crop is not so good as fall crop. But sugar beet is not good as last year. Well sir, Mr. Adams from Kaysville, a sheep man, is shearing his sheep up to the Broad Canyon last week. And he is loading his wool at Washakie siding. He load two car here. Mr. Jacob Peyope was return home from shearing sheep out Wyoming country. He made a good money that. Some of our boys just return home from shearing sheep, about last week. Mr. Thomas [Pabawena] was return home from Idaho to shear sheep and he was the boss of the gang. . . . Mr. Enos Pubigee was a proud parent. The baby boy born [Ervin Andrew, b. May 19, 1926] his home last week ago. . . . Most of our people working in sugar field just now down north Garland Sugar Factory. But there was a [lot] of us home now. . . . Mr. Dick Arritch is return home from his Idaho trip, and he gone about week or 10 days ago. Mr. Henry Woonsook been down Tremonton first part of this week. And he was after his grand ma home too. . . . I was been over to Logan City first of the week and to see Journal people over there and also on especial business too. While I was over, Mr. J. C. Allen, Editor of Journal to enquire me going up Lewiston to the big boxing contest that night. And I was return home same night. But coming home with my neighbor, Mr. Nick Peterson, from Union, Utah. Well sir, we got home about 3 o'clock in morning. Mr. Seth Pubigee and Chester Ottogary went up Idaho Reservation about last week ago. But they may return home this week. They was looking for some work up there. Well, our baseball team played with Garland League team last Saturday—they played good. But have a gather [rather] good baseball team here last spring. It was all young fellows too, etc. [1926-05-29 LJ]

WASHAKIE, JUNE 1, 1926. The people are . . . going out for the work in the sugar beet field just now . . . some . . . working their own beet. The summer nearly here now and the crop looking pretty promising so far. I expect we are going have a good crop grain this year. We having a real horse training race horse here for coming this fall. I expect we are going have a good horses this fall. Our baseball team went over to Clarkston, Utah, last Saturday played with league team over there. We lose game to score of 10 to 6 in favor of Clarkston team. This was a good game. I went over with the boys and I seen some acquainted, Mr. Thompson was my old acquaint. I and him used to play baseball together.

    Mr. Chief Harry Dixon is here now with his brother. But he is looking for work other day and going over to Mr. S. [Sye] B. Marble in Sugar Company Farm. He expect stay until July. This [his] home at Elko, Nevada. Mr. Willie Neaman hit with ball while playing over to Clarkston. The ball hit his right eye and a small cut above his eyes and he improved nicely now. But he unconvenienced a few minute. Mr. Soquitch and wife was remain down at my place down Elwood. Mr. Seth Pubigee was return home from Idaho trip. Mr. Jim Wagon and wife has new born boy baby last week ago. Mr. Mose Neaman and Jim Pabawena was went over to watch the game ball over to Clarkston. . . . Some been celebrate a Memorial Day and decorated the our cemetery ground. But they doing it every year. Miss Susie Low is coming our town some time ago last week. Her home at Elko and she visit her husband grave last Sunday and doing decorating too. . . . [1926-06-05 LJ]

WASHAKIE, JUNE 1926.   Our crop is looking pretty good . . . other day have a little rain here didn't amount any thing. It is looking pretty dry just now. Our people say they going a big celebration on the fourth July and they haven't decided yet whether they going have a celebrate yet. I expect we are going have some Indians from Fort Hall to come down to help celebrate here. Our people getting through the sugar beet and every body return home from work. I expect going have a good crop wheat this year. Our people is much sickness so far and everybody is well now. Mr. Elias Pubigee and wife went out Nevada and visiting his wife relatives and friend. But he may return home before 4 July. He went out last with Mr. Johny Thompson from Wells, Nevada. Mr. Harry Dixon and with brother still here working . . . for Mr. Sye Marble at Deweyville, Utah. He will going home soon as getting through. Mr. Harry Dixon, I and more other mens been down to Ogden last Saturday, on the matter of business. Mr. George P. Sam went up Idaho Reservation some time this week on the important business. . . . Master Chester Ottogary is purchase a new Ford car. He expect going make a trip to Wyoming some time after 4 July and to visit some his relatives over there. Mr. Chief Oh Henry Woonsook [reference to O'Henry the author] and Mr. Nephi Zundel motoring down Ogden City about last week. . . . [1926-06-19 LJ]

WASHAKIE, JULY 1926.   . . . Weather is getting pretty warm now and some our wheat crop are getting pretty dry just now, and some places are looking going have a good crop. The sugar beet look pretty good now. I expect have good crop beets this year. Our people want celebrate fourth July here at our town. They haven't made arrange yet. Some people West Portage have a Whoop[ing] Cough. . . . Well sir we may celebrate here our town after all. Some people want going up Wyoming before Twenty fourth to see some Shoshone Sun Dance. We letter from some one, letter said there was lots of Indians are there now from different places country, and these going join in Sun Dance. I thought we might going Wyoming too to see that big Sun Dance. Mr. George P. Sam went to Idaho Reservation last week on the espe-cial business. He may return home this coming week. And also Mr. Harry Dixon with his brother return home about two wk ago. He going attend business same business as Mr. Geo. P. Sam. . . . I have made a business trip over to Cache Valley other day and return last Tuesday. The [boys] still fighting now, next bout be at Richmond [UT] on the 5 July and then some of our boys are going box at Tremonton on the 5 July again. Mrs. Tom Elk coming from from Idaho last wk, she is sick now with all her children. But her husband stay up Idaho reservation and he is lease land from Indian agent. . . . Mr. Henry Woonsook and Catch Toyahdook went to Idaho Res. about last Sunday . . . on the matter of business. Nobody sick just now. . . . Nearly everybody putting their hay [up] now. The hay crop is much good this year. The water is kind scarce this year. But we didn't have any rain for long time now. [1926-07-26 LJ]]

WASHAKIE, JULY 26, 1926.   The people are doing fine this times. And [I] return from Wyoming last week ago. I was kind sick when I returned my trip. Well sir our farmer harvesting their grain just now. But the Indians are put up their first crop hay. And nearly all through by this time. I hope they through already. Then they going have a real Sun Dance after get with their hay. But second crop hay nearly all ready in the Wyoming, . . . Mr. Nephi Perdash and his wife and father been out Wyo. too. And also Mr. Catch Toyahdook and wife more other are return home too last week. We haven't any celebrate this year. But we had a big dinner on the 24th July. Then we went up to West Portage to see some horses races up there. Well sir, some Indians boys visiting our little town on the 24th July, all return home next day. And Mr. George Mich [?] is here looking for thief. There was three Indians from West come here they went up the on the Reservation and making a bad check. And he was looking for them with one white man. They return to Idaho some day, they was here on the 24th July. Mr. Moroni Timbimboo is proud owners of a new Ford car. [1926-07-31 LJ]]

WASHAKIE, AUGUST 4, 1926.   The Shoshone are here doing very fine. No one sick just now. But there is one baby girl died here about last Thursday morning she was 2 days old. This was Mr. Seth Pubigee little girl and buried at Washakie Cemetery. We have a splendid harvesting this year and grain is good, and three buyers is buying some of our grain I expect have a good price this year. They paying $1.25 per bushel this year and they start on their second crop, hay now. Nearly all grain cut by this time. Some our people are attending . . . Malad Stake Conference . . . last Saturday and Sunday. . . . Mr. Catch Toyahdook and wife been up to Fort Hall Reservation last week and visiting his relatives and friends. He return other day. Mr. Enos Pubigee want going up with his race horse. He expect [go or be] up there on the 12, 13 of this Month. Mr. Fred Jensen been over to Washakie last Sunday. He expect getting some our baseball players over to Logan next Saturday on 7 and 8 August But we telephone him this morning, and our boys will going over on Saturday, our boys going to play with a Jap boys team from Ogden, Utah. I expect some of our people are going over to Logan City to join the celebrate big day.

Mr. Dick Arritch just return from Idaho Reservation last week. But was motoring up there some time last week. I and Mr. Ammon Pubigee was a little hunting trip up to Grace, Idaho, about last week ago. . . . [1926-08-07 LJ]]

WASHAKIE, AUGUST 10, 1926.   . . . The crop is all harvest just now and they sold the grain in town. One the grain buyers here buy all our grain. The grain is about $1.20 per bushel this year I think it is good price for the grain. Well some our Indians want job pretty bad. And our agent from Fort Hall is coming down here to going build new school over little town. And he figuring going start on it right away. They have ready for coming school year.

They are start today working on it today. Well they need 4 men work on it about 4 week. I expect going have a good school house this coming year. Our rejoice over the new school house. Our baseball team was play over to Logan city last Saturday. But are going down Layton, Utah next Saturday August 14, 1926. I expect we are going good old time down there I expect some our folks and children going down too. But we did not have good time over to Logan last because they was so many been over there. On the Pacific Island Day Celebrate. There was about 400 people was attend the meeting at Logan City. The Tabernacle will with some Island missionary present from different part of the State. The first speaker was Mr. Gordard. Also 2 speaker Mr. Pres. H. J. Grant [Heber J. Grant, President, LDS Church], and also have a nice programme too. Mr. Timus Perdash a proud owner a new Ford car. He purchase one car last wk. Mr. Moroni Timbimboo and wife been to Logan City to see a big celebrate last Saturday. And also Mr. Catch Toyahdook and family been to Logan two to see a big Ball game. Mr. Johny Dick and with his brothers been to Logan City about last week ago. . . . [1926-08-14 LJ]

WASHAKIE, AUGUST 18, 1926.   Our people are going join in big Peach Day in Brigham City on the 17 and 18 inst. Our horse mens is getting their horses ready for that big day. But we have about 6 good horses here in our town. I hope we are have a good time down [there]. The harvest is over with now. The wheat is all sold. The fall work soon be here. The weather getting little bit colder just now. Last Saturday on the 14 August base ball team been down Layton, Utah a play, and in the favor Layton boys. But our ball team didn't have a good show account our boys didn't play for long time. It is about 3 month haven't played, this was second time our boys holding a ball such long time didn't touch ball inside 3 for [or four] month. We will do better next time, going down again. But mighty glad to have them fellows treating a [us] fairly. Them sure them people are good people. I expect the Adams Bros make this play.

Our people are good condition so far. Some our men are working the foundation of our new school house. They start last week. They agent getting through before the school start for this year. Mr. Moroni Timbimboo and wife motoring up Idaho Reservation and he return home today, and also visiting some his own relatives and friends. Mr. Dick Arritch just return from Idaho Reservation about last week. Mr. Catch Toyahdook and wife visiting some his friends up Idaho some time ago. Mr. William Hootchew and wife is motoring over to Cache Valley some time ago last month and return home. His home up Idaho. . . . Mr. Jim Wagon and wife has not return home yet from Yellowstone Park. He may come after season close. [1926-08-21 LJ]

WASHAKIE, AUGUST 25, 1926.   The wheat harvest is not so good this year on account we have a dry weather. Well sir . . . the sugar beet wasn't any good. I hope we doing better next year. . . . The Government is building a new school for the coming year. The working add it all last week on it. But soon our people put in fall wheat, and getting the ground ready plant. Mrs. [or Miss] Ethel Perdash was took sick last and take her down Garland. They been operated on Saturday. She have a appendicitis, and she attack pretty bad last week then operation form so quick on her. But she improving pretty nicely now. And she down Garland hospital now. Mr. Nephi

Perdash that her [father] and mother [Jessie Zundel Perdash] was down last Monday to see how she getting along. She doing pretty fine and her grandma, Miss Cohn Zundel was visit her last Monday too. Mr. William Hootchew and wife is stay at Mr. Warren Wongan place just now. But he motoring over to Logan. His leg take with rhemtismn [rheumatism]. He was laid up for several days now. His home is up Idaho Reservation. . . . Mr. Timus Perdash and Henry Woonsook been down to Ogden on matter of business. Mr. George Elk and family went out west for hunting some pine nuts yesterday. Mr. Ralph Stayner is Ford dealer was been up here doing some collecting. Mr. Jack Hooper and his partner went home last week ago. Their home at Nevada. Mr. Moroni Timbimboo family under quintiner [quarantine] here in our town. They had a Black Spot Measle and they soon getting over now. . . . Mr. Ammon Pubigee lease his dry farm to Mr. George Evans from West Portage for several year, and he is getting ready for planting now. [1926-08-28 LJ]

WASHAKIE, SEPTEMBER 2, 1926. . . . The farmers are getting too busy put in fall wheat. But the threshing all done about last week ago. A new school house building up soon. The is two carpenters working on it now all the time. I expect they getting through building next three week more. Mr. Moroni Timbimboo and wife visiting Idaho Reservation some time ago about two weeks. . . . Mr. Warren Wongan take some wheat to the mill of Garland other day. Mr. Nephi Perdash and wife visiting his daughter down Garland hospital she been operated on for appendicitis about week ago. She is doing nicely. . . . Mr. John Dick going out Nevada and looking for some work. He may return home before sugar beet topping time. . . .

Mr. Willie Neaman still working up Idaho Reservation. Mr. George Tomock and family went to Raft River and hunting some pine nuts and also Mr. Yeager Timbimboo and wife going out west on the same business. They expect return home before Peach Day. Well sir, some our people are going join celebrate on Peach Day Parade. And they going have a War dance on street on the 17 and 18 in the evening. Don't miss that big War dance, and they getting their war feathers ready now. Mr. Soquitch Timbimboo and family visiting my little [farm] down here at Elwood now. But he expect stay here until Peach Day. . . . Master Kickapoo Dan and his brother, Custer, going boxing contest in moving picture house in Malad City tonight. Mr. [Ray] Diamond still mail carrier for Washakie town. The sugar beet is not so good this year here now. Mr. Ammon Pubigee lease his farm to Mr. George Eacken [Evans] from West Portage for several year. But has [not] doing any thing now, and he took job on the school building. [1926-09-04 LJ]

WASHAKIE, SEPTEMBER 14, 1926. The people are good wheat crop this year, but the sugar beet crop is pretty bad this year. It is not worth digging and it poor crop. Our farmers put the fall crop in just now, and nearly all done now. The weather getting colder now. Some people going a big Parade on the Peach Day celebrate, and are have a good horses to take down Brigham City.[20] I expect our horses put in track down there. We have one race horse pretty fast [Buckskin Nelly]. It is hard to beat. She was own by Mr. Enos Pubigee. But she winner all the races last year.[21] Mr. Yeager Timbimboo and wife hasn't return yet, they hunting some pine nuts out west. And also Mr. George Elk and family has not return home yet. They was doing some [or same] business. It is about 70 miles west from here. They may return before Peach

Day. . . . Mr. Hyrum Wongsaw is visiting my old farm down Elwood. Mr. George P. Sam went up Idaho and doing some matters of Business. Mr. Moroni Timbimboo went up to Idaho and going [visit] his relatives and friends. Mr. Charlie Perdash went to Fort Washakie and matter of business and accompanied his son, Mr. Timus Perdash. He expect return return soon as can. Miss Ethel Perdash is return from Garland Hospital about last week ago. Master Chester Ottogary been down Salt Lake City and he is fighting Mr. Hardy K. Downing. The first fighting in ring for coming winter, he meet Master Lee Gerry from Seattle Oregon. Lee Gerry was a clever boxer, [but] Kickapoo Dan get decision. Mr. Thomas Pabawena out Nevada and looking for work. . . . Mr. John Dick coming home from Nevada and doing some work out there.

Mr. Thomas Pabawena just return home from Nevada. But he visiting some his relatives and friends out there, etc. [1926-09-18 LJ]

Willie Writes from Shelly, Idaho

SHELLY, IDAHO, SEPTEMBER 28, 1926.   We are coming here about one week ago. But and coming for work. There is so many people here from every where. The some Mexican, white hobs [hobos] and some Indians from different places of the country. Some of them can even getting job. We been here long enough get job. But can [not] getting job just now.[22] This country is great potatoes raising country. Well it is plenty spuds for this year and sugar beet isn't good. There is about 20 from our town here now, and looking for job. I expect more come up here in few day. These white day school stop yesterday. They want put school children put work in spuds. Well I guess we going work in few day yet. The weather is getting colder here in last few day. And the freeze later apples around Blackfoot, and Shelly. They didn't pick soon enough. The frost has been so early this year. Well sir, have acquainted many white people are here this country. Mr. Catch Toyahdook and family coming up yesterday. Mr. James Pabawena and with his brothers is coming here pretty soon. Mr. Seth Pubigee and Chester Ottogary went down Salt Lake last Thursday and doing fighting down there. Well they come back yet. They expect return Tuesday. I have met Mr. Lewis William here in this town today. He was my school chum. He was a life insurance man. But he making his home at Boise, Idaho. I have new acquainted some people around here. I expect we many remain here about three week or more. [1926-10-02 LJ]

Willie Ottogary at Pocatello

POCATELLO, IDAHO, OCTOBER 14, 1926.   The weather is getting pretty cold now. We been up there to Idaho Falls working in spuds. The all our went home yesterday, and they all through with work up Idaho. There is about 30 our people from Washakie up here work. There some from Nevada, Wyoming, Montana. Mr. Catch Toyahdook is still working up Idaho Falls now and rest Indians went home and some Indians from Fort Hall Reservation working too. I have seen quite lots Indians are here at Fort Hall Reservation. I am visiting at home of Mr. Doan place this nice morning. But Mr. Enos Pubigee and Chester Ottogary left home yesterday afternoon for Washakie. Mr. Seth Pubigee and family stay at Pocatello today, and he doing some business here. Mr. Tom Elk and family went home yesterday. But they is working spuds up around Blackfoot, and more other Indians with him. The farmer up around Idaho Falls raise most potatoes and sugar beets. They start harvesting sugar beet crop last week. The sugar beet isn't as good this year. Well sir, I will soon return home, in the few day. I have a accquainted many of the Indians here. Mr. Bill Williams and wife is coming here yesterday. He is pretty sick and he come here for medicine treatment. His home is about 80 miles west Great Salt Lake City. The place named Skull Valley, and two boys from Ibakaho [Ibapah] is accompany him. He expect will be here about one month or more, etc. I will be soon home again, etc. [1926-10-16 LJ]]

WASHAKIE, OCTOBER 23, 1926.   The people are working out Idaho. Nearly all return home yet. There was a few fellows out the Idaho but they working in spuds and now going in sugar beet topping. I expect be here about next week some time. The crop is up Idaho is spuds. And the sugar beet pretty poor. And some places is not worth digging. When I return from Idaho and find my people are doing nicely. Our new school house is nearly finished by this time. Probably next week some time. Only one white man working on it now. Mr. Ammon Pubigee is working on this building. He is only Indian man on it this fall. They use a old house for school now. The weather get colder now. But winter soon be here. George P. Sam had his eye trouble and he laid up for week or more. Mr. George Tospanguitch motoring over to Logan some time ago. Mr. Dick Arritch got hurt other day, but he fell off from his spring wagon. But he getting all right now. Mr. Tom Elk and family went up Idaho Reservation first of this week. Mr. Timus Perdash divorce his wife about three week ago and he married another girl from Nevada and she run away from him again. But she was first married widow of Mr. Amos Moemberg. He live her about two week. Mr. Moroni Timbimboo and family made trip up in Oregon state about two week ago. But he left one his girl up there to Indian school [Chemawa School at Forest Grove, Oregon]. . . . Mr. Jim Wagon build a house this fall. He expect going up Yellowstone Park again next coming summer. Master Chester Ottogary getting line up to fight up Pocatello, Idaho on the 7th Nov. But he is going boxing with Tuffe Edward from Pocatello. I guess next match be at Malad City on the 11 Nov. But he start training for fight now. [1926-10-23 LJ]

WASHAKIE, OCTOBER 28, 1926.   The people are good condition now, and weather getting colder now. Our new school nearly finish now. There was little working inside. Well I expect be done next week, and ready to use about week more or so. . . . All the boys return from Idaho. They working in spuds and sugar beet up there. I and Mr. Seth Pubigee return from Idaho last night, and we peddle some apple. I expect going up again tomorrow again. Mr. Tom Elk still up Idaho now. Here release [leased] land from Indian up there to Bannock Creek, and working on it. Mr. Dick Arritch got hurt last week and fell off from his spring wagon. But he is well as ever now. . . .

Mr. Catch Toyahdook and wife went up Idaho Reservation to hunting [and] some trap on the Snake River, and Mr. Henry Woonsook accompany him. Mr. Jimia Arimo the son of Chief Arimo went home last Monday. And he visiting our little town last week to see some relation and friends too. Some his relatives live here in our town. Mr. Ammon Pubigee is doing some hunting here. Mr. Jim Wagon and hunting some trapping up Idaho. Mr. Billy Neaman still up . . . there to Idaho working. Mr. Elias Pubigee baby girl [probably Catherine] died here about last Tuesday afternoon, and she was about 5 month old. She buried yesterday at

Washakie cemetery. Mr. Chief Black Hawk died at his home near Gibson station last Saturday and buried. And he was well known all over the country. Mr. Seth Pubigee hauled his team on truck last week, and he is to keep at home now. Some our people working sugar beet down near Garland Factory. The Indians big time last Sunday having horses races, and going having next Sunday again. Well sir, we might going up again. Master C. R. Ottogary or Kickapoo Dan, going fighting Pocatello on next Monday night on the 1 Nov. He meet Master Max Boyatt, Pocatello 4 round bout at Lyric Theatre. The people are pretty anxious to see him fight and also Indians too. I expect there will be a great crowd be there to see him fight, and he line up fight to at Malad City on the 11 November. [1926-10-30 LJ]

WASHAKIE, NOVEMBER 25, 1926.   Our people all through their work now and they getting some winter wood now. I see in Salt Lake Telegram the Kickapoo Dan in [boxing] card last Monday night. But Mr. Kid Davis is fail to pay Mr. Seth Pubigee, manager to Master Chester Ottogary. But he didn't pay enough, and he was call over to phone last Wednesday. So we didn't come down to Salt Lake City. I expect they fool the people down there to Salt Lake City.[23]

Mrs. Jane Pabawena was died here last Tuesday night, and widow of Mr. Tom Pabawena for many year. Her funeral service held Washakie ward meeting house. . . . She was about 80 year old. She came to Utah about 40 year ago, and she convert the Mormon Church in year 1886. She reside here ever since that time. But left 5 grown children and 7 great grandchildren too.

Mr. Kippetchew Noragan went over to Paradise and doing some trapping over there.

Mr. George P. Sam is sick now he is getting little better now.

Mr. Danyhay and wife is visit Mr. Mose Neaman place.

Mrs. Emy Neaman [Emma, or Pan-Do-Wee Brain] is very low now. She been sick for long time, over year. We expect not been live any longer. . . .

Mr. Jim Wagon is building new house for winter.

Our day school is used a new school here. This was build by the Government for us. There was about 20 or more children attended school here.

But weather is getting colder here now, and winter soon be here.

The people are very quiet here on the Thanksgiving Day here. [1926-11-27 LJ]

WASHAKIE, DECEMBER 1, 1926.   The weather is getting very cold just now. But the fall crop looking pretty good. But I expect the wheat crop be good next year. Our day school very good. There is about 20 or more children went school this year, and the school is very nice now. We had sad news today. Our old sister died here last Sunday night. But her name is Mrs. Emy Brain and she is widow Mr. Frank Brain [father of Moses Neaman]. He been dead long time ago. She come from Wyoming about 40 year and her making home since that time. Will join Mormon church since came after here. She was about 80 year old. But was still member of church until her death. The funeral service held at . . . Washakie ward meeting house . . . entement [interment] at Washakie Cemetery.

Mr. Kippetchew Noragan and wife been over to Logan City and also he made some trapping too.

Mr. George Tospanguitch motoring over to Cache valley last week.

Mr. Catch Toyahdook and wife went up Idaho yesterday.

Mr. Danyhay and wife went home yesterday. The was been here about and they down see Mrs. Emy Brain. His wife is neice of this death woman. . . .

I and boys been over to Logan City last Monday to Mr. J. C. Allen at the Journal office. To fix up for fight over there, some time next week.

Mr. Pabboo is visiting our town other day. But his wife is very sick. And he figuring taking a medicine treatment here. . . . [1926-12-04 LJ]]

WASHAKIE, DECEMBER 8, 1926.   We have a snow storm here last night. But snow about half inch here, and didn't amount anything. Our people are good condition now. There was about two death this fall, both the older sisters, and also one old man died here lately. Our people are talking about Christmas now. They are going a Christmas programme here. Well sir I hope we going good time on Christmas day. Seem to every body rejoice over the Xmas. Mr. Ernie Adams wrote letter to Kickapoo Dan to ask him about his fight business, and he wrote back telling his condition. But he want to our place to stay all winter long. Perhaps he been back East and doing some boxing. He wants know he come to Utah and training with the boys here at our place, Elwood, Utah, and training some boxing here. I do not know weather [whether] is coming or not. Mr. Catch Toyahdook and wife is return from Idaho a few days ago and he was visit some his own brothers and friends up on the reservation. Mr. George P. Sam and wife motoring over to Logan some time last two week ago. Mr. Tom Elk is still up there to Idaho, and he was lease and one Indian land up in Bannock Creek about last spring. Mr. George Tomock and with his boys motoring down Tremonton last part of the last week ago. Mr. Seth Pubigee been down Brigham City and manager of the Kickapoo Dan, and sign for fight, on the 14 day of December at Brigham City, Knudson Building. . . . Mr. Jacob Peyope is doing some trapping up around here on the foot hills. Mr. Pabboo is visit our town here last week ago. But still he remain here now. Mr. Thomas Pabawena and his brothers working up canyon just now, etc. [1926-12-11 LJ]]

WASHAKIE, DECEMBER 14, 1926.   The weather getting prety cold over here now. We have a regular snow storm last Monday. The big wind come from South and it blow like 38 mile per hour and freeze everything around here. I guess thermometer went about 20 below here and we have snow here about 3 or 4 inch now. The people are very poor condition in food line. The crop is fail last summer. I expect the winter is now. Our people is getting ready for winter now. Mr. Soquitch Timbimboo is getting pretty good now and also he doing some Christmas shopping down Tremonton last . . . week. Mr. George P. Sam was sick about two week ago. But is up around again, and was his eye trouble. . . . Mr. Jim Wagon little boy took sick some time ago last week. But he taking a Dr. Treatment now. . . . Mr. Catch Toyahdook and wife return home from Idaho Reservation about last week. He was visiting his own relation and friend up there. Mr. Nephi Perdash was motoring down Tremonton about first part of last week. Mrs. Neatze Moemberg and daugther was motoring down Garland last week ago. Mr. Seth Pubigee been down Tremonton and doing Christmas shopping and also Mr. Hyrum Wongsaw accompany him. Some our boys been doing some winter trapping. There will be a new fighter coming out Utah soon, his name Ernie Adams, his home is Ely Nevada. He figuring going stay here our place at Elwood, Utah. But want training with my boys all winter. Mr. Yeager Timbimboo is craple [crippled] up with rheumatisum here about couple month ago. He could not getting around very well. Our day school pretty good this year . . . there is about 27 children attend school here our little town. [1926-12-21 LJ]

WASHAKIE, DECEMBER 22, 1926.   The people are good condition now. But we have a snow about 6 inch last night. Our people are rejoice over the Christmas is coming now. Well, sir, we have good such winter now. Now is time snow coming now. It is seem to me getting late to have snow. Our people going have Christmas program. They going [have] a program commence at and 10 o'clock Saturday morning and going have a big dinner at the ward hall. Mr. Elias Pubigee and wife been Tremonton and doing some Christmas shopping other day. . . . Mr. Mose Neaman went over to Logan city with family and going spend Xmas over there. Mr. Moroni Timbimboo and wife attend meeting up Malad city Friday night. But his girl nearly died with heart trouble.[24] But she is doing all right while he was up to Malad city. . . . Mr. Seth Pubigee and Mr. Henry Woonsook made a business trip down Tremonton other day. Mr. George P. Sam is up again. But his eyes getting better now. Mr. Warren Wongan lost his little son. He died here about last Monday. Funeral service held at ward meeting house Wednesday. There is no one sick just and [none] of them under the weather. Mr. George Mose is living here now. But his children went school now. . . . [1926-12-24 LJ]

Willie Ottogary Writes to The Journal From Washakie

WASHAKIE, DECEMBER 29, 1926.   The winter is here now, but old year is passed now, and we looking for the new year. The New Year make a people glad whole world. While we waiting for New Year some of us our people are passed away. There is about three or four death this old year while we looking for New Year our heart so happy. I hope we be a prosperous people after New Year here. The weather is getting pretty cold just now here. Some our people away and spend Christmas some place, and Salt Lake City. They was return other day, and having a splendid time. Mr. Mose Neaman and wife was spending Christmas over to Logan City. But hasn't come back yet. Mr. Joe Woonsook is getting good now. He was pretty sick last two week ago. But he was under Dr. treatment here, while back. Mr. Seth Pubigee and whole family spend Christmas time down Salt Lake City. They was return home yesterday. Mrs. Amos Moemberg went down last week and take her little boy [Tracy Moemberg] under went operation on his lip, and upper was a big gap [a harelip] he was born that way. But he doing nicely. He operated at the Salt Lake City, L. D. S. Hospital. He been hospital for three days and all return home already now. Mr. Kippetchew Noragan and wife been down Salt Lake City and buying some deer hide. Mr. Moroni Timbimboo is write to his girl [Joana] at Oregon. But she was home sick she want coming home right away. But attending school up there she went up last September. Her sister is sick just now. That reason she want coming home. Mr. Soquitch Timbimboo is doing some New Year shopping up to West Portage. [1927-01-01 LJ]

7

"Our People Haven't Got Any Land for Their Own,"[1] 1927–1929

WASHAKIE, JANUARY 5, 1927. We have a lovely weather here yesterday. It is feel all most like spring weather. But the night is pretty cold now. The is five inch snow here now. We held New Year programme here . . . and evening was a big dance for every body. . . . We haven't fighting down Salt Lake City for such long time. But we made a contract with Mr. Kid Davis last fall. We mad [made contract] like our own old Indian custom way, but he broke our contract. So we didn't fight in Salt Lake City any more. But like see Mr. Kid Davis once more. But he didn't pay what he agreed to pay. We got to fight some place just now. Mr. Seth Pubigee been up to Malad City on matter of business and also he made a business trip down Brigham City first part this week. Mr. Mose Neaman and family is return Logan

Ray Diamond and Amy Hootchew Timbimboo, Washakie, Utah, 1938. "He learned to read and read the Bible daily—never joined any church." *Courtesy Mae Timbimboo Parry.*

City he spend Christmas and New Year's over there. I was made a business trip over to Logan City middle part of last week ago. Mr. Charlie Dick and Mr. James Pabawena had a bad trouble last week go. But Charlie shot Jim Pabawena dog. Then he hie [hit] Charlie breast and back his head and took a shot gun away from his hand and the stop trouble then and Mr. Charlie didn't do anything to Mr. James Pabawena. They doing fine now. . . . Miss Edward is spending New Year with her aunt, Miss Susie Highyou here in little town. She went home last week ago. Her home is on Fort Hall Reservation. Mr. Tom Elk still up Idaho. He was a leased Indian land on the Bannock Creek. He may stay winter up there. Mr. [Ray] Diamond is still carrying mail our town now. I hoping we will have a good year this year. [1927-01-08 LJ]

WASHAKIE, JANUARY 12, 1927.   The weather is get warm here just now. But we didn't have much snow now. We have about 5 inch snow now. . . . But some of our people say going have a easy winter this winter. . . . Some of us under the weather they getting good now. Mrs. John [Cohn] Zundel received a bad news from Fort Washakie, Wyoming. Her uncle was died out there about two week ago. But he was well know this part of this country. His name was Mr. Pa-zo-quita. I expect he was about 75 year of age. He leave his wife and some children behind him. But he was not church member. Mr. Seth Pubigee made a business trip up to Pocatello, Idaho, first part of this week. And accompany his brother-in-law. . . . Mr. Moroni Timbimboo and wife went down Salt Lake City. But his girl was sick for three week ago. I expect going see Dr. down there, and he take Master Tracy Moemberg with. But he been down Salt Lake City some [time] ago. The Dr. been operated on his lip. But Dr. look him once more. The lip is doing very splendid now. I have made a business trip up to Washakie to day. There was about 3 death ever since this fall. Mr. Mose Neaman and his boys been hunting some Jack Rabbit today and they slaughter so many. . . . Our day school running very splendid just now. Mr. Soquitch Timbimboo purchase a second handed stove today. He bought this stove from Mr. Lawrence Hansen Elwood, Utah. [1927-01-15 LJ]

WASHAKIE, JANUARY 20, 1927.   The people are here good condition just now. The weather get warm here about all last month. . . . We haven't got much snow left it is about inch ice covered the ground. Well we a storm other night but tise not amount anything. I expect soon we a regular storm one these days. Some our people say they going have easy winter this winter a big part this month is gone now. Well sir, I was been over to Logan City on matters of business. The Elks have a fighting programme last Friday night. I expect is programme is a splendid. . . .[2] Mr. Yeager Timbimboo was been down Salt Lake City to buying some deer hide. And return last week ago. Master Martin Soldier was visiting our little town here away to the Fort Hall Reservation. He was raised here and went school here when he was a little boyhood. But he moved away from here about 9 year ago, and making his home out Deep Creek, Utah; about 120 miles west Salt Lake City, and he accompany Mr. Dewey Moon and there was two automobile car passed through our town going up Idaho Res. They taking a sick man. I expect going have a Dr. treatment up there. Last night one my boy boxing with Mr. Con Hansen from Bear River City. They put up fine show. Every body was satisfied. They box for draw. I see 5 important mans to present at the Boxing contest last night from Logan City, Utah. Mr. Moroni Timbimboo and wife return from Salt Lake City. But take their little girl to Salt Lake City to have Dr. treatement. She seem to didn't get any better. [1927-01-22 LJ]

WASHAKIE, JANUARY 26, 1927.   The weather is change little. Last Friday and Saturday is coldest we every had this [winter], I know it is zero weather them two days. . . . Not much sickness among us this winter. Nearly every-body is well. Only we had a flue but didn't [seem] so serious. There was a big rabbit hunt last Friday. The boys was choose side and they said the lose side going pay for the dance ticket. They have a dance last Friday night. The boys lose pay for ticket. Mr. Soquitch Timbimboo is kind of sick now on account begin [being] old age. . . . Mr. Moroni Timbimboo been Malad City first part of the week. Miss Jonana [Joana] Timbimboo expect coming home from school at Shamwa [Chemawa] Indian school, Oregon. Mr. Enos Pubigee, Mr. Seth Pubigee and more other been down middle part and buying some ammunition for hunting. Mr. Martin Soldier is returning home last week he didn't visit our town this time. His home at Deep Creek Reservation, Utah. Mr. Seth Pubigee the manager of the fight boys here at Washakie. He went down Salt Lake City last Sunday to fight. Master Chester Ottogary is going fight Mr. Jack Andrews at Manhattan Club Hippodrome Theatre on the Monday night, Jan. 24, 1927. The fight going off is usel aways [usual way]. Mr. Seth Pubigee just return from Salt Lake City last night. And accompany Mr. Chester Ottogary and his brother Mr. Enos Pubigee. Master Chester Ottogary meet Jack Andrews again Manhattan club at Hippodrome Theatre Salt Lake City. But Jack Andrews is decision over him. But my boy just a kid he is about some 19 on the 30 this month. I expect the Andrews is out his class. Well he start fight on the 9 January last year, 1926. Mr. Kid Davis seems to me bush [push] him pretty fast, and he was boxing out his class. But the Mr. Jack Andrews is star boxer of the State Utah. And he is well train in ring more experience then Master Kickapoo Dan.[3] [1927-01-29 LJ]

WASHAKIE, FEBRUARY 2, 1927.   We having a nice warm weather here almost like spring weather the snow is thawing pretty fast, the snow nearly all gone just now. I expect this was real good because the hay was scarce here our town. We haven't much crop hay last summer. The money was short and hay short too. We don't know what going to do in future time on account the dry weather last summer. I expect going have a good season next summer and plenty every thing. There was not much sickness among us all winter, and everybody feeling pretty good so far. I heard going have another dance. But the Bishop of this ward put up a dance to raise fund to [buy] some books with. It will be next Friday night. Mr. James Pabawena and wife was been [made] member of church. They was received a baptism last Saturday afternoon, and become the member Church of Christ latter day saints, and also Mrs. Alice Pubigee and with her two sisters was convert. . . . They was received baptisum about some last week ago. Miss Jeenna [Joana] Timbimboo hasn't return home yet. . . . Mr. Seth Pubigee is just return home from Salt Lake City last night. . . . Master Chester Ottogary doing fighting down Salt Lake City, at the Hippodrome Theatre. He met Mr. Ernie Kid, Ross [Ernie Kid Ross] from

Casper, Wyo. They fight a draw about 6 round bout. I expect this put up good show, and also I was witness the fight. Mr. Jim Wagon was been down Tremonton last week ago. Mr. Geo. P. Sam up around again. But he was sick last month. Mr. [Ray] Diamond still carrying U. S. mail for our little town. He is carry for the about 9 year this coming summer. [1927-02-05 LJ]

WASHAKIE, FEBRUARY 10, 1927.   . . . Almost big part the winter is gone. We had a fairly this winter. One thing is good for us. We didn't much hay for our horses. The people having not much disease this year only had such a bad cold. I expect winter wheat going winter kill on account having much snow. If it have more warm weather be a good. I guess some of the families have a German measel too. Mr. George P. Sam received a bad news from Skull Valley. That his relation died out Skull Valley. But he was middle age man. He going school about year 1883. Then their parent moved away from here they live out since that. But he haven't any children, only had a wife. Mr. Nephi Perdash and wife been down Salt Lake City last week ago and buying some deer hide. And return same days. . . . Mr. Soquitch Timbimboo is sick in bed. I expect he getting better now. . . . Mr. Bishop Yeager Timbimboo was putting up dance and raise some money to buy some book for meeting house. I expect going have another dance be next Friday night too for the old and young. Miss Louise Ottogary sick now. She took sick last Saturday night. She getting better now. Mr. Ammon Pubigee was motor down Elwood and he visited my home at Elwood while he was down. . . . [1927-02-12 LJ]

WASHAKIE, FEBRUARY 17, 1927.   We have a . . . stormy weather since last week ago, and still rain here today. Well our people are here good condition just now. But some of us people had a German measles there only one case here report last week. . . . Our people are rejoice over the spring time soon be here. We have a dance last Friday. Every-body have a enjoyable time. . . . Mr. Seth Pubigee has been on my place down Elwood first part this week ago and also Master Chester Ottogary accompany him. . . . Mr. Seth Pubigee made a business trip up Pocatello last week ago and accompany Master Ottogary and return last Monday. Mr. Ammon Pubigee visit my place down Elwood today. He return home tonight. Mr. Moroni M. Ward is sick ever since last fall. But he was getting pretty bad condition now. They expect can live any longer. He was man doing some good work for our people. And teach them how to farm and doing missionary work among our people several year. I guess about over 50 year. Then he moved down Riverside, about 20 year ago. And he making his home [since] that time. Mr. George M. Ward, his son, took his place as Bishop in our ward for several year now. He can talk in our language well as I can. Mr. [Ray] Diamond still carries mail for Washakie of quite number of years. Mr. Tom Elk still up Idaho yet. He supposed to come home for winter. Mr. Soquitch Timbimboo is getting better now. But he was sick last week and he up around again. But he is olderest man in our town. [1927-02-19 LJ]

WASHAKIE, FEBRUARY 25, 1927.   . . . Our people are rejoice over the spring is coming now. Our fall crop look pretty just now. We have such lovely weather this winter not much snow. There is about 4 or 5 inch snow here all winter long. But last two weeks ago have snow and rain together. Well our short food and hay. But we didn't much crop last year on account being so dry last summer. I expect have a nice crop this year plenty of everything. Some of us are pretty poor can buy hay for their stock. Mr. Nephi Perdash was been down Salt Lake City last two weeks ago and buying some deer skin. Mr. George Mose still living our town. But [his] children went to school here just now. He expect return home when spring open. Mr. Seth Pubigee was been down my place down Elwood first part this week. Mr. Moroni Timbimboo was made a business trip down Salt Lake City some time last month. . . . Mr. Moroni Ward is pretty sick. But he was man learning our people how to farm, and doing some mission work among us people for many year probably 40 year, and he great friend to Indian, and also he is Indian interupter [interpreter] too. . . . [1927-02-26 LJ]

WASHAKIE, MARCH 17, 1927.   . . . Our rejoice over the spring here. . . . Well our grain looking pretty good. I expect going have a good crop this year. The hay is pretty scarce here just. We raise not much hay last year, on account being so dry season. We had a stormy weather other day . . . but didn't last long. It is all gone now. Master Chester R. Ottogary was down my place yesterday. Brought me a very sad news. That my uncle [Soquitch Timbimboo] died Washakie yesterday. He been sick about month. But he was so old. I guess he was about 80 year old. But left his wife and one brother behind. But he was splendid worker in Church. Well he was the help white settlers in early day. The funeral service not arranged yet. Mr. Moroni Timbimboo going up Malad getting his coffin yesterday. Mr. Yeager Timbimboo is going take care his brother widow later on. She was old woman. And she was sick too. But is getting better now. . . . Mr. George Mose still living here with his dad-in-law. But his little children went school here this winter. Master Custer Ottogary been away from home several days. But he was visit some his relation up Washakie. He return home other day. Some of the boys doing some winter trapping here. Some of our people are under the weather now. I expect he getting better later on when weather get change again. Mrs. Tom Elk is sick. She getting better now, and Mr. Tom Elk going up Idaho again about last month. [1927-03-19 LJ]

WASHAKIE, MARCH 22, 1927.   The spring is here just now. But the people are rejoice over the spring is here. We have warm weather. Our grain crop is looking splendid now. . . . We lose our older man here last week ago, his name is Mr. Soquitch. His funeral service held Washakie ward meeting house last Friday about 11 o'clock morning. Conduct service by Bishop Geo. M. Ward. They was born good testimony our death brother. But he was very splendid churcher worker. He is man act good scout for the white people in the early day.

The funeral service held at Garland . . . for the Mr. Moroni Ward. He was took missionary work among Indians at Washakie for the 40 year. But he is man doing big work for our people, and doing some the land work for the our people. Some our people attended his funeral service down Garland. He was the man got friend every where. The was a big part his friends and relatives attended his funeral. . . . Mr. Clawson was talking his funeral service born good testimony toward him. The about 6 more speakers too. . . . Mr. Chief Gonseaulas [Gonzales] is here at Washakie. I was made a business trip over to Logan first day this week, and doing some shopping, and return same day. Mr. Chester Ottogary return home last week ago, at Elwood, Utah. Miss Louise Ottogary at my home now. But she is going school at Elwood school first part next week. She is about return our home when Mr. Soquitch Timbimboo died. Well will stay here along as school last. . . . [1927-03-26 LJ]

WASHAKIE, APRIL 8, 1927.   We have a early spring this year, and the weather getting good here just now. We start our spring work now. . . . I hope we going have a good crop this year. Well everything looking splendid just now. The hay is scarce just now. But we haven't hay this winter. Some of our people went down for Conference down Salt Lake City, and return home already now. . . . Mr. Seth Pubigee is manager of Washakie fighter is coming up from Salt Lake City last night. But he been down for fight. But Master Chester Ottogary fighting down Salt Lake City last Monday night. He clash with Mr. Noble Cerventes [Cervantes] around bout at Manhattan Club Hippodrome Theatre. But he fight for draw, and also Mr. Enos Pubigee and Custer Ottogary accompany Mr. Seth Pubigee. But he sign up another fight already now at Brigham City. Next week I expect going have three boys fight at Brigham City on the 15 April.

Mr. Nephi Perdash and wife been down conference Salt Lake City. He return last Monday. Well there was only three death this winter. There was lot sickness among us all this winter and nearly every-body is well now. Our day school running pretty good this year. . . . [1927-04-09 LJ]

WASHAKIE, APRIL 13, 1927.   The weather . . . cold here right now. But we had a stormy weather here last all last week. But it is so cold nobody want doing any farming. I expect some our farmer to raise sugar beet here this year. But the beet was fail last year. Well expect going have good year for sugar beet here. The roads impossible to travel through here now. Our last fall crop looking pretty good so far. We expect to going a good crop this coming summer. And our people are very good condition now. Nobody sick just now. But there was three old people died here last winter. . . . Last fall Mr. Bill Williams and wife was [made] his last visit at Mr. Towhee place at near Tyhee Station, Idaho. When he return then he died suddenly. . . . Master Chester, with his brother, Master Custer E. Ottogary, been home down Elwood on the Sunday and Monday and coming up here yesterday. They training up here coming next Saturday. The three boys going fight down Brigham City on the 16 April 1927. I hope they are going put a splendid show, and they match up with the boys from Salt Lake City. I expect lots people to see this big Boxing contest next Saturday night. Well it is be at the Knudson Building, Brigham City. Commence at 8:30 o'clock sharp. There was lots people want going see this Boxing around the Elwood and also Tremonton, so on etc. [1927-04-16 LJ]

WASHAKIE, APRIL 28, 1927.   The summer is soon be here now. But the weather is pretty warmer. Well our people rejoice the summer is coming. The grain crop is looking pretty good. I hope we are going a good this year. The every body getting pretty good so far. No death just now. Mr. Ammon Pubigee been down my place at Elwood and also made some business. Mr. Seth Pubigee and with his brother

Enos Pubigee been over to Logan on some business first part of this week. Master Custer Ottogary stay with Mr. Enos Pubigee and doing some training up to Washakie. Well been home last Sunday in Elwood, Utah. Mr. Elias Pubigee is motor down my place at Elwood today and return home tonight, and also Master Chester Ottogary is accompany Mr. Elias Pubigee today. But he is stay with his cousin Seth Eagle Pubigee up to Washakie. This my boy are going fight down Salt Lake City next Monday night. Well hope they will have a good luck down there. Mr. Martin Soldier is going up to Pocatello Reservation. He stop at Washakie over night and he going have a Dr. treatment up there. Well home at Deep Creek, Utah, at 150 miles west Salt Lake City. [1927-04-30 LJ]

WASHAKIE, MAY 25, 1927. . . . We had a splendid rain here last ago, and help us in the grain field. But the grain crop looking pretty good just after this rain we had. Our farmer rejoice over this rain. I expect we going have a nice crop this year, away the thing looking. Well sir, this was a good thing prospect just now. Mr. Enos Pubigee is getting prepare for the his race horse for coming big race down to Brigham City next Saturday. But he expect won all that race. And more other horse are getting prepared too. I expect we going put on the race about ten horses. Well we will going down watch the big race.[4] Mr. George Bran is still here at Washakie now with his sister. They stay at Mr. Charlie Perdash place. His home out Wyoming. He expect going [stay] for this coming summer. He has own farm in the Sage Creek north the Fort Washakie about twelve mile. Mr. James Pabawena is down town other day and doing some shopping. Mr. Mose Neaman was motor down Garland first part of this week. Mr. John Pabawena and with his brother Mr. Dave Pabawena looking for some job down Garland other day, for thinning sugar beet. . . . Our boys are rig up a base ball team here while back. They expect going play around here this summer. [1927-05-28 LJ]

WASHAKIE, JUNE 16, 1927. The people are here real good condition, and some of them working in the sugar beet field. Well around the Garland, Riverside, etc. . . . Seem to me everything growing pretty slow this spring. It is so cold this spring. Some of us raise sugar beet here too. . . . Mr. George P. Sam trade his old overland car off for two horses about last two week ago. Mr. George Tospanguitch is getting better now. But he was real sick man here last couple week ago. But is up and around again. Mr. George Mose has return again here about last two week. But with his family and he been home out Nevada to see his parents and brother. Mr. George Prann [Bran], and with brother-in-law went home to Wyoming a week ago. But was here our all winter along. . . . Mr. Seth Pubigee and Mr. Chester Ottogary made a business trip over to Logan city about last week ago. And also they try to get our ball team to play to on the 4th July too. Our boys are play good this year. Mr. Nephi Perdash was motor down Tremonton last Saturday. Mr. Jim Wagon want go to Yellowstone Park pretty soon, but he working for man down Ogden or Mr. Smith. Mr. Nephi Zundel girl return from her school. She went school at Fort Hall industrial school. Mr. Moroni Timbimboo was return home about last he been up Oregon and fetch his girl home. She been school up there to Cammawa [Chemawa Indian] School. Mr. Enos Pubigee is getting his little Buckskin Nell for race at

Logan on the big celebrate 4th July. Our boys played [baseball] with Plymouth boys last Saturday the was pretty good game there. [1927-06-18 LJ]

WASHAKIE, JUNE 29, 1927.   The weather pretty warm just now. . . . But some of us thinning their own sugar beet now. The grain looking pretty good this year. I expect we going have a good harvest this year now. Well the sugar beet crop look pretty good also. One little baby girl died here middle of last week. This baby, Miss May Perdash, and at Washakie Cemetery. This was first [death] for last spring. Well was sick about week. Mr. Enos Pubigee and family went up Idaho here other. And to see big Sun Dance up on the Fort Hall Reservation. He expect return in few days, and also Mr. Mose Neaman and boys going up tomorrow too on the same business. Mr. Seth Pubigee was motor down my place this morning, and accompany his family. I expect are going have a two [day] celebrate 4 and 5 July at West Portage, and our going join the big celebration. . . . They going a horse races on the both day, and also going have a fight. But Master Chester Ottogary and his brother Master Custer on the programme too. Come over to West Portage who want to see boxing. Don't miss it now. Mr. Harry Dixon To-Touna [hereafter Tootiaina] is visit my farm down Elwood and he going up to Idaho, for awhile, then he return Nevada after visit some his relation up Idaho. Mr. Seth Pubigee and Mr. Warren Wongan was motor down Ogden last Saturday. Mr. Enos Pubigee was down Brigham City last Saturday and he joining the parade and get $5.00 prize down there and with all his family. Mr. Kippetchew Noragan and wife was motor over to Logan city last week ago. Mr. George Tospanguitch still sick just now. But he is getting little better. Master Chester Ottogary going fight over to Logan city on the 4th July, Commence at 8:30 o'clock. . . . I am going over to Logan city 4th July on matter of the business. [1927-07-02 LJ]

WASHAKIE, JULY 8, 1927.   . . . Our people are join celebrate 4th July with West Portage 4 and 5 July and having good time. There was a horse racing and riding buck contest. It is was a real good time. The Black Foot Indians baseball team played with our boys.[5] The score was about 4 to 1 in favor of Washakie baseball team. The Black Foot Indian team is good. Well it was a good game. We have a some vistor from different part country. Some our people are been up Idaho Indian having a Sun Dance up there. But they already return now. Mr. Harry J. Dixon Tootiaina get hurt about last week and he was through off from hay stack and broke his left leg, and broke left wrist and he improved fine. But his folks is stay at my place at Elwood now. Mr. George Tospanguitch died up to Idaho Reservation last Monday. But he was going buried up Idaho today. Mr. Enos Pubigee purchase a second hand Buick car last two week ago. He motor down Tremonton yesterday. . . . Mr. Thomas Pabawena and [family] went to Idaho Reservation yesterday to attend Mr. George Tospanguitch funeral. Mr. George Tospanguitch was well known all over the country. He was 80 year old. Mr. Nephi Perdash was motor down Garland other day. Mr. Warren [Wongan] purchase a second hand Ford car here couple day ago. I and boys been over to Logan city on the 4th July. Master Chester Ottogary was fight with Jack Andrews and bout was 10 round to a draw. Then he fight with Mr. Michel from Colorda [Colorado], lightweight champion and six round to draw, at West Portage and Master Chief Custer Ottogary fight with Fred Neeley from Malad, and Custer decision over him. Mr. Mose Neaman with his boys been up to Idaho Reservation to see the Sun Dance up there, and also one Indian man died up there. He was middle age man. Mr. Nephi Zundel has not return from Idaho Reservation yet. Mr. John Phillip [Phelps] is here now. He come from Winter River Reservation, Wyoming. He expect stay here for while, and also few visitors from Elko, Nevada. Mr. Warren Wongan was motor down Ogden last week ago. [1927-07-09 LJ]

WASHAKIE, JULY 13, 1927.   The warm weather is still here, the sugar beet crop is doing all right this year, and the grain crop be good. . . . Our people are good condition, only one man died up Fort Hall Reservation about a week ago. Mr. Nephi Zundel is still up Idaho Res. Mr. Elias Pubigee and wife motor down Brigham City last Tuesday. . . . Mr. James Pabawena and more others was been down Tremonton on matter of business. Mr. Elias Pubigee was purchase a second handed Ford car last week ago. Mr. Chief Harry Dixon is getting better now. But he was a broken leg and wrist. He laid up over week at Garland Hospital. Mrs. Harry Dixon is working in sugar beet field north Field, and with her grandson, Master Ray Hack. Their home was at Elko, Nevada. Mr. Moroni Timbimboo has been up Idaho Reservation with accompany Mr. Thomas Pabawena and his family and visiting some his relation up there. Miss Iba [Ivy] Hootchew come home from school two week ago. She stay with her sister Miss Timbimboo [Amy Hootchew Timbimboo] at Washakie. Mr. Enos Pubigee and wife and his father been up Lava Hot Springs, Idaho last part last week. He return home same day. . . . Master Chester Ottogary was visit Washakie last Sunday. Mr. John Phillip [Phelps] still our town yet. He come from Wyoming. . . . Mr. George Mose return from Nevada about couple weeks ago. But he play ball with our boys here. Our boys going down Layton, Utah, on the Pioneer Day play ball. Mr. Joe Woonsook and wife been up Lava Hot Spring about week ago, on account being sick. Some our people are buy some fruit down Brigham City now. Mr. Seth Pubigee motor down Ogden here about week ago, and accompany Mr. Warren Wongan and his wife too. [1927-07-23 LJ]

WASHAKIE, JULY 28, 1927.   The grain crop all harvesting just now. But nearly all over with. Well, we having a good harvest this year, and wheat crop is very splendid, and also the sugar beet is good too. The weather is getting pretty hot. Everything dry now. Some of our went over to Logan city and spent 24 July there. And some went over to Holbrook, Idaho, spent Pioneer Day over there. Mr. Enos Pubigee took his race [horse] over to Holbrook. She was lose on the 3 1-8 [three-eighths mile] race and Spark Plug win the race; and also having real good time over [there]. But our boys was play ball with Holbrook, and score was about 6 to 8 in favor of our boys. And also some of our people went to Malad City 25 July. But we was join Parade. We have a Ford truck hauled our warriors and have a head gears [headdresses] on. It was looking fine. The boss of this gang was Mr. Seth Eagle [Pubigee]. He took all charge of our business. Then our boys played [ball] with Malad boys. It was a real good game. The game was start about 2:30 o'clock on the 25 July, 1927. Then fight come about 5 o'clock at the Star Threata [Theatre], Malad City. Master Chester O. Kickapoo Dan boxing with Mr. Billy Mark, Casper, Wyo. But he was a half breed Navajo Indian. Mr. Kickapoo Dan was out box him. He weight about 175 lbs. he overweight. Mr. Kickapoo Dan but he was decision over him. Then Master Chief Custer Ottogary, his brother, fight with Wyne [Wayne?] Huff, Union [?], and he decision over him in 4 round bout. Mr. Huff only last three round. . . . The was a Tremonton ball club come over to Washakie on last Sunday, try to get our boys to play ball with last Monday. But they was all line up to Malad City so they didn't go over. Then he prospond [postponed] for next Sunday. Well I expect our boys will going over to play with them. . . . Mr. Moroni Timbimboo and family also his father and mother with over to Holbrook and Malad City and having a splendid good time both places. Mr. Catch Lion [Toyahdook] purchased a second hand Cherelete [Chevrolet] car last week. . . . Mr. Tom Elk went over to Logan and spent 24th July over there and accompany his family, etc. [1927-07-30 LJ]

WASHAKIE, AUGUST 3, 1927.   The harvest all done. The crop turn out pretty good this year. The weather been so dry this summer. We didn't have rain since last spring. But I expect going have rain in the few day or so. The our boys play with the Trenton [UT] about last Sunday. Well hay is so much this year. But kind scarce around our place or here now. . . . Mr. Ammon Pubigee been up to Reservation on the matters of business. But he also [visiting] his relation up there, etc. Mr. Thomas Pabawena gone out Nevada for work, and his brother Mr. Dave Pabawena. They expect return home in this month. . . . Mr. Harry Dixon Tootiaina still at Garland Hospital now. But he will go out about next week, and his wife is visit him last week ago. Mr. Chester R. Ottogary and his brother Mr. Custer E. Ottogary been up Fort Hall Reservation last part last week on the matters of business. Mr. Enos Pubigee went Wyoming to going visit his friends and relation out there. . . . Mr. Egpe [?] and family visit his relation Mr. Jacob Peyope here in our town and he return to his home after 24 July. Mr. Tom Elk and family move back from Idaho about two week ago. But he may remain about another month. . . . [1927-08-06 LJ]

WASHAKIE, AUGUST 18, 1927.   The harvesting all over now. But harvest pretty good this year, and also sugar beet is good too. The grain nearly all sold just now. We have very dry summer this year, and Relief Society having a party at meeting [house] other night and gave a Grand Ball and good old time everybody enjoyed themself. The weather is warm here. But big part summer is gone now. Mr. Harry Dixon Tootiaina, Chief of Western Indians tribe layed up for broken left leg. He was in Garland hospital for six week. But he is getting little better and he was very weak, didn't up around yet, his leg get all right just now. . . . Mr. Seth Pubigee and family visit Mr. Harry Dixon Tootiaina and wife down Elwood at my place, and he make another visit about last week too. Mr. Hyrum Wongsaw visit him too. . . . Mr. Catch Lion [Toyahdook] and wife went up Yellowstone Park last week ago. He hasn't return home yet, and Mr. Henry Woonsook accompany him. They expect return home next week. . . . Mr. Joe Woonsook is going blind and his eyes so bad now and could not see anything. Mr. Enos Pubigee was trade car with a fellow from Ogden here other day, both the cars was same make as Chevrolet. Mr. Catch Lion purchase a new salden [sedan] Chercolet [Chevrolet] car. Mr. Warren Wongan visit Chief Harry Dixon Tootiaina last week ago. Mr. George P. Sam went down

Chester Ottogary in parade dress, ca. 1927, possibly for a 24th of July celebration at either Brigham City or Logan Utah. *Courtesy Clyde S. Ottogary.*

Ogden last Tuesday on the matters of buisness and return same day. . . . I was made buisness trip over to Logan about ago. Master Chester R. Ottogary going fight down Ogden tomorrow night. . . . [1927-08-20 LJ]]

WASHAKIE, AUGUST 31, 1927.   Some of our out hunt some pine nuts out west about 80 miles from here. They went last Monday morning. But I expect out about one week or ten days. The school soon start for winter time and expect same man teach school this year. We all our people are good condition just now, no sick. But some one just gone away for work. Mr. Seth Eagle Pubigee made buisness trip down Salt Lake last week ago. Mr. Enos Pubigee made a buisness trip to Idaho Reservation last part last week ago, and accompanied Mr. Warren Wongan. Mr. Moroni Timbimboo made buisness trip down Brigham City last week ago. Mr. Seth Pubigee made buisness trip on the last Monday. But he line up for the fight on the Peach Day, Sept. 9, 1927. Then he made another trip up Malad City today on the same buisness. Mr. Chester Ottogary and his brother Custer Ottogary made a nice vacation last week ago up to the Deweyville mountain. . . . Mr. Ammon Pubigee expect going out west and trying hunt some pine nuts too. Mr. Charlie Perdash and his wife gone out west and hunt some pine nuts. Mr. Harry Dixon Tootiaina still in the bed for two month ago today. He was broke his left leg on the 30 June. He is improving pretty slowly. But he was under Indian Dr. treatment here about couple days ago. They have much grain this year and sugar beet too, and the weather change now. The weather getting little colder. Well sir some people are going down Brigham City on the Peach Day and help join Parade. Mr. Thomas

Hazel Timbimboo Zundel and her husband, Wallace Zundel, picking pine nuts near Yost, Utah. *Courtesy Mae Timbimboo Parry.*

Pabawena hasn't return from his Nevada trip yet. . . . I made a business trip up to Washakie yesterday. [1927-09-03 LJ]

WASHAKIE, SEPTEMBER 17, 1927.   We have a splendid rain here . . . two day ago. It is help our fall grain, and the people are very good condition just now. We start our fall working now and put in grain. The weather getting little bit colder. . . . All our people are return from Brigham City Peach Day.[6] We having very good time down there too. Mr. Eddie Drinks and Indian man been down to Brigham City they was come late for Peach Day will return last Tuesday. Their home up on Reservation, Idaho. Mr. Ammon Pubigee and one of his went out west to hunt some pine nuts. Mr. Chester Ottogary and his brother, Master Custer Ottogary accompany him. Mr. Harry Dixon still in bed . . . but he getting better just now. Mr. James Pabawena and with brother John Pabawena accompany made a business down to Elwood today, and also Mr. George P. Sam to visit my place down to Elwood today. . . . Mr. Enos Pubigee gone out west to hunt some pine nuts. He may return next Saturday. Mr. Yeager Timbimboo and wife has not return from Raft River. Mr. Samboo is stayed with Mrs. Thomas Pabawena place not [yet]. But he lost his wife about three month ago. Mr. Chief Harry Dixon Tootiaina has received a important [news] from McMermitts [Fort McDermitt on the Nevada/Oregon border] Indians last Tuesday. These people want him coming out there to Nevada. There was a great gathering out there. . . . I made a business trip over to Logan City on Tuesday last. Mrs. Elias Pubigee doing nice she born baby in the last Monday last. . . . [1927-09-17 LJ]

WASHAKIE, SEPTEMBER 30, 1927.   We all our fall crop put in now, and the weather are getting pretty cold now here. The people are getting alright now. Some of our people are going to Idaho for work. Well, Mr. Yeager Timbimboo and wife come back from west other day. Mr. Nephi Zundel went up to American Fall to attend County fair, and also his brother-in-law went [with] him too. Mr. Jacob Peyope and his boy went to American Falls too. I am at Idaho Reservation and been down to American Falls to see big fair. And acquainted many Indians are here too and visits some my own relation too. Indians are good condition here on the Reservation. Mr. Willie Dan little girl died here at Tinchhee place. Mr. Seth Pubigee went Idaho Fall to work with family, and several other boys with him too. Mr. Thomas Pabawena and his two brothers hasn't return home yet from Nevada. Mr. Tom Elk went back to Idaho, about two week ago. Some our people are attend Tremonton Fair last week and also Malad City fair too. . . . [1927-10-01 LJ]

WASHAKIE, OCTOBER 18, 1927.   We was visiting Indians out Nevada. It was all Indians out there Paiute. They was a big gathering Indians out to McDermitt from different places of state, and having a real Indians Dance about six nights. This was a small Reservation. But their only 40 or 50 families living in this small Reservation. It takes about two good day get over there about 422 miles out there to Ft. McDermitt. I expect 5 different states was there to the big time. We getting out on the 6 Oct., 1927. . . . I was return home on the night Friday night. Then went up Idaho Reservation last Monday and Tuesday and seen some my relation and friends, and made some business. Well I made a very short visit at Industrial School at Fort Hall, and seen some Indians working spuds. There was plenty job up there. I return home this afternoon, everybody is doing [well]. Some of them working sugar been north Garland factory. Well sir, the people are been Conference at Salt Lake City last week. And return week ago. But having good time while they been down. I and Mr. James Pabawena been up to Fort Hall Reservation in few days. Mr. Mose Neaman is sick in bed now. Mr. Willie Neaman and with brother Master Linford Neaman came home last Monday while they father was sick. Mr. Enos Pubigee still working up to Idaho Falls now. Mr. Frank West [was] kill up to Pocatello on the last Monday and by automobile and instantly kill. Mr. Chief Harry D. Tootiaina out to Fort McDermitt. But he was broke his left leg here last summer. But he went out with me about week ago last Saturday, he broke his leg again and he fell in water ditch. He was in Indian Hospital at Fort McDermitt just now. His wife is here, she working sugar beet field now. I acquainted so many Paiute out Nevada while out. There was about 5 different chief there at McDermitt from part of Reservation. [1927-10-22 LJ]

WASHAKIE, OCTOBER 28, 1927.   The people here working in the sugar field down around Garland factory. But some is digging their own crop beets. Some of them went up Idaho working spuds up around Idaho Falls or some other places. We put in all our fall crop in already. But we have a real nice rain other day. It help all fall grain. There was quite lot sugar beet raised here our town this year. Our day schoool is start up last two week ago. Mr. Catch Lion [Toyahdook] and family work up Idaho. He been home here last week ago. Mr. Thomas Pabawena layed in bed for two week ago, and his eyes . . . improving pretty slow now. Mr. Mose Neaman is took sick last week. He getting little better today. I expect get work again few days. Mr. Ammon Pubigee with his older son visit my place down Elwood last Sunday. Mr. Seth Pubigee a business trip down Ogden City last Monday. Mr. Enos Pubigee and family short visit my place down Elwood last Tuesday. . . . Mr. Geo. P. Sam made a business trip down Tremonton last part last week. Mr. Moroni Timbimboo made a business trip down Tremonton last part last week. Mr. Elias Pubigee and wife made short visit at my place in Elwood some time ago. Mr. Warren Wongan and family coming home Idaho about last week ago. Mr. Harry D. Tootiaina is still at McDermitt . . . broken his leg again and he is at Indian hospital out there. But I like hear from him. I was made a business trip over to Logan last Sunday. Mr. James Pabawena made a business trip up Idaho Reservation some time ago. Mr. Jim Wagon return from Idaho Falls. He was working in spuds. Mrs. Harry D. Tootiaina still here. But was topping sugar beet here. She expect going Nevada after get through topping. [1927-10-29 LJ]

WASHAKIE, NOVEMBER 3, 1927.   The people are here working sugar beet crop. Well some of them work their own sugar beet and some work for the white people down near sugar factory. We have a good crop sugar beet this year, and better than last year. But all crop being so good this year. The weather get change now, and winter soon come here. Our fall crop wheat looking [good] now. I expect we going have another good crop next year. I received letter here other day from Mr. Chief Harry Tootiaina. He was doing fine out to Nevada. . . . Mr. Jack Johny [Johny Jack] just return from Idaho Reservation here about last Sunday, and also Master Herbert Pabawena accompany him. . . . Mr. Jacob Peyope is hunt his boy last Monday night. But his boy run away his second hand Ford car. Mr. Enos Pubigee and wife was short visit down Elwood my place about last week ago. Mr. Shear Bronchwast [Sear Poncho] and Mr. Mule Pocatello, and short visit here in our town, etc. Mr. Chester Ottogary and with his brother Master Custer Ottogary still up there to Idaho and working in spuds. They expect come down soon as get through. But the weather getting cold just now. [1927-11-05 LJ]

WASHAKIE, NOVEMBER 9, 1927.   The weather getting change just now. And winter soon be here. We have nice little rain about two week ago, and helps great deal our full [fall] crops, and it up now. But looking like splendid for next year again. The threshing is pretty well done now. The sugar [beet] nearly all done just now. But most our people topping beet for white people down north sugar factory now. I expect soon be through with them. And some of us have good crop beet this year. Our people been [good] condition just now since Mr. Geo. Tospanquitch died. And most the old people are pass away now, there is 1–4 old people been live here in our little town just now. There was a very stormy weather since last couple weeks ago. Mr. Seth Pubigee made a business trip down Brigham about last Thursday. Mr. [Jacob] Peyope made trip up Idaho Reservation last Sunday. But his 16 year old boy stole his second hand Ford car, and run up to Idaho Reservation. But brought to car back last Monday night. Mr. Warren Wongan is hauling him around Garland, Tremonton and looking him all over for him. Finally, went up Idaho and catch him up there and left the boys up there too. Mr. Enos Pubigee been down Trenton about last Saturday night and doing some Sunday shopping. . . . I made business trip down Ogden City today. Mr. James Pabawena received letter from Mr. Harry D. Tootiaina he said in his broken legs is getting better now. But he his want wife home at Elko. Nev. soon as can. She is working in sugar beet field at Fielding, Utah. I expect she soon return home when done with beet. . . . Master Linford Neaman and Orvan [Evans] Peyope just return home from Idaho last Monday. These boys was stole Mr. Jacob Peyope Ford car last Sunday and he left them up to Reservation. [1927-11-12 LJ]

WASHAKIE, NOVEMBER 17, 1927.   We had very stormy weather all time now. But and helping on our dry farms. The fall wheat crop looking good so far. Some our people working sugar beet field now. They get through later part this month. It is pretty dirty job work now and the weather keeping bad all time last week ago. The sugar beet harvest nearly through by this time. There [are] some dig their own beet just now, they all get through last week ago. The beet isn't so good this yr are around our vicinity.

Mr. Nephi Zundel and his family is working at Mr. Jim and Mr. George Steed place, near Fielding Station. Mr. Nephi Perdash purchase a new saddle pony about couple week ago. . . . Mr. Seth Pubigee been down Brigham City on matters of business. I was down to Brigham City on business. Mr. Thomas Pabawena still has eyes get bad. But he went down Ogden City last week and to see Dr. Harding, and he expect getting little improving yet since he seen Dr. Mr. Harry D. Tootiaina still out Ft. McDermitt, Nevada. But his leg leased [least] getting better. He said in his letter come home on next month or more. And Mrs. Harry D. Tootiaina went to home last week ago, She left here on Sunday morning, and she accompany Miss MoNno. Mr. Dave Pabawena taken these woman taken over to Deweyville station. . . . [1927-11-19 LJ]

WASHAKIE, NOVEMBER 24, 1927.   . . . We have a pretty cold weather here about 2 week ago. Some of our people are still working sugar beet field now, around north Garland factory, and it is pretty bad weather getting sugar beet out of the ground. There was about three crows [crews] are work for white men sugar beet. They expect getting through next week some time now on. Well sir, and there was quite lot beet in the ground yet. We had little bits snow here last week ago. Mr. Jim Wagon and wife to attend the court last Tuesday and more other do too. Miss Alice Pubigee and Miss Louise Ottogary broke in house [owned] by Mr. George Mose and stole some clothes, shawl, hand chief [handkerchief], bead necktie, and more other article too. The hearing was on the 22 Nov. in the room 1 in the County Commissioner room at Brigham City, and hold jevinel [Juvenile] Court. These girls was found guilty before the jevinel [Juvenile] judge. They sent to jail for len [ten] days and there is two more girls from Washakie in jail too, at Brigham City. These girls ran away, the sheriff pick up. Master Evan Peyope was stole Mr. John Pabawena saddle and rifle and he sold them to Mr. Brigg Johns from West Portage. Then he catch a pluss [probably bus] at West Portage and went up Fort Hall Res. But his dad sent word to Fort Hall and arrested the boy, and put to industrial school at Fort Hall. Mr. Nephi Perdash been down Brigham City on the matter of business. . . . I and Mr. Elias Pubigee attend court down Brigham City on the 22 Nov. or on Tuesday. . . . Mr. Thomas Pabawena eyes getting little bit better and is improve pretty slow. Mr. Harry D. Tootiaina still out McDermitt now but he said [in] letter his leg getting better and getting strong every-day now. He expect coming home on the 28 this month. Mr. Towhee was visit here our country some time ago. But he purchase a second hand Ford car down Ogden City. But he stay here three [days] and took his car home. His home is near Tiau-hee [Tyhee] Station. Master Custer E. Ottogary and his brother Master Chester R. Ottogary still up Idaho Reservation. They expect be home on the middle of this month. They hasn't show up yet. . . . [1927-11-26 LJ]

WASHAKIE, NOVEMBER 30, 1927.   The people are here good condition now yet. The is getting pretty cold and the winter is here now. We had very stormy day all last week, and some time rain and some time sun shine. I expect the rain help great deal for the fall grain. But it is looking pretty green now. Well I hope we will have a good crop next year. All our people nearly return home from their work. There is some still working in sugar beet yet. . . . Mr. Enos Pubigee is plowing for Jap down to Riverside. Mr. George Tomock just return home from his work yesterday. Mr. Nephi Perdash was motor down Tremonton other day and he [see] his daughter at Fielding station. But his daughter [Ethel Eliza Perdash] got married down Ogden about two week ago, and she married to Mexican boy. They making their home at Fielding Station. Miss Irene Tomock was in jail last week ago for runaway. Her trail [trial] go be at Brigham City today. Mr. James Pabawena was down Tremonton yesterday on some business and he accompany his two brothers. I made a business trip to Washakie yesterday, and am doing much business just now and busy all time. Mr. Seth Pubigee is looking for the Master Chester Ottogary or Kickapoo Dan every day now. But they still up Idaho Reservation now. They expect coming home any time now. Mr. George P. Sam was down Tremonton other day and doing some shopping. Mr. Nephi Zundel and family return from work last week ago. Mr. Thomas Pabawena still eye sick now some time his pretty good or bad. Mr. Mose Neaman getting better now and he was sick two week ago. Mr. Tom Elk is still up Idaho Reservation. He lease land some Indian land up there. Mrs. Elias Pubigee got out jail yesterday and Mr. Charlie Cheal bring her up far as Riverside, and she take evening train up to Washakie. [1927-12-03 LJ]

WASHAKIE, DECEMBER 23, 1927.   We had very cold weather now. The first snow fall about 4 inch, and snowed here more than 4 inch now. I guess about 6 inch right now, and there is coldest weather ever had for many years. The Malad River frozen over last week. Mr. Bishop Geo. M. Ward through threshing alfalfa seed last week ago. and also Mr. Moroni Timbimboo too and two more others. Mr. Nephi Perdash been up Idaho Res. on matter of business and he been down Ogden too. Mr. Seth Pubigee down Ogden some time ago last week and accompany his brother-in-law too.

Mr. Mose Meania [Neaman] went over to Logan about week ago and he expect spent Christmas time over there and all his family. Mr. Kippetchew Noragan motor down Ogden other day. Mr. James Pabawena with his two brothers been down Ogden and matter of business today and return in the evening. Mr. Enos Pubigee was chaffer [chauffeur] for these man. Mr. Jim Wagon was visit Logan City about last week. Master Herbert Pabawena been down Salt Lake City about week and he looking for fight down there. And he return last week. Mr. George P. Sam been over to Logan. [The next four sentences were apparently typeset incorrectly and should read as follows:] Mr. Moroni Timbimboo was been over to Logan City and work temple and accompany his wife, and also Mr. Warren Wongan and his wife too. Mr. Jacob Peyope is doing some trapping some coyote. Our boys was a big rabbit hunt last Wednesday. . . . Mr. Ammon Pubigee been down Elwood and visit my place yesterday. . . . Mr. George Mose were home about two week ago. He making his home Nevada. But he left his children and wife here at Washakie, and he expect return here in the spring. [1927-12-24 LJ]

WASHAKIE, JANUARY 20, 1928.   The people are now good condition now. But nobody sick now, since last fall. The weather is getting little bit warmer now. The big part winter is gone right now. And we have much snow here. The snow is about 6 inch. The hay is scarce around here just. I have been up Idaho Reservation about 2 week ago on the matter of business, and also made a business trip out west on the last weeks ago. I have seen my old accquainted out around Elko, Nevada, and seen Mr. Chief Harry D. Tootiaina, Western Shoshone. He had his leg broken twice last summer and he is get well and his legs. But he is up around and his leg is perfectly well and he expect coming here early in spring. But he working pretty hard on this Indians land matter. He is well known Indians Chief of the west. There was about 800 hundred [Indians] scarrated [scattered] over the Nevada. I visiting different places of the Nevada last week ago. And return home about last Friday or Saturday. Mr. Nephi Perdash been down Ogden last on the matter of business. Mr. George Tomock and wife been down industrial school at north Ogden to [see] their girl. . . . Mr. Wilford Peyope return home from Idaho Reservation about last week ago. Mr. Seth Pubigee and Mr. Chester Ottogary made a business trip down Brigham last week. . . . Last Wednesday night the boys was on the boxing contest. Mr. Chester Ottogary or Kickapoo Dan meet Mr. Con Hansen, 4 round bout, they fought draw. And we had another little fighter, his name is Ed. Wagon. He was fight last Wednesday night. [1928-01-28 LJ]

WASHAKIE, FEBRUARY 2, 1928.   The Indians say we are going early spring this year. One old man is good weather profit [prophet], he said in month of December. He told some Indians up Fort Hall Reservation going have a fair winter not much snow, not much cold. It is come out that acately [actually] what he said. Some of them satisfied what he said to them. I believe he was prophsite [prophesied] the weather and he is one of the [that] Kind Doctor. The weather kind warm here put near [colloquialism: pert'near] till this winter. We have had about 5 inch snow here right now. We are going have a big reservation here at Washakie in future time. Well had some land claim against United States. I higher [hire] me two attorney awhile back last about 6 year ago, and all our Lawyer working on it now, and also Congress[man] D. C. Colton [Don B. Colton, Utah], Washington, D. C.

Mr. Nephi Perdash girl married to Mexican boy last fall. But she was married [without] her parent consent. But her father was refuse her married, then he take up [matter] with [Utah] Governor [George H.] Dern about last week ago. Mr. Dern retradition [extradition] paper. She went out to Los Angeles, California before Christmas. Well the Law provides the Mexican men can[not] married Indians. It was prohited [prohibited]. Now she arrested at Los Angeles last Saturday. The Box Elder Co. Sheriff going out to bring her back to Utah again. Her name is Eathel E. [Ethel Eliza] Perdash. But her husband was refuse her after get married and raise so many trouble. Mr. Nephi Perdash made a business down Ogden last week. Mr. Seth Eagle was motor up to Malad City last part of last week, and accompany Mr. Kickapoo Dan Ottogary. . . . Mr. James Pabawena and with his two Brother made a business trip down sugar factory Garland. . . . Mr. Wilford Peyope was motor up Idaho Reservation two week ago and he has return last week. . . . Mr. Jim Wagon made a business trip down Ogden about last week ago. Mr. Moroni Timbimboo made a business trip to Malad City last week. Mr. George Elk been down to visit his daughter north Ogden. She was in the industrial school Ogden, and she been every since last November. Mr. Timus Perdash and Mr. Henry Woonsook motor down Ogden couple week ago. Our day school running good this year. The school children gaving a party last Friday night and everybody have enjoyable time. The is no body sick to speak of, etc. [1928-02-04 LJ]

WASHAKIE, FEBRUARY 9, 1928.   The people are very good condition just now, and spring be here. The weather getting warmer every day. Some of our people think the spring is here just now. We haven't got much snow right now and snow is nearly all thawing out. Last Friday night had a Grand Ball here at ward meeting house, and everybody is having a jolly time. The hay is pretty scarce. But the winter wasn't hard this year. It seem to feel like spring all winter along, perhaps we may get cold weather later long. Mr. Bishop Yeager Timbimboo wife is pretty sick here last week ago. Mr. Kippetchew Noragan made a business trip down Ogden last week ago. Mr. Warren Wongan and wife motor down Salt Lake City about week ago. Mr. Ammon Pubigee and his son Mr. Seth Eagle made business trip over to Logan City yesterday. . . . I and Mr. James Pabawena and his brother Mr. Thomas Pabawena has been over to Logan city too. Mr. Seth Eagle made a trip down Salt Lake City last Tuesday. But he was the manager of the Kickapoo Dan, and last Monday night fight down Salt Lake City at McCullough arena last Monday. He fought with Billy McCann. But Mr. Downey Hardy was referee the fight. The decision was given to Billy McCann, etc. I was accompany my two sons while they down Salt Lake City and return home on the last Tuesday evening. I got letter from Mr. Annies Tommy yesterday. He stated in his letter some Indians boys had a trouble white man begin killing deer last fall. He expect need help out to Ibapah. It is about 150 mile west of Great Salt Lake City, and there is about 30 families living out there now. I have visit Journal office last Wed. I have great surprise to see that new automatic printer. Now is it installed in the Journal Building, and it [began] operate on last Saturday. I think it is great thing to human name make. In this our world, and it not big machine. But this machine weigh about 70 or 90 pound. Well I going tell my people about the machine. They said this was great machine. They heard this kind before. They want know how far this carries message, and I told them carries about many hundred miles and ask me again, and said to them by wire not by air. The machine is get good business or work order. [1928-02-11 LJ]

WASHAKIE, FEBRUARY 23, 1928.   The weather is ittle bit cold just now. But our say going have a spring is coming now. They people here very good condition now. Only one death this winter. No one sick just now. The snow nearly gone here now. There is very little on the ground yet. We a good time yesterday a celebrate George Washington Birthday, and we had a nice programme at ward chapel . . . [and] they have children dance after dinner. . . . Mr. Danyhay and his wife were here at place of Mr. Jacob Peyope. His wife is sick about two month, and wife take under Dr. care, now other day they went down Ogden city to see Mrs. Dr. Peaucanon [Buchanan]. But she is getting little [im]prove now. But their home near Tyhee Station, Idaho. Mr. Willie Neaman went up Idaho and looking for some work. He gone last week ago. . . . Mrs. George Tomock and her daughter return home other night. They been motor down Ogden City three days. I and Mr. James Pabawena his two brother made business trip down Ogden last Monday. Mr. Jacob Peyope son and two other boys run away with his ford car. While he is celebrate [Washington's birthday]. Then he go after them. He catch the boys in Garland and took his car away from them, and boys walked home last night. They walked about 18 miles. Mr. Seth Eagle made business trip Samaria, Idaho, last week ago. Mr. Warren Wongan and Mr. Catch Lion [Toyahdook] was been down Ogden other [day] on the matter of business. [1928-02-25 LJ]

WASHAKIE, MARCH 1, 1928.   Our people are rejoice over spring is here now. But the weather is change now. There some our people been Brigham City other day to attend court. We had trouble with 3 boys here on Washington['s Birthday]. They stole Mr. Jacob Peyope Ford car and they arrest the boys here last Saturday and hearing come off last Tuesday afternoon and they release one boy and other are found guilty by Mr. Judge Neilsen from Logan.[7] I and Mr. Catch Lion [Toyahdook] he is one special gaurdine [guardian of] boy. He high [hire] Mr. Chez to employee to appeal at court again.[8] But he said us going appeal court in side ten day, them [then] another hearing again. Mr. Jacob Peyope was attend Juvenile Court last Tuesday afternoon. He willing he [his son] attend industrial school two year. But he said before judge [he] is bad boy. Mr. George M. Ward was interrupted [interpreted] for them. Mr. James [Pabawena] and I and his two brother been down Ogden important business. Mr. Geo. P. Sam, Mr. Jacob Peyope, and Mr. Warren Wongan was motor down Ogden city last Tuesday. Mr. Seth Eagle was made a business trip down Ogden yesterday. Mr. Chester R. Ottogary was been down Brigham City. But he start walked to his former home Elwood last Tuesday night. He was so all in when reach home. . . . Mr. Thomas Pabawena and I visit Miss Pabayou place at Ogden yesterday morning and doing some business with her. Mr. Tan-hee [Danyhay] and wife return home last week ago, and his wife getting little better. They expect back some time next month. Mr. Moroni Timbimboo and wife motor up Malad city other day. Some Samarites [probably Lamanites [9]] coming over from Washakie and act of miss[ion]ary work on the third week March, 1928. Mr. Bishop Tom Perry of North Ward [Logan] want us people coming to preach to people there. But we going arrangements with [him] now. If we come we will let knowing them so they coming to meeting hear our teaching. All you people read Journal know when we come, we invited everybody, coming at 9 ward meeting. Remember the date on the 18 Mar. 1928. Well I can[not] mention their names yet. [1928-03-03 LJ]

WASHAKIE, MARCH 9, 1928.   The people rejoice over the Spring is here. They soon start their farm work now, again. The snow is all gone by this time, the warm is here yet. Our day school running pretty nice this year. Mr. Tom Elk just return from Idaho. He was visit his relatives up there. Mrs. Jacob Peyope is also been up Idaho Reservation and he [Jacob] was attend his sister funeral service last Wednesday he was return home other day.

Mr. George P. Sam has not return home yet. He was went on especial business. Also he visit his nephew, Mr. Albert Scobby. He was pretty sick in the hospital at Fort Hall. Mr. Wilford Peyope is been up to Idaho Res. and return other day. Mr. Ammon Pubigee and wife been down Ogden last Thursday and doing shopping and also his son, Mr. Elias Pubigee and wife accompany him. I and Mr. James M. Pabawena is been down Ogden on the important business. . . . Mr. Enos Pubigee been over to Logan first of the last week ago on especial business, and also Master Custer Ottogary him too. . . . Mr. Moroni Timbimboo and wife just return home from Salt Lake City last Tuesday, and he is visit his sister-in-law, she was kind sick, she live in Salt Lake City. [1928-03-12 LJ]]

WASHAKIE, MARCH 15, 1928.   . . . The people pretty poor this spring. And pretty scarce around here now. The spring soon be here. They some of us over to Logan City on the matter Sunday School works. . . . Mr. Jacob Peyope and Warren Wongan visit his son Master Evans Peyope down to industrial school north Ogden last week ago. Mr. Kippetchew Noragan wife been down Brigham City first part this week, on the importance business. Mr. Catch Toyahdook and his wife was in courthouse last Monday and doing and to atubered [adopted] him by Mr. Jim Wagon and wife. He name is Master Edward Tiretooke [Toyahdook] now . . . . Mr. Mose Neaman has return from fort Hall Reservation last week ago. But visiting his relatives and friends up there. Mr. Geo. P. Sam was return home from Idaho Res. and visiting his friends and relatives there.

I have received from Mr. Jim Lewis from Burns, Oregon. He stated in his letter there was a flue among those Indians up there and some of them died with it, and also received letter from Chief Harry D. Tootiaina too. He said in his letter the Indians out there is pretty poor condition this year no work for them right now. There is about 6 thousand Shoshone Indians of the state Nevada is homeless. They are pretty poor condition today. They earn their living by working for the Rancher men all over that country.

Remember the Journal reader, some of us coming over to Logan City and act part on the program on the 25 March. It comes on the Sunday Evening, at Nine Ward [9th Ward] of the Logan be sure come see us and it will do you good and gave you more idea, etc. [1928-03-17 LJ]]

WASHAKIE, MARCH 22, 1928.   The spring is here now, our people are rejoice. . . . Some our spring work is start. Some our people keep busy right now and put in spring grain. . . . Mr. Jacob Peyope and Mr. Warren Wongan been down Brigham City on some business. Mr. Catch Toyahdook made a business down Ogden today. Mr. Seth Pubigee accompany him. . . . Mr. Chief Harry D. Tootiaina expect coming here at Washakie pretty soon, and his family. . . . Mr. Enos Pubigee and wife is working for Jap down near Riverside . . . he got job all summer long. . . . Mr. Chester Ottogary just move down Elwood first part last week ago with his family. Miss Louise Ottogary move down to [her] father ranch in Elwood. . . . I have made a business trip down Ogden today. The some of our people wanted over to Logan, and as going take a part on the evening program next Sunday night. There will be a ward conference held here at our ward next Sunday March 25, 1928. I expect some visitors will be present to this conference. Then we will coming over to Logan after noon. I hope we will have a real good time. All your Journal reader must remember date we were coming to our part on the program. The program will be 1st, 3 fellows dress old custom, sing their own language. 2nd, 5 girls sing on Sunday songbook. 3rd will give a short speech about the Mormonism. We will corridely [cordially] invite every body. It will held at nine ward Logan about 7:30 o'clock in evening, etc. [1928-03-24 LJ]

WASHAKIE, MARCH 30, 1928.   The most of the people are with a good condition so far. There was nobody sick just now, since old Miss Moemberg died here about last month ago. The spring is here right now. But had pretty wet weather here all last week. The storm weather hangs around pretty well it make everything coming fine now. Our fall grain looking pretty good. We have a splendid rain here other day. The road is impossible to travel so much muddy right now. . . . Last Sunday night I and 5 more boys was made [trip] over to Logan. But was part on the program in evening meeting. But there was about more than 700 attended. Meeting that night, at Ninth Ward Logan. The people are great surprise for the speak Select reading and songs we [do] over there that night. We are showing new thing for Church. As we are the belong members of the church of Jesus Christ of Latter-day Saints. Bishop Perry Ninth Ward is well satisfied and more other people. Well our subject was about Gospel of the Latter Saint. There was about 5 boys, 5 girls been over to Logan City. Mr. Moroni Timbimboo and his family been up Malad City . . . he was taken up them some religion class worker up there last Sunday night too. But he was promised to come with to Logan, so he can come us on account that.

Well Mr. Chief Harry D. Tootiaina, want come here on Utah pretty soon. But he want to see our people here once more. He was been here along Jan[uary], but he want us fellows come out there people there around Elko, Battle Mountain, Carlin, Wells, and Ruby Valley too. . . . Mr. Jacob Peyope visit his son Evans Peyope down North Ogden or Industrial school. . . .

Our day school here run pretty good this year. There was about 25 or more pupil attended all winter long. Mr. Tom Elk is still here now. But he was [working] land up Fort Hall reservation. And his lease expire one more year. Mr. Dave Pabawena was trade his old Ford car for the other Ford car and pay money [for] different [difference].

Our spring work soon start. But the weather is bad could [not] do any work just now. The ground is so wet cannot do thing. I expect we will have good weather so we can work up the ground and seeded too, etc. [1928-04-04 LJ]

WASHAKIE, APRIL 5, 1928.   The people are very good condition just now . . . not much sickness amongst us now. Our Spring is here right now. But we soon work up our ground to plant something. I hope our grain crop good this year again. Our fall crop look good. Well if get enough wet this year We will have good crop again. We have had bad wet weather here all last week ago. Some of us want going to Salt Lake City for conference next week.

I expect we going have land allotted by Government pretty soon. Our people haven't got any land for their own. If case coming through court this we will soon have land and home. The people are interested in this land claim. These belong to the Northwestern land [band] of Shoshone tribes of Indians. We have two Lawyers working on our case. But Northwestern Band Shoshone against United States, accordance the treaty July 30, 1863. We will win the case in future time. I expect going have a big reservation here at Bear River Valley, about year or two. . . .

Mr. Seth Pubigee made a business trip down Ogden City first part of this week. Mr. Catch Toyahdook was take sick on last Sunday he and wife been down Ogden to see Dr. and he visit his adopted son, Eddie Toyahdook at industrial school north Ogden. . . . Mr. George P. Sam is sick in bed last week he getting better now. Mr. Harry D. Tootiaina was send letter to me last week and telling some bad news . . . happened out to Western Shoshone Indian Reservation. And he expect coming out Utah pretty soon. . . . Mr. Ell [Al] Steel and family visit our town here some time ago last month going up Idaho. . . . Mr. Jim Wagon, was made [trip] down Ogden on the matter of business. Mr. Enos Pubigee and family visit my farm down Elwood last Tuesday morning. [1928-04-07 LJ]

WASHAKIE, APRIL 11, 1928.   The weather is getting cold here two or three days ago, and had stormy weather last week ago. Some of our people are been down Salt Lake City and attended General Conference last Sunday. They return last Monday. Mr. James Pabawena with his two brothers return from Salt Lake City last Monday. Mr. Jim Wagon and wife motor down Salt Lake City return home on the Monday and accompany Mr. Nephi Zundel. Mr. Nephi Perdash motor down Tremonton trade new Sheblete [Chevrolet] car here other day. . . . Mr. Seth Pubigee been down conference and with family and return home last Monday. Mr. Kippetchew Noragan been Conference too. Our day school pretty good this year. There was about 25 or more attend school this year. . . . [1928-04-14 LJ]

WASHAKIE, APRIL 21, 1928.   . . . The weather getting too warm just now. The spring work soon done. There was two men been here from Logan, on the last Sunday. I expect Mr. N. C. Crookston the Indian Committee was make arrange for the big celebrate for 24th July. And they told our people getting ready for big celebrate, and want ready for old custom, and more other stuff. The people are all agree to come help celebrate next coming 24th July, or Pioneer Day. Well I expect we are going have real good old time. . . . Mr. Jacob Peyope and Warren Wongan made business trip Brigham last part last week. . . . Mr. Catch Toyahdook want going up to Fort Hall Reservation and visit his relation and friend too. Mr. Jim Wagon want going up Yellowstone pretty soon on the 1st June. . . . Mr. Enos Pubigee still working for Jap down to Riverside now, and his little [?] took sick last week then he came home for awhile. But he return to work yesterday. Mr. Dewey [Moon] is still here in town just now. But he may return some time last part this month, his home up to Idaho. The day school pretty fine this year. Mr. Seth Pubigee was visit my farm down to Elwood middle part of last week. The was about only three old pioneer still living in our town right now. There are good for next two or three year more. [1928-04-21 LJ]

WASHAKIE, APRIL 26, 1928.   . . . Nearly all our spring work done here now. The weather is change and warm weather is here. Our people are very good condition nobody sick just now. Our fall grain looking fine. I expect we are going real good crop this year. Well Mr. Lane, Probate agent is here now. And working for Probate some land belong to the died mens here at Washakie. But he stayed here about two days now. Getting straight the land for the Indians. He sent here by Mr. Wm Larre, Probate Chief from Washington, D.C. He expect getting in few days I was seen him last Tuesday and some good work for our people and also one man from Salt Lake City Chief Railroad here too, and he buy some land for Railroad. Some Indian giving free right away [of way] about 20 years ago. Then he buy it from Probate agent and allowance $40.00 for acre for it. Then pay the Indians for the land now. Mr. Catch Toyahdook was visit his relatives and friend up Idaho Reservation about last week ago. And also Mr. Seth Pubigee accompany him. . . . Mr. John [Jim] Wagon and wife went down to Hot Spring last Sunday and one his boy nearly drowned in spring. But his dad pull him out the water and save his little boy life. Mr. Seth Pubigee and with Mr. Chester Ottogary been over to Logan on the matter of business on last Tuesday. Mr. James Pabawena and with his two brothers been to Logan City importance business. I and Mr. James M. Pabawena want going out Nevada on the important business. We might gone for week or more days. Mr. John Pabawena and Mr. Dave Pabawena going Nevada pretty soon and looking after their mine claim. . . . Mr. Tom Elk went up Idaho to start farm up there. Mr. Mose Neaman went up Idaho about last month he has not return home yet. But he is looking some work. [1928-04-28 LJ]

WASHAKIE, MAY 13, 1928.   We have a splendid rain here yesterday morning and it still raining now. But helps our fall grain crop. I expect have about 4 inch rain here. This rain surprise us because was not expecting rain. But everybody rejoice over this rain. I hope we are going have a big crop this. We all one our water ditch cleaning about last week ago. I hope we get enough water for our hay crop this year. Mr. Mose Neaman was return home from Idaho here about week ago. But he work on the farm up there for white. The some of the working for Adam Sheep Company and they shear sheep up the Broad Canyon. Mr. Seth Pubigee been up to Malad City last Wednesday on matter of business. . . . Mr. John [Jim] Wagon expect went up Yellowstone Park on the first June, on the matter of business. Mr. Moroni Timbimboo was motor up to Malad here about week ago. Mr. Chester R. Ottogary been down Salt Lake City middle part of last week on the matter of business and return home last part last week. Mr. George Tomock and wife was motor down Tremonton last week ago. Mr. Jacob Peyope went out Rock Spring [WY] about week ago to shearing sheep out there. Mr. Warren Wongan and wife motor down Tremonton about last week. Mrs. John Pabawena went out Wells, Nevada and little was sick out there and she accompany her daughter, Mrs. Louis Brown. But might return home next two week or more. Mr. Ammon Pubigee motor down

Tremonton some time last week. Mr. Toyahdook was motor down Ogden last week ago. Mr. Enos Pubigee still down Riverside working for Jap. He got all summer job. Mr. James Pabawena and his brothers hasn't return home yet. They may return home some time next month. They went out Nevada some time ago and went out the matter of some business. Mr. Seth Pubigee was visit my farm down Elwood some time ago last week. Mr. Nephi Perdash and wife motor down Ogden some time ago last week. Mr. Timus Perdash took sick about week ago and he getting better now. But was take a ineflusez [influenza]. . . . Mr. Ammon Pubigee and Mr. Catch Toyahdook is working for Mr. John D. Hess and they put up fence for him up around Mount Springs [UT]. They nearly done by this time now. I was received letter from my attorney Washington, D. C. about claim here now. He said in his letter we are sure getting Senator King bill through this [session].[10] I expect he will giving us home and land later on. I am mighty glad this is coming. [1928-05-19 LJ]

WASHAKIE, MAY 24, 1928.   The summer is here right now. We have had a nice little rain other day. The wheat crop look pretty so far, and our spring grain is so good now. The people are here rejoice the over nice weather having just now. The people are good condition no sick just now since death of Mrs. Mernbery [Moemberg]. Some of our went off for work just to work in sugar beet field just down near sugar factory. Mr. Chief Harry [Dixon] soon coming to Utah now. He live at Elko, Nev. Mr. James M. Pabawena and with his two brothers return from Nevada trip, about last week ago. Mr. John Pabawena boy dead at Dee Hospital Ogden last week ago. The funeral service held at Washakie Ward chapel. Mr. Jim Thompson was visit our town here last Saturday.[11] Then he went up Idaho to his relatives and friends up there. He expect went home soon he come back from Fort Hall reservation. . . . Mr. Catch Toyahdook was been visiting his brother up to Fort Hall Reservation a week ago. Mr. Seth Pubigee made a business trip down Ogden last part last week. Mr. Jacob Peyope visit his boy down industrial school north Ogden yesterday. Mr. John [Jim] Wagon been up Idaho last week and home this week, and expect go up Yellowstone in the first June, 1928. Mr. Ammon Pubigee made a business trip over to Logan last week ago and accompany Mr. Yeager Timbimboo a two week to see about the big celebration on 24–25 July, 1928. They made already arrange to come over to Logan help home celebration. I expect all our people are coming the big home celebration. . . . Mr. John Pabawena and wife went up to Idaho to visit their friend and relation up there. He may return next week. [1928-05-26 LJ]

WASHAKIE, MAY 29, 1928.   The summer is here now. But cold weather all gone. The people are poor condition just now. The grain is look pretty good, I hope we going have a good crop this and every look so good. Some of our people are going up the Idaho Reservation for the Memorial Day, and to visit some their relation and friend up there. I expect they may return home some time this week. Our people visit today. But most people working in sugar beet field now. Mr. Tom Elk is pretty sick just. His folk expect can able to live no longer he took sick just few days ago. Mr. Dave Pabawena return home yesterday from his Nevada trip. He was been for week or ten day ago. But he bring Mrs. Thompson home, and also three children his brother, Mr. John Pabawena. Mr. Jim Thompson was visit town here some time he return home last week. His at Wells, Nevada, and he made a business trip up Idaho Reservation before he return home. Mr. Nephi Zundel motor down Garland first part last week ago. . . . Mr. George Tomock is working down Deweyville on the sugar company farm. . . . Mr. John [Jim] Wagon expect going to Yellowstone in side four weeks more. He expect going around by Lander, Wyoming. . . . Mr. James M. Pabawena with his brother Mr. Thomas Pabawena and family motor over to Cache Valley. They hasn't return home yet. Mr. Ammon Pubigee and Catch Toyahdook and Mr. Yeager Timbimboo has been appointed committees on the big home celebration of Logan City. There will be lots our people come over to Logan City on the 24 and 25 July. I was been over Thursday attend a pioneer meeting also take part in the program. . . . Mr. Jacob Peyope was return last week. He was shearing sheep out Wyoming about two week ago. . . . Some our men doing Earigate [irrigate] their hay crop just now, and some the hay ready to cut now. [1928-06-02 LJ]

WASHAKIE, JUNE 26, 1928.   The people are very anxious to getting ready for the 24 July Come celebration at Logan just. I expect every thing ready by this time, and they are fixing their war bonnet now. Well it come pretty time fast now. All our dry farm seem to pretty dry. Well we have a nice shower here last week ago. Some place the grain crop touched by the frost about last week ago, in our vicinity. I expect we have a good here. The weather is getting too warm now. Now we getting our first hay up now. No sugar beet raise in town this year. And the water is pretty scarce right now. Mr. Timus Perdash nearly died here. But he getting better and up around again this week. Mr. Beans Indian and family is visit my place last Monday, and he return Tuesday morning. His home at Elko, Nevada. I and Chief Harry D. Tootiaina is in the Logan City this morning and we were on the fishing trip over to Bear Lake country. Mr. Harry Tootiaina expect stay here at Washakie all summer. Mr. Warren Wongan and wife motor down Tremonton last week. Mr. Seth Eagle made a business up to Malad city here last week. Mr. Moroni Timbimboo and family been down Elwood to buy some cherries on the Monday last. Mr. Enos Pubigee been down my place at Elwood here first part of last week. Mr. Nephi Perdash and wife motor down Tremonton some time ago. Mr. Ammon Pubigee, with his son Mr. Elias Pubigee, made little hunting trip in the Grace, Idaho, last week ago. Mr. Mose Neaman was purchase second hand baby overland car here last week. . . . Some Indian from Nevada are around here last week. They all went home now. Our people are join West Portage people are going celebrate on the 4th July and 5th. Everything line up all ready just. The horse races and bucking contest, and foot races, and relay horse race. I hope our people having real good time. But my boys are line up fight on the fourth July now. [1928-06-30 LJ]

WASHAKIE, JULY 5, 1928.   The people enjoyed celebrate here at West Portage 4th July yesterday. They have all kind sport in the afternoon. But we join with West Portage people and some Indians from Fort Hall Reservation here now. Well they have two days celebration here. They have best horse races in the country. Mr. Timus Perdash is died down Garland hospital yesterday afternoon. His funeral arrange for tomorrow morning. Mr. Nephi Perdash went to Fort Hall Reservation today and gave notice for their relatives and friends too. He return today. But he [Timus Perdash] sick ever early in spring, and under Dr. care for two weeks. Mr. Walter Smooks and wife visit our home town yesterday and return yesterday. His home at Bannock Creek, Idaho. . . . Mr. Geo Mose came here last week and went home last week and took wife home. His home at Ruby Valley. I and Chief Harry D. Tootiaina return home from our fishing and hunting trip out Bear Lake last. We come home last Monday. Mr. Warren Wongan and Mr. Charlie Perdash went down Tremonton on the matter of business this week. . . . Mr. Custer E. Ottogary have boxing contests over to Downey, Idaho yesterday afternoon he was match with Doab Talbot 8 round bout. But they sposed [supposed] to be draw and both my boys going fight tonight and more other three boys too. Our grain turning pretty fast now and soon harvesting time here. I expect going have a good crop. [1928-07-07 LJ]

WASHAKIE, JULY 27, 1928.   The harvest grain is getting start last week, and crop turn out pretty good. . . . Well grain buyer start buy grain around here just now. It bring good price, all farm raise dry land wheat. All our people are over to Logan and join in the big Home Celebration on the 24 and 25 July, and having real good time. Our old custom [costume] getting nice, which were worn in the big parade. It was the first class condition. This was made by our people at Washakie also our tents or wigwam in the good condition too.

Some of our people just from Logan last night, and some hasn't returned home yet. It was real good big parade on the July 24, and our people nearly all join parade. Mrs. High-top Joshua is pretty bad sick here last week. But she is getting little better now. She was about 80 year of old. Mr. Amwillie and wife is visit our people over to Logan on the 24 day July with his son and wife is retain here at Mr. Mose Neaman place. Mr. Tom Elk come home for 24 July last week from Idaho and he is going return in the few days now. Well he lease land from Indian up on the Bannock Creek.

Mr. Chief Harry D. Tootiaina made a business trip up Fort Hall reservation here last week. Mr. James Pabawena and his wife also made business in the Idaho and visiting some his friend and relatives up there. Mr. Elias Pubigee and his wife made business trip up Idaho last week. Mr. Nephi Zundel was motor up to Idaho Reservation last week ago. . . . I and Mr. Harry D. Tootiaina was received letter from Mr. Buckerro [Buckaroo] Jack here last week, us come out to attend big meeting they want attend. This was real business meeting going have out to Fort McDermitt, on the 20 Sept. He want invite us come out to see them in that date. We are decided going out there on the 20th. Mr. Buckerro Jack want some Indian chief to attend his business council out there Fort McDermitt. He wants some from Bidwell, Calif. [Fort Bidwell Indian Reservation]; Burns, Oregon [Burns Indian Reservation]; Shrus [Shasta?], Calif; and Warm Springs from Oregon and many other places country, etc. [1928-07-28 LJ]

WASHAKIE, AUGUST 10, 1928.   The harvesting nearly all over now. But most of them harvest their grain. The crop pretty good harvest this year. I guess the grain over is raise 25,000 bushel this year. The grain gave only 90c 80c per bushel, and the weather is too warm here couple day ago. But night kind cold now. Soon fall working begin

Left to right: Maureen Pubigee, Andrew Pubigee, Norman Woonsook, Emily Woonsook, Katherine Timbimboo, and Grace Timbimboo, Ogden, July 24, 1935. The children appear to be dressed for a Pioneer Day parade or celebration. *Courtesy Mae Timbimboo Parry.*

Frank Timbimboo (*left*) and Catch, or Ketch, Toyahdook. *Courtesy Mae Timbimboo Parry.*

Hitope Joshua, 1934. *Courtesy Mae Timbimboo Parry.*

now and no sugar beets raise in this place this year. Well sir, Mr. Harry Tootiaina was took sick after 24 July but he getting all right again. Last week ago he was visit my farm down Elwood, Utah. He expect to stay here until 15 day next month his old home at Elko, Nevada. Well Mr. John Pabawena and family went out for Nevada on the last Saturday. He expect not stay out very long and going visit some his relation and friend out to Nevada. . . . Mr. Jacob Peyope expect be going up big rado [rodeo] at Soda Springs commence 14 and 15th this month. . . . Mrs. Hitope Joshua was sick here about last two week but she improving just now, she is well now. Mr. Catch Toyahdook was a purchase a second hand chevelate [Chevrolet] car about last week ago and went down Ogden bought. . . . Mr. Chester Ottogary and wife making their home at Washakie just now.[12] Mr. Tom Elk was down here for the 24 July and he return on the Idaho again about three weeks ago. . . . [1928-08-13 LJ]

WASHAKIE, AUGUST 18, 1928.   The people are good condition just now. But nobody, just one old woman sick here. It being in so old age. She is getting improving right now. There was no death since last death along the summer. Some our people been up Soda Springs and they all return home now. Mr. Seth Pubigee return from Soda Springs on the last Sunday and he was motor to Tremonton some [same] day. And also Mr. Chester Ottogary accompany him to. Mr. Chief Harry D. Tootiaina also been Soda Springs. He was been that country before, that is first time, and he lives out Elko Nevada. He come to Utah on the 10 July and stay ever since that time. But he like Utah better than Nevada. He expect return home on the 18 Sept. Well he expect having a good time here all summer, and visit my farm down Elwood a few time along in summer. . . . Mr. John Wagon and wife still up to Yellowstone Park and he doing some business up there. . . . Mr. Jim John Neaman purchase a second hand Ford car here two weeks ago. . . . All Indians live up here are home-less. They haven't got any land for their own name, there was only 13 Indians got homestead land up here. But we living on the church land up here. Church owns about 500 acres and we divide up amongst us. They getting about 30 acres each man and head the family. Most this church land is dry farm. No sugar beet raise here. This year is pretty good crop this year etc. [1928-08-18 LJ]

WASHAKIE, AUGUST 28, 1928.   The people are here all done their harvesting just. Some of them went up to Idaho Falls. They was return last ago, and bring their horses with them. They load their grain here on car. They nearly all grain sold here, and through harvesting now. Mr. Bishop G. M. Ward made a business up the Idaho Reservation some time about a week ago. . . . Mr. Thomas Pabawena and Chief Harry D. Tootiaina was visit my farm down Elwood on the first day this week. . . . Mr. Charles Perdash sold load wheat Tremonton last Monday. . . . Mr. Johnny Thompson is still here. But come from Nevada about two week ago. He may stayed here all this month. His home at Wells, Nevada.[13]

There was bad news come at farm down Elwood, by the last Wednesday morn-ing. My boy baby boy [Chester's son, Ernie Steele Ottogary, b. 16 Dec. 1927] died on the last Tuesday up to the Idaho Falls on 22 August. He bring his body down to Washakie. But he arrange funeral service here on Wednesday. The funeral was held at ward meeting house about 12 o'clock on Friday, the first speaker was Bishop Yeager Timbimboo 2 asst. Bishop, Catch Toyahdook, and also Bishop Geo. M. Ward. They more testimony was same all to gather, and also made a good talk. . . . Well, he was only 8 month old. They don't know what cause the death the little baby. He might catch bad cold, and only sick in half day and died. . . .

Mr. John Pabawena and family made trip out Nevada about first week this month and he was return home about couple week ago. Mr. Peter Bird was sick. He came here with Mr. Johnny Thompson. I expect he had consumption. He was been sick all summer along, and he stay with his sister, Mrs. Charley Dick on the east Washakie. Well he may live all this fall. Mr. Johny Dick was been seen Dr. down Ogden city here some time ago, and was sick here some time ago. [1928-09-01 LJ]

WASHAKIE, SEPTEMBER 7, 1928.   The harvesting all over with thus far, and fall work is coming now. But they are getting ready for seed their ground right away. The weather getting little colder just now. Everybody is good condition so far. But soon the summer will be gone by this time now, and fall soon be here. Mr. Harry D. Tootiaina is still here now. Well expect return next month. But he is doing some business here just now. Mr. Catch Toyahdook was motor down Ogden yesterday and accompany Mr. Chief Harry D. Tootiaina. Mr. Nephi Zundel and with his nephew Mr. Wilford Peyope went up Idaho Reservation last week ago. He may come back in few days, and expect going visit his relatives and friend up there. Mr. Nephi Perdash and wife was motor down Tremonton first part this week. Mrs. George Tomock went down Ogden and she is going visit her daughter at industrial school. Mr. Catch Toyahdook was visit his adorbed [adopted] son, Master Eddie

Toyahdook, and he was send to industrial [school] last spring down to Ogden, and he will come home in the first next month. Mr. Seth Pubigee and Master Custer Ottogary trucking race horses up to Preston, Idaho, about last Wednesday and going running up there. These horses owns by Mr. Enos Pubigee and Mr. Nephi Perdash. Mr. Moroni Timbimboo was motor down Tremonton other day. Mr. Warren Wongan motor down Ogden last week ago. Mr. Jacob Peyope also visit his boy at industrial [school] down Ogden last part of last week. Mr. Peter Bird is sick now. He stayed at his sister place East Washakie. But he about 60 year of old now. Mr. Johnny Thompson is still here now. He come here from Nevada some time ago last month. I expect he will stay all this fall. Mr. Mose Neaman was motor down Garland yesterday. . . . Mr. Johny Pabawena was been doing some shopping down Tremonton other day. [1928-09-08 LJ]

WASHAKIE, SEPTEMBER 13, 1928.   The fall crops are put in all ready just now. Soon the fall weather is here. The weather getting colder here right now. And the grain all sold here and the money nearly all spent. Some our people over to Preston, Idaho, the big rodeo they have up there, and the all return home last part of the last week. Mr. Enos Pubigee horses up there. Mr. Nephi Perdash was take his race horse down Brigham City. Also Mr. Enos Pubigee take his race horses up to Malad City, Idaho, today. Mr. John Pabawena little boy died here on the Monday after-noon about 2 o'clock. And funeral service were held at ward meeting house on the last Tuesday. He was about year old. Mr. Harry D. Tootiaina motor down my farm Elwood last Friday. Mr. Elias Pubigee and wife been down Brigham City and buy some peaches. Mr. Hyrum Wongsaw was motor down Brigham City other day. Mr. Chief Harry D. Tootiaina is went out west and hunting some Indian pine nuts. He expect be gone about week. Mr. Thomas Pabawena and his brother Mr. Jim Pabawena made business trip down Ogden last week. Mr. Catch Toyahdook been over to Preston, Idaho, last Saturday to see rodeo and return home same day. Mr. Kippetchew Noragan motor down Tremonton other day. Mr. Tom Elk was return home from Idaho Reservation and lease Indian land up there. . . . Mr. Johnny Thompson still here now. Well he may stay here all this fall. Mr. Lyn Perry is here now. But he divorce his wife some time ago last summer. But she got married and she died up Idaho Reservation. She was raise and born here at Washakie. Then she get married to Mr. Lyn Perry they moved to Fort Hall Reservation. Mrs. George Tomock was motor down Ogden and she visit her daughter Miss Irene Tomock. Mr. Charlie Perdash went down Brigham City Peach Day yesterday. Mr. Jacob Peyope was motor down Brigham City other day. I made business trip over to Logan about last week ago. Mrs. Enos Pubigee went down Brigham City to Peach Day celebrate, she expect going buy some peaches while she was down, for putting it up for winter. [1928-09-15 LJ]

WASHAKIE, SEPTEMBER 21, 1928.   The people are good condition so far. But some our people gone down to Tremonton to attend Box Elder Co. Fair and big Rodeo there. Some Fort Hall come down yesterday to see a Rodeo, and some the Indians boy rider down to Rodeo and riding wild horses. There is one man rope tripping in the rodeo.[14] Well Mr. Chief Garfield Pocatello is here now from Fort Hall Reservation. Mr. Moroni Timbimboo is take [daughters] down California here about two week ago and she is going school at Riverside instantied [Sherman Institute at Riverside].[15] Mr. Enos Pubigee and Mr. Nephi Perdash bring their running horses yesterday down to Tremonton. Mr. Jacob Browning motor down Brigham Peach Day celebration about last week ago. And also many other Indians from Idaho Reservation. Mr. George Tomock was motor down Brigham City other day. Mr. Jim Pabawena get through his fall work done. But he went down big Rodeo yesterday and his family. Mr. Chief Harry D. Tootiaina is stay with me down to Elwood on the farm. He expect went home next month or more. But he stay in the Utah all summer. Mr. Nephi Zundel was return home from Fort Hall Reservation other day. Mr. Kippetchew Noragan and wife been buy some peaches down Brigham City last week. . . . Mr. Bishop Yeager Timbimboo went to Rodeo yesterday afternoon. Mr. Henry Hootchew and wife come from Idaho yesterday and he went to Rodeo and he expect stay here a few days. And he raise and born here. Then he move Idaho and get married up there. He own some land there. Mr. Tom Elk still here at Washakie, and he expect going back Idaho in few day more. He lease Indian [land] up there. . . . Mr. Jim Wagon and family return home from Yellowstone about last week ago. Mr. Samboo is visit our town here last week. He expect stay all winter here with his niece. Mrs. Thomas Pabawena, Mr. Johnny Thompson still here and he want going up to Idaho to visit his relatives and friends too in few week. [1928-09-22 LJ]

WASHAKIE, OCTOBER 10, 1928.   The weather is getting pretty bad now. But the winter soon come. The people are say going hard winter this year. Yesterday have stormy weather here. But it is pretty cold today. And some our people went up to Idaho to work in spuds now. They haven't return yet. Some gone down to Garland factory to work for the same white men around north sugar factory. We have just return from Nevada trip. But been out there some matter of business. We are among Paiutes Tribe. Well I and Chief Harry D. Tootiaina return with me on the Utah. But he like Utah better than Nevada. There was a different places of Nevada be present, and about 6 Chief Paiute was a big Council. Mr. Dave Pabawena was retain at Wells. Mrs. Harry D. Tootiaina is stay at Catch Toyahdook place while he been out McDermitt. The [Those] people are bad condition now. They didn't raise any crop this year. Some Paiutes have any land, they just roam around like old time. The especial Indian Agent from Reno did not looking after them. That reason they are pretty poor. We find them the agent didn't take good care of them. We know that Indian agent is steal some thing from Paiute. That reason want come out there to assist them to explain all the trouble they had. They say the government did not pay for their game yet, even the state didn't pay for game. Then white men say we got same as white. Well now they talking matter over and find out and big white father or government. But made a agreement with our wars [warriors] and chief all over the United States. Some day may Indian have big law suit with government. Now they study up these thing. I am sorry I missing two week now. [1928-10-13 LJ]

Seth Eagle Pubigee and Jacob Peyope working on Nephi Zundel's
home, Washakie, Utah, 1940. *Courtesy Mae Timbimboo Parry.*

WASHAKIE, OCTOBER 18, 1928.   We have stormy weather here last week, and getting
pretty cold just now. I hope winter soon be here. We have had frost here about week
ago, and took everything now. But some of our people went Idaho Reservation on
some work, and some went down Garland work in the sugar beet for the white men.
And no sugar beet here this year. Mr. Jim J. Neaman return home from Idaho and
he was work Idaho. Mr. Tom Elk return to Idaho last Monday, and he been home
about one month. He expect harvest his crop for this year. Mr. Catch Toyahdook is
return home last Saturday and return to Idaho in same day. Mr. Jim Wagon and wife
return home from Yellowstone Park about month ago, and he working for Mr.
Smith from Ogden. Mr. Nephi Perdash and wife just return home from Idaho. He
was working in spuds up there to Idaho Falls. . . . Mr. James Pabawena and his crew
work in sugar beet North Garland factory. Mr. George Elk and wife is visit home
from his work on the last Monday. . . . Miss Ida Zundel return last Friday and she
was visit some relation and friend on the reservation. Miss Ethel Perdash get married one of the Idaho boy about last week. She may make her home up there. Mr.
Chief Harry D. Tootiaina and wife is here now. But expect return home some time
next month, soon as sugar beet work done. Mr. John Pabawena has family working
for Mr. Arb Roots, East Garland. Mr. John Pabawena and with brother Mr. Thomas
Pabawena been visit Mr. Zip Brown, Idaho, and he was pretty sick, and he still sick,
and, also been down Brigham City on the matter of business. Mrs. Hightop Joshua
is getting well now. But she was sick all summer. Mr. Samboo is still here. But he
may stay here all winter with his niece Mrs. Thomas Pabawena. His home up to
Bannock Creek, Idaho. [1928-10-20 LJ]

WASHAKIE, OCTOBER 25, 1928.   The people are good condition just now. We had storm weather here last night. I expect they help us on our dry farm yet. It might bring fall wheat up and good thing have little rain. Our people looking winter is coming soon. Some hasn't coming home from there works up to Idaho. They might come any time now on. . . . Mr. Chief Harry, D. Tootiaina was motor down to Tremonton yesterday. Well he stay here another month. His wife work in the sugar field now. . . . Mr. Jacob Peyope and family went to Mr. L. Larsen place last week and getting sugar beet topping there. Mr. Seth Pubigee has not return from Idaho, the manager for fight and Ottogary brothers. These boys is with him up there. I expect be here any time. . . . Mr. Henry Woonsook been home last week and then went up Idaho. Mr. Catch Toyahdook still up Idaho working. These our people never been deer hunt when season open. They was afraid to hunt deer about [around] white men. I have got extra paper with this letter to print too. [The "extra paper," a letter, is included here in its entirety without corrections.]

(Extra paper) Sept. 29, 1928. and also action of the four nation and tribe. But also proclaiming themselves independent and autonomous nation. We propose to demand of the Government to show cause why it should not repect provision of the treaties with our people all of which absolute independent for the red men does not able want the citizenship yet until gets our right and these right were promised to treaties with both English and American Government. United States promised to pay of the band Showshone nation good many years ago from today. The red mens has been find out short time ago. And for the driving away the game. The white the destruction of the game, and also timber been cuting off and also water right. The state been not pay yet. The state has owing the Indians for the water right yet and made red men poor. We suppose look into that matter now today. All these ting and wild animal game is belong to the Northwestern band of Shonshone today. These all animals with out brand on, which was never set-tlement yet with different Indians nation of the United States of America. And also of the timber belong to the Shonshone Indian today. The Government has not buy the mineral land or rail roads and under ground never been settle yet, and either the state has not pay for our game yet. And having arrested the Indian over there for get the game not branded now day. The state up against to the Indians which ground the state stand on to fight against the Indian and the Indian should hunting there own game anytime the year. accordance the law of the treaties or any state by right away to the Indian tribe. The white people keep us bothering. But even we did not bothering white people yet so etc.

Willie Ottogary.
[1928-10-27 LJ]

WASHAKIE, NOVEMBER 1, 1928.   Today is stormy weather and rain earning last night. Well I suppose soon be a winter is coming, all people put near [pert'near] come home now. But Mr. Seth Pubigee still up to Idaho yet. Miss Irene Tomock return from industrial school last week ago. But she be down nearly a year since she took her down. Mr. Catch Toyahdook was return home Idaho last week first part this week. Mr. Henry Woonsook came home last week. He been visit some his relatives and friends Idaho Reservation some time ago last week. . . . Miss Ida Zundel been sick here about week ago. She hasn't get any better yet. Mr. Johnny Thompson still here at Washakie now, his home out Wells, Nevada. Mr. Dave Pabawena doing some prospecting out Nevada now. . . . Mr. Ammon Pubigee was doing hunting about last week ago. But he didn't see anything. Mr. Thomas Pabawena his eye getting better now. But he was nearly blind last summer, and he getting better condition. I was made a business trip at Washakie last week. . . . Miss Ethel Perdash get married one Fort Hall boy she make [meet] her up on the Reservation. Mr. Chief Harry D. Tootiaina motor over to Logan City about week ago. Mr. [Ray] Diamond still carry mail at Washakie. Mr. Chester Ottogary still remain up Idaho now and also his master Custer too. Miss Susie Highyou still stay down Brigham City yet. I expect this nice rain we had here [help] our fall grain. . . . Mr. Portage is helping Mr. Thomas Pabawena in sugar beet. He come here from Austin, Nevada, last summer. He expect to remain in Idaho this winter. I have letter from Mr. Harry, Johnny, George [one person] some time ago last week. He said in letter and still living out Ely country right now and also some Indians still living there. [1928-11-03 LJ]

WASHAKIE, NOVEMBER 8, 1928.   We had very storm and rain here yesterday today. But the road is impossible to travel through. It is so muddy. Some the down near Garland Factory. They soon through the sugar beet probably next week or more. The flue amongst us now. Well some had flue now. It is not so bad and not heard nobody died yet. Mr. John Pabawena was nearly died with flue. But was sick here for two weeks and he is getting better now, and also all his family had it too. They soon through with. Mr. Ammon Pubigee and wife was motor down Tremonton other day. He return yesterday. Mr. Mose Neaman motor down Tremonton yesterday with his three sons. . . . Mr. Hyrum Wongsaw motor down Tremonton yesterday and accompany Mr. [Ray] Diamond mail carrier at Washakie. Mr. Seth Pubigee the fighting manager for Ottogary brothers and going have fight up to Malad City, Idaho, next Saturday night Nov. 10. Gen Custer Ottogary match with Mr. Reed Peterson from Tremonton. It is good match. Mr. Chief Harry D. Tootiaina, expect going stay here at washakie this winter, and he figure the Utah is good country and cheap living than Nevada. Mr. Nephi Perdash visit his home for Sunday from his work. Mr. Moroni Timbimboo was motor up to Malad City other day. Mr. Wilford Peyope was purchase another car here last week. . . . Nobody sick here at Washakie, everybody is good condition. Mr. George P. Sam was sick awhile back. Then he is getting well. I expect this rainy weather make fall grain come up. Mr. Bishop G. M. Ward Washakie was down Tremonton on the matter of business yesterday. The Indian are not registered to be vot[e], by the according to Law the treaties of the United States, etc. [1928-11-10 LJ]

WASHAKIE, NOVEMBER 14, 1928.   We have nice summer this yr. But also have good harvesting grain. But no sugar beet raise here our town this yr. The weather is bad and rainy today. The road impossible to travel through. Our people think the winter is pretty near now. The people are very good condition so far. Nobody since died since Mr. Perdash death [Timus Perdash, see 1928-07-07 LJ]. And is under the flue just now. Mr. Elias Pubigee boy baby is very sick last week ago. Master Evans Peyope return from industrial School about two weeks ago and also Master Eddie Toyahdook too. Mr. George Mose is come back here some time last week from Nevada. . . . Mr. Johny Dick is still working for Mr. Bill Mason at Mount Spring, and doing some fall plowing too. . . . Mr. Thomas Pabawena made as especial trip down Ogden City last. But he went down to his attorney about some trouble come up on middle part of this month. . . . Mr. Hyrum Wongsaw was been down Tremonton in matter of business. Master Eddie Toyahdook is come back on his business again and he was fight last Saturday night up to Malad city. Mr. John Wagon brought some deer hide from Mr. Smith from Ogden City some time ago. Miss Susie Highyou just return home here last week ago. She stay at Brigham City for three month. Mr. Chief Harry D. Tootiaina expect going stay here Washakie all winter now. But cannot return home and he and his wife like Utah best than Nevada. I hope had some relation and friends living in our town. Mr. John Thompson expect to return home soon probably next month. It is good weather for our fall crop and bring the grain up for the next year coming. That means a good crop. Our people thinking about the winter and it hard winter this year. The Indian all way tell true about the weather, etc. [1928-11-17 LJ]

WASHAKIE, NOVEMBER 30, 1928.   The winter soon here this part of the country and weather pretty cold just now. The people are coming from their works and they get through all last week, some our people are had flue pretty bad, and nobody died with is [it] just now. Well, the people are going have a hard winter this year. Mr. Enos Pubigee been down Ogden on the matters of business and accompany his brother, Mr. Seth Pubigee. Mr. Warren Wongan baby was pretty sick just now but he getting little bit better today. Mr. Moroni Timbimboo and family been California just return home last Saturday and he is visit his daughter Indian School at Riverside, California, and he say like California pretty good. But he bring one his girl. Mr. Enos Pubigee with his father visit my little farm down Elwood other day. Mr. Mose Neaman was down Tremonton other day and doing some Thanksgiving shopping. Mr. Harry D. Tootiaina was motor down Tremonton first of the week. I and one of my boys been over to Logan City last Wednesday on the matter of business and to see some my old accquaintance there. . . . Our people are poor condition just now, not much grain here last summer. Mr. Chester Ottogary was stay my farm couple day and went back Washakie for Thanksgiving. I spent Thanksgiving over to Stone, Idaho, with Mr. Albert Knudson, and having good time. The well spent Thanksgiving yesterday. [1928-12-06 LJ]

WASHAKIE, DECEMBER 12, 1928.   The winter is here right now. But we had snow here other day and snowed about 5 inch here around this valley. And still snowing this morning, and people think this winter going be hard winter. We had stormy weather and cold now. Some of our boys were shooting Jack rabbits yesterday. They slaughter quite lot rabbit yesterday, about 3 hundred or more I expect going big hunt again tomorrow too.

Mr. Mose Neaman went over to Logan last week ago. And Mr. Jacob Peyope is doing some trapping now. Mr. Tom Elk return home about last month ago, and he going remain all winter long. Mr. Samboo was return home last month ago, and was working in the sugar beet field. . . .

The Norther Western Band Indians Committee been down Ogden City about last and attended their business down there. The matter of the land business. . . . But some our people getting under the flue here just now. Mr. Johny Pabawena went down Tremonton the matters of business some time ago last week. Mr. Henry Woonsook been down to Ogden City first part last week ago, and his wife to Dr. She is get little bit better just now. [1928-12-20 LJ]

WASHAKIE, DECEMBER 21, 1928.   The winter is here now and we had have very cold weather. A snow is about 4 inch just now. Our boys been big rabbit hunt here about couple days ago and slaughter quite bit jacks. Some of our people have a flue now. Nobody died yet with it. Some getting alright now. They another big hunt today. I expect they doing some good this year and they sell rabbit fur. Mr. Robert Harris buying a rabbit fur from them. He paying about 9¢ each for them. Well this good price rabbit fur. They like hunt now. Mr. Jack Johnson and son come here last week ago. He come from Fort Hall, Idaho. His home is down Elko, Nevada. . . . Miss Susie Perwhat is pretty sick now and she is low. But her folk expect cannot live long, and she was older woman in our little town. Mr. Nephi Perdash and wife had auto wreck here about last Saturday. His wife in face broken glass. But she alright now. Didn't hurt car. This was man from Twin Falls. His name Mr. Williams and he hit Mr. Nephi Perdash car. Mr. Jim Neaman motor down Tremonton yesterday, and with his brother.

Master Linford Neaman and Miss Margaret Perdash got married here last week ago. Mr. Geo. M. Ward, Bishop was doing ceremony. . . . Mr John Wagon been down to Tremonton doing some Christmas shopping. Mr. Jacob Peyope and Kippetchew Noragan been down Tremonton yesterday and doing Christmas shopping. Mr. Mose Neaman went over to Logan city and stay over until Christmas. Mr. Jacob Peyope and doing some trapping this winter, and also Mr. Tom Elk doing thing. Our day school running fine this year. There was about 25 children attend school here just now. Mr. Chief Harry D. Tootiaina expect live here all winter with our people. Our people very poor this. But we haven't got land for own, and the hay is scarce around here now. The is worth about $13.00 per ton right now. I and one of my son pretty busy this week selling some Christmas trees, around this town Tremonton and many other places. Some of our people seen attend union meeting up to Malad City last Sunday. Mr. George Sam doing fine now, and was pretty sick last month. [1928-12-26 LJ]

WASHAKIE, DECEMBER 26, 1928.   The winter is very cold just now, and our people are good condition. But Miss Susie Perwhat was died here last week, and her funeral service held at Washakie ward chapel one o'clock last Monday after noon, and she was a good church member. She was a well known all the country and her age was about 104 years old and she was older woman in our town. She left two daughter, and several grandchildren, etc. and many great grandchildren, and boys been hunt rabbit today they slaughter grade [great] many of them, and they will another time this week. We had nice time on the Xmas day. But we have nice programme before noon, and we had big feast in the ward chapel afternoon, then have a children dance commence at 2 o'clock and evening Christmas dance. The everybody have a real good time. Mr. Nephi Zundel and Mr. John Wagon motor down Tremonton on the Xmas day. Mr. Enos Pubigee, Mr. Henry Woonsook, and Mr. Wilford Peyope motor down yesterday and having a good time. Mr. Jerry Jackson with his father come here about couple weeks ago. They expect stay here after New Year. Their home out Butte Mountain on Elko, Nev. Master Pratt Eagle is visit our town now. He live out Skull Valley, Utah. He expect to stay until New Years. Mr. Catch Lion [Toyahdook], motor down Tremonton yesterday. Mr. Jim John Neaman was return from Logan yesterday. But he and his Mr. Linford Neaman and family went over to Logan city spend Christmas over there. Mr. Mose Neaman and family went over couple week ago, and spend Christmas over there and he going return home after New Yr. Mr. Nephi Perdash motor downtown yesterday. Mr. Jacob Peyope is still trapping coyote now. And also Mr. Tom Elk still trapping too. Mr. Harry D. Tootiaina went up to Malad city and two more other fellows and matters of business. Mr. Warren Wongan been down Tremonton and doing some New Year shopping yesterday. Mr. Bishop Geo. M. Ward and wife spent Christmas down to Riverside with his only folk and friends. Mr. Jim Wagon been down Ogden City last week ago, on the matter of business. [1928-12-29 LJ]

WASHAKIE, JANUARY 9, 1929. We had very cold weather just now, and last snow we had about three inch here now and that is last snow storm we had and all together is about 6 inch snow that is deep we got here. Our people are good condition now. But only two death here this winter. And one little girl died here on last Friday . . . she buried last Saturday. The boys has been big rabbit other-day, and slaughter quite lot of the bunnies. The boys go out shoot rabbit pretnear [pert'near] every day. But we had spend New Year pretty well this year and carried very nice programme on the New Year Day, which was select reading, comic speech, song, and music select, etc., and it was well spend. Master Pratt Eagle is visit our little town before Christmas time and also New Year Day too. He expect return home in few days. He live out west of Salt Lake City in the place name Skull Valley. Mr. Mose Neaman was motor over to Logan City before New Year. Well he come home after Christmas day. . . . Mr. Seth Pubigee and Master Custer Ottogary made business trip down Tremonton last week. . . . Mr. Jacob Peyope was visit his daughter down Tremonton hospital last week. She been operation about two week ago and she is doing fine. She was operation for appendicitis. . . . Mr. Sotank Johnson is still here now, expect going home after New Years. But he stay with Mr. Thomas Pabawena folks, and also Mr. Johnny Thompson still here in our town now. He may return home next spring. But he stayed at his son-in-law place east Washakie. Mr. Harry D. Tootiaina was motor up to Malad city about week ago, and accompany Mr. Thomas Pabawena. Miss Mone Thompson little girl died with flue here last Friday and buried last Saturday. She was about one year old. . . . I been visit Washakie town on the Christmas Day and also New Year Day, and return home after New Years in the Elwood on the South east Tremonton. [1929-01-12 LJ]

WASHAKIE, JANUARY 17, 1929. The weather is getting bitter cold now. But the Indians are pretty bad condition. Our people are pretty poor, and haven't much wheat crop this winter. I hope we going have a good crop next year. Our boys been hunt rabbit make their living this winter and earn little money that way, and they hunt rabbit nearly every day.[16] We had stormy weather today and cold weather, too. The snowing start this early this morning. Well, last Saturday Mr. Seth Pubigee nearly shot his left hand off. But he is doing fine and dandy in the Tremonton hospital, and he come down same night, and Mr. Dr. White dress his wound and put 4 stitch on side of his left hand. He may stay couple day more to stay then he went home. Last Monday his family been visit him down Tremonton hospital. Mr. Warren Wongan was visit Mr. Seth Pubigee in hospital yesterday that is his friend. Mr. Catch Lion [Toyahdook] and wife and wife's sister accompany him visit their relation and friends on the Fort Hall Reservation last week and return home in few days ago. Mr. Chester R. Ottogary and wife visit my farm down Elwood last Monday night. . . . Master Pratt Eagle is still here now, and his home is out Skully Valley, 80 miles west Salt Lake City. Mr. Warren Wongan was attend Stake Conference up to Malad City, and also Mr. Harry D. Tootiaina and Mr. James Pabawena accompany him attended conference at Malad City last Sunday, and many of attend too. . . . Mr. Ammon Pubigee was visit his son, Mr. Seth Pubigee at Tremonton hospital last Monday. [1929-01-19 LJ]

WASHAKIE, FEBRUARY 2, 1929.　The people are good condition just now. But some our people under the weather. We had very cold weather here this winter. The road is pretty bad to travel through to valley. I hope soon road cut through. Our boys been hunt jack rabbit nearly everyday, and earn their living. Mr. Robert Harris buy all the rabbit skin around here. Our day school is running good condition this year. Most all the children went school here. Last night ward amusum [amusement] committee gave a dance. But everybody enjoyed themselves. Mr. Seth Pubigee went down Tremonton to see Dr. White. But was been hospital about week and he shot one his hand with 16 gauge shotgun, and Dr. White address his wound today and he coming fine now, but healing good now. . . . Master Pratt Eagle is still here now. He expect went home after New Year. But he nearly forgot his home. I am going up visit Washakie tomorrow, and forgot to write early. [1929-02-04 LJ]

WASHAKIE, FEBRUARY 7, 1929.　The winter nearly over with here. The cold weather still here and spring soon come. The people are pretty poor this year. But doing some rabbit hunting everyday here and earn their living that way. There is one death here other night, a small boy died. He was about month old. But he was born before his time about month early. But he was buried here today. There was much sickness among us. Almost the children sick, here with flu and it stayed us pretty well. Miss Julia Pabawena is pretty sick now and also Miss Katie Neaman sick bed. Mr. Johnny Thompson is Doctor them now. This Indian Doctor, Johnny Thompson with treated some sick people and he was from Nevada. He may return in the spring. Master Pratt Eagle went home last Saturday morning. Mr. Seth Pubigee doing very nicely. His hand is healing pretty faster. Mr. Jim Wagon motored down Tremonton other day and accompany Mr. Nephi Zundel. Mr. [Jack or Sotank] Johnson went home last Sunday morning. He home Elko, Nev. . . . Mr. Moroni Timbimboo is sick now and he doing nice and soon up around again now. Mr. Chief Harry D. Tootiaina still live here now, and his people want him come

Left to right: Rhoda Moemberg Woonsook, Eleanor Neaman, Ben Pabawena, Katherine Timbimboo, Helen Pubigee, Clara Alex (or Elk), Emily Woonsook, Ester Peyope, Geneva Alex, Grace Timbimboo, and Amy Timbimboo. Several of the children were born between 1926 and 1928. Photo taken at Old White Church, Washakie, Utah. *Courtesy Mae Timbimboo Parry.*

home right away. Master Ray Hank is come here last week. He come from Elko, Nevada. . . . Mr. [Ray] Diamond, mail carrier, was change hand now, Mr. Yeager Timbimboo took his place now. I and my son Master Custer E. Ottogary made a business trip up to Washakie in the few day ago and return home yesterday at Elwood. Our land business coming fine. I and Mr. Chief Harry D. Tootiaina talking about our business other day. We are going have a big Reservation on the northern part Utah in future. It might come toward spring time. But we have against government about our claim and game. We the Indians supposed to be paid for our game and timber. But government promised pay for it, accordance the 1863 treaty. We are Indians are try study about the government work. But we find something about government work. It don't treated us right. We should draw money from government each year. But we do not get money yet for game and timber and other stuff etc. [1929-02-11 LJ]

WASHAKIE, FEBRUARY 14, 1929.   The storm we had here about today. It is pretty cold, and cold weather nearly all over with us. And the people are not good conditions, some of them pretty sick just now. The flue is still here now, and nearly all over with us, most children had the flue just now. Some of us pretty sick now. Miss Katie Neaman is pretty sick just now. Mr. Johnny Thompson is Dr. her last. But little bit worse now. Also Miss Julia Pabawena is sick too. . . . Mr. Fish Bishop visit our town yesterday and his three boys. They went up to Idaho Reservation today.

Left to right: Leland Pubigee, Jim John Neaman, Melvin Alex, Katherine Timbimboo, Devere Perdash, unidentified girl behind Devere, Jessie Pocatello. *Courtesy Mae Timbimboo Parry.*

They expect return here in few day they come here on matter of business. They are going Mr. Any Tomy [Annies Tommy] and he was act Chief. He is going down with them. Their home out to Ibapah, Utah. . . . Mr. Tom Elk is doing some trapping this winter again. Mr. Seth Pubigee getting better now and healing pretty fast. We having been celebrated Sirchin [Lincoln?] Birthday yesterday, and wrendered a nice programme, in evening and we had nice luncheon and after luncheon, dance, and everybody enjoyed very much. Mr. Charlie Skidmore Supt. School was visit our day school here last Tuesday afternoon and accompany Mr. Tylar [Tyler] too. [1929-02-16 LJ]

WASHAKIE, FEBRUARY 21, 1929. The people are good condition now. They are happy spring is here. Well the weather is getting warmer. Then feel like spring soon here. The hay is pretty scarce just, and price stay well up to date. Price of hay some around $12.00 per ton. The snow is going down grantiadly [gradually] now. But we had nice winter . . . only 2 death this winter. I hope we are going have a good year, and look like that, and plenty snow. The people pretty poor condition this year and have much of the crop. I was made a business trip over to Logan city yesterday and meet some my white friends over there. I expect and went up to Washakie today and help them celebrate George Washington Birthday. The going hold met [meeting] at ward chapel and have a programme and commence at 10 o'clock sharp, and which is song, select readings, dialogues, and comic speech, so on, etc. Mr. Annies Tommy was visit our town here last Sunday and he is way home, and his nefew and his wife accompany him. They went home last Tuesday. Their home out to Deep Creek, Utah. He was doing some business up to Idaho Reservation. Mr. Fish Bishop come here about ago and trying doing some business with our head men. They having some trouble out Deep Creek Reservation. Mr. James Pabawena, Chief Harry D. Tootiaina went down Ogden City on the matter of business last Tuesday. Mr. Catch Lion [Toyahdook] and Mr. Henry Woonsook motor down Salt Lake city last Tuesday. Mr. Seth Pubigee went down Tremonton to see Dr. White about his hand and coming pretty good and healing pretty nicely. Mr. Warren Wongan motor down Tremonton last week. Mr. Chester Ottogary left his wife [at home] and went up Idaho Reservation last Tuesday. But he expect remain there a rest of the winter. Mr. Nephi Zundel motor down Tremonton last week some time ago. [1929-02-23 LJ]

WASHAKIE, FEBRUARY 28, 1929.   The winter hasn't gone yet. The weather so cold now. We had stormy weather here other [day], and the snow nearly gone. It is about 4 inch left yet. I hope the spring soon be here. Well some of us sick and they getting better now. The flue stay pretty well here all winter along. Most children had flue. Our day school pretty well running this winter. The government helping school children here and gaving them something to eat at dinner time. The children likes that too. The getting pretty poor this, no food stuff and no hay too. I expect our people are starve soon. There is no work tall [at all] for them. Well spring open then we might getting job do some thing, and earn some things, and living. . . . Mrs. Katie Neaman was pretty sick here last month. She is getting better now. . . . Mrs. Julia Pabawena is well now, She is wife of Mr. Thomas Pabawena, and she sick all winter long. Mr. Chester Ottogary was return home and visit his mother [Nancy] up Fort Hall Reservation. . . . [1929-03-05 LJ]

WASHAKIE, MARCH 7, 1929.   The spring is here right now. The weather getting change just now. The people are here very poor condition this yr. They out hay and money too. . . . It is pretty hard to get hay right now, and we lost some of our stock. I expect we are going have a good summer this year. We heard from Senator Wm. H. King from Washington, D.C. about our land matter. That his letter read like this. ["]The Conference report on my Bill Senate 710 in behalf of Shoshones approved today. Believe it will be signed by the President with in a day or two.["] But our people pretty anxious the hear more about our land business. It means to going have big Reservation here around Washakie. . . . Mr. Johnny Thompson still wintering here. Mr. Harry D. Tootiaina motor down Garland yesterday. Mr. Jacob Peyope and Kippetchew Noragan motor down Ogden last week ago. Mr. Nephi Zundel motor down Tremonton last part last week. Mr. Moroni Timbimboo made business trip up to Malad City first of this week. Mr. Chester Ottogary motor down Tremonton last week. . . . I made a business up to Washakie last of last week. Mr. [Ray] Diamond change off hand. Mr. Yeager Timbimboo took his job to carried mail at Washakie now. This Mr. Diamond been carrying mail for 7 year here, he was retired here last month. He was about 80 year of age and he was one of the pioneer here our town Washakie. [1929-03-09 LJ]

WASHAKIE, MARCH 14, 1929.   The people are pretty good condition right now. The winter is going away here now and spring is here this morning our getting rejoice when this spring come here once more. Well this will last winter we seen. But every body saying to winter, goodbye and come again in 9 month, Mr. winter. Some our people under the weather now, and nearly everybody getting well just now. Some of our people going out hunt jack rabbit last month. There is quite lot rabbits been kill here this winter. I expect 4000 kill been this winter. They make good money on the rabbit's fur. Some our spring work be here soon. Mr. Harry D. Tootiaina motor down Garland last week ago. Mr. Johnny Thompson still here for winter. He expect return home in the spring. He live out Wells, Nevada. Mr. John Wagon made a business trip down Ogden City last week and he expect going out Yellowstone again along 15 June 1929. Mr. Kippetchew Noragan been down Tremonton and doing some shopping last part last week and he was accompany Mr. Silas [Elias] Pubigee and also Mr. Ammon Pubigee. Mr. Warren Wongan and wife was down visiting Tremonton town other day. Mr. James M. Pabawena with his two brother motor down Tremonton other day. I am in Brigham City today, and come for the one of my son is going on the fight ring once more. But he is not been fight for this year. Well sir, I don't know whether he could stand fight or not. He hasn't not training yet this winter. I am mighty glad to see some my old acquaints here in Brigham City. Mr. Hyrum Wongsaw is kind sick because he was old age and he was one of the pioneers Waskakie. I expect is very few old timers living in our little town today. The Relief Society giving their annual meeting held at ward chapel, on the 16 of March, 1929. And they going carried a nice programme before noon commence at 10 o'clock sharp. I hope they going splendid time.

 Willie Ottogary.

 [1929-03-19 LJ]]

[The following letter was probably written by an editor of *The Journal*.]

The Journal
Logan City, Utah, Saturday, March 23, 1929.
Willie Ottogary Answers the Grim Reapers Call

 Word reached The Journal late Friday afternoon of the death and burial of Willie Ottogary of Washakie, the faithful Indian scribe of this paper for over twenty years. Many a reader has read the regular letters of this prominent Indian over this period of years and have been entertained and amused by the unique way in which he handled the English language.

 A telephone communication to Washakie brought the news that Willie died at his Elwood home early Monday morning, March 18, and that burial services were held Thursday at 12 o'clock in the Washakie meeting house with the entire Indian tribe in mourning.

 Willie Ottogary was about 55 years of age.[17] He was well educated for an Indian and more than once he went to Washington, D.C., to intercede for his people for rights he believed Uncle Sam had taken from them. His death was due to a sudden heart attack. He had not been ill long. The last letter directed to The Journal was written in Brigham City on March 14, the day he went to the Boxelder county metropolis to watch his son Custer in a boxing contest.

 Besides his two sons, Chester and Custer, he is also survived by a daughter, Louise Ottogary, who resided at the Ottogary home at Elwood. [1929-03-23 LJ]

Willie Ottogary's grave, Washakie, Utah.
Photo by Matthew E. Kreitzer.

Conclusion

WHEN I READ MARK TWAIN'S CLASSIC YARN OF THE WEST, *Roughing It,* I found it entertaining reading but negative in its treatment of the Shoshoneans of Utah and Nevada, whom he called "the wretchedest type of mankind . . . ever seen."[1] Twain's perspective was undoubtedly influenced by late nineteenth century Social Darwinism, which viewed Indians and other ethnic groups collectively as lower races. Twain was reflecting beliefs common in much of white American society during the late nineteenth century in attempting humor at the expense of Western Indian groups.

Not long after reading *Roughing It,* I read *The Shoshoni Frontier and the Bear River Massacre,* by Brigham D. Madsen. As I finished reading it, I considered that although Madsen dealt with the Shoshone branch of the same Shoshonean family (which also includes Utes, Paiutes, and Goshutes), the Indians in his account were quite different from those portrayed in *Roughing It.* Contrasting perceptions from different times created the distinction. *The Shoshoni Frontier* was published a hundred years or so after *Roughing It.* It was more objective because it was influenced not by the Social Darwinism of Twain's era but by the more ethnically enlightened attitudes of the 1980s.

Twain and Madsen each gave their readers literary sustenance drawn from kernels of real-world experience. What about the native perspective of the Shoshone themselves, though? Who would provide pine nuts to the literary diet? Pine nuts were the perfect food for the Shoshone and continued to be harvested even after Willie Ottogary's lifetime. Harvests were prepared and cached as a critical ration for winter, and the nuts provided much of the necessary energy for Shoshone men and women to perform their daily routines, which included traditional storytelling at night during the long winter months. The passing on of culture through stories is, of course, not simply a form of recreation. Storytelling was an obligation to future generations of one's culture group—a means to preserve the knowledge vital to a group's cultural, as well as physical, survival. Willie Ottogary knew this. He provided the literary pine nuts. His efforts at writing and storytelling were not done to amuse white audiences. They transformed certain aspects of Northwestern Shoshone culture into print and thereby preserved them, communicating important messages to future generations.

Since Columbus and other Europeans took credit for "discovering" America, whites have been the major providers of information on Native Americans. Yet when the Pilgrims arrived in American, they were met by an English-speaking native, Squanto. For hundreds of years, bilingual Native Americans have been the norm rather than the exception. In parts of the United States some natives could speak and understand not only their own and perhaps several other Indian dialects or languages but English and French and/or Spanish as well. At an early date some could read and write as well. European-run "Indian schools" for young natives and eventually even a few colleges disseminated such skills.

As a result, by the 1800s several Native Americans had established themselves as writers. The better-known eastern writers were often the second or third generation of a bilingual family. Among the successful Indian writers and orators in English were John Ross (Cherokee, 1790–1866); Kah-ge-ga-gah-bowh, or George Copway (Chippewa, 1847–1889); and Green McCurtain (Choctaw, 1884–1909).[2]

Fur trappers and explorers of the early 1800s introduced the English language to the Shoshoneans of the intermountain region. Western natives learned some English in order to communicate with trappers regarding geography, animals, and trade, but opportunities to employ the language were brief and sporadic. Then the Mormon pioneers moved west and settled in the heart of the Shoshonean domain in 1847, creating greater need for the Indians to speak English effectively and regularly. As the Mormons established permanent homes in the Great Basin, the English vocabulary of neighboring Indians grew. However, there were few published Shoshone writers in the area until Willie Ottogary.

Ottogary's parents did not speak English. He learned the language, as a boy, in a Mormon-run day school at the Washakie settlement. In contrast to other Native American writers of his day, such as Alexander Lawrence Posey (Creek, 1893–1915) or Carlos Montezuma (Apache, circa 1887–1922),[3] Ottogary was raised by two native parents and never attended college. He was the first generation of his family to speak, read, and write in a foreign tongue. He also published, for twenty-three years, a column in that same foreign tongue. This significant accomplishment required a tremendous amount of determination, self-confidence, patience, and practice, not to mention the effort and research required to keep informed on Washakie and Shoshone events. He was, to a large degree, alone in his efforts.

Willie Ottogary was a unique individual who faced many difficulties. Although learning the English language was one of the most difficult challenges he had to overcome, Ottogary also dealt with personal crises and losses. There was the emotional trauma of losing his first wife and their two children to untimely deaths. He also lost, to premature death, the first two children of his union with Nancy, his second wife. By the end of 1916, Nancy had left him, and he had filed for divorce. When his grandson, Chester's boy, died, Willie, able to empathize with his son and daughter-in-law's loss, went to Idaho for the funeral. Another misfortune was smallpox.[4] Ottogary contracted the disease in 1920 and lost a friend and other acquaintances in this outbreak.

Ottogary also had to overcome prejudice and dishonesty. He and his family occasionally encountered callous forms of racial bias. In church meetings, they sometimes had to put up with whites who refused to sit on the same pew with Indians.[5] This form of hypocrisy, exhibited in the church he loved, must have been especially challenging for Ottogary, although he said nothing of it in his letters. The other problem, dishonesty, hurt all the Shoshone. Many whites used questionable means to secure Indian allotment land from the Shoshone. Some descendants of the Washakie Shoshone believe that white officials profited from these illicit land deals. In his columns, Ottogary campaigned against deceptive land deals.

Considering the obstacles he faced, it is a wonder that Ottogary was able to achieve as much as he did. His sources of strength included the positive and nurturing traditional Shoshone upbringing his parents supplied. His family remained important to him, and his sister, Eliza, and her husband, Ammon Pubigee, remained close to Willie and his children. His children were also a source of great emotional and physical support. Close friends, Indian and white, provided further strength and support. His faith in God seemed secure and lasting, and through his faith he surely believed that justice would eventually (whether in this life or the next) prevail.

He also learned the power of a positive attitude. He had a yearning for knowledge and was excited by life and its challenges and rewards. He felt that his life and the lives of others of his generation represented a bridge between two key eras. His letters reflect this belief that his was the generation of change, of transition. Aware of the critical issues facing his people during this time, he worked hard to make *them* aware of these issues. He was sustained, as a leader, by his conviction that he had a commission to fulfill: to regain the Northwestern Shoshone homeland.

Though Ottogary apparently had an enduring faith in the potential goodness of humanity, he was not so naive that he overlooked the two common vices of greed and lust for power. He learned quickly that, in the white world, land often meant power, having seen that kind of power used against his people. Ottogary loved his homeland in northern Utah. He looked forward to the day when it would be given back to his people. He was a visionary. Two of his greatest assets were his stamina and self-confidence. His journalistic career spanned twenty-three long years, which is a tremendous achievement. Throughout his life, he never gave up. He kept trying, working, and hoping that his efforts would be successful.

Many questions remain unanswered about Ottogary's methods, such as how he went about preparing his columns. Did he have a favorite time of day to write? A favorite place? How much preparation had preceded when he sat in front of a blank sheet of paper? Did he just begin writing? Did he have notes on what he wanted to cover and an outline of how to present the information? Did he go out and interview his kinsmen, or did they come to him? Perhaps he gathered material for his letters after Sunday church meetings as people visited with each other, or maybe he gained information by attending social functions or by visiting individuals in their homes. What parameters, if any, did editors place on his writings, such as on length and content? He seems to have been able to write freely, but manuscript copies of his letters have not been found to compare with the printed versions. What, if any, newspaper columns did he use as models for his column? Was he coached by newspaper editors? What books and papers did he read? Stan Andersen remembered from his childhood that the Ottogarys subscribed to the Sunday *Denver Post*,[6] but what other papers did he read? Did he read the Book of Mormon? The Bible? Other books? We don't know. It also would be interesting to know what he thought of some of the key events in Native American history that occurred during his lifetime (1869–1929), such as the Battle of the Little Bighorn (1876), the Ghost Dance Movement and its demise at the Wounded Knee Massacre (1890), or the destruction of Shoshone Mike's band in Nevada (1911).

LDS Relief Society members and children, *left to right*, Cohn S. Zundel, Frank Timbimboo (little boy), Mary Woonsook, Amy H. Timbimboo, Nellie Pabawena, Verna Pabawena (little girl), and Lucy Cojo Peyope, May 14, 1939. *Courtesy Mae Timbimboo Parry.*

Standing outside the Washakie meetinghouse, *left to right*, Henry Woonsook, Nephi Perdash, Moroni Timbimboo, and Jim John Neaman: "All Indian Bishopric of LDS Church, Washakie Ward." *Courtesy Mae Timbimboo Parry.*

Ottogary's columns also do not reveal how he felt about other major events, such as Prohibition, that had an impact on the lives of all Americans.

Some conclusions can be drawn regarding the contribution Ottogary made through his columns. His letters chronicle his leadership of the Washakie Shoshone, though he chose not to refer to himself as a "chief," and his efforts to correct those problems that hurt the Northwestern Shoshone, especially his ongoing efforts to get their lands back. He also recorded much information on the culture of his people. He wrote of their ceremonial practices during an era of transition. History and anthropology texts offer views of these traditions as seen by outsiders or at least shaped by their writing, but Ottogary provides an insider's account. He wrote of ceremonies that were performed in an atmosphere of social contempt from government officials, religious leaders, and other whites. His descriptions of the Shoshone subsistence culture that continued to be important during his writing career were unparalleled, though other economic activities increasingly supplemented or replaced traditional practices.

His authoritative look at continuing food gathering traditions is an important addition to published anthropological and ethnohistorical accounts. That his name is not mentioned in the citations in those reports may demonstrate that anthropologists of his day were so interested in salvaging "lost" or disappearing cultural texts that they deemed reports from a culture in transition less significant. Ottogary's reports may not have been as scientific, but as firsthand observations from a member of the culture, they were certainly just as valuable. His writings help bridge an information gap on the status of Shoshone culture between the late nineteenth and mid-twentieth centuries and do so from a Native's perspective.

Willie Ottogary's legacy takes various forms. In interviews and other research for this book, I found that many people knew Ottogary's letters but did not know him personally. Moreover, some people remembered things Ottogary wrote that, based on my research, were never written or at least never published. Ottogary was remembered by some as a symbol, perhaps even an archetype of the misconceived modern Indian, and thereby he became for them less real, more mythical. Over the years what people remember from sixty years prior has become distorted in their memory, and perhaps they choose to remember a story in the form they want. The following anecdote is an example: Ottogary was known to be outspoken, and he was also known for his unique way of putting things. In Mormon tradition, high councilors (ecclesiastical leaders) speak at church meetings every month, on the third Sunday. They are famous in Mormon folklore for giving long and boring presentations. According to a white informant, a friend recalled that Ottogary once wrote: "The high Councilor came over to Washakie, he talked a long time but didn't say anything."[7] This anecdote illustrates Ottogary's wit as recalled in legend. His sense of humor thrives in the folk traditions of some of northern Utah's elderly citizens.

Ottogary's legacy, though, also includes real contributions (aside from those mentioned) to the body of historical evidence regarding the Northwestern Shoshone. Ottogary composed an Indian social history that is unexcelled for its period in Western America. His contributions to folklore are significant; through his articles the vernacular culture of the Shoshone of northern Utah in the early

1900s was accurately and thoroughly presented. Because of the detail Ottogary's columns provided, it is possible to recreate the Washakie of his lifetime. The genealogical data found in his writings complements, often corroborates, and sometimes challenges evidence that exists in other records. His legacy is a record of a people, a time, and a place, a significant microcosm that warrants serious attention and continued study.

Willie Ottogary opened a window to the Northwestern Shoshone world. Yet that metaphor seems awkward in reference to a time when the Shoshone were still learning about opening and closing windows in frame houses. As I sought a metaphor that would have more meaning to the Shoshone of Washakie, I was struck by how difficult it must have been for Ottogary not only to write in a new language but to think in it as well. Subsequently, *voice* seemed to me a metaphor that he would have felt more comfortable using to express his relationships to the Washakie community and his audience. As the voice of Washakie, Willie Ottogary was a living interpreter of his people and their ways of life to the white world that had surrounded them and attempted to squeeze their culture out of existence.

As a Native American journalist, Ottogary preserved a history of the Northwestern Shoshone and spoke out against injustices against them. He faithfully recorded the social history of his people during a crucial era and thereby added a priceless account to the store of knowledge regarding the West's native populations. Had he lived just a few more years, he might have been able to complete his quest for a federally recognized Washakie Reservation in Utah, but death silenced his voice first. Shoshone no longer live at Washakie, which was sold by the Mormon Church after most of its residents had departed, but if enough interest in Ottogary's vision could be mounted now, the Northwestern Shoshone could return "home," to where the bones of their ancestors testify of perpetual ownership.

In 1993 I was invited to attend the yearly gathering of the Northwestern Shoshone. The tribal council conducted the sessions, and I was impressed by the depth and breadth of the issues they discussed and the decorum that existed in the meetings. After the scheduled activities of the day were over, several members of the group retired to Leland Pubigee's home to visit. Those present, including tribal elders, their wives, several children, and me, sat in a rough circle. Occasionally someone would speak in Shoshone. The oldest man there spoke with a slight speech impediment that had been a part of his life since birth. I knew that because Ottogary wrote over sixty years ago in one of his columns about a boy who was taken to Salt Lake City to have an operation on his harelip. It only took a moment or two after meeting this gentleman to make the connection between him and Ottogary's reference to him as a boy. Many other scenes from the Washakie colony's past entered my mind—all remembered from Ottogary's letters.

We swapped stories about the Northwestern Shoshone and about Willie Ottogary. Then I brought out my bound copies of Ottogary's letters and, with deep respect, handed them to the two oldest men. I gave a brief introduction about how the letters were organized and, as they put on their glasses and began to read, sat back and watched. Their reactions were reflective, enthusiastic, and serious. They smiled and laughed as they remembered people, places, and events from their childhoods. Their brows furrowed as they considered the deeper issues encoded in the passages written so long ago.

The events of that afternoon made me more aware of one aspect of the Ottogary letters' significance. Though they were originally intended to address a mostly white audience, they were also written for future generations of Shoshone. Ottogary may have understood that his letters would not be fully appreciated until long after he died. Today, through this edition, Ottogary's voice speaks out clearly from the past, with simplicity, confidence, and purpose, of the dignity, beauty, and endurance of the Northwestern Shoshone.

Appendix A

SHOSHONE TREATIES, 1863

The following treaties are reprinted from Charles J. Kappler, *Indian Affairs: Laws and Treaties*, vol. 2, *Treaties* (Washington, D.C.: Government Printing Office, 1904), 848–51.

TREATY WITH THE SHOSHONI—NORTHWESTERN BANDS, 1863

Articles of agreement made at Box Elder, in Utah Territory, this thirtieth day of July, A.D. *one thousand eight hundred and sixty-three, by and between the United States of America, represented by Brigadier-General P. Edward Connor, commanding the military district of Utah, and James Duane Doty, commissioner, and the northwestern bands of the Shoshonee Indians, represented by their chiefs and warriors:*

ARTICLE 1. It is agreed that friendly and amicable relations shall be re-established between the bands of the Shoshonee Nation, parties hereto, and the United States, and it is declared that a firm and perpetual peace shall be henceforth maintained between the said bands and the United States.

ARTICLE 2. The treaty concluded at Fort Bridger on the 2nd day of July, 1863; between the United States and the Shoshonee Nation, being read and fully interpreted and explained to the said chiefs and warriors, they do hereby give their full and free assent to all of the provisions of said treaty, and the same are hereby adopted as a part of this agreement, and the same shall be binding upon the parties hereto.

ARTICLE 3. In consideration of the stipulations in the preceding articles, the United States agree to increase the annuity to the Shoshonee Nation five thousand dollars, to be paid in the manner provided in said treaty. And the said northwestern bands hereby acknowledge to have received of the United States, at the signing of these articles, provisions and goods to the amount of two thousand dollars, to relieve their immediate necessities, the said bands having been reduced by the war to a state of utter destitution.

ARTICLE 4. The country claimed by Pokatello, for himself and his people, is bounded on the west by Raft River and on the east by the Porteneuf Mountains.

ARTICLE 5. Nothing herein contained shall be construed or taken to admit any other or greater title or interest in the lands embraced within the territories described in said treaty in said tribes or bands of Indians than existed in them upon the acquisition of said territories from Mexico by the laws thereof.

Done at Box Elder, this thirtieth day of July, A.D. 1863.

James Duane Doty,
Governor and acting superintendent of Indian affairs in Utah Territory.

P. Edw. Connor,
Brigadier-General U.S. Volunteers, commanding District of Utah.

Pokatello, his x mark, chief.
Toomontso, his x mark, chief.
Sanpitz, his x mark, chief.
Tosowitz, his x mark, chief.
Yahnoway, his x mark, chief.
Weerahsoop, his x mark, chief.
Pahragoosahd, his x mark, chief.
Tahkwetoonah, his x mark, chief.
Omashee, (John Pokatello's brother,) his x mark, chief.

Witnesses:
Robt. Pollock, colonel Third Infantry, C.V.
M.G. Lewis, captain Third Infantry, C.V.
S.E. Jocelyn, first lieutenant Third Infantry, C.V.
Jos. A. Gebone, Indian interpreter.
John Barnard, jr., his x mark, special interpreter.
Willis H. Boothe, special interpreter.
Horace Wheat.

TREATY WITH THE EASTERN SHOSHONI, 1863

Articles of Agreement made at Fort Bridger, in Utah Territory, this second day of July, A.D. one thousand eight hundred and sixty-three, by and between the United States of America, represented by its commissioners, and the Shoshone nation of Indians, represented by its chiefs and Principal Men And Warriors of the Eastern Bands, as follows:

ARTICLE 1.   Friendly and amically relations are hereby re-established between the bands of the Shoshonee nation, parties hereto, and the United States; and it is declared that a firm and perpetual peace shall be henceforth maintained between the Shoshonee nation and the United States.

ARTICLE 2.   The several routes of travel through the Shoshonee Country, now or hereafter used by white men, shall be and remain forever free and safe for the use of the government of the United States, and of all emigrants and travellers under its authority and Protection, without molestation or injury from any of the people of the said nation. And if depredations should at any time be committed by bad men of their nation, the offenders shall be immediately seized and delivered up to the proper officers of the United States, to be punished as their offences shall deserve; and the safety of all travellers passing peaceably over said routes is hereby guaranteed by said nation. Military agricultural settlements and military posts may be established by the

President of the United States along said routes; ferries may be maintained over the rivers wherever they may be required; and houses erected and settlements formed at such points as may be necessary for the comfort and convenience of travellers.

ARTICLE 3.   The telegraph and overland stage lines having been established and operated through a part of the Shoshonee country, it is expressly agreed that the same may be continued without hindrance, molestation, or injury from the people of said nation; and that their property, and the lives of passengers in the stages, and of the employes of the respective companies, shall be protected by them.

And further, it being understood that provision has been made by the Government of the United States for the construction of a railway from the plains west to the Pacific ocean, it is stipulated by said nation that said railway, or its branches, may be located, constructed, and operated, without molestation from them, through any portion of the country claimed by them.

ARTICLE 4.   It is understood the boundaries of the Shoshonee country, as defined and described by said nation, is as follows: On the north, by the mountains on the north side of the valley of Shoshonee or Snake River; on the east, by the Wind River mountains, Peenahpah river, the north fork of Platte or Koo-chin-agah, and the north Park or Buffalo House; and on the south, by Yampah river and the Uintah mountains. The western boundary is left undefined, there being no Shoshonees from that district of country present; but the bands now present claim that their own country is bounded on the west by Salt Lake.

ARTICLE 5.   The United States being aware of the inconvenience resulting to the Indians in consequence of the driving away and destruction of game along the routes travelled by whites, and by the formation of agricultural and mining settlements, are willing to fairly compensate them for the same; therefore, and in consideration of the preceding stipulations, the United States promise and agree to pay to the bands of the Shoshonee nation, parties hereto, annually for the term of twenty years, the sum of ten thousand dollars, in such articles as the President of the United States may deem suitable to their wants and condition, either as hunters or herdsmen. And the said bands of the Shoshonee nation hereby acknowledge the reception of the said stipulated annuities, as a full compensation and equivalent for the loss of game, and the rights and privileges hereby conceded.

ARTICLE 6.   The said bands hereby acknowledge that they have received from said Commissioners provisions and clothing amounting to six thousand dollars, as presents, at the conclusion of the treaty.

ARTICLE 7.   Nothing herein contained shall be construed or taken to admit any other or greater title or interest in the lands embraced within the territories described in said Treaty with said tribes or bands of Indians than existed in them upon the acquisition of said territories from Mexico by the laws thereof.

Done at Fort Bridger the day and year above written.

James Duane Doty,
Luther Mann, jr.,
Commissioners.

                                        Washakee, his x mark.
                                        Wanapitz, his x mark.
                                        Toopsapowet, his x mark.
                                        Pantoshiga, his x mark.
                                        Ninabitzee, his x mark.
                                        Narkawk, his x mark.
                                        Taboonshea, his x mark.
                                        Weerango, his x mark.
                                        Tootsahp, his x mark.
                                        Weeahyukee, his x mark.
                                        Bazile, his x mark.

In the presence of–
     Jack Robertson, interpreter.
     Samuel Dean.

Appendix B

This appendix provides an opportunity to compare Ottogary's letters to a typical social column from a white community, Brigham City, Utah. This is from *The Box Elder Journal*, March 18, 1918. Each short paragraph was separated by a series of dashes.

Local Brevities

Send us your family washing and have it done right. Brigham Steam Laundry.

John Knudson of Deweyville, was in Brigham on business matters Saturday afternoon.

A son registered at the home of Mr. and Mrs. Charles Stoddard of Corinne Saturday.

Thomas Young, who has been residing in Logan for the past two months, returned yesterday evening.

Miss Christina Hansen had her tonsils and adenoids removed at the Pearse & Cooley hospital a few days ago.

Frank Greenhalgh has accepted a position with the Studebaker Bros. and is now busy selling wagons.

If your boy balks at using a hoe this season, escort him to the woodshed and do unto him as you were done by in your youthful days. It may pain him, but it will train him—and he'll hustle.

P. W. Bott returned Friday from a trip to Idaho and Wyoming, representing the John H. Bott & Sons.

Mrs. John Jensen on South Main street is entertaining some of her friends at a quilting bee this afternoon.

The Turner, Yonk & Jardine Auto Co. recently sold a Chevrolet car to Mrs. Kirk of Mantua and one to Lorenzo Peterson of Brigham.

The Misses Barbara Larsen and Maud Hibbard, two young school "marms" of Deweyville, visited in Brigham City over Sunday.

Walter Sudbury of Deweyville, one of the soldier boys, a member of A Company, 20th Infantry, stationed at Fort Douglas, was a Brigham visitor Saturday.

Miss Nina Nixon of Salt Lake City, who is taking training in the L. D. S. hospital, was in the city for a few days last week visiting with her brother, Dr. J. W. Nixon.

Abel S. Rich will deliver a lecture on genealogy at the regular Relief Society meeting Tuesday at 3 P.M. at the Second ward chapel. A good attendance is desired.

Mr. and Mrs. D. Jardine went to Idaho Falls Friday evening to visit friends for a few days.

Mrs. S. W. Jacobsen went to Rock Springs, Wyoming, Saturday for a few days visit. Mr. Jacobsen is at present employed in that vicinity.

In these days of scarcity of foodstuffs there is no room for the professional beggar of the hobo. Give him a hoe or the boot.

Mrs. D. R. Wright and Mrs. J. A. Lee went to Ogden this morning. Mrs. Wright will remain a few days to visit with her daughters, Mrs. Earl Furniss and Mrs. Roland Farr.

Appendix C

Information on Ottogary's travels was taken from his published letters. He may have visited these (and other) places at other times. Numbers at right indicate the number of times Ottogary wrote of visiting each place.

Utah		Nevada		Idaho	
Bear Lake	1	Austin	1	American Falls	1
Blacksmith's Fork Canyon	2	Battle Mountain	2	Blackfoot	1
Brigham City	2	Cherry Hill	1	Burley	2
Cache Valley	1	Edgemont	1	Fairfield	1
Clarkston	1	Elko	7	Fort Hall	8
Deep Creek	6	Ely	1	Hailey	1
Garland	1	Fort McDermitt	2	Holbrook	1
Lewiston	1	McGill	1	Malad	5
Logan	36	Owyhee	7	McCammon	1
Mantua	1	Ruby Valley	1	Pocatello	2
Ogden	6	Wells	2	Shelley	1
Penrose	1	White Rock	1	Shoshone	1
Promontory	1			Soda Springs	1
Saint John (Tooele County)	1			Stone	1
Salt Lake City	11			Twin Falls	1
Skull Valley	5				
Tremonton	5				
Uintah Basin	1				

Wyoming		Miscellaneous (listed from East-to-West)	
Fort Washakie	10	New York City, NY	1
Jackson Hole	1	Washington, DC	3
Lander	2	Pittsburg, PA	1
Wind River	4	Cincinnati, OH	1
		Chicago, IL	1
		St. Louis, MO	1
		Kansas City, [MO or KS?]	1
		Haskell (Indian School), KS	1
		Council Bluffs, IA	1
		Oklahoma (3 weeks in 1921)	1
		Lawton, OK	1
		Cach, OK	1

Appendix D

No.	Name	Acres					
		Dry Wheat	Dry Barley	Dry Alfalfa	Irrigated Alfalfa	Beets	Ready To Seed
	James Joshua	60	15	4	9		50 [?]
1	Yeagah Timbimboo			5		3	40
2	Joseph Wonsook		20		3		17
3	Moroni Timbimboo	45	40	15		9 ½	45
4	Catch Queyembitch	11	26	8	2	4	
5	Hyrum Wongasaw		8		6		
6	Frank West	13		7			
7	Dick Arratch	8	2	9			10
8	Lewis Colisim	9	5				9
9	Charley Broom						
10	Geo. P. Sam				2		
11	Joseph Piniboo	13	29	6	4		13
12	Sam Jack				4		
13	Jim Jack				6		
14	Seth Pubigee		16	9			
15	Ammon Pubigee	19	20		6		19
16	Enos Pubigee		10				
17	Soquitch Timbimboo	6		4	6		8
18	Johnny Timmock	13	8	4	2	4	6
19	Tom Elk			6			19
20	Thos Pabowena				4		
21	Geo Elk	2			4	6	
22	Charley Perdash		8			8	16
23	Nephi Perdash		24		2	3	
24	Tiamas Perdash		12	18	4	3	26
25	Kippechuckoo Noragan	11	30	20	4	6	15
26	Joseph Moemberg	10	10	10	5	5	
27	Jacob Peyope		13		2	3 ½	
28	Nephi Zundel		14	10	2	8	
29	Tommy Tyboats		14	10			
30	Wm. Hootchew		13	5	5	3	10
31	Lorenzo Hootchew					6	
32	Henry Hootchew					10	10
33	Gcor. Tosapanguitch	10					
34	Warren Wongan		19		3	3	
35	Henry Woonsook		10			10	
36	Moses Neaman		13	2	2		
	[Totals]	230	388	152	87	82	263

Teams	Wagons	Buggies	Plows	Harrows	Seed Drills	Cultivators	Harness	Unknown	
3	2	2	2	1	1	1	2		
1	1	1			1		1		
2			2	2			2	30	
2									
1	1	1	1	1			1	30	
1								10	
1	1		1	1	1		1		
2	1	1	1		1		1		
1	1						1		3
2	2		1	1			2		
1	1	1	1				1	10	
								10	
2		1	1	1			1		
1	1		1	1	1		1		
2		1					1		
1	1	1	1				1		
2	2	1	1	1	1	1	2		
2	1		1		1		1		13*
							1	32	
1	1		1				1	13	
1	1			1		1	1	15	
1	1						1		
1			1				1		4 8
2	1	1	1	1	1	1	2		
2	1	1	1	1	1		2	30	
1	1		1				1		
1	1		1				1		2
	1		1	1			1		
1			1		1		1		
1		1					1		
1			1			1	1	20	
1	1	1	1				1		
1	1						1	13	
1	1			1			1	10	
1				1			1		1 ½
44	26	14	24	15	10	5	38	223	5

Appendix E

Box Elder News
Thursday, April 1, 1915
Willie Ottogary Goes East Again

On Tuesday evening of this week, our esteemed friend and famous Indian correspondent, Willie Ottogary left for Washington, D.C. over the Union Pacific for
the purpose of completing the work which he has been doing for some time past
in behalf of his red brethren. Willie returned from the nation's capital only a few
weeks ago to get further data and this he is now carrying with him in a big suitcase
for the enlightenment of the department of Indian affairs.

The Indians throughout the north and west of the United States, have formed
one big league to petition the Government to grant them certain privileges. The
matter of making citizens of the Redmen has been discussed and suggested and this
they are not anxious to have happen to them, according to our Indian correspondent the natives do not want to become citizens of the United States, tho they
desire to live under the protection of the stars and stripes and as wards of Uncle
Sam. But there are certain obligations attendent [sic] upon citizenship which the
Indians do not care to assume, some of which are the payment of taxes on land and
otherwise having their present rights circumscribed to the extent that they fear
they will be reduced to the level of common beggars and will have to go about in
poverty asking for something to eat. Mr. Ottogary states that his people want to
become independent and they feel that the government owes them at least what
has been promised thru treaties at various times, which includes lands, hunting,
fishing and timber privileges. He also declared that the Redmen want a flag of their
own. He cited the fact that all nations on the earth have a flag except the Indians
and now they want one of their own. The design has been determined upon by a
council and is a red and yellow back ground with an American eagle and a star in
the upper corner.

Referring to the recent Indian uprising in southern Utah, and in fact to all the
great Indian wars since the Redmen became wards of the government, Willie
declared that they were all instigated by the government Indian Agents who make
a practice of oppressing their charges until patience ceases to be a virtue and they
go on the war path. He cited one case in particular which he laid before the
Department on his recent visit to Washington, where the Government had supplied the Indians on a certain reservation in this state with some $3,000 worth of
machinery and farm implements, which is in keeping with the Government-
Indian treaty, and the agent then went among his charges and informed them that
he was supplying them with machinery and tools and they would have to pay him

back in work or farm produce which they did. Mr. Ottogary waxed eloquent when speaking of this circumstance and he declared that the Department would be made acquainted with the complete facts in order that it might be understood just how the Indians are mistreated.

When asked what the treaty of the Washakie Indians had to say about land grants, Willie stated that thru it the government gave his people the whole of Box Elder County for hunting and fishing and also land privileges. The hunting and fishing as well as free timber privileges have never been rescinded but the land grant has and now the Indians desire the privilege of going out and taking up land without cost in order that they might sustain themselves and not be forced to beg, a condition which Willie declared would be most objectionable to he and his people.

Since his return from Washington, Mr. Ottogary has visited the Indians in practically every part of the state and secured their thumb prints opposite their names which he has recorded on large sheets of paper and had the combined document sworn to by a notary public. He secured from the Utah Indians at Deep Creek 189 names and thumb prints; 89 from Washakie and 42 from Skull Valley. These will be presented to the Commissioner of Indian Affairs at Washington along with the petition asking for exemption from citizenship, a national flag and the treaty rights which have been unobserved in the past. A company of Indian delegates from each of the other northwestern states departed for Washington a few days ahead of Mr. Ottogary but he will meet them in Washington.

Speaking of his recent visit to the White Father, whom by-the-way, he was not permitted to meet, Willie stated that while he enjoyed the experience he was mighty glad to get back to Utah. He said it made him dizzy to go up to the top of the Washington monument as well as rather sick at the stomach. The visit to the many governmental buildings was interesting as was his attendence [sic] at Congress while that body was in session. Speaking of the President, Willie stated that no one was allowed to see the Executive "on account of the war" but that he proposed to pay a visit to President Wilson this time. He stated the ride across the continent was very tiresome and meals on the dining car were very expensive. The expense of Willie's pilgrimages are borne by the Indians collectively by popular assessment.

Appendix F

These winners had already competed in the Deep Creek Indian Fair held on the Deep Creek Reservation, Ibapah, Utah, September 20–22, 1915. At the Utah State Fair, Salt Lake City, these Indians (and others from the Scattered Bands) combined their entries for a special Indian exhibit.

Lorenzo D. Creel, Special Agent for the Scattered Bands Indians in Utah reported to his superiors: "It is with great satisfaction that I am able to report that for the first time in the history of the State Fair of Utah, recognition of equal rights with the white man was given to the Indians. This Exhibit was not entered in competition, yet the State Fair Association awarded Special Prizes, amounting to $25, to individual Indians. The following are the names and amounts awarded to each Indian.

Class 1.

				[cash prize amt.]
Annies Tommy,	wheat,	first prize	grain	1.50
Catch [Toyahdook],	wheat,	second	grain	1.00
Geo. Brown,	wheat,	third	grain	.75
Kip Norango [Noragan]	oats,	first prize	grain	1.50
Joe Trim,	oats,	second	grain	1.00
Moroni Timbimboo,	Sugar beets,	first prize		1.00

Class 2.

Belle Moody,	bread,	first prize	.75
Lucy Bear,	bread,	second	.75
Mrs. Heinks,	bread,	third	.75
Alice Brown,	Canned peaches,	first prize	1.00
Maggie Elk,	Canned beets,	first prize	1.00
Anna Hamilton,	Canned pears,	first prize	1.00
Nancy Ottogary,	Canned cherries,	first prize	1.00
Minnie Zundel,	Canned peas,	first prize	1.00
Yampitch Timbimboo,	C. [Canned?]	first prize	1.00

Class 4.

Mrs. Blackbear,	dress,	first prize	.75
Lillie Benson,	dress,	second	.50
Mamie Clover,	apron,	first prize	.75
Amy Timbimboo,	quilt,	first prize	.75
School Children, Deep Creek,	quilt,	first prize	.75
Bertie Clover,	Drawn work,	first prize	.75
Lucy Bear,	tatting,	first prize	.75
Nora Pugi,	hemstitching,	first prize	.75
Minnie Zundel,	embroidery,	first prize	.75
Ione Wongon [Wongan],	embroidery,	second prize	.50
Children,	cross stitch,	first prize	.75
Michie Tommy,	sofa Pillow,	first prize	.75

Class 5.

| Mrs. Annies Tommy, | basket, | first prize | .75 |
| Mrs. Blackbear, | beadwork, | first prize | .75 |

Appendix G

"Malad Idaho Stake Centennial History Book, 1888–1988." Author is not listed, but Hubert Gleed was chairman of the Centennial History Project. The following is reproduced verbatim from this text.

Washakie Ward
1880–1966

Bishops	Years Served
Isaac E D Zundell	1880–1890
Moroni Ward	1890–1902
George M. Ward	1902–May 12, 1929
Joseph Parry	May 12, 1929–Jan 22, 1939
Moroni Timbimboo	Jan 22, 1939–Mar 11, 1945
Glenn Morris	Mar 11, 1945–Feb 2, 1947
Newel Cutler	Feb 2, 1947–Sep 26, 1960

1st Counselor	Years Served
Alexander Hanakie	1880–1890
Yegah Timbimboo	1902–May 12, 1929
Moroni Timbimboo	May 12, 1929–Jan 22, 1939
Nephi Perdash	Jan 22, 1939–Nov 10, 1940
Jim John Neaman	Nov 10, 1940–Mar 11, 1945
Henry Woonsook	Mar 11, 1945–Feb 2, 1947
John Popoweenie [Pabawena?]	Feb 2, 1947–Sep 26, 1960

2nd Counselor	Years Served
Moroni Ward	1880–1890
Catch Toyahdook	1902–1912
James Jashua [sic]	1912–May 12, 1929
Warren Wongan	May 12, 1929–Sep 9, 1934
Henry Woonsook	Sep 9, 1934–Jan 22, 1939
Jim John Neaman	Jan 22, 1939–Nov 9, 1940
John Popoweenie [Pabawena?]	Nov 9, 1940–Mar 11, 1945
Russel Armstrong	Mar 11, 1945–Sep 26, 1960

Presiding Elders	Years Served
John F Conley	Sep 26, 1960–Nov 7, 1960
Chester Neal	Nov 7, 1960–Jan 2, 1966

1st Counselor	Years Served
Vernon Lamb	Nov 7, 1960–Jan 2, 1966

2nd Counselor	Years Served
Lamar S. Cutler	Nov 7, 1960–Jan 2, 1966

Ward Clerks	Years Served
Warren Wongan	1902–May 12, 1912
Ammon Pubigee	1912–1929
Henry Woonsook	May 12, 1929–Jan 22, 1940
Grant Parry	Jun 3, 1940–Mar 11, 1945
Dwight Woonsook	Mar 11, 1945–Feb 2, 1947
Verne Oreme	Feb 2, 1947–Mar 29 1953
Jim Jon [sic] Neaman	Sep 26, 1960–Jan 2, 1966

R.S. Presidents	Years Served
Elizabeth Zundell	May 20, 1883–Apr 9, 1890
Mary A Ward	Apr 9, 1890–1917

Primary Presidents	Years Served
Pheline Zundell	May 20, 1883–

S. S. Presidents	Years Served
Ammon Pubigee	1902–1908
Moroni Timbimboo	1908–1917

YMMIA Presidents	Years Served
Yegah Timbimboo	1902–1917

Appendix H

NEWSPAPER ACCOUNTS OF TWO OF THE OTTOGARYS' EARLY BOXING MATCHES

The Deseret News
Saturday, April 10, 1926.
Indian Fighters Are Featured on Downing's Card
[preliminary paragraph omitted]
Washakies Are Coming

Probably the most interesting announcement in connection with the new program is the invasion of Salt Lake by all of the Washakie reservation's warriors. The list includes the best fighting Indians ever seen in the local ring. They are Chester "Kickapoo Dan" Ottogary, General Custer Ottogary, Enos Pabigee and Chief O'Henry [Woonsook]. All have fought in matches either here or in Brigham or Tremonton. Only one of them have ever lost a contest and that was Chief O'Henry, who was knocked out after a valiant effort in a tought [sic] battle here. The rest of them have won every start.

Kickapoo Dan battles in the semi-windup of the new program, a four round bout. He meets Jack Brooks, the fighting barber. Brooks has a reputation for terrific slugging and for his ability to take them. He will have a tough time with the little redskin, however, for Kickapoo Dan takes em as well as anybody and fights back so hard that he is mighty tough to keep away from as well as to hit.

Battle Royal
General Custer Ottogary, Enos Pabigee and Chier [sic] O'Henry clash in a battle royal team match with Bob Young, Badnews Taylor, and Knockout Kiefer, three big colored boys who have had plenty of experience. . . .

The Deseret News
Tuesday, April 13, 1926

Farrell Wins On Foul In Boxing With Kronick
[preliminary paragraphs omitted]
Ottogary Wins.

. . . Chester Ottogary, the Washakie indian kayoed Jack Brooks, the battling barber, in the second round of their scheduled four verser. Brooks hit hard while he lasted, but he seemed unable to damage the Redskin and Chester wore him down with his ponderous mauling by the end of the first round, and he was in prime shape to receive the knockout punch soon after the opening of the second canto.

Black Boys Lose.

. . . The battle royal of the evening featuring three Indians General Custer Ottogary, Chief Pabigee and Chief O'Henry versus three negroes. Bob Young "Bad News' Taylor and Knockout Keifer, lasted almost four minutes, at the end of which time the black boys had all been draped in horizontal postures at various angles of the mat.

The Deseret News
Friday, April 16, 1926
Indian Fighter Takes Big Stride in His Profession

. . . CHESTER "Kickapoo Dan" Ottogary, the fighting Indian from Washakie, and "Wild Bill" Farrell, of Salt Lake will meet in the feature bout of a triple-header at the Hippodrome theatre next Monday night according to the announcement made this morning by Promoter Hardy K. Downing. The bout will mark the peak of the career of the little Indian boy, who has stirred local fistic circles as no one has since Jack Dempsey left the Manhattan club behind and sauntered forth in search of fistic fame. . . ."

The Deseret News
Tuesday, April 20, 1926
Kickapoo Dan' Gets Draw in Bout with 'Wild Bill'
Indian Fighter Surprises With Fine Showing

. . . "Wild Bill" Farrell, famous local pugilistic performer, had some of his ferocious traits removed, not painlessly either, by Kickapoo Dan, the slugging Washakie Indian, in the six round main event of Downing's weekly Manhattan club offering at the Hippodrome last night. The bout was nothing less than six rounds of terrific battering, with the boys so worn out at the end that they could hardly stand up to get their draw decision.

The Indian looked a trifle better in the first part of the bout, but he failed to follow up his opportunities and Farrell survived the critical part of the bout allright. In the last couple of rounds Bill got going himself, and the Indian found the going pretty tough. Dan landed a number of solid body blows during the course of the affair, but most of his head punches glanced off Bill's solid knob without doing much damage. . . .

This last article from *The Deseret News* included stories about Jim Thorpe and Jack Dempsey alongside the story about Ottogary.

Notes

Preface

1. Edlef Edlefsen, *Willie Ottogary's Letters to "The Journal" Logan, Utah* (Davis, Calif.: Danewel Publications, 1967).

Introduction

1. Brigham D. Madsen, *The Shoshoni Frontier and the Bear River Massacre* (Salt Lake City: University of Utah Press, 1985), 186.
2. Lorene Washines, "Lee Neaman Oral History," Dec. 2, 1979, Special Collections, Merrill Library, Utah State University, Logan, Utah (hereafter, USU Special Collections), 5.
3. Leland Pubigee, interview by Matthew E. Kreitzer, Brigham City, Utah, May 20, 1993; Mae Timbimboo Parry, "Massacre at Boa Ogoi," appendix B, in Madsen, *Shoshoni Frontier*, 238; Clyde S. Ottogary, telephone interview by Matthew E. Kreitzer, Pocatello, Idaho, May 22, 1993.
4. See herein appendix A: "Treaty with the Shoshoni—Northwestern Bands, 1863."
5. See entry for Peter Ottogary in Biographical Register.
6. Leland Pubigee interview, Brigham City, Utah, May, 20, 1993.
7. Brigham D. Madsen, *Corinne: The Gentile Capital of Utah* (Salt Lake City: Utah State Historical Society, 1980), 282–87.
8. Joshua T. Evans, "The Northwestern Shoshone Indians, (a) Under Tribal Organization and Government, (b) Under the Ecclesiastical Administration of the Church of Jesus Christ of Latter-day Saints as Exemplified at the Washakie Colony, Utah" (master's thesis, Utah State Agricultural College, 1938), 79.
9. Ibid., 81.
10. "Bishop Zundell's Wards: The Shoshone Progress toward Civilization," *Deseret News*, 9 September 1884.
11. Stan Andersen, *The Andersens of Elwood: A Family History* (San Francisco: Stan Andersen, 1990), 21; X. Y. Z. (pseud.), "Washakie: Description of the Lamanitish City in Malad Valley," *Utah Journal*, December 4, 1883.
12. Washines, "Lee Neaman Oral History," 4.
13. Matthew E. Kreitzer, "The Spirit Never Dies: An Examination of Supernatural Experiences of Northwestern Shoshone and the Relationship of These Experiences to Mormon Theology," unpublished research paper, 1993.
14. Box Elder County, Utah, Recorder's Office, Deed Records, Book J, p. 63 (homestead certificate 2584).
15. Federal manuscript population census schedule, 1900, Utah: Box Elder County, West Portage Precinct, sheet 14 A.
16. The 1880 federal manuscript population census schedules for Plymouth and Portage Precincts, Box Elder County, Utah, note only one other child (a one-year-old) named Willie or Billy. The only Shoshone youth that could read and write named Willie or Billy was listed as Willie Ottoger.

17. X. Y. Z., "Description."
18. Stan Andersen, San Francisco, letter to Matthew E. Kreitzer, March 15, 1993.
19. Ottogary letter to *The Journal*, January 9, 1915. Hereafter citations from Ottogary's letters will be abbreviated year-month-day with abbreviated name of publication: e.g. 1915-01-09 LJ.
20. 1916-10-21 LJ.
21. Northwestern Band Tribal Council, "Historical Record of the Northwestern Band of Shoshone Indians," July 10, 1937, 1, 2, copy in possession of Clyde S. Ottogary, Pocatello, Idaho.
22. Northwestern Band Tribal Council, "Agreement or Certificate," (noting transfer of leadership from Willie Ottogary and Harry D. Tootiania to Chief Custer Ottogary and Harry D. Tootiania), tribal meeting, September 16, 1929. Carbon copy in possession of Clyde S. Ottogary, Pocatello, Idaho.
23. See herein appendix C, "The Travels of Willie Ottogary."
24. David L. Wood, "Gosiute-Shoshone Draft Resistance, 1917–1918," *Utah Historical Quarterly* 49 (1981): 173–88; "Willie Ottogary, Educated Indian, Held for Conspiracy," *Deseret Evening News*, February 21, 1918.
25. Willie Ottogary v. Albert Saylor, First Judicial District Court, civil case no. 2382, Box Elder County, Utah, 1918.
26. Fifty Indians called on President Harding at the White House and asked him to appoint a Native American as commissioner of Indian affairs. After the meeting they were photographed together. See *New York Times*, March 13, 1921, p. 22.
27. Charles E. Dibble, "The Mormon Mission to the Shoshoni Indians" *Utah Humanities Review* 1 (July 1947), 290.
28. Willie Ottogary, "Family Record Book of Willie Ottogary." Original in possession of Clyde S. Ottogary, Pocatello, Idaho.
29. Andrew Jenson, "Manuscript Histories of Wards: Washakie Ward, Box Elder County, Utah," 1900, Descriptive History, Collection LR 9928, LDS Church Archives, Salt Lake City.
30. "Historical Records and Minutes," Washakie Ward, Box Elder Stake, LR 9928, series 11, LDS Church Archives, Salt Lake City.
31. "Sealings of Previously Married," Book A: November 21, 1900 to July 31, 1913. Logan Temple Records, Logan, Utah. Ottogary and his wife, Nancy, were sealed January 5, 1912.
32. Owen Rasmussen, interview by Matthew E. Kreitzer, Elwood, Utah, March 22, 1993.
33. "Wm. Ottogary Dies Suddenly at Ranch Home: Great White Spirit Calls Noted Indian to Happy Hunting Ground," *Bear River Valley Leader*, Tremonton, Utah, March 21, 1929.
34. Leland Pubigee, interview by Matthew E. Kreitzer, Washakie, Utah, May 31, 1993.
35. Mae Timbimboo Parry, telephone interview by Matthew E. Kreitzer, May 12, 1993.
36. Willie Ottogary v. Nancy West Ottogary, First Judicial District Court, civil case no. 2211 (decree of divorce), Box Elder County, Utah, 1917. See herein appendix D; "Exhibit of Acreage and Produce," for a comparison of Ottogary's farming peers at Washakie.
37. "Sealings of Children to Parents," Book D: January 5, 1912. Logan Temple Records, Logan, Utah.
38. "Records of Members of LDS in Washakie Ward, Malad Stake of Zion," film 027,406, LDS Family History Center, Logan, Utah.
39. Marriage license of Willie Ottogary and Nancy West, October 26, 1903, Box Elder County Recorder's Office, Brigham City, Utah.
40. Ottogary Family Record Book.

41. Rasmussen interview.
42. "Missionary Index," 1971–1973, LDS Church Archives, Salt Lake City.
43. *Andersens of Elwood.*
44. "Wm. Ottogary Dies Suddenly."
45. Edlefsen, *Willie Ottogary's Letters.*
46. Clyde S. Ottogary, interview by Matthew E. Kreitzer, Pocatello, Idaho, November 21, 1992.
47. Leland Pubigee, telephone interview by Matthew E. Kreitzer, May 5, 1993.
48. Julian H. Steward, *Basin-Plateau Aboriginal Sociopolitical Groups*, Smithsonian Institution Bureau of Ethnology Bulletin 120 (Washington: Government Printing Office, 1938), 241–43.

Chapter 1: "I Will Write a Few Line," 1906–1910

1. Hereafter abbreviated as TT with date shown in the form year-month-day newspaper.
2. Sherman was probably the editor of the *Tremont Times* at the time this letter was published. A complete listing of all the individuals mentioned by Ottogary is included in the Biographical Register. Biographical information, where known, regarding key individuals is included in this register.
3. In Ottogary's writing style the words "and" and "but" are often used interchangeably to begin sentences. In this sentence the word "And" would appear a more appropriate choice than "But." I have included the more appropriate choice in brackets early on so the reader will become accustomed to Ottogary's style.
4. Most letters concluded with this signature line. With a few exceptions, I have omitted these.
5. Ottogary maintained a home and farm in Elwood, Box Elder County. This residence was the homestead of his father, O-Ti-Cot-i, Peter Otahgary. Peter's homestead was lot no. 9 of section 18, township 11 north, range 2 west of Salt Lake Meridian in Utah Territory. For more information on the O-Ti-Cot-i patent, see Box Elder County Recorder's Office, Deed Records, Book J, p. 63 (homestead certificate 2584). Willie lived in Elwood and made numerous trips to Washakie, about 18 miles north of Elwood, to visit kinsmen. He apparently also lived there at times. Ottogary wrote letters from various other locations including, on occasion, newspaper offices.
6. Ottogary often visited Deeth and Ruby Valley, Nevada. These and other Western Shoshone lands played key roles in Ottogary's writings.
7. *Fandango* is a Spanish loanword that the Shoshone eventually adopted as an alternative name for their traditional round dances. These celebrations served cultural, social, and political functions. See Steven J. Crum, *The Road On Which We Came=Po'i Pentun Tammen Kimmappeh: A History of the Western Shoshone* (Salt Lake City: University of Utah Press, 1994), 40, 41.
8. Portage is a small farming community about two miles north of Washakie, just south of the Idaho border.
9. There was a Union Pacific Railroad stop (or siding) at Washakie. From this stop residents could board the train or load goods for market.
10. Rabbits could mean economic ruin to a farming community, whether Indian or white. To meet the threat, rabbit drives were organized during the winter months. Towns would divide into teams and wager on which team would kill the most rabbits during the day. In the evening a dance was held, the music being paid for by the losing side. The rabbit pelts were sold to be tanned into furs. The meat was eaten, dried for winter use, or delivered to the needy.

11. Moroni Timbimboo married Phoebe Shoshonitze, but they later divorced. He married Amy Hootchew Nov. 29, 1910. Mae Timbimboo Parry, letter to Matthew E. Kreitzer, Nov. 1997; Mae Timbimboo Parry, correspondence to Matthew E. Kreitzer, July 1999; Marriage Licences for Box Elder County, Utah, 1887–1966; Index to Marriage Licences and Certificates, film 0480310, LDS Family History Library, Salt Lake City (hereafter LDS FHL). Printed copy available at Box Elder County Recorder's Office.

12. Wood was used for cooking and heating. The nearest wood was located in the foothills and mountains west of Washakie in Broad Canyon or Portage Canyon. The trees are juniper and pinyon. Though sage brush can also be used for fuel, specific mention of wood gathering trips by Ottogary suggests the consistent use of wood by the Washakie Shoshone for fuel. He also notes the gathering of cedar posts, used for fencing, and the seasonal cutting of Christmas trees.

13. George M. Ward succeeded his father, Moroni Ward, as bishop of the Washakie Ward. In Mormon ecclesiastical hierarchy, a bishop is the administrator and spiritual leader of a church unit called a ward which is comparable to a parish. A stake is comprised of several wards and is comparable to a diocese.

14. A header was a horse-drawn piece of farm machinery that cuts grain heads off the stalk.

15. Both steam- and horse-driven threshers were used in Washakie in the early twentieth century. The horse-driven thresher used a circular mechanism called a "horse power." The three to five horses, each harnessed to the "horse power," maintained a constant movement around the circle. Each had to step over the driveshaft as they came to it, and a stumble could be disastrous to man and beast. Steam-powered tractors were much more expensive, so tractors and threshers were often hired to go from farm to farm until all the threshing was done. Threshing was a labor intensive activity that was often followed by an informal community gathering complete with a potluck feast.

16. Fall crops were typically grains such as wheat (winter wheat) and rye. Planted in the fall, they grew to eight to ten inches before the fall frost. They would reappear early in the spring, grow rapidly, mature, and were harvested in July. They could be dry-farmed or irrigated. Spring crops included barley, oats, spring wheat, corn, sugar beets, and beans.

17. Harvest time brought Shoshone laborers from their homes in Idaho, Wyoming, and Nevada to northern Utah. These farm laborers and often their families dwelt in tipis on the outskirts of white communities. Some stayed with Shoshone relatives at Washakie or at Shoshone homesteads in the Elwood area such as the Ottogary farm. When the seasonal work was completed, they usually returned home.

18. When two letters were printed in the same issue of a newspaper, they are identified as A and B.

19. Some Shoshone farmers made contracts with white farmers for mature crops.

20. Hereafter abbreviated as LJ with date shown in the form year-month-day newspaper.

21. This show was held at Tremonton, Utah, a community near Elwood. Anxious to see mythical portrayals of the "real" American West, audiences, including Indians, flocked to Wild West shows. Ottogary notes that acquaintances were being made between the several tribes and that hour-long dances capped off events.

22. The Islanders were a group of Hawaiian Mormons who had come to Utah to be near the Salt Lake Temple. The Church established a ranch (about 1,300 acres) for them in Skull Valley in 1889. They called the colony Iosepa (Hawaiian for Joseph), in honor of President Joseph F. Smith. The colony struggled for over twenty-five years to build a successful farming and ranching enterprise. The experimental colony ended when the church announced it would construct a temple in Laie, Oahu. Many of these Hawaiian Latter-day Saints accepted the church's offer of assistance to return home.

See James B. Allen and Glen M. Leonard, *The Story of the Latter-day Saints* (Salt Lake City: Deseret Book Company, 1976), 420.

23. Brigham City's Peach Day was first celebrated in September 1904. Free peaches, music, and a parade, with prizes awarded for best floats, were part of the annual celebration. See Lydia Walker Forsgren, *History of Box Elder County, Utah, 1851–1937* (Utah: Box Elder County Daughters of Utah Pioneers, 1937), 68, 69.

Chapter 2: "Willie Ottogary Breaks Silence," 1911–1913

1. Hereafter abbreviated as BEN with date shown in the form year-month-day newspaper.
2. The photograph on page 43 of Ottogary, standing alone, accompanied this article.
3. This letter and the following one are nearly identical. Both are included for comparison, but hereafter, only the "best" of duplicate letters will be included, with the exception of 1913-01-16 LJ and 1913-01-16 BEN. See note 33 below.
4. Blacksmith Fork Canyon is located about seven miles southeast of Logan. It is a beautiful mountain canyon frequently used for hunting and fishing trips.
5. Prior to this, the *Box Elder News* spelled his name as Ottegary.
6. The $20 loss represented a tremendous economic burden for Noragan. For example, the ticket price on the Oregon Short Line was 50¢ from Brigham City to Ogden one way, 90¢ round trip; Brigham City to Salt Lake City was $1.50 one way, and $2.70 round trip. See the *Box Elder News*, October 5, 1911.
7. This letter provides a somewhat curious editorial note in parentheses after the title: "Washakie. (Written by an Indian.)" Did the editor think readers would suspect a non-Indian wrote the letter, or did the editor believe newspaper sales would increase if readers knew an Indian wrote them?
8. Ottogary's letters were sometimes published simultaneously in two or more papers. Often the only differences were changes probably made by the editors. Where no significant information is added, the letter is excluded from this collection but the citation is given along with the bracketed comment [Not included].
9. See Seth Pubigee v. Jennie Wanswook Pubigee [Pojennie Woonsook], First Judicial District Court, Box Elder County, Utah, civil case no. 1423, 1911. Though the case was filed, no documentation exists in the case folder to show the marriage was legally dissolved. Census and other documents suggest the couple stayed together.
10. Ottogary's remarks on this shooting are strictly objective, and he does not indicate whether the incident was accidental or deliberate. According to Leland Pubigee (interview May 5, 1993), his father, Enos (age 14 at the time), was the boy who was shot.
11. The injured boy was apparently Seth Pubigee, see 1912-03-21-A LJ.
12. According to Mormon theology, certain ordinances for salvation must be performed in temples. If a person dies without receiving these ordinances, a living individual (usually a relative) can perform them vicariously. The Ottogarys and the Joshuas were at the Logan Temple doing these ordinances for their deceased relatives and friends.
13. Samuel Whitney was a pioneer and friend to the Indians. He was also the favored interpreter in northern Utah for Chief Washakie. See "Lest We Forget: History of Samuel Alonzo Whitney," n.d., USU Special Collections.
14. Probably Utah State Agricultural College in Logan.
15. Two letters appear in this issue of *The Journal*, one dated March 19, the other March 20, 1912. Accordingly, they are listed as A and B.
16. Jesse Earl was president of the Earl and England Publishing Company, publisher of *The Journal*. See Noble Warrum, editor, *Utah Since Statehood: Historical and Biographical* (Chicago and Salt Lake: S. J. Clark Publishing Company, 1919) 4: 165.

17. Movies shown at the Lyric Theatre that week were *The Sheepman's Escape, Tom Tilling's Baby, St. John's Newfoundland,* and *A Question of Seconds.* Ten cents was the price of admission. The entire reference states: "Splendid Program for the week end patrons, featuring a splendid western drama, 'The Sheepman's Escape,' A human story portrayed with excellent skill." See *The Journal,* March 14, 1912.

18. Sons of Chief Sagwitch through different mothers. They were Soquitch (b. ca. 1846), Yeager (b. ca. 1848), and Frank (later known as Frank Timbimboo Warner, b. ca. 1861). Each survived the harrowing Bear River Massacre.

19. Frank Timbimboo graduated from Brigham Young College and served as a teacher for many years. He taught penmanship and perfected the art of calligraphy on greeting cards. He served three missions (in Montana and Canada) for the LDS Church before his death in January 1919 in the flu epidemic. As a child, he had been sold to Solomon Warner of Willard, Box Elder County, by an errant relative while Frank's father, Sagwitch, was away. The boy was later traded to Warner's brother Amos, who provided the child, now known as Frank Timbimboo Warner, with a good education. Scott R. Christensen, *Sagwitch: Shoshoni Chieftain, Mormon Elder, 1822–1887* (Logan: Utah State University Press, 1999), 67; Mae Timbimoo Parry, telephone interview by Matthew E. Kreitzer, July 20, 1997; John C. Dowdle Journal, 1844–1908, typescript, USU Special Collections, 201.

20. Ottogary's letters are organized according to the date each letter was written. In order to avoid confusion where a letter's code appears to be out of sequence, I have included an explanation in brackets.

21. Movies shown at the Crystal Theatre that week were *The Guardian Angel, The Law of the Range,* and *The Guilty Baby.* Admission was 5¢ for children and 10¢ for adults. See *The Journal,* March 30, 1912.

22. The only Jim John mentioned in census documents was Jim John Neaman, but he was born July 14, 1901. The editor of the paper probably made a transcription mistake and Grouse Creek Jack and family were going to the farm of his son, Jim Jack.

23. Grubbing sage means to clear the land of sage by pulling it up by the roots. The process also requires hauling off rocks. The task is time-consuming and physically taxing. "Jim John" was apparently preparing his land for cultivation.

24. It is unclear if the store was Ward's privately owned business or if it was an LDS bishop's storehouse. Bishop's storehouses were administered by local bishops to help provide for the needs of poor members. This social welfare concept is a hallmark of Mormonism.

25. Publishers of *The Journal,* Charles England and Jesse Earl asked Ottogary to write a biographical sketch of his life.

26. Ottogary's death certificate (filed March 19, 1929) records that he was born July 6, 1869, in Mantua, in Box Elder County.

27. George Washington Hill was an early LDS Indian missionary in northern Utah. See the Biographical Register and Christensen, *Sagwitch.*

28. This reference is to the Indian mission established by the Mormon Church to the Northwestern Shoshone, initially under the leadership of George W. Hill. See Brigham D. Madson, *Chief Pocatello: The "White Plume"* (Salt Lake City: University of Utah Press, 1986), 93.

29. The three children Eliza Wongan left were probably Iona (or Tish-E-A-Wipe, b. 1896), Warren (b. 1898), and Eunice (b. 1905).

30. Brown and the others performed in the Sioux Indian Medicine Show. See 1910-02-15 LJ.

31. The Relief Society is an auxiliary organization of the LDS Church whose motto is "Charity Never Faileth." Aside from their concern for the less fortunate, Relief Society women also organize social and educational gatherings.

32. Ottogary, Ammon Pubigee, and Charlie Broom (later mentioned by name) were called to preach to the people of Washakie and to other outlying Shoshonean communities such as Ibapah, in Tooele County. Stake presidents have the authority to call individuals on short term missions. Those called preach the gospel of Mormonism within the boundaries of the stake.

33. This letter (1913-01-16 LJ) and the next (1913-01-16 BEN) are good examples to compare editing practices between two newspapers. In these cases, no editorial changes have been made to the published text.

34. Old Folk's Day was a formal Mormon celebration to honor contributions of the elderly and was respected wherever Mormons gathered. The best source is Brian D. Reeves, "Hoary-Headed Saints: The Aged in Nineteenth-Century Mormon Culture" (master's thesis, Brigham Young University, 1987).

35. This was probably Grouse Creek Jack. His sons were Jim (b. 1886), Sam (b. 1891), and Stanguitch (or Panguitch, b. 1894).

36. Ottogary sent the photo on page 57 along with this letter to the *Box Elder News*. The photograph of "Wah-Hah-Gun-Ta" appeared in *The Journal* January 16, 1913, and the caption repeated much of the information from this letter. However, Ottogary says more here than was in the caption. He had to have obtained the details from another news source, possibly from another newspaper. According to a neighbor of Ottogary, Stan Andersen, he subscribed to the Sunday *Denver Post*. See *The Andersens of Elwood: A Family History*, (San Francisco: Stan Andersen, 1990), 21.

37. Mrs. Joe Moemberg was Sarah Pocatello. Her father was Tom Pocatello, brother to Chief Pocatello. See Brigham Madsen, *Chief Pocatello: The "White Plume"* (Salt Lake City: University of Utah Press, 1986); Family Group Records (batch 1553338 and F884096 032), LDS FHL.

38. Grippe is an acute viral disease such as influenza.

39. Probably in the Broad Canyon area.

40. Allotments were made available on the Fort Hall Reservation by an act of Congress March 3, 1911. Since Ottogary remained in Utah the allotment request was apparently denied. See Brigham D. Madsen, *The Northern Shoshone* (Caldwell, Idaho: The Caxton Printers, 1980), 148.

41. See "Ringling Circus Draws Big Crowds: Everybody and His Little Brother Packs Big Top at Both Shows," *The Ogden Examiner*, August 3, 1913.

42. The only Neaman born about this time was Everett Neaman, born Nov. 30, 1913 at Washakie, to Moses and Katie Neaman.

Chapter 3: "I Am Going Tell Some News," 1914–1920

1. Taken from 1918-03-19 LJ.

2. The only Indian doctor Ottogary mentioned by name was Johnny Thompson. See 1929-02-11 LJ.

3. Also Te Na-pa-ch. See Biographical Register.

4. See Martha C. Knack, "Philene T. Hall, Bureau of Indian Affairs Field Matron: Planned Culture Change of Washakie Shoshone Women," *Prologue* 22 (Summer 1990): 150–67.

5. The Agriculture Round-Up was a forum held annually at the Utah State Agricultural College in Logan. Participants attended to learn the most up-to-date farming ideas and procedures. They camped-out on the Quad in tents and attended daily lectures. Lectures and demonstrations were presented by knowledgable individuals in the region. Ottogary's comments offer his unique perspective—that of an American Indian farmer.

6. John A. Widtsoe was president of the Utah Agricultural College from 1907 to 1916. See Biographical Register.

7. This is the first recorded attempt by the Northwestern Band of the Shoshone Nation to establish a tribal council.

8. It is unclear what Ottogary is saying when he uses the word civilized. Taking a broad view, based on all his writings, it appears that "civilized" meant to him to accept an agrarian lifestyle, a reasonable amount of land for each Shoshone, the protection of certain rights held by Indians (such as hunting and fishing on traditional lands), freedom from being taxed, and enjoying the priviliges associated with contemporary life in northern Utah.

9. See related article in appendix E, "Willie Ottogary Goes East Again," 1915-04-01 BEN.

10. Oakley is on Goose Creek in Cassia County, Idaho.

11. Ottogary's spelling of Wilson's first name as "Windrow" may be agriculturally based. A windrow is created by raking hay or other cut vegetation into rows for drying, thus making it easier for later gathering. Perhaps Ottogary heard the name and spelled it Windrow because, as a farmer, he was familiar with windrows. Another possibility is that Ottogary was making a political statement by calling the president Windrow Wilson.

12. Tossing bundles of grain onto the thresher's conveyor belt.

13. See appendix F, "Awards and Prizes Presented for the Special Indian Exhibit of the Utah State Fair, Fall 1915." Several award winners were from Washakie, Utah.

14. This paragraph may refer to some Shoshone desiring to move to their farms north of Brigham City, at a location once called Indian Town. Other Shoshone, according to Ottogary, continued to lease their lower farmlands to white farmers, a common practice. See Kenneth Hunsaker, "Indian Town, Utah: A Pre-Washakie Settlement," 1983, USU Special Collections.

15. Willie filed for divorce December 2, 1916. See Willie Ottogary v. Nancy West Ottogary, First Judicial District Court Box Elder County, Utah, civil case no. 2211, 1917.

16. E. Saylor could be Albert Saylor. In the fall of 1916, Albert Saylor hired Willie Ottogary, George P. Sam, and Johnie Tomock to research the heirs of Shoshone land patent holders. Saylor was apparently using them in a scheme to help acquire the property. Their agreement included a reasonable payment for services performed, but Saylor failed to follow through. The following August Ottogary filed suit and won the case. See Willie Ottogary v. Albert Saylor, First Judicial District Court, Box Elder County, Utah, civil case no. 2382, 1918.

17. See David L. Wood, "Gosiute-Shoshone Draft Resistance, 1917–1918," *Utah Historical Quarterly* 49 (1981):173–88.

18. See "Many Injured in Bad Wreck," *Box Elder Journal*, November 8, 1917.

19. Ottogary's letter writing routinely tapered off during the harvest season; he was a single parent, a full-time farmer, a tribal leader and spokesman, as well as a part-time journalist.

20. Ottogary may be making a reference to the "War Garden" concept of World War I.

21. A worldwide influenza epidemic of this year left nearly 22 million people dead.

22. As a child, Eliza Pubigee (Ottogary's sister) took ill and "died" but came back from the dead. She said she saw God and Jesus Christ, was instructed on how to live, and was told to go back to her body. She came back, related her story, and was honored for some time to come. The community's celebration of her experience was later stifled by Bishop Isaac E. D. Zundel. See Charles E. Dibble, "Mormon Mission to the Shoshone," *Utah Humanities Review* 1 (1947): 290.

23. Ottogary may be suggesting that the young runaway couple might make a positive behavior change at some other place.

24. See Biographical Register. The daughter was Rose Parago-Sam (b. Oct. 13, 1906, d. June 17, 1919).

25. For more on Harry Preacher, see Crum, *Road*, 62, 75–76.

26. When Ottogary uses the word "Jap" in this context, he is merely following a common practice of his day.

Chapter 4: "I Will Start on My Stories," 1921–1922

1. Taken from 1921-09-05 LJ.

2. Catch Quipitch was known by several names. Hereafter he appears as Catch Toyahdook. See Biographical Register.

3. Much of this was evidently quoted from a letter Ottogary received from Louis Mann, a reporter from North Yakima, Washington. Mann appears to have been an American Indian who, like Ottogary, was working for the rights of his people.

4. Ottogary highlights his trip to Washington, D.C. He attended President Harding's inauguration and, on March 8, 1921, participated in an Indian delegation meeting where he shook hands with the president. See Biographical Register for more information about individuals mentioned.

5. Moroni Timbimboo stayed on Fort Hall Reservation for a few months but returned to Washakie. In 1922, Ottogary again wrote that Moroni moved to Fort Hall. According to Moroni Timbimboo's daughter, Mae Timbimboo Parry, he never moved there permanently.

6. Many Washakie residents were involved in traditional craft work. Some made gloves and other items from buckskin. Others did beadwork. Pubigee acted as middleman, supplying a friend with beads.

7. The Promontory Range and Rozel Flats are areas fairly close to one another on the northern end of the Great Salt Lake.

8. Bright's disease is one of several kidney diseases.

9. Hunt dances often followed sparrow and rabbit hunts.

10. Hite Spring on Kessler Creek in Idaho County (north-central Idaho) is much further away than the seven miles north which Ottogary suggested. Another possibility is Hot Spring, though he does not give enough information to tell which hot spring he is referring to.

11. The article mentioned by Ottogary regarding Senator Key Pittman's speech was not included in the newspaper. See Biographical Register for more information on Key Pittman.

12. There are Thirteen Articles of Faith, or principle beliefs, of the LDS Church. The fourth Article of Faith is: "We believe that the first principles and ordinances of the Gospel are: first, Faith in the Lord Jesus Christ; second, Repentance; third, Baptism by immersion for the remission of sins; fourth, Laying on of hands for the gift of the Holy Ghost." Joseph Smith, "The Wentworth Letter" (The Articles of Faith of the Church of Jesus Christ of Latter-day Saints), *History of the Church of Jesus Christ of Latter-day Saints*, 2nd ed. revised (Salt Lake City: Deseret Book Company, 1978) 4: 535–41.

13. It is unclear whether these Washakie representatives recited the first or the fourth Article of Faith (or both) at the general conference. The First Article reads: "We believe in God, the Eternal Father, and in His Son, Jesus Christ, and in the Holy Ghost."

14. These men were probably functioning as ward teachers (or home teachers as they are called now). Ward teachers visited members of the ward periodically, typically once a month, and presented a spiritual message and offered assistance where needed.

15. The Interurban Car was a public transportation system in Logan otherwise known as the electric rail system. See related article in *Box Elder News*, March 4, 1912.

16. See Biographical Register for more information regarding June Neaman.

17. Ottogary may have been "on assignment" to cover the Elks Club Convention (Benevolent Protective Order of Elks, B.P.O.E.).

18. These Shoshone were purchasing cherries for winter use, maintaining their traditional food preservation customs. The cherries could be dried or bottled, a more contemporary method. See also 1922-09-28 LJ for drying peaches.

19. Chokecherries were harvested during the end of June through early July and buffalo berries were gathered closer to fall, according to Leland Pubigee (interviewed May 5, 1993).

20. Harry Dixon was elected the new chief at this council, replacing Joe Gilbert. Crum, *Road*, 77.

21. Ottogary may have missed the visit to Brigham City of Man-a-wntze (wife of Chief Pocatello) because he was away on business, see "Distinguished Visitor Here; 112 years Old," *Box Elder News*, Oct. 3, 1922.

22. It appears that Ottogary is combining the Box Elder Treaty of 1863 (see Charles J. Kappler, *Indian Affairs: Laws and Treaties* 2: *Treaties*, [Washington: Government Printing Office, 1904], 850–51) and a letter written by Assistant Commissioner of Indian Affairs Edgar B. Meritt, reaffirming Shoshone rights to hunt and fish whenever they want on their aboriginal homelands.

23. See Danyhay in Biographical Register.

24. Ottogary may have been in Logan so often to gather news for his column, to collect payment for his columns, or simply to visit old acquaintances.

25. According to Mae Timbimboo Parry, her father Moroni never joined the Baptist Church.

Chapter 5: "We Expect Get Some Land from Our Big White Pop in Future Time," 1923–1924

1. Taken from 1924-03-08 LJ.

2. The mail carrier is probably Ray Diamond. See Biographical Register.

3. Ottogary may have written to the publisher of *The Journal* (England) for an advance on his paycheck, to remind him of payday, or to ask for a short term loan.

4. Faithful members of the LDS Church are expected to pay 10 percent of their increase to the Church as a tithe. Washakie members earned a distinctive honor when they reached a near-perfect level of full-tithe paying.

5. Seth Pubigee may have been administrating the estate of a deceased relative.

6. Seth Pubigee and others apparently played the role of wild Indians in a stage holdup as part of the Malad City Carnival.

7. Ottogary and Pubigee may have been prospecting for gold or silver. Ottogary later writes of a prospecting venture in Wyoming, see 1924-10-18-B LJ.

8. Hereafter abbreviated as OCE with date shown in the form year-month-day newspaper.

9. Ottogary may refer either to the front as a line of military engagement or to Mr. Bird serving as a front, or point, man. While discussing military experiences and Washakie veterans, Korean War veteran Leland Pubigee mentioned that he too was "point man" when his company was on patrol. Interview, Brigham City, Utah, May 20, 1993.

10. Youcup Moemberg was a daughter of Tom Pocatello. The granddaughter mentioned here was probably Amy Broom, daughter of Charlie Broom and Neatze Moemberg. See Biographical Register for Moemberg, Mrs. Joe (Sarah), and Broom, Charlie.

11. They may have been planning a birthday celebration honoring George Washington.

12. Ottogary seems to support the sale of Indian land at Fort Hall while working to gain land for the people at Washakie. Perhaps he felt the Fort Hall Reservation was large enough to support its residents while the Washakie area was not.

13. Ottogary makes a clever reference to the president as "big white pop."

14. Ottogary is indicting the federal government for not living up to obligations under the Treaty of 1863.

15. Most LDS meetinghouses are equipped with a cultural hall where activities such as dinners, dances, games, and receptions are held. These halls are sometimes referred to as ward halls.

16. The last three sentences of this letter appear to be quoted from an advertisement.

17. Samaria Lake is about fourteen miles northwest of Washakie, in Oneida County, Idaho. A canal dug from this lake fed irrigation ditches in Washakie. Much of the land under cultivation at Washakie was dry farmed (see 1926-04-10 LJ). The remaining fields were irrigated.

18. Ottogary is asked by an insurance salesman to mention him in his column. The salesman may have recognized the readership Ottogary's column carried.

19. Ottogary is once again on a special assignment for *The Journal*.

20. William Donner was superintendent of the Fort Hall Reservation, Idaho. See also chapter six, note 3.

21. Both Mound Spring and Mountain Spring are about three miles southeast of Washakie.

22. In this and other letters, note that Ottagary mentions traditional food gathering activities (e.g., pine nut gathering and wild cherry picking) coinciding with poor wheat and sugar beet harvests.

23. Pubigee appears to have wanted his son to buy hay in Idaho and sell it in northern Utah, a strategy to profit by adjusting supply to demand.

24. The phrase, "all under water," means water rights were available.

Chapter 6: "You People May Read My Writing Long as I Work," 1925–1926

1. Taken from 1925-09-26 LJ.

2. See appendix G for more information on ward leadership positions held by Washakie Shoshone.

3. After Tom Elk was arrested, Ottogary explained to officials that according to the Treaty of 1863, the Indians could hunt with few restrictions. William Donner, superintendent of the Fort Hall Reservation, failed to support Ottogary on this issue, so the two had a confrontation. Ottogary wrote a letter of complaint to E. B. Meritt, assistant commissioner of Indian affairs, Washington, D.C.(Feb. 2, 1925). Mr. Elk received a suspended sentence and was required to pay ten dollars in court costs, based on future good behavior. For Ottogary's complaints against Donner, see Central Classified Files, Records of the Bureau of Indian Affairs, National Archives Record Group 75, file 8760, 1925, Scattered Bands in Utah or Fort Hall Agency, classification no. 115.

4. Ottogary notes the severity of the economic situation at Washakie by suggesting no one had enough money to even purchase a setting hen—perhaps for a family meal.

5. Hereafter abbreviated as BEJ with date shown in the form year-month-day newspaper.

6. Probably Za-Ko-Na-Cok-Paw (Bob Smith), father of Ottogary's ex-wife, Nancy. According to family tradition, Bob Smith was an army scout during the Bannock War of 1878, see Biographical Register under Ottogary, Nancy.

7. Ottogary signs on as a correspondent for the *Box Elder Journal*, the fifth newspaper to publish his column on the Washakie colony.

8. Ottogary demonstrates his objectivity in journalism by reporting on a heinous crime involving three Indians in the Pocatello, Idaho, area. He confirms, once again, his desire to keep his readers abreast of Indian news.

9. Under ideal circumstances, three crops of alfalfa hay can be cut during the growing season in northern Utah and southern Idaho.

10. Scholars have not sufficiently examined the role lawyers have played in Shoshone land claims, a critical issue for Ottogary. For example, we know little of the work of Charles H. Merillat. We know more about Ernest L. Wilkinson, the lawyer who took over from Merillat. Wilkinson eventually enjoyed a sterling career as president of Brigham Young University, see Woodruff J. Deem and Glenn V. Bird, *Ernest L. Wilkinson: Indian Advocate and University President* (Provo, Utah: privately published by Alice L. Wilkinson, 1982).

11. A sulky plow is a two-wheeled plow with a seat for the driver.

12. Warm Dances were held in winter months to ". . . ask the maker for help . . . [regarding the weather] be lenient to the people." Grass Dances were in the spring, to seek divine intervention ". . . to speed up nature so everything be good in summer, hurry things up." Leland Pubigee, telephone interview by Matthew E. Kreitzer, May 5, 1993.

13. Bracketed clarifications in this sentence provided by Mae Timbimboo Parry, summer 1997.

14. The child was Joseph Amos Moemberg, born Jan. 21, 1926.

15. See Biographical Register for more information on Charlie Harris. His gift of a phonograph leads to the especially provocative idea that a wax recording of Ottogary's voice might exist.

16. This letter introduces readers to the boxing Ottogary brothers. Both Chester and Custer experienced notoriety for their talents in the ring. Their father noted with pride the bouts the boys fought during the boxing season, which ran throughout the winter months, usually beginning in January. Their exploits were covered in various papers of northern Utah, particularly after 1926. See appendix H, "Newspaper Accounts of Two of the Ottogarys' Early Boxing Matches."

17. This racial expression was widely used during Ottogary's day.

18. The schoolhouse, first mentioned by Ottogary in May 1925, still had not been built. Ottogary reported construction was completed in November 1926.

19. Ed Wagon was adopted by Catch Toyahdook and his wife in 1928.

20. "A large delegation of Washakie Indians, under the direction of Thomas Pabawena, arrived in Brigham City yesterday for the big Peach Day celebration to be held Friday and Saturday. They brought with them their dogs and ponies, and a beef steer for a barbeque. The Indians have pitched their tents on the western outskirts of the city, near Pioneer park, and are looking forward to the big festival with enthusiasm. A group of these Indians, in primitive costume and war paint, will be featured in the big parade Friday morning, and during the celebration will participate in the program each day, giving native war dances, sham battles, etc. They will also give an exhibition of pony racing, broncho riding, etc." See "Washakie Indians Arrive for Peach Day Celebration," *Box Elder News*, Sept. 14, 1926.

21. Not only did Enos Pubigee enter a horse, but Nephi Perdash and T. (Thomas?) Pabawena did also. With names such as "Indian Tom," "Red Cloud," "Flirt," "Strawberry," and, of course, "Buckskin Nelly," Washakie horses placed well at the Peach Day Races. A purse of $1097.50 was awarded for both days (22 races). Of this, 21 percent was won by the Washakie group. For more details, see "Peach Day Horse Racing: New Racing Course at Pioneer Park Opened Friday Afternoon," *Box Elder News*, Sept. 21, 1926.

22. Migrant farm workers converged in Idaho to work during the potato harvest.

23. Ottogary complains that his son Chester was not paid enough for a fight. He thought Chester's character was under attack by the press for not showing up for his fight.

24. According to Mae Timbimboo Parry, Moroni and Amy Timbimboo did not have any daughters who had heart problems.

Chapter 7: "Our People Haven't Got Any Land for Their Own," 1927–1929

1. Taken from 1928-04-07 LJ.

2. Ottogary reports on boxers who competed at this event, but does not mention his sons or any boxers from Washakie. He may have been scouting future opponents or covering a news story for the paper.

3. Ottogary admits his son, Chester, was outclassed in the ring by a more experienced boxer.

4. Enos Pubigee entered two horses, Buckskin Nelly and Bobby, and won $22.50. Buckskin Nelly tied in the half-mile race. "This race was one of the best put over during the afternoon and caused considerable excitement." See "Horse Racing Draws Crowd," *Box Elder News*, May 31, 1927.

5. It is unclear whether the Washakie team played an Indian team from Blackfoot, Idaho, or a team comprised of Blackfoot, or Blackfeet, Indians.

6. For details, see "Race Program The Best Ever: Fast Horses From Utah and Idaho Compete; Vaudeville a Feature." *Box Elder News*, September 13, 1927.

7. Juvenile Judge L. E. Nelson heard the case and committed Evans Peyope (age 16) and Ed Wagen, or Wagon (age 12), to the state industrial school. Wallace Zundel (age 14) was given a suspended sentence. See "Two Indian Boys Sent to The State Reform School," *Box Elder News*, March 2, 1928.

8. This is probably Joseph Chez, past attorney general for Utah. After Ottogary died, Chez worked on Shoshone legal issues with the Ernest L. Wilkinson law firm. See Deem, *Ernest L. Wilkinson*, 151 n. 67 .

9. This reference is probably to Lamanites, not Samarites, from Samaria, Idaho. A Logan bishop requested a group of Washakie Indians come to Logan to present a gospel-centered program to local whites. According to LDS belief, Lamanites were descended from groups of ancient Israelites who migrated to the Americas (circa 600 B.C.). See *The Book of Mormon*. Popular Mormon belief held that American Indians descended from these Lamanites.

10. Senator William H. King introduced a bill (S. 4396) in the 69th Congress, 1st Session, June 4, 1926. This bill was rejected, but another (S. 710) was introduced by King in the 1st Session of the 70th Congress, December 6 (calendar day, December 9), 1927. This bill was approved and signed into law by the president, February 28, 1929. Public Law 854, 70th Congress, 1st sess.

11. This may be the same Thompson who used to play baseball with Willie Ottogary (1926-06-05 LJ), and he may be related to John Pabawena since Nellie Thompson married John S. Pabawena. Hence, Jim Thompson may have been at Washakie for the Pabawena boy's funeral.

12. Chester's wife was Vida Pubigee, daughter of Seth Pubigee and Pojennie Woonsook.

13. "The medicine man of Starr Valley was Johnny Thompson, son of Poongorah, signer of the Treaty of 1863." Edna B. Patterson, Louise A. Ulph, and Victor Goodwin, *Nevada's Northeast Frontier* (Sparks, Nevada: Western Printing & Publishing Co., 1969), 34.

14. This may have been a calf or steer roping event where the roper attempts to rope the head or the head and back feet of the animal in a timed contest. Another possibility is that the man was engaged in rope tricks.

15. Moroni Timbimboo took daughters Joana, Hazel, and Mae to the Sherman Institute, a Bureau of Indian Affairs school at Riverside, California.

16. Rabbit furs were selling for as high as $1.10 per pound, see "Many Rabbits Killed in Box Elder County," *Bear River Valley Leader* (Tremonton, Utah), January 16, 1929.

17. Ottogary's birth certificate notes he was born July 6, 1869, making him 59 years and 8 months old at the time of his death.

Conclusion

1. Mark Twain, *Roughing It* (New York: Harper and Brothers Publishing, 1913), 1:131.

2. Daniel F. Littlefield, Jr., and James W. Parins, *A Biobibliography of Native American Writers, 1772–1924* (Metuchen, New Jersey: Scarecrow Press, 1981), 34–37, 92–93, 153–55.

3. Ibid., 100–107, 135–40.

4. See 1920-05-29 LJ.

5. Rasmussen interview.

6. Anderson, *Andersens of Elwood*, 21.

7. This story was told to me by an informant, but it could not be found in extant copies of Ottogary's letters or otherwise verified. Since my intention here is not to challenge his veracity or embarrass him, I have omitted the informant's name. The narrative is included because it illustrates that Ottogary's legacy lives on in folklore.

Bibliography

BOOKS

Allen, James B. and Glen M. Leonard. *The Story of the Latter-day Saints*. Salt Lake City: Deseret Book Company, 1976.

Alter, Cecil J. *Utah, the Storied Domain*. Chicago & New York: American Historical Society, 1932.

Andersen, Stan. *The Andersens of Elwood: A Family History*. San Francisco: Stan Andersen, 1990.

Christiansen, Scott R. *Sagwitch: Shoshone Chieftain, Mormon Elder*. Logan: Utah State University Press, 1999.

Crum, Steven J. *The Road On Which We Came = Po'i Pentun Tammen Kimmappeh: A History of the Western Shoshone*. Salt Lake City: University of Utah Press, 1994.

Deem, Woodruff J. and Glenn V. Bird, *Ernest L. Wilkinson: Indian Advocate and University President*. Provo: privately published by Alice L. Wilkinson, 1982.

Edlefsen, Edlef. *Willie Ottogary's Letters to "The Journal" Logan, Utah*. Davis, Calif.: Danewel Publications, 1967.

Forsgren, Lydia Walker. *History of Box Elder County, Utah, 1851–1937*. Box Elder County Daughters of Utah Pioneers, 1937.

Johnson, Ruth. *Patchwork: Early Pioneer, Indian, and Faith Promoting Latter-day Saint Stories*. A Privately Printed Presentation Edition Limited to one hundred and fifty copies, 1973.

Jorgensen, Joseph G. *The Sun Dance Religion: Power for the Powerless*. Chicago: University of Chicago Press, 1972.

Kappler, Charles J. *Indian Affairs. Laws and Treaties*, vol. 2, *Treaties*. Washington: Government Printing Office, 1904.

Littlefield, Daniel F. Jr. and James W. Parins. *A Biobibliography of Native American Writers, 1772–1924*. Metuchen, New Jersey: Scarecrow Press, 1981.

Madsen, Brigham D. *Chief Pocatello: The "White Plume."* Salt Lake City: University of Utah Press. 1986.

_____. *Corinne: The Gentile Capital of Utah*. Salt Lake City: Utah State Historical Society, 1980.

_____. *The Northern Shoshoni*. Caldwell, Idaho: Caxton Printers, 1980.

_____. *The Shoshoni Frontier and the Bear River Massacre*. Salt Lake City: University of Utah Press, 1985.

Miller, Wick, R. *Newe Natekwinappeh: Shoshone Stories and Dictionary*. University of Utah Anthropological Papers 94. 1972.

Patterson, Edna B., Louise A. Ulph, and Victor Goodwin. *Nevada's Northeast Frontier*. Sparks: Western Printing & Publishing Co., 1969.

Peterson, Charles S. *Utah: A History*. States and the Nation Series. American Association for State and Local History, Nashville, Tennessee. New York: W. W. Norton and Company, 1984.

Quatannens, Jo Anne McCormick, compiler. *Senators of the United States: A Historical Bibliography: A Compilation of Works by and about Members of the United States Senate 1789–1995*. Washington: Government Printing Office, 1995.

Smith, Joseph. *History of the Church of Jesus Christ of Latter-day Saints.* 2nd ed. rev. Salt Lake City: Deseret Book Company, 1978.

Steward, Julian H. *Basin-Plateau Aboriginal Sociopolitical Groups.* Smithsonian Institution Bureau of Ethnology Bulletin 120. Washington: Government Printing Office, 1938.

Twain, Mark. *Roughing It.* New York: Harper and Brothers, 1913.

Warrum, Noble, editor. *Utah Since Statehood: Historical and Biographical.* Chicago and Salt Lake City: S. J. Clark Publishing Company, 1919.

Widtsoe, John A. *In a Sunlit Land: The Autobiography of John A. Widtsoe.* Salt Lake City: Deseret News Press, 1953.

ARTICLES

Dibble, Charles E. "The Mormon Mission to the Shoshone Indians." *Utah Humanities Review* 1 (1947).

Knack, Martha C. "Philene T. Hall, Bureau of Indian Affairs Field Matron: Planned Culture Change of Washakie Shoshone Women." *Prologue* 22 (1990): 150–67.

Wood, David L. "Gosiute-Shoshone Draft Resistance, 1917–1918." *Utah Historical Quarterly* 49 (1981): 173–88.

THESES AND DISSERTATIONS

Christensen, Scott R. "Sagwitch: Shoshoni Chieftain, Mormon Elder, 1822–1884." Master's thesis, Utah State University, 1995.

Evans, Joshua T. "The Northwestern Shoshone Indians, (a) Under Tribal Organization and Government, (b) Under the Ecclesiastical Administration of the Church of Jesus Christ of Latter-day Saints as Exemplified at the Washakie Colony, Utah." Master's thesis, Utah State Agricultural College, 1938.

Kreitzer, Matthew E. "Willie Ottogary: Northwestern Shoshone Journalist, 1906–1929." Master's thesis, Utah State University, 1993.

Reeves, Brian D. "Hoary-Headed Saints: The Aged in Nineteenth-Century Mormon Culture." Master's thesis, Brigham Young University, 1987.

GOVERNMENT DOCUMENTS

American Indian Census Rolls, 1885–1940. Records of the Bureau of Indian Affairs, Record Group 75. National Archives, Washington, D.C.

Biographical Directory of the United States: 1774 to Present. BIOGUIDE (http://bioguide.congress.gov/). Accessed December 1, 1998.

Box Elder County Recorder's Office. Deed Records, Book J, p. 63 (homestead certificate 2584).

————. Marriage Licenses. Willie Ottogary and Nancy West, October 26, 1903.

Box Elder County, Utah. First Judicial District Court. Seth Pubigee v. Jennie Wanswook Pubigee [Pojennie Woonsook], civil case no. 1423, 1911.

————. Willie Ottogary v. Nancy West Ottogary, civil case no. 2211, 1917.

————. Willie Ottogary v. Albert Saylor, civil case no. 2382, 1918.

Central Classified Files. Records of the Bureau of Indian Affairs, Record Group 75. National Archives, Washington, D.C.

Northwestern Band Tribal Council. "Agreement or Certificate," (noting transfer of leadership from Willie Ottogary and Harry D. Tootiania to Chief Custer Ottogary and Harry D. Tootiania). Tribal meeting September 16, 1929. Carbon copy in possession of Clyde S. Ottogary, Pocatello, Idaho.

————. "Historical Record of the Northwestern Band of Shoshone Indians," July 10, 1937. Copy in possession of Clyde S. Ottogary, Pocatello, Idaho.

U.S. Center for Legislative Archives: 70 Stat 1407-(PL 854).

U.S. Department of Interior. Bureau of the Census. Utah. Manuscript population census schedules, 1880, 1900, 1910, 1920.

U.S. *Statutes at Large*. Vol. 45, pt. 1 (December 1927–March 1929). Concurrent Resolutions of the Two Houses of Congress and Recent Treaties, Conventions, and Executive Proclamations. Washington: Government Printing Office, 1929.

Utah. Vital Records. Death Certificates. State Board of Health. Box Elder County.

Utah. Vital Records. Marriage Licenses for Box Elder County, 1887–1966. Index to Marriage Licences and Certificates, LDS Family History Library, Salt Lake City, film 0480310. Hard copy available at Box Elder County Recorder's Office.

INTERVIEWS, CORRESPONDENCE, AND CONVERSATIONS

Andersen, Stan, San Francisco. Letter to Matthew E. Kreitzer, March 15, 1993.

Crapo, Richley. Department of Anthropology, Utah State University. Email correspondence received by Matthew E. Kreitzer, October 8, 1997.

Menta, Alene. Pocatello, Idaho. Informal conversations with Matthew E. Kreitzer at a Native American Literature workshop at the University of Utah, July 7–11, 1996.

Ottogary, Clyde S. Interviews by Matthew E. Kreitzer (telephone and in person), November 21, 1992, December 12, 1992, January 26, 1993, February 20, 1993, May 22, 1993, Pocatello, Idaho.

Parry, Mae Timbimboo. Telephone interviews by Matthew E. Kreitzer, May 12, 1993, July 20, 1997, and Aug. 28, 1999.

_____. Letter to Matthew E. Kreitzer, November 1997.

_____. Correspondence to Matthew E. Kreitzer, July 1999.

Pubigee, Leland. Interview by Matthew E. Kreitzer, Brigham City, Utah, May 5, 1993 (telephone) and May 19-20, 1993; Washakie, Utah, May 31, 1993.

Rasmussen, Owen Y. Interview by Matthew E. Kreitzer, Elwood, Utah, March 22, 1993.

MANUSCRIPTS

Dowdle, John C. Journal, 1844–1908. Typescript. Special Collections, Merrill Library, Utah State University, Logan, Utah.

Elwood Ward Church Records. Film 025634, LDS Family History Library, Logan, Utah.

Family Group Records. Film 1553338, LDS Family History Library, Salt Lake City.

Hill, George W. "Autobiography and Indian Missionary Journals of George W. Hill. . . ." Copy in Utah State University Special Collections, Logan.

"Historical Records and Minutes." Washakie Ward, Box Elder Stake. No. 9928, series 11–20, LDS Church Archives, Salt Lake City.

Hunsaker, Kenneth D. "Indian Town, Utah: A Pre-Washakie Settlement," 1983. Utah State University Special Collections, Logan.

Incorporation of Washakie Ward, 8 March 1886, Member List p. 204, 205. Film 048066, LDS Family History Library, Salt Lake City.

International Genealogical Index Version 3.02 (1993 Edition), IGI.

Jenson, Andrew. Journal History of the Church of Jesus Christ of Latter-day Saints, 1820–1972. LDS Church Archives, Salt Lake City.

_____. "Manuscript Histories of Wards, Washakie Ward, Box Elder County, Utah, 1900." Descriptive History Collection. LR 9928, LDS Church Archives, Salt Lake City.

Kreitzer, Matthew E. "The Spirit Never Dies: An Examination of Supernatural Experiences of Northwestern Shoshone and the Relationship of these Experiences to Mormon Theology." Unpublished research paper in possession of Matthew E. Kreitzer, 1993.

"Lest We Forget: History of Samuel Alonzo Whitney." [no author listed]. Unpublished biographical paper, n.d., Utah State University Special Collections, Logan.

Logan Temple Records. "Baptisms for the Dead, 1912." Logan, Utah. Indexed, Film 0177869, LDS Family History Library, Salt Lake City.

_____. "Living Sealings." Book A: May 21, 1884 to November 21, 1900. Logan, Utah.

_____. "Sealings of Children to Parents." Book D: December, 10, 1909 to November 21, 1912. Logan,Utah.

_____. "Sealings of Previously Married." Book A: November 21,1900 to July 31,1913. Logan, Utah.

"Malad Idaho Stake Centennial History Book, 1888–1988," n.p. 1988. The manuscript lists Hubert Gleed as Chairman of the Centennial History Project. Copy from Ricks College Library, Special Collections, Rexburg, Idaho. A variation is located in Utah State University Special Collections, Logan.

"Missionary Index." 1971–1973, LDS Church Archives, Salt Lake City.

"Record of Members Collection 1836–1970." No. CR 375 8, LDS Church Archives, Salt Lake City.

Salt Lake City Temple, ord. 7216. Film 183527, p. 205, LDS Family History Library, Salt Lake City.

"Seventies Quorums, Records, 1844–1975." No. 499, reels 144, 145, 395, LDS Church Archives, Salt Lake City.

Washakie [Utah], 1891-1909. Film no.179,951, LDS Church Records, LDS Family History Library, Logan, Utah.

"Washakie Church Records, Records of Members Early to 1931. Records of Members in Washakie Ward, Malad Stake of Zion." Film 027,406. LDS Family History Library, Logan, Utah. Also available at LDS Church Archives, Salt Lake City.

"Washakie Ward Historical Record, 1880–1965." [To 1948]. Film 027,406, LDS Family History Library, Logan, Utah.

"Washakie Ward, Malad Stake, Record of Members (Record of Indians) Before 1900." A record of temple ordinances performed in the Logan Temple for Indians led by Washakie. Includes a 1938 census of the Washakie Ward, Malad Stake, Idaho. Film 0599816, item 2, LDS Family History Library, Salt Lake City.

Washines, Lorene. "Lee Neaman Oral History." 1979. Special Collections, Merrill Library, Utah State University, Logan, Utah.

PRIVATELY OWNED MATERIAL

Funeral Program of Chester R. Ottogary. Services held Nov. 11, 1987. Copy in possession of Matthew E. Kreitzer.

Ottogary Letters. Copies of letters collected from microform sources held in Utah State University Special Collections, Logan. Photocopies in possession of Matthew E. Kreitzer.

Ottogary, Willie. "Family Record Book of Willie Ottogary." Original in possession of Clyde S. Ottogary.

Parry, Mae Timbimboo. Family history records. Information includes extensive records relating to Washakie families.

Washakie Cemetery data collected by Matthew E. Kreitzer from grave markers at Washakie, Utah, 20 July 1997.

NEWSPAPERS

Bear River Valley Leader. Tremonton, Box Elder County, Utah.

Box Elder Journal. Brigham City, Box Elder County, Utah.

Box Elder News. Brigham City, Box Elder County, Utah.
Deseret Evening News, The. Salt Lake City, Utah.
Deseret News, The. Salt Lake City, Utah.
Journal, The. Logan, Cache County, Utah.
New York Times, New York City, New York.
Oneida County Enterprise. Malad, Idaho.
Tremonton Times. Tremonton, Box Elder County, Utah.
Utah Journal, Logan, Cache County, Utah.

Biographical Register and Index

THIS BIOGRAPHICAL REGISTER AND INDEX INCLUDES the individuals mentioned by Ottogary, along with the dates and newspapers within which their names were published. Since many surnames have been recorded in different ways, a method of standardization has been employed to avoid confusion. Traditional names were usually transcribed according to the recorder's interpretation of the sound each syllable made; hence, Shoshone names could be recorded in many different ways. From available evidence, Ottogary's own spellings, and, in some cases, preferred spellings obtained from living descendants, the most consistent and appropriate spelling has been selected. Various other spellings are included in parentheses. These spellings, along with traditional meanings of names, are included at the first instance they occur.

Some success was achieved in finding the meanings of traditional names. This was a difficult task since spelling changes have nearly always taken place. While complete accuracy was the goal, it is not guaranteed.

Biographical information, where known, has been included for each individual; namely, birth, marriage, children, and death information. Where parents are noted, father appears first, mother second. Gender is noted only where there may be confusion. Other significant information appears for those individuals who had a lasting influence on Ottogary's life or the Washakie Colony. Since Ottogary's letters focus on the Shoshone of Washakie, Utah, and surrounding areas, only those whites who played key roles in the Washakie saga are featured with biographical data. References for each entry, including names of informants who supplied traditional meanings of names, are abbreviated in brackets. Full citations are included in the bibliography.

Square brackets enclose references. In the interest of space, I have used two-letter abbreviations for states. For example, Utah is abbreviated as UT.

GUIDE TO ABBREVIATIONS OF FREQUENTLY USED SOURCES

AICR. American Indian Census Rolls, 1885–1940. National Archives microcopy 595, RG 75, LDS Family History Library (hereafter LDS FHL), film 576856. Information regarding specific Shoshonean individuals was obtained from the following: (a) "Census of the Shoshone Indians of Goshute Agency (Washakie, UT), Utah on June 25–27, 1917, taken by Geo. M. Ward, Bishop." (b) "Census of the Shoshonie Indians of Goshute Agency, Utah on June 30, 1920. Living at Washakie, Utah. Taken by N. Conner, Supt. & S.D.A." (c) "Census of the Goshute Indians of Ibapah, Utah, Agency, on June 30, 1919, taken by N. Conner, Supt. & Sp'l .D.A." (d) "Census of the Goshute Indians of Goshute Agency, Utah, on June 30, 1920, taken by N. Conner, Supt. & S.D.A." (e)

"Census of the Goshute Indians of Goshute Agency, Utah, on June 30, 1921. Living at Skull Valley, Iosepa, Utah. Taken by Nick Conner, Superintendent."

BAPT. Logan Temple Records, "Baptisms for the Dead, 1912." Indexed. LDS FHL, film 0177869.

BEJ. *Box Elder Journal*. Brigham City, Box Elder County, Utah.

BEN. *Box Elder News*. Brigham City, Box Elder County, Utah.

BIOGUIDE. Biographical Directory of the United States: 1774 to Present (http://bioguide.congress.gov/), Accessed 1 December 1998.

CCFEX13. Central Classified Files. Bureau of Indian Affairs, Record Group 75, National Archives, file 113732-15—Scattered Bands in Utah-150, exhibit 13, "Census of Indians at Washakie, Utah."

CCF. Same as above, except different file numbers follow to the correct corresponding file. For example: CCF 31378-28-Shoshoni-350, refers to file no. 31378, year 1928, group: Shoshoni; classification no. 350 deals with estates-heirship cases. This particular file deals with Dick Arratch, deceased.

CR 375 8. LDS "Record of Members Collection 1836–1970." LDS Church Archives, call no. CR 375 8.

FGR. Family Group Records at LDS FHL, film 1553338.

IGI. LDS International Genealogical Index (TM), 1993 Edition, Version 3.02. CD-ROM copies available in most branches of the LDS Family History Library system.

INF_____. Informant name. For example; INF Parry, Mae Timbimboo.

JRNLH. Jenson, Andrew. Journal History of the Church of Jesus Christ of Latter-day Saints, 1820–1972.

KAPPLER. Kappler, Charles J. *Indian Affairs: Laws and Treaties, vol 2, Treaties*. Washington: Government Printing Office, 1904.

LJ. *Journal, The*. Logan, Cache County, Utah.

MALADSTKHST. "Malad Idaho Stake History, 1888–1977," n.p. 1988. USU Special Collections.

MTPFHR. Mae Timbimboo Parry, family history records. Information includes extensive records relating to Washakie families.

NOSHOS. Brigham D. Madsen. *The Northern Shoshoni*. Caldwell, Idaho: Caxton Printers, Ltd., 1980.

OFRB. Ottogary, Willie. "Family Record Book of Willie Ottogary." Original in possession of Clyde S. Ottogary.

OCE. *Oneida County Enterprise*. Malad, Idaho.

OL. Ottogary Letters. Copies of letters collected from microform sources held in USU Special Collections. Photocopies in possession of Matthew E. Kreitzer.

ROAD. Crum, Steven J. *The Road On Which We Came=Po'i Pentun Tammen Kimmappeh: A History of the Western Shoshone*. Salt Lake City: University of Utah Press, 1994.

SAG. Christensen, Scott R. "Sagwitch: Shoshoni Chieftain, Mormon Elder, 1822–1884." Master's thesis, Utah State University, 1995.

SAW. "Lest We Forget: History of Samuel Alonzo Whitney." Unpublished paper, n.d. USU Special Collections.

SENATEUS. Quatannens, Jo Anne McCormick, compiler. *Senators of the United States: A Historical Bibliography: A Compilation of Works by and about Members of the United States Senate 1789–1995*. Washington: Government Printing Office, 1995.

SLNGS. LDS Temple Sealing Records.

LV. "Living Sealings." Book A. 21 May 1884 to 21 November 1900. Logan Temple Records.

CTP. "Sealings of Children to Parents." Book D. 5 January 1912. Logan Temple Records.

TT. *Tremont Times*. Tremonton, Box Elder County, Utah.

USFC____. United States Federal Census manuscript [date]. Dates include 1880, 1900, 1910, and 1920. Microfilm copies of population census manuscripts are available at LDS FHL. Unless otherwise noted in text or Biographical Register, the manuscripts used deal with Utah, Box Elder County, West Portage or Portage Precinct, Washakie (City, town, or village).

VRDC. Vital Records, Death Certificates. State Board of Health. Box Elder County. Death Certificate for Peter Otahgary: filed 6 February 1910. For William Ottogary: filed 19 March 1929.

VRML. Vital Records, Marriage Licences for Box Elder County, 1887–1966. Index to Marriage Licences and Certificates, LDS FHL film 0480310. Hard copy available at Box Elder County Recorder's Office.

WARRUM. Warrum, Noble, editor, *Utah Since Statehood: Historical and Biographical*. Chicago and Salt Lake: The S. J. Clark Publishing Company, 1919.

WASHCEM. Data collected by Matthew E. Kreitzer from grave markers at Washakie Cemetery, 20 July 1997.

WCR E-1931. "Washakie Church Records, Records of Members Early to 1931. Records of Members in Washakie Ward, Malad Stake of Zion." LDS FHL (Logan), film 027,406.

WWROM. "Washakie Ward, Malad Stake, Record of Members (Record of Indians) Before 1900." A record of temple ordinances performed in the Logan Temple for Indians led by Washakie. Includes a 1938 census of the Washakie Ward, Malad Stake, Idaho. LDS FHL, film 0599816, item 2.

BIOGRAPHICAL ENTRIES

Adams, Ernie. Boxer from Ely, NV, who wanted to train with Chester and Custer Ottogary. [OL]. *1926:* 12-11 LJ, 12-21 LJ.

Adams, Mr. Sheepman from Kaysville, UT, who employed Washakie Indians during shearing season. [OL]. *1926:* 05-29 LJ; *1924:* 05-03 LJ.

Adams, W. (Will?) A. Beet farmer from East Garland, UT, who made sugar beet contracts with at least one Washkie resident, Jim Wagon. [OL]. *1907:* 11-21 TT; *1923:* 04-14 LJ, 06-16 LJ.

Adney, C. G. Agricultural Round Up speaker from Box Elder County, UT. [OL]. *1914:* 02-10 LJ.

Alex. See Elk or Alex.

Allen, J. C. Editor of *The Journal* and boxing promoter. [OL]. *1926:* 03-27 LJ, 05-29 LJ, 12-04 LJ.

Allen, Miss. *1913:* 01-30 BEN.

Ammon, Governor. Agricultural Round Up speaker, governor of Colorado. [OL]. *1914:* 02-03 LJ.

Amwillie, Mr. *1928:* 07-28 LJ.

Anderson, Casper. Farmer from Elwood, UT, who owned and hired out a steam thresher. [OL]. *1922:* 09-05 BEN; *1924:* 08-23 LJ.

Andrews, Jack. Boxer. *1927:* 01-29 LJ, 07-09 LJ.

Arimo. From Fort Hall area. "Edmo" is the English version of "Arimo" [INF Menta, Alene]. *1924:* 07-26 LJ.

Arimo, Eugene. From Fort Hall Reservation. [OL]. *1924:* 07-26 LJ.

Arimo, Jimia [Jim]. *1926:* 10-30 LJ.

Arritch (or Arratch), Dick. Born ca. 1840, WY. Married to Sigoratch (or Sig-go-tooch, b. 1842 or 1848, ID). Both married four times. No children listed. Arritch was a farmer. The following information regarding the name, Arritch, is provided by Richley Crapo, USU, Logan, UT: "Arritch, Arrach, originally ata-cci (Uncle: ata which would sound like ara to an English speaker, is a reciprocal kinship term meaning both 'mother's broth-er' and 'a man's sister's child'). The 'uncle' in question was likely the first man who is listed in records as bearing this 'family name,' and after him it was simply passed on as a family name." [CCF 113732-15-SB-150; INF Crapo, Richley; USFC 1910; see also heir-ship case file CCF-31378-28-Shoshoni-350 for details about family history]. *1907:* 03-28 TT; *1911:* 12-21 BEN; *1921:* 01-22 LJ; *1922:* 02-04 LJ, 05-20 LJ; *1923:* 03-17 LJ; *1924:* 05-24 LJ; *1925:* 04-18 LJ, 06-29 LJ, 10-23 BEJ, 11-21 LJ; *1926:* 05-29 LJ, 08-07 LJ, 08-21 LJ, 10-23 LJ, 10-30 LJ.

Arritch, Sig-go-tooch. This wife of Dick Arritch died of smallpox in May 1920. [OL]. *1920:* 05-29 LJ.

Arrtanip (Arranip), Mrs. Rose. This is probably Palm-bouk Arra-nip, who was born in 1825 in Wind River, WY, and sealed Feb. 17, 1886 to Yo-go-boo from Humbolt Wells, NV. [SLNGS LV]. *1919:* 07-26 LJ.

Atwin, Chief James. Ute Ottogary met in the Uintah Basin in October, 1919. [OL]. *1919:* 11-10 LJ.

Bachlor, L. *1914:* 01-31 LJ.

Ball, E. D. *1914:* 02-10 LJ.

Ball, Mr. *1914:* 02-10 LJ.

Baniboo. See Paniboo, Joseph.

Bannock, Frank. See Frank, Bannock.

Barbar, Mr. Battling, "Battling Barbar." Boxer. [OL]. *1926:* 04-17 LJ.

Barlow (Barralow in text), J. H. *1914:* 01-31 LJ.

Barry, Dave. From Wind River Reservation. [OL]. *1922:* 06-03 LJ.

Bates, C. H. Accompanied Ottogary on a tour of Mount Vernon, VA, in 1921. [OL]. *1921:* 03-25 BEN.

Bell, A. D. This may be E. D. Ball. *1914:* 02-14 LJ.

Benson, Bessie. From Deep Creek, UT. [OL]. *1913:* 04-24 BEN.

Big Elk. From Fort Hall Reservation. [OL]. *1925:* 08-10 LJ, 08-22 LJ.

Billy, Mr. From Fort Hall Reservation. It is unclear if this is a surname or a given name. [OL]. *1924:* 07-26 LJ.

Bird, Dock (Doc). Shoshone World War I veteran from NV. [OL]. *1924:* 01-19 LJ, 03-08 LJ, 03-15 LJ, 04-10 OCE.

Bird, Peter. From NV. [OL]. *1924:* 11-29 LJ; *1928:* 09-01 LJ, 09-08 LJ.

Bishop, Fish. From Ibapah, UT. [OL]. *1929:* 02-16 LJ, 02-23 LJ.

Black, Dr. Physician at Tremonton Hospital. [OL]. *1923:* 05-12 LJ.

Black Hawk, Chief. Died at his home near Gibson Station. [OL]. *1926:* 10-30 LJ.

Boyatt, Max. Boxer. *1926:* 10-30 LJ.

Boyle, Louis. *1914:* 01-29-B LJ.

Brain, Emma (Emy A. or Pan-Do-Wee). Emma was known as Se-ba-pa-chee at Washakie, the traditional meaning of which was "rabbit brush." Born ca. 1840, she came to Washakie, UT, from WY about 1886 and married Frank Brain. Their only child recorded was Mose Neaman. [IGI; INF Parry, Mae Timbimboo; OL; USFC 1910; WWROM]. *1923:* 12-24 LJ; *1926:* 11-27 LJ, 12-04 LJ.

Brain, Frank (Redman, or Onda-Bow-low-se). Preceded his wife Emma (Emy A. or Pan-Do-Wee) in death. "Onda-Bow-low-se might come from *onta-ppoto-cci*, 'yellow-stick,' meaning 'little (digging or walking) stick,' probably 'little walking stick,' since Frank was male." [INF Crapo, Richley; OL]. *1926:* 12-04 LJ.

Bran (or Prann), George. Owned a farm in the Sage Creek area, about twelve miles north of Fort Washakie, WY. [OL]. *1927:* 05-28 LJ, 06-18 LJ.

Broncho, Jim. From Fort Hall Reservation. Owned a large cattle ranch in West Pocatello. Died March 1925. [INF Menta, Alene; OL]. *1925:* 03-17 LJ.

Broncho, Sear. See Poncho, Sear.

Bronies (possibly also Browning), Jacob. From Bannock Creek, ID. [OL]. *1906:* 12-06 TT.

Broom, Charlie (Charles). A farmer of beets and grain, Broom was a cousin to Willie Ottogary, probably because his mother, Kan-An-Zuc (Kanazo or Karajo, also known as Ba-Ti-See, b. ca. 1850), married Peter Ottogary after leaving Charlie's father, James (Jim) Broom (b. ca. 1850). Charlie was born in 1871, Box Elder County, and died 18 April 1920. He married Neatze (or Neadge) Moemberg (b. 1876 to Joseph Moemberg and Sarah Pocatello) and their children were Amy (Feb. 19, 1890– July 15, 1966) and Emily (Feb. 12, 1893–Apr. 8, 1895). After this marriage ended he married Annie Hootchew (b. ca. 1872). The 1910 census lists the children in their household as Henry Hootchew (stepson, b. ca. 1892), Amy Hootchew (stepdaughter, b. ca. 1894), Ivy Hootchew (stepdaughter, b. ca. 1898), and Eva Widgagee (niece, b. ca. 1908). Broom and Annie were later divorced. [CCF 113732-15-SB-150; FGR; IGI; OL; MTPFHR; USFC 1910]. *1907:* 11-21 TT; *1908:* 02-06 TT, 02-06 TT; *1909:* 06-15 LJ, 07-27 LJ; *1911:* 04-25 LJ, 10-05 BEN, 10-12 BEN; *1912:* 03-14 LJ, 04-16 LJ; *1913:* 01-02 LJ, 01-09 LJ, 04-24 BEN; *1916:* 05-23 LJ, 10-10 LJ; *1919:* 05-15 LJ; *1920:* 05-29 LJ.

Brown, James S., Jr. (known as Chip Brown). A farm laborer who was unemployed for twenty-five weeks in 1909. Born ca. 1889 to James Brown (b. 1850, Elko, NV) and Pap-a-riss (b. 1863, near Elko, NV). Married Saddie Timoke (Nov. 24, 1904, Brigham City, UT) and Alice Smith (b. Mar. 1892, sister to Nancy Smith, wife of Willie Ottogary). [CCF 113732-15-SB-150; INF Ottogary, Clyde; SLNGS LV; USFC 1900; VRML]. *1916:* 05-23 LJ, 06-24 LJ, 08-15 BEN, 08-22 LJ.

Brown, James [Sr.]. Father of James S. Brown Jr., this farmer of small grain was born in 1850 (Elko, NV) and married to (LDS Sealing) Pap-a-riss (b. 1863, near Elko, NV) on Mar. 4, 1885. Only child known is James S. Brown Jr. [SLNGS LV; FGR; USFC 1910]. *1906:* 08-23 TT, 10-10 TT; *1907:* 04-25 TT, 05-09 TT; *1910:* 02-15 LJ, 03-08 LJ; *1911:* 03-07 LJ, 05-11 BEN; *1912:* 09-28 LJ; *1913:* 01-02 LJ; *1914:* 01-29-A LJ; *1915:* 01-09 LJ, 01-18 BEN; *1924:* 07-05 LJ.

Brown, John. From Wind River Reservation, WY. [OL]. *1923:* 09-29 LJ, 10-13 LJ, 12-08 LJ.

Brown, Mrs. Louis. Daughter of Mrs. John Pabawena. [OL]. *1928:* 05-19 LJ.

Brown, Zip. From Idaho. [OL]. *1928:* 10-20 LJ.

Brownie (or Browning), Jacob. From Ross Fork, ID. [OL]. *1914:* 01-01 LJ; *1928:* 09-22 LJ.

Buchanan, Dr. Mrs. Physician from Deweyville, UT. Her name was spelled in various ways by Ottogary, such as Buecannon, Beconnan, Peucannon, and Prue-Cannon. [OL]. *1922:* 05-12 BEN; *1923:* 04-07 LJ, 10-20 LJ; *1924:* 02-21 OCE, 05-24 LJ; *1926:* 01-23 LJ; *1928:* 02-25 LJ.

Burton, Mr. *1913:* 07-03 BEN.

Caine, John T., III. *1914:* 02-07 LJ, 02-10 LJ, 02-10 LJ, 02-14 LJ.

Call, B. C. [OL]. Attorney. *1925:* 02-07 LJ.

Cannon, C. Y. *1914:* 02-14 LJ.

Carlyle, C. W. *1914:* 02-10 LJ, 02-10 LJ, 02-14 LJ.

Carsen, Mr. *1923:* 09-22 LJ.

Cerventes (or Cervantes), Noble. Boxer. *1927:* 04-09 LJ.

Charlie, Susie. *1925:* 03-10 LJ.

Charley. This may be Buckskin Charley, chief of the Southern Utes, who served ca. 1890–1930. Ottogary met him in the Uinta Basin in October, 1919. [See Joseph G. Jorgensen, *The Sun Dance Religion: Power for the Powerless* (Chicago: University of Chicago Press, 1972), 24; OL]. *1919:* 11-10 LJ.

Cheal, Charlie. *1927:* 12-03 LJ.

Cheyenne Indians Chief. *1925:* 07-18 LJ.

Chez, Mr. Attorney. Probably Joseph Chez, attorney general for the state of Utah who later worked on Shoshone legal concerns with the Ernest L. Wilkinson law firm. *1928:* 03-03 LJ.

Chicken, Jimmy (Jim). Died 1 Feb. 1922. [WCR E-1931]. *1921:* 10-24 LJ; *1922:* 02-04 LJ, 02-18 LJ.

Chickey, Mr. From Fort Hall, ID. [OL]. *1925:* 08-22 LJ.

Christensen, George. Insurance salesman from Tremonton, UT. [OL]. *1924:* 07-05 LJ.

Clawson, Mr. *1927:* 03-26 LJ.

Cole, Mr. Manager of Garland branch of Riter Bros. Drug Company. [OL]. *1917:* 03-23 LJ.

Colton, D. C. (Don Byron). Utah attorney who was elected as a Republican to Congress (serving from Mar. 4, 1921 to Mar. 3, 1933). Born Sept. 15, 1876, he died Aug 1, 1952. [BIOGUIDE; "Throngs Attend Two-Day Peach Carnival In Brigham," *Box Elder News,* Sept. 13, 1927]. *1928:* 02-04 LJ.

Comanke (Comlank, Comalang, Comnake, or Comankee), George. Traditional meaning of Comanke: "Rabbit ears." Born 1856. Married Susie Widgiguitch (b. 1856). English name: George McGee. [AICR 1917; INF Parry, Mae Timbimboo]. *1911:* 07-13 LJ, 07-13 BEN; *1913:* 07-03 LJ; *1916:* 09-12 LJ; *1918:* 06-01 LJ.

Compton, Jane S. From Brigham City's Compton's Photo Studio. [OL]. *1925:* 09-18 BEJ, 09-19 LJ.

Compton, Jennie (Jeanie). Daughter of Jane Compton. [OL]. *1925:* 09-18 BEJ, 09-19 LJ.

Comrath, Mr. From Fort Hall Reservation, ID. [OL]. *1925:* 11-28 LJ.

Coolidge, Calvin. U.S. president. *1925:* 02-21 LJ.

Corsium (Coralison, Colisim, Collasin, or Colisin), Lewis. Born ca. 1865, WY. Married Mary C. (b. ca. 1875, WY, the daughter of Maggie Pupugawat (or Maggie Igocoite)). Their children were Mason (b. ca. 1898), Vida (b. ca. 1909), and Mabel (b. 1915). [AICR 1917 and 1920; CCF 113732-15-SB-150; USFC 1910]. *1907:* 03-28 TT, 09-19 TT; *1912:* 09-12 BEN; *1913:* 01-02 LJ; *1920:* 11-13 LJ, 12-24 LJ; *1921:* 01-10 LJ, 02-08 LJ.

Creel, Lorenzo D. Special agent of Indian affairs for the scattered bands of Indians in Utah. [CCF 103366-14-SB-047]. *1914:* 06-09 LJ, 07-14 LJ; *1915:* 01-18 BEN.

Crockett, J. A. *1922:* 05-06 LJ.

Crookston, N. C. From Logan, UT. [OL]. *1928:* 04-21 LJ

Curel, Wm. (Bill). Express businessman from Logan, UT. [OL]. *1922:* 07-18 BEN; *1923:* 05-05 LJ; *1925:* 04-11 LJ.

Dan, Dr. John. *1926:* 01-02 LJ.

Dan, Willie. From Idaho Reservation. [OL]. *1927:* 10-01 LJ.

Daniel, Daniel. *1915:* 12-23 LJ.

Danyhay (Dandy, Timhay, Tinhay, Tonyhay, Tan-by-hay, Tanyha, Tan-hay, Tan-hee, Ton-hee, or Tandhay). From Ta-hee Station, Fort Hall Reservation, ID. Mrs. Danyhay was the niece of Emma Brain. [OL]. *1922:* 12-02 LJ, 12-15 BEN, 12-26 BEN, 12-30-B LJ; *1923:* 01-13 LJ, 02-17 LJ, 03-10 LJ, 04-07 LJ, 04-28 LJ, 05-05 LJ, 06-02 LJ; *1926:* 11-27 LJ, 12-04 LJ; *1928:* 02-25 LJ, 03-03 LJ.

Davis, Kid. Boxer. *1926:* 11-27 LJ; *1927:* 01-08 LJ, 01-29 LJ.

Davis, Owen. *1907:* 04-25 TT.

Dern, George H. Utah governor (1925-1932). Appointed by President Franklin D. Roosevelt as secretary of war. [UTAH]. *1928:* 02-04 LJ.

Diamond, Ray. Also known as Ray Diamond Womenup, or simply Diamond. Mail carrier at Washakie from at least 1922 until 1929. Born ca. 1830, Utah, to Be Sue and Pay Way Keep, Diamond was Chief Sagwitch's youngest sister's son. His wife was known as Mrs. Womenup. The couple had one child, a daughter, whose name "sounds like Chinaman"—she married a man named Ballard from the Fort Hall area. Ray Diamond Womenup's name means, "left him behind, bear was chasing him." Diamond learned to read, and he read the Bible daily, though he never joined any church. He died in 1940. [CCF 113732-15-SB-150; IGI; INF Parry, Mae Timbimboo; MTPFHR; OL; USFC 1920; WASHCEM]. *1913:* 01-16 LJ, 01-16 BEN, 01-30 BEN; *1922:* 08-08 BEN; *1926:* 01-23 LJ, 09-04 LJ; *1927:* 01-08 LJ, 02-05 LJ; *1928:* 11-03 LJ, 11-10 LJ; *1929:* 02-11 LJ, 03-09 LJ.

Dick, Charlie. Laborer from NV. Census records indicate he was born ca. 1870 and married to Lizzie (b. ca. 1868). His household included Mary Dick, mother, (b. ca. 1838). [USFC 1920, NV, Elko County, Tuscarora Precinct]. *1927:* 01-08 LJ; *1928:* 09-01 LJ.

Dick, John. *1924:* 12-06 LJ; *1925:* 10-16 BEJ, 10-17 LJ; *1926:* 08-14 LJ, 09-04 LJ, 09-18 LJ; *1928:* 09-01 LJ, 11-17 LJ.

Dioves (or Tovier), Jim. *1914:* 01-15 BEN, 01-17 LJ.

Disquime, Mr. *1925:* 07-18 LJ

Dixon, Harry (suffix surname "Tootiaina" first added by Ottogary July 1927). Also listed as Too-toamee by Ottogary (see *1928-11-14* LJ). Western Shoshone leader and close associate of Ottogary during the 1920s. Born May 22, 1872 in Austin, Lander Co., NV; his parents were Pa-Ze-Nar and Maggie. Harry married Nellie Charlie (b. 1865, Austin, Lander Co., NV, daughter of Wild Charley and Mollie Tom) on Feb. 28, 1935. The couple came to Washakie from Nevada. He was Paiute and Shoshone. [FGR; IGI; INF Parry, Mae Timbimboo]. *1922:* 09-30 LJ, 10-03 BEN; *1923:* 07-07 LJ, 09-22 LJ, 10-06 LJ, 10-13 LJ, 10-20 LJ, 11-03 LJ, 12-08 LJ, 12-24 LJ; *1924:* 06-19 OCE; *1925:* 02-02 LJ, 10-16 BEJ, 10-23 BEJ, 10-24 LJ, 11-07 LJ, 11-21 LJ; *1926:* 02-06 LJ, 06-05 LJ, 06-19 LJ, 07-26 LJ; *1927:* 07-02 LJ, 07-09 LJ, 07-23 LJ, 08-06 LJ, 08-20 LJ, 09-03 LJ, 09-17 LJ, 09-17 LJ, 10-22 LJ, 10-29 LJ, 11-05 LJ, 11-12 LJ, 11-19 LJ, 11-26 LJ; *1928:* 01-28 LJ, 03-17 LJ, 03-24 LJ, 04-04 LJ, 04-07 LJ, 05-26 LJ, 06-30 LJ, 07-07 LJ, 07-28 LJ, 07-28 LJ, 08-13 LJ, 08-18 LJ, 09-01 LJ, 09-08 LJ, 09-15 LJ, 09-22 LJ, 10-13 LJ, 10-20 LJ, 10-27 LJ, 11-03 LJ, 11-10 LJ, 11-17 LJ, 12-06 LJ, 12-26 LJ, 12-29 LJ; *1929:* 01-12 LJ, 01-19 LJ, 02-11 LJ, 02-23 LJ, 03-09 LJ, 03-20 LJ.

Doan, Mr. From Pocatello, ID. [OL]. *1926:* 10-16 LJ.

Donner, Wm. Superintendent from Fort Hall Reservation. Responsible for Washakie, Utah, where he made monthly visits. [NOSHOS, 101; OL]. *1924:* 08-23 LJ; *1925:* 06-06 LJ.

Dorman, J. E. . *1914:* 02-07 LJ, 02-10 LJ.

Doutch (Dortch), J. H. Indian affairs official from Washington, D.C. [OL]. *1916:* 10-21 LJ.

Downing, Hardy K. Boxing promoter. *1926:* 09-18 LJ.

Drinks, Eddy. *1922:* 12-30-B LJ; *1927:* 09-17 LJ.

Eagle, David (Dave). From Skull Valley, UT. Born 1836. Married first to Lizzie (b. 1862) and second to Kate (b. 1872). Children: Dan (b. 1902), Pratt (son, b. 1908), Beatrice (b. 1911, d. Apr. 1, 1921). [AICR 1921, Census of Goshute Indians living at Skull Valley, Iosepa, UT]. *1913:* 04-24 BEN.

Eagle, Frank. From Skull Valley, UT. Born ca. 1893. His wife, May (b. ca. 1892) had a daughter b. ca. 1914. [AICR 1921, Census of Goshute Indians living at Skull Valley, Iosepa, UT; CCF 103366-14-SB-047]. *1913:* 03-06 BEN.

Eagle, Pratt. From Skull Valley, UT. Born 1908. [AICR 1921, Census of Goshute Indians living at Skull Valley, Iosepa, UT]. *1928:* 12-29 LJ, *1929:* 01-12 LJ, 01-19 LJ, 02-04 LJ, 02-11 LJ.

Earl, Jesse. An LDS Democrat, Earl was president of Earl and England Publishing Company, publisher of *The Journal* at Logan. Born Oct. 30, 1870, Logan, UT, to Jacob Earl (of St. John, New Brunswick) and Fannie Cummings, who died in 1911. Earl married Mae Needham of Salt Lake City, Apr. 18, 1894. [WARRUM 4: 165]. *1912:* 03-21-B LJ, 04-02 LJ, 05-23 LJ.

Edward, Miss. From Fort Hall Reservation. Niece of Susie Highyou. [OL]. *1927:* 01-08 LJ.

Edward, Tuffe. Boxer. [OL]. *1926:* 10-23 LJ.

Egpe, Mr. Relative of Jacob Peyope. [OL]. *1927:* 08-06 LJ.

Eldredge, B. . *1914:* 02-07 LJ.

Elk, George. A farm laborer whose family lived in an aboriginal dwelling. Elk was born 1861 (d. Nov. 18, 1932), NV, to Pah-Lea-Ah-Au-Gitse and Ank-A-Poey (traditional meaning of Ank-A-Poey: "red eye.") . He married Maggie (b. 1876, Hamilton, White River Co., NV), daughter of Na-ne-ur-der and Herb-chip-A. Their children were Creel (son, b. Dec. 19, 1914), Irene (b. Sept. 22, 1916), Lucille (b. ca. 1918). According to the 1910 census, neither George nor his wife could speak English. [FGR; INF Parry, Mae Timbimboo; USFC 1910]. *1922:* 08-12 LJ, 09-01 BEN; *1923:* 06-16 LJ; *1924:* 06-12 OCE; *1926:* 03-27 LJ, 08-28 LJ, 09-18 LJ; *1928:* 02-04 LJ, 10-20 LJ.

Elk, Mrs. George (Maggie). *1913:* 03-06 BEN; *1919:* 03-13 LJ.

Elk or Alex, Tom. Tom was born Feb. 13, 1872, Deeth, Elko Co., NV, to Elk or Alex (b. ca. 1836, Deeth, Elko, NV, d. Dec. 18, 1932) and Yumba-Gorbuyap Jane (who became Jane Pabawena when she married Thomas Pabawena, b. 1836, Deeth, Elko Co., NV, d. Nov. 16 or 18, 1926 at Washakie). Married Lucy Zundel (b. 1885, d. July 31, 1966, daughter of Moroni and Cohn Shoshonitch Zundel). Tom and Lucy had three children living with them that were Lucy's from a previous marriage to George Peyope. These three children were Esther P. (b. ca. 1903), Steven P. (b. ca. 1906), and Wilford P. (b. ca. 1910). Tom and Lucy's children were Marjorie (b. 1915), Joseph Young (b. 1918), Geneva (b. 1925), and Melvin A. (b. 1931). Marjorie Elk told Mae T. Parry when they were in high school that the family changed their name from Elk to Alex. [AICR, 1920; CCF 113732-15-SB-150; FGR; INF Parry, Mae Timbimboo; WWROM]. *1919:* 03-13 LJ; *1922:* 03-18-B LJ, 07-11 BEN, 07-25 BEN, 08-08 BEN, 08-19 LJ, 12-15 BEN; *1924:* 02-09 LJ, 06-05 OCE, 06-19 OCE, 08-23 LJ, 11-08 LJ]; *1925:* 02-02 LJ, 02-07 LJ, 02-17 LJ, 03-17 LJ, 04-14 BEJ, 05-16 LJ, 05-22 BEJ, 05-23 LJ, 06-02 LJ, 06-13 LJ, 06-29 LJ, 09-19 LJ, 09-26 LJ, 10-16 BEJ, 10-24 LJ, 12-28 LJ]; *1926:* 01-16 LJ, 03-06 LJ, 04-17 LJ, 05-08 LJ, 07-26 LJ, 10-16 LJ, 10-23 LJ, 10-30 LJ, 12-11 LJ]; *1927:* 01-08 LJ, 02-19 LJ, 03-19 LJ, 07-30 LJ, 08-06 LJ, 10-01 LJ, 12-03 LJ]; *1928:* 03-12 LJ, 04-04 LJ, 04-28 LJ, 06-02 LJ, 07-28 LJ, 08-13 LJ, 09-15, LJ, 09-22 LJ, 10-20 LJ, 12-20 LJ, 12-26 LJ, 12-29 LJ]; *1929:* 02-16 LJ.

Elk, Mrs. Tom (Lucy). *1926:* 07-26 LJ; *1927:* 03-19 LJ.

England, Johny. *1921:* 02-03 LJ.

England, Charles. Manager of *The Journal,* published at Logan, owned and operated by Earl and England Publishing Company. Son of William England, Charles was born Oct. 6, 1863, in Tooele, UT, and married Phebe Almyra Woolf of Hyde Park, UT, in the Logan Temple on June 10, 1886. [WARRUM 4: 158]. *1912:* 05-23 LJ; *1923:* 03-03 LJ.

Evans, George. From West Portage, UT. [OL]. *1926:* 08-28 LJ, 09-04 LJ.

Findall, K. H. *1914:* 01-29-B LJ.

himself." Charlie became a key figure in Logan commerce when he organized Harris Music Company in 1889. He was also president and manager of the Logan Garage and Supply Company, which sold and serviced automobiles (Hudson Super Six, Essex, and Nash). He was also president of the American Steam Laundry Company. Well liked, Harris was active in social circles and such civic organizations as the Commercial Club and Rotary Club. Music played a key role in his life. "He [was] . . . an accomplished violinist, having studied in New York, Chicago, and Berlin under celebrated teachers. . . ." Charles M. Harris was born Nov. 29, 1866 (Logan, UT) to Alma Harris (b. Ohio) and Sarah Earl (b. Canada). Both parents were musically inclined and gifted. His father played the violin and his mother ". . . at the age of eighty-four can sing and dance like a young girl." Charles married Marguerite Shirley Barrett, a talented pianist from Lakota, North Dakota. [WARRUM 4: 360-63; OL]. *1926: 02-06 LJ*.

Harris, Frank. Probably a sibling of Charles Harris, vice president of the Harris Music Company. [WARRUM 4: 360-63]. *1922: 04-01 LJ*.

Harris, Mr. A commissioner of Indian affairs at Washington, D.C. [OL]. *1915: 01-09 LJ*.

Harris, R. *1907: 09-12 TT*

Harris, Robert. Bought rabbit pelts from Washakie hunters. [OL]. *1928: 12-26 LJ; 1929: 02-04 LJ*.

Harris, W. T. Along with Bert Hall, Harris installed gas lighting at Washakie church meeting house. From West Portage, UT. [OL]. *1911: 03-07 LJ*.

Harry, Johnny, George. See George, Harry Johnny. *1928: 11-03 LJ*.

Hass, R. P. Indian agent working at Fort Washakie, WY. [OL]. *1925: 07-17 BEJ, 07-18 LJ*.

Hawkins, E. B. *1914: 02-03 LJ*.

Haws, J. K. *1924: 09-20 LJ*.

Haws, Peter. *1906: 08-23 TT*.

Heize, Paul. *1924: 06-19 OCE*.

Hess, [Hess boys]. *1922: 06-06 BEN*.

Hess, Charlie. *1922: 11-04-B LJ*.

Hess, John D. *1928: 05-19 LJ*.

Highyou (Highyo, Hiowidguitch, Hiwagagea, Waghee, or Widgiguitch), Susie. Came to Washakie from NV. Her father came to Washakie also. Born ca. 1855, Susie was listed as a sixty-year-old widow in 1915; however, in 1917 she was listed as spouse to George Comalang (b. 1856). It is likely she had a previous marriage before she wed Comalang sometime between 1915 and 1917. [CCF 113732-15-SB-150; AICR 1917, Washakie; INF Parry, Mae Timbimboo]. *1919: 05-15 LJ; 1922: 11-14 BEN; 1924: 04-14 LJ; 1925: 03-28 LJ; 1926: 01-16 LJ; 1927: 01-08 LJ; 1928: 11-03 LJ, 11-17 LJ*.

Hill, George R. *1914: 01-29-B LJ*.

Hill, George W. LDS missionary to the Northwestern Shoshone. He was called in April 1873 and served for many years. He achieved considerable success during 1875. Helped organize the Indian farm near Corinne. Hill probably baptized Ottogary's parents Aug. 1, 1875 on the "Horseshoe Bend" of the Bear River. [NOSHOS, 239; "Autobiography and Indian Missionary Journals of George W. Hill. . . ," copy in USU Special Collections]. *1912: 05-23 LJ*.

Hogson, Miss. Teacher at Washakie Day School. *1926: 02-13 LJ*.

Holmes, Will R. Editor and manager of the *Box Elder Journal*. [OL]. *1925: 03-27 BEJ, 03-28 LJ*.

Hooper, Jack. From Nevada. [OL]. *1926: 08-28 LJ*

Hootchew, Annie C. Traditional meaning of Hootchew: "bird." Born Sept. 3, 1871, Elko, NV, to Cah Mase Vah (b. 1849, NV, d. 1895, NV) and Dusky (b. 1851, NV, d. ca. 1885 or 1891, NV). Annie married Don Carlos Hootchew who died at about age twenty-eight. Their children were Elmer (d. in infancy), Henry (b. 1891, d. 1970), Amy (b. 1893,

d. May 1999), Lewis (b. ca. 1893), Ivey (Ivy, b. 1895). She then married Charlie Broom but they had no children. Annie's third husband was Ono Johnny, and they had six children: Ruby (b. Oct. 25, 1900, d. Dec. 19, 1900), Ruth (b. Aug. 9, 1901, d. Aug. 10, 1901), Jimmy (b. Feb. 1, 1902, d. Feb. 18, 1902), Johnnie (b. Jan. 5, 1903, d. Jan. 10, 1903), Mae (b. Jan. 5, 1904, d. Jan. 17, 1904), and Lara (b. Mar. 22, 1905, d. Apr. 2, 1905). These children have the Hootchew surname at the Washakie cemetery, but they were Annie and Ono Johnny's children. Annie died June 28, 1925, Pocatello, ID. [CCF 113732-15-SB-150; INF Parry, Mae Timbimboo; MTPFHR; WASHCEM]. *1920:* 01-02 LJ; *1922:* 11-14 BEN.

Hootchew, Henry. Born 1891 to Don Carlos Hootchew and Annie Cah Mase Vah Hootchew. Married Minnie Woonsook (b. ca. 1896, daughter of Joseph and Mary Woonsook). Child: Andy Alma Hootchew (b. ca. 1914). Henry died in 1970. [CCF 113732-15-SB-150; MTPFHR; WASHCEM]. *1916:* 08-22 LJ; *1928:* 09-22 LJ.

Hootchew, Ivy. See Annie Hootchew. Ivy Hootchew and Moroni Ward Jr. receive third place in an essay contest on tuberculosis. The prize was an inscribed pin that said: "Health—Indian Schools—1912," [*Box Elder News*, Aug. 1, 1912]. *1927:* 07-23 LJ.

Hootchew, Lorenzo (Ren). Born ca. 1880, ID, to William Hootchew (from NV) and Julia (from UT). Married Co-Mah, Feb. 20, 1902 at Brigham City. Federal records list Goody (or Goodeg, b. ca. 1885), daughter of Pugahjunip Jack (Grouse Creek Jack), as his spouse. It appears that Co-Mah and Goody (or Goodeg) were the same person. The 1910 census says the couple had been married for seven years (married ca. 1903). Lorenzo was listed as a sugar beet farmer living with his wife in an aboriginal dwelling. No children were listed. [CCF 113732-15-SB-150; USFC 1910; VRML]. *1916:* 05-23 LJ.

Hootchew, William. Born ca. 1850, NV. Married Julia (b. 1850, Soda Springs, ID). Sealed Feb. 10, 1886 in Logan Temple. Julia was called I-ya-gwa-za (toad). The 1910 census says they had been married for forty years and had thirteen children, only two of whom were still living, Lorenzo (b. ca. 1880), and Phoebe (b. 1881). William's occupation was listed as farmer of beets and grain. [CCF 113732-15-SB-150; INF Parry, Mae Timbimboo; SLNGS LV; USFC 1910]. *1907:* 01-10 TT; *1921:* 10-10 LJ; *1922:* 09-05 BEN, 09-28 LJ; *1923:* 05-26 LJ; *1926:* 08-21 LJ, 08-28 LJ.

Horn, Minnie. From Fort Hall Reservation, ID. [OL]. *1925:* 07-17 BEJ, 07-18 LJ.

Horsely, Mr. *1921:* 03-22 LJ.

Hower, Oliver. Superintendent of St. Michael's Mission, Fort Washakie area, WY. [OL]. *1925:* 08-01 LJ, 08-04 BEJ.

Hows, Dean. Farmer residing near Tremonton, UT. [OL]. *1923:* 03-17 LJ.

Huff, Wayne. Boxer. [OL]. *1927:* 07-30 LJ.

Hurren, J. W. From Hyde Park, UT. [OL]. *1914:* 01-31 LJ.

Hyer, A. L. *1914:* 01-29-B LJ.

Impitch, Catch. See Toyahdook, Catch.

Inarich, Mr. From near Blackfoot, ID. [OL]. *1925:* 05-16 LJ.

Indian, Beans (Mr. Beans Indian). From Elko, NV. His name was Quagigant, meaning "to have a tail." [INF Menta, Alene; OL]. *1928:* 06-30 LJ.

Indian, Ben. From Wind River Reservation, WY. [OL]. *1924:* 02-23 LJ.

Indian, Charley. Probably from Deeth, NV, area. [OL]. *1924:* 05-03 LJ, 06-05 OCE.

Indian Dr. Indian doctor. *1927:* 09-03 LJ.

Indian, Dick. From NV. [OL]. *1922:* 10-03 BEN.

Indian, George. From Wind River Reservation, WY. [OL]. *1923:* 02-17 LJ.

Indian, Maggie (Indian Maggie). *1917:* 11-24 LJ.

Indian, Rachel (could be Rachel Perdash). *1924:* 02-23 LJ, 02-28 OCE.

Indian, Wash. Ute from the Uinta Basin, UT. [OL]. *1919:* 11-10 LJ.

Indians, Willie. *1925:* 08-01 LJ.

Ingshing, Dom. From Fielding, UT. [OL]. *1923:* 12-24 LJ.

Jack, Agnus (Agnes, Agnes Woogagee). Born ca. 1892, she married Jim Jack July 21, 1910 at Brigham City, his second marriage, her first. The couple married according to traditional Shoshone customs before applying for a civil marriage license on July 21, 1910. A note written by George M. Ward to the county clerk was attached to the license, saying "Dear Sir: This couple desire to get a marriage license. Also want you to perform the ceremony." The 1910 census says they had been married for four years. Their children were Delia (Julia, b. ca. 1906), Gilbert (b. May 1909), and Bessie (b. ca. 1913). [CCF 113732-15-SB-150; OL; USFC 1910; VRML]. *1912:* 01-11 BEN.

Jack, Antelope. Probably Jake Antelope from Deep Creek, UT, a widower who was born in 1821. [AICR 1920]. *1913:* 04-24 BEN.

Jack, Buckerro (Buckaroo). From Fort McDermitt Reservation, NV. [OL]. *1928:* 07-28 LJ.

Jack, Grouse Creek (Pugahjunip Jack). Born 1833, Grouse Creek, UT. Met Brigham Young when about fifteen years old. Married at about age twenty-five but his wife died young. He worked with mortar on the Logan Temple, where he married his first wife's sister after its dedication. She died in the 1930s. They had five children, two of whom were still living in 1941. Federal census records note Jack was married three times. He married Ankapompy (or Aukapompy, "red hair," b. 1851, NV) ca. 1880, and they had eight children, four of whom survived, Jim (b. 1886), Sam (b. ca. 1890), Stanquitch (or Panguitch; later known as Wilson Jack; b. ca. 1894). Records also note a daughter, Goody (or Goodeg, or Co-Mah) Jack (b. ca. 1885 or 1893), who married Lorenzo Hootchew Feb. 20, 1902 at Brigham City. Grouse Creek Jack's activities included farm laboring, trapping, and pine nut gathering. In 1910 he and his wife were living in an aboriginal dwelling in Washakie. [AICR 1917; CCF 113732-15-SB-150; INF Parry, Mae Timbimboo; JRNLH; USFC 1910]. *1907:* 11-28 TT; *1909:* 07-27 LJ; *1912:* 04-04 LJ; *1913:* 01-02 LJ, 01-23 BEN, 08-14 LJ; *1915:* 12-23 LJ; *1916:* 01-29 LJ, 08-15 BEN, 08-22 LJ, 10-20 BEN, 11-11 LJ, 12-08 BEN; *1922:* 09-05 BEN, 09-19 BEN; *1923:* 05-19 LJ, 05-26 LJ.

Jack, Happy. From Uinta Reservation, UT. [OL]. *1919:* 11-10 LJ.

Jack, Jim (Jimmy, James). Born ca. 1885, son of Grouse Creek Jack and Ankapompy Jack. For Jim's wife and children see Agnus (or Agnes Woogagee) Jack, his wife. Jim was married twice. With his first wife Iva (Ivy, or Ivai) Pojennie Woonsook, he fathered a daughter, Tena (Teannie, or Tenie, b. June 10, 1902), who was listed as single in the "Census of Indians at Washakie, Utah." Jim's occupation: farm laborer. [AICR 1917; CCF 113732-15-SB-150; USFC 1910; VRML]. *1909:* 05-29 LJ; *1911:* 09-12 LJ; *1916:* 05-23 LJ.

Jack, Johny. This may be Johny Dick. [OL]. *1924:* 09-20 LJ; *1925:* 03-10 LJ, 10-16 BEJ, 10-17 LJ; *1927:* 11-05 LJ.

Jack, Mrs. Johny. See Johny Jack. *1923:* 05-19 LJ.

Jack, Monkey (Monkey Jackson). [OL]. *1911:* 04-25 LJ, 05-11 BEN.

Jack, Sam. Born 1891, son of Grouse Creek Jack and Ankapompy Jack. [AIRCR 1917]. *1909:* 06-15 LJ; *1912:* 09-28 LJ; *1915:* 12-23 LJ; *1916:* 05-23 LJ.

Jack, Sig-g-ye-gant. Died 1915. [OL]. *1915:* 12-23 LJ.

Jack, Stanquitch (or Panguitch, although Stanquitch is the more traditional spelling. It is based on *painkwi,* or "fish." When Ottogary spells Tospanguitch, he uses the "g" instead of "q." These differences are maintained in this volume. Later known as Wilson Jack). Born 1894 (son of Grouse Creek Jack and Ankapompy Jack). Married Mary (b. ca. 1896), and, as Wilson Jack, later (in the 1960s) married Nancy Smith, former wife of Willie Ottogary (they divorced in 1916). [AICR 1917; CCF 113732-15-SB-150; JRNLH; Miller, Wick, R. *Newe Natekwinappeh: Shoshone Stories and Dictionary,* University of Utah Anthropological Papers 94, 1972]. *1916:* 05-23 LJ, 06-24 LJ; *1918:* 01-24 LJ; *1921:*

10-31 LJ]; *1922:* 06-30 BEN, 07-11 BEN, 07-18 BEN, 07-25 BEN, 08-08 BEN, 08-12 LJ, 09-01 BEN, 09-19 BEN; *1924:* 06-05 OCE.

Jackson, George. From Wind River Reservation, WY. [OL]. *1922:* 09-28 LJ, 11-04-A LJ.

Jackson, Jerry. From Butte Mtn., near Elko, NV. [OL]. *1928:* 12-29 LJ.

Jackson, Monkey. From Pocatello, ID. See Jack, Monkey. [OL]. *1913:* 07-03 LJ.

Jensen, Dr. *1922:* 04-29 LJ.

Jensen, Fred. Possibly from Logan, UT. [OL]. *1926:* 08-07 LJ.

Jensen, Mr. Probably from Plymouth, UT. [OL]. *1925:* 03-28 LJ.

Jim, Broncho. See Broncho, Jim.

Jim, Mr. Riey. From NV. [OL]. *1925:* 01-17-B LJ, 02-17 LJ, 02-21 LJ, 06-06 LJ, 06-13 LJ.

Jim, White. From White Rock, NV. [OL]. *1922:* 01-06 LJ.

John, Jim. *1912:* 04-04 LJ.

Johns, Brigg. From West Portage, UT. [OL]. *1927:* 11-26 LJ.

Johnson, Jack. From Elko, NV. [OL]. *1928:* 12-26 LJ.

Johnson, Sotank. From Elko, NV. [OL]. *1929:* 01-12 LJ, 02-11 LJ.

Johny, John (or Johny). *1923:* 06-02 LJ, 06-30 LJ; *1924:* 02-23 LJ, 04-14 LJ, 05-03 LJ.

Joseph, Harry S. Born in Cincinnati, Ohio, on 14 June 1866 to Soloman and Augusta Bamberger Joseph. Harry became a prominent figure in Utah mining and civic affairs. [ALTER]. *1922:* 06-13 BEN.

Joshua, Hightop (Hitope, Hitope Ankegee). Traditional meaning of Hightop, or Hittappah: "flat," "to flatten something," possibly meaning "frybread." Born Nov. 25, 1843, WY, to fa. Gwy-Woot (Qui-What, or Qui-wat, which means "without wife," b. ca. 1820, WY), and Ma-Ca-Jo-What (meaning "middle finger gone," b. ca. 1823, WY). A marriage certificate shows that James Joshua (Joshua or Tyboatz) married Hitope Broom May 12, 1892, suggesting that Hightop was previously married to a man named Broom. The 1910 census notes that James and Hightop Joshua had six children and none were living. On Mar. 5, 1912 Hitope was baptized vicariously for a deceased daughter: Julia Na-Maw-jane (Na-Maw-jane was apparently the name of a previous husband) who was born ca. Apr. 8, 1880, WY, and died Apr. 24, 1891. Hightop was also baptized for Almira Joshua. See James Joshua for other children. Hightop is listed as stepmother. It is obvious that both Hightop and James were married and had issue from prior unions. Also on Mar. 5, 1912, James Joshua was vicariously baptised for four males, each with the last name of Na-Maw-jane (in the "Relation to the Dead" column James is listed as stepfather). These four males were: Ankatooah (b. Sept. 8, 1873, WY, d. July 29, 1895), Mo-ja-yah (b. ca. Mar. 15, 1878, WY, d. Jan. 10, 1893), George (b. Apr. 20, 1881, WY, d. Mar. 25, 1890), Stewart (b. ca. Feb. 20, 1884, UT, d. ca. Aug. 15, 1892). It appears that Hightop Ankegee was married to Na-Maw-jane first, then to Broom, and finally to James Joshua. She died Feb. 4, 1942. [BAPT; CCF 113732-15-SB-150; FGR; INF Crapo, Richley, Parry, Mae Timbimboo; USFC 1910; VRML; WASHCEM]. *1922:* 02-18 LJ, 06-03 LJ; *1925:* 09-26 LJ; *1928:* 07-28 LJ, 08-13 LJ, 10-20 LJ.

Joshua (or Tyboatz), James (or Jim). Born Apr. 10, 1850, Salt Lake City, son of Toa-Wah-Cha (b. ca. 1820, UT, probably stepfather) and Che-Nah (b. ca. 1825, UT, traditional meaning of Che-Nah, or probably Ze Nah: "potato."). According to Mae T. Parry, James Joshua's father was white, though he was raised by an Indian father. The 1910 census lists James as half Indian, half white, and his father's birthplace is ambiguously listed as "unknown." James married Hitope (or Hightop) Broom May 12, 1892. His children with an unknown spouse were Almira (b. ca. 1886, UT, d. July 30, 1894), Danny (b. ca. 1888, UT, d. 1893), unnamed male (b. 1890, UT, d. Sept. 8, 1891). A notation on an LDS family group record reads, "Jim Joshua and wife was first Indian Missionary from Ft. Washakie." James's occupation was listed as grain and beet farmer. He died Oct. 1, 1920.

[BAPT; CCF 113732-15-SB-150; FGR; INF Parry, Mae Timbimboo; OL; USFC 1910; VRML; WASHCEM]. *1906:* 08-23 TT; *1907:* 08-22 TT; *1909:* 06-15 LJ; *1911:* 01-31 LJ; *1912:* 03-14 LJ; *1914:* 01-17 LJ; *1919:* 05-15 LJ; *1920:* 10-20 LJ; *1922:* 06-03 LJ.

Kelley, Jack. Boxer from Salt Lake City. [OL]. *1926:* 03-20 LJ.

Kickapoo Dan. See Chester Ottogary.

King, William Henry. U.S. senator (Democrat) from Utah. Born 1863. Died 1949. Served in the Senate from 1917 to 1941. Proposed Senate Bill no. 710 on behalf of the Shoshone of Utah, Dec. 1927. [OL; SENATEUS]. *1928:* 05-19 LJ; *1929:* 03-09 LJ.

Knudson, Mr. Albert. From Stone, ID. [OL]. *1928:* 12-06 LJ.

Knudson, W. O. *1914:* 01-31 LJ.

Lambert, C. M. *1914:* 02-07 LJ, 02-10 LJ.

Lane, Mr. Probate agent from Washington, D.C. [OL]. *1928:* 04-28 LJ.

Larre, William. Probate chief from Washington, D.C. [OL]. *1928:* 04-28 LJ.

Larsen, Mr. L. *1928:* 10-27 LJ.

Lasalle. See Pocatello, Mr. Mule.

Leach, Jim. Elected chief of Battle Mountain, NV, at a Shoshone council held in 1922. [OL; ROAD, 60]. *1922:* 10-03 BEN; *1923:* 07-07 LJ.

Lewis, Jim. From Burns, Oregon. [OL]. *1928:* 03-17 LJ.

Lindsay, C. W. *1914:* 02-10 LJ.

Linford, Mrs. J. H. *1914:* 02-03 LJ.

Lion, Catch. See Toyahdook, Catch.

Loader, Young. Boxer from Bingham Canyon, UT. [OL]. *1926:* 02-17 LJ.

Lofthouse, Mr. From Paradise, UT. [OL]. *1922:* 04-01 LJ.

Low, Susie. Came to Washakie from Elko, NV. [INF Parry, Mae Timbimboo; OL]. *1926:* 06-05 LJ.

Low, Tip. From Deeth, NV. According to family lore, Tip's daughter Alice and other children heard an owl hooting outside their window one night. The owl was saying, "Children who are sleeping in there are going to be without a papa." When they awoke the next morning, their father had died in his sleep at Washakie. [INF Parry, Mae Timbimboo]. *1916:* 01-29 LJ, 05-23 LJ; *1918:* 01-25 LJ, 06-01 LJ; *1919:* 05-15 LJ.

Luke, Don. Boxer, son of Dr. Luke of Tremonton, UT. [OL]. *1926:* 03-27 LJ.

Luke, Dr. O. D. Doctor working at Tremonton Hospital. Father of Don Luke, the boxer. [OL]. *1923:* 04-14 LJ, 05-12 LJ; *1924:* 05-24 LJ; *1926:* 03-27 LJ.

Mack, Charlie. Ute from the Uinta Basin, UT. [OL]. *1919:* 11-10 LJ.

Mann, Louis (Indian). Reporter from North Yakima, WA. [OL]. *1921:* 02-11 LJ.

Marble, Sye. From Deweyville, UT. [OL]. *1924-06-19* OCE, *1926:* 06-05 LJ.

Mark, Billy. Navajo boxer from Casper, WY. [OL]. *1927:* 07-30 LJ.

Marsh, C. D. *1914:* 01-31 LJ.

Marsh, George. From Promontory area, UT. [OL]. *1923:* 12-08 LJ.

Mason, Walt. *1917:* 11-24 LJ.

Mason, Bill. From Mount Spring, UT. [OL]. *1928:* 11-17 LJ.

Mason, William. From Riverside, UT. [OL]. *1916:* 05-23 LJ.

Mc-Conihe, Mr. Indian agent from Washington, D.C., who met with Washakie Shoshone, Oct. 1915. *1916:* 10-21 LJ.

McCackey (McCaskey), Charles. Probably from Owyhee area, NV. [OL]. *1923:* 07-28 LJ.

McCann, Billy. Boxer. *1928:* 02-11 LJ.

McCaskey, James. From Owyhee, NV. [OL]. *1907:* 05-30 TT, 06-13 TT.

McGill, Cleave. From Ibapah, UT. Son of Pete and May McGill, born 1910. [AICR 1919]. *1913:* 04-24 BEN.

McGill, Peter. Ottogary mentions McGill and family were residing at Fort Hall, ID, and Fort Washakie, WY. From Ibapah, UT. Born in 1871, he married May McGill (b. 1871). Their children were Jerry Wm. (b. 1896), William (b. 1908), Cleve (son b. 1910), Jimmy (b. 1911), Arrow (son b. 1913), Clarence (b. 1916), Harold (b. 1918). [AICR 1919; OL]. *1925:* 07-18 LJ, 08-01 LJ, 08-04 BEJ, 08-10 LJ.

McLaughlin, W. W. *1914:* 01-31 LJ.

Merillat, Charles H. Attorney at Washington, D.C., employed by Shoshones to work on land claims. [OL]. *1925:* 10-24 LJ.

Meritt, Edgar B. Assistant commissioner of Indian affairs. [OL; ROAD, 80, 81]. *1922:* 11-14 BEN.

Mich, George. *1926:* 07-31 LJ.

Michel, Mr. Boxer from Colorado. [OL]. *1927:* 07-09 LJ.

Mickey, Johnny. From Fort Hall Reservation, ID. [OL]. *1920:* 12-04 LJ.

Moemberg, Amos. Born 1889, Washakie, UT, to Joseph Moemberg, who was born May 1858 to John Moemberg (and Po-Be-Hup or Popahope), who was born 1824, Promontory, UT. John's father was Ti-wats-E, which may mean "losing things.") and Sarah Pocatello or Sarah Youngap (b. Feb. 1860, daughter to Tom Pocatello). Amos married May (also known as Mary) Nanakey (b. 1896, Box Elder Co., daughter of Jonny Nanakey and To-Fib-Ah). Their children were all born at Washakie: Dwight (b. Aug. 24, 1913, d. Feb. 9, 1914), Rhoda Elnora (b. Oct. 20, 1914, married Henry Woonsook Sept. 8, 1931), Tracy (son, b. Aug. 1, 1918), unnamed male (b. Mar. 4, 1921, d. Mar. 4, 1921), Gladys (b. Nov. 15, 1922, d. June 5, 1927), Joseph Amos (b. Jan. 21, 1926, d. Aug. 2, 1931). Amos was a farm laborer who also owned his own farm. He died Dec. 4, 1925. [AICR 1920 Washakie; CCF 113732-15-SB-150; FGR; IGI; INF Ottogary, Diane; USFC 1900, 1910]. *1916:* 10-10 LJ; *1922:* 03-18-A LJ; *1923:* 02-10 LJ; *1925:* 01-17-B LJ, 12-12 LJ; *1926:* 10-23 LJ.

Moemberg (or Mo-go-berge), Bill. Born 1865, Brigham City. Sealed in Logan Temple to Rosalia Pow-en-tag-qwen-ey (b. 1864 in WY) on Feb. 10, 1886. [SLNGS LV]. *1908:* 02-06-B TT.

Moemberg, Mary (May Nanakey), came to Washakie from NV. Married Amos Moemberg. She went by the name of Bessie also. She married several times. Moved to Fort Hall Reservation and died there. See Amos Moemberg. [CCF 113732-15-SB-150; FGR; INF Parry, Mae Timbimboo]. *1923:* 05-12 LJ, 05-19 LJ, 05-26 LJ; *1925:* 12-28 LJ; *1926:* 02-06 LJ; *1927:* 01-01 LJ.

Moemberg, Miss. *1928:* 04-04 LJ, 05-26 LJ.

Moemberg, Neatze (or Neadge). First child (b. 1876, UT) of Joseph Moemberg and Sarah Pocatello Moemberg. Neatze was sister to Amos Moemberg. Married to Charlie Broom, later divorced, they had one daughter, Amy Broom (b. ca. 1895). Neatze and Amy raised Tracy Moemberg, son of Amos and May Moemberg. In 1910, Amy was living with her grandmother, Mrs. Joe [Sarah] Moemberg, in an aboriginal dwelling. [CCF 113732-15-SB-150; FGR; INF Parry, Mae Timbimboo; USFC 1910]. *1925:* 01-17-B LJ, 06-20 LJ, 06-29 LJ; *1926:* 12-21 LJ.

Moemberg, Mrs. Joe (Sarah). Sarah Pocatello (or Youcup, or Sarah Youngap) was born Feb. 1860, UT, (d. Feb. 8, 1928) to Tom Pocatello, a chief from Bannock Creek, ID, area. Sarah married Joseph Moemberg (b. May 1858). See Amos Moemberg. Children born to Sarah and Joseph: Neatze (Neadge, b. 1876), Amos (b. 1889), Annie (Ann, b. 1891), and Andrew (b. 1893). [FGR; IGI; USFC 1900, 1910]. *1913:* 02-08 LJ; *1924:* 02-09 LJ.

Moemberg, Tracy. Born Aug. 1, 1918, Washakie, Box Elder Co., to Amos Moemberg and May (Mary) Nanakey. [FGR]. *1927:* 01-01 LJ, 01-15 LJ.

MoNno, Miss. *1927:* 11-19 LJ.

Moody, George. From Skull Valley, UT. Born ca. 1866. Married Laura Beel (or Bell, b. ca. 1871). Both apparently had been married before. Only two children are mentioned under this couple: one male, one female (names and ages are unclear from source). [CCF 103366-14-SB-047]. *1913:* 04-22 LJ; *1917:* 01-18 LJ, 03-30 LJ, 11-24 LJ; *1919:* 02-26 LJ, 11-10 LJ; *1920:* 01-02 LJ; *1921:* 12-08 LJ; *1922:* 01-06 LJ; *1923:* 03-10 LJ.

Moon, Dewey. Born ca. 1896. [CCF 103366-14-SB-047]. *1927:* 01-22 LJ; *1928:* 04-21 LJ.

Morgan. From Nevada. [OL]. *1920:* 10-23 LJ.

Mose, Brownie D. From Ruby Valley, NV. Born ca. 1884. Married to Maggie (b. ca. 1888). Children: Ruth (b. ca. 1911), Teddy (b. ca. 1913), Alfred (b. ca. 1915), Pansy (b. ca. 1917), Eddie S. (b. ca. 1918 or 1919). Both parents could read, write, and speak English. Brownie was a farm laborer and his wife a washer woman. The two oldest children were enrolled in school. [USFC 1920/NV/Elko/Ruby Valley Precinct]. *1925:* 11-06 BEJ, 11-28 LJ.

Mose, George E. A farm laborer from Ruby Valley, NV, George was a traditional leader of the Western Shoshone and a descendant of a signer of the Ruby Valley Treaty. His family spent considerable time in Washakie, UT, where George broke horses and did other farm work, and their children attended school. Born ca. 1892, George married Lucille E. (b. ca. 1895), and their children were Gladys (b. ca. 1916) and George H. (b. ca. 1918). He and his wife could read, write, and speak English. [OL, USFC 1920/NV/Elko/Ruby Valley Precinct; ROAD, 130]. *1920:* 10-23 LJ; *1925:* 10-03 LJ, 10-06 BEJ, 10-16 BEJ, 10-23 BEJ, 12-28 LJ; *1926:* 01-11 LJ, 01-16 LJ, 01-30 LJ, 02-06 LJ, 02-27 LJ, 03-27 LJ, 12-24 LJ; *1927:* 02-26 LJ, 03-19 LJ, 06-18 LJ, 07-23 LJ, 12-24 LJ; *1928:* 07-07 LJ, 11-17 LJ.

Murdock, [Mr.] . *1914:* 02-10 LJ.

Murray, T. E. *1914:* 02-14 LJ.

Na-do-yo-kar, Mr. From Cache, OK. [OL]. *1925:* 09-05 LJ.

Nampy-dooah, Mr. Traditional meaning of Nampy-dooah: "foot's son." From Fort Washakie, WY. [INF Parry, Mae Timbimboo; OL]. *1925:* 08-10 LJ, 08-15 LJ, 08-22 LJ, 09-05 LJ.

Neaman. *1907:* 09-19 TT; *1914:* 01-01 BEN.

Neaman, Jim (James or John). Born July 14, 1901, in Washakie, to Moses Neaman and Rebecca Widgagee, he married Emmeline Pabawena, a daughter of John Spencer Pabawena and Ida North Peter (Ida Northfork Pete) ca. June 1924. Their children were Lee Allen (b. Mar. 15, 1925, Washakie), Eleanor (b. ca. 1927), Jim John Jr. (ca. 1931), Raymond Orlein (b. Apr. 18, 1934, Washakie), Reed Willie (b. May 29, 1936, Washakie), Kenneth L. (b. ca. 1937). Jim John Sr. was a laborer and an LDS-ordained seventy. He could speak English since he was eight years old. [WWROM; IGI; INF Parry, Mae Timbimboo; USFC 1910]. *1922:* 04-08 LJ, 09-19 BEN; *1923:* 12-08 LJ; *1924:* 06-05 OCE, 06-05 OCE, 07-05 LJ; *1925:* 01-24 LJ, 03-28 LJ, 04-14 BEJ; *1926:* 03-27 LJ; *1928:* 08-18 LJ, 10-20 LJ, 12-26 LJ, 12-29 LJ.

Neaman, Johnny. *1919:* 05-15 LJ.

Neaman, June (Louis Jones, or Louis June). Born June 10, 1906, Washakie, to Moses Neaman and Betsy Padzipe. Traditional meaning of Padzipe: "water holder." June's mother died ca. 1908. From the time he was about two years old, he was raised by his grandparents, Soquitch Timbimboo and his wife, Towange. Louis June died Apr. 29, 1922 after a three week illness, possibly influenza. [CCF 113732-15-SB-150; WWROM; IGI; INF Parry, Mae Timbimboo; OL; USFC 1910]. *1919:* 05-15 LJ; *1920:* 02-16 LJ; *1922:* 04-01 LJ, 04-04 BEN, 04-08 LJ, 04-22 LJ, 04-29 LJ, 05-12 BEN.

Neaman, Katie. Born Sept. 10, 1874, Star Valley, Elko, NV, to Elk or Alex and Yumba-Gorbuyap Jane (known later as Jane Pabawena). Katie was married first to Pagagonah Sho-sho-nitch. Their daughter Phoebe Ann later married Willie Neaman. Katie then married Moses Neaman July 15, 1910, Brigham City. Children of Katie and Moses

Neaman were Linford (or Lenford, b. May 1911), Everett (b. Nov. 30, 1913). Prior to her marriage to Moses Neaman, Katie was living with her widowed mother, Jane, in an aboriginal dwelling in the Washakie area. [CCF 113732-15-SB-150; FGR; USFC 1910; VRML]. *1919: 05-15 LJ; 1920: 02-16 LJ; 1929: 02-11 LJ, 02-16 LJ, 03-05 LJ.*

Neaman, Linford (or Lenford). Born May 1911 to Moses Neaman and Katie Pabawena. Married Margaret Perdash (b. Aug. 11, 1913 to Nephi Perdash and Jessie Zundel). Linford died 1962. [CCF 113732-15-SB-150; OL; WASHCEM]. *1927: 10-22 LJ, 11-12 LJ; 1928: 12-26 LJ, 12-29 LJ.*

Neaman (or Neamon), Mose (or Moses). Born Aug. 1, 1872, Fort Washakie, WY, to Redman (or Onda-Bow-Low-Se, or Frank) Brain and Emma (or Pan-Do-Wee) Brain. Married to Annie (or Melantie) Dewey-watz. Their children, both born in Washakie, UT, were Willie (b. 1895) and Lucy (b. 1897, later md. a man named Drinks). Mose then married Rebecca Widgagee, and their children were Foster (or Fostner, b. July 1, 1899), (James) Jim John (b. July 14, 1901), son Neman (Neaman) (b. ca. 1903, died before naming), Lucine (b. Sept. 24, 1904). He then married Betsy Padzipe. Their children were (Louis) Jones (or Louis June) (b. June 10, 1906), unnamed child (b. July 4, 1909). He finally married Katie Elk or Alex (or Pabawena) July 15, 1910, Brigham City. Their children were Linford (or Lenford, b. May 1911) and Everett (b. Nov. 30, 1913). Mose was a farmer of grain. His mother, Emma Brain lived with Mose for some time after she was widowed. [CCF 113732-15-SB-150; OL; USFC 1910; VRML]. *1911: 05-25 BEN, 12-21 LJ; 1912: 01-30 LJ; 1913: 01-02 LJ; 1915: 12-23 LJ; 1916: 05-23 LJ; 1919: 03-13 LJ, 05-15 LJ; 1920: 02-16 LJ; 1921: 12-08 LJ; 1922: 03-18-B LJ, 05-20 LJ, 06-03 LJ, 07-11 BEN, 07-25 BEN, 08-08 BEN, 09-05 BEN, 09-19 BEN, 10-21 LJ; 1923: 11-03 LJ, 12-24 LJ; 1924: 01-12 LJ, 04-10 OCE, 04-14 LJ, 06-05 OCE, 06-12 OCE, 08-16 LJ, 11-29 LJ, 12-06 LJ, 12-27 LJ; 1925: 01-03 LJ, 01-17-A LJ, 05-02 LJ, 06-13 LJ, 06-20 LJ, 06-29 LJ; 1926: 06-05 LJ, 11-27 LJ, 12-24 LJ; 1927: 01-01 LJ, 01-08 LJ, 01-15 LJ, 05-28 LJ, 07-02 LJ, 07-09 LJ, 10-22 LJ, 10-29 LJ, 12-03 LJ, 12-24 LJ; 1928: 03-17 LJ, 04-28 LJ, 05-19 LJ, 06-30 LJ, 07-28 LJ, 09-08 LJ, 11-10 LJ, 12-06 LJ, 12-20 LJ, 12-26 LJ, 12-29 LJ; 1929: 01-12 LJ.*

Neaman, Phebe (or Phoebe) Ann. Born ca. 1892 to Pobagonah Sho-sho-nitch and Katie Elk (or Alex). See Willie Neaman. [CCF 113732-15-SB-150; WWROM]. *1919: 05-15 LJ.*

Neaman, Thomas. *1922: 04-29 LJ.*

Neaman, Willie (Billy). Born 1895, Washakie, UT (or WY), to Mose (or Moses) Neaman and Annie Melantie Deweywatz. Married Phoebe Ann (daughter of Pabagonah Sho-sho-nitch and Katie Pabowena. Katie later married Moses Neaman. There is a discrepancy between documents for their children—CCF files note a son, Linford, age eight, and a daughter (unclear, but looks like Earrett, age six); census records maintain Lenford (Linford) is son of Moses and Katie. [CCF 113732-15-SB-150; WWROM; USFC 1920]. *1919: 05-15 LJ; 1922: 05-20 LJ, 06-06 BEN, 07-18 BEN, 09-01 BEN; 1923: 04-21 LJ, 05-19 LJ, 06-16 LJ, 06-23 LJ, 06-30 LJ; 1924: 11-08 LJ; 1925: 03-10 LJ, 05-16 LJ, 05-22 BEJ; 1926: 06-05 LJ, 09-04 LJ, 10-30 LJ; 1927: 10-22 LJ; 1928: 02-25 LJ.*

Neeley, Fred. Boxer from Malad, ID. [OL]. *1927: 07-09 LJ.*

Neilsen, Judge. Judge from Logan. [OL]. *1928: 03-03 LJ.*

Nelson, Bailey. From Richmond, UT. [OL]. *1914: 02-07 LJ.*

Nickdore, Fred (Japanese). Farmed south of Garland, UT. [OL]. *1920: 02-26 LJ.*

Noragan (Noragun, Norigan, or Nologan [however; there are no "L" sounds in the Shoshone language]), Kippetchew (Kippe-chugo, or Kip). Born Aug. 2, 1865, Logan, UT, to Pa-Sawe-itse (or Noragan, b. 1800, d. 1872) and Mogaguitch (Mogaquitah, or Mojo-quitch, b. 1822, Elko, NV, d. Jan. 9, 1922). Kip Married Posetz (or Bosats-za, or Positz, b. Nov. 15, 1871, Granger, WY, to So-go-put-Sie and Yah-Ro-quitch). Kip had been married twice, his wife in 1910 was Positz (or Posetz). The couple had been married for twenty years and had no children. Kip was also listed as owning and operating his own farm. Posetz died April 15, 1950 and Kip June 10, 1950. [CCF 113732-15-SB-150; IGI; MTPFHR; SLNGS LV; USFC 1910; WCR E-1931]. 1907: 04-04 TT; 1911: 09-12 LJ; 1912: 03-02 LJ, 04-16 LJ; 1914: 02-03 LJ; 1920: 12-24 LJ; 1922: 04-08 LJ, 04-22 LJ, 08-19 LJ, 12-30-A LJ, 12-30-B LJ; 1923: 01-06 LJ, 01-23 BEN, 04-07 LJ, 04-14 LJ; 1924: 01-10 OCE, 09-27-A LJ, 11-29 LJ, 12-27 LJ; 1925: 01-03 LJ, 02-17 LJ, 04-18 LJ; 1926: 01-11 LJ, 02-06 LJ, 02-13 LJ, 02-27 LJ, 11-27 LJ, 12-04 LJ; 1927: 01-01 LJ, 07-02 LJ, 12-24 LJ; 1928: 02-11 LJ, 03-17 LJ, 04-14 LJ, 09-15 LJ, 09-22 LJ, 12-26 LJ; 1929: 03-09 LJ, 03-20 LJ.

Nordoff, Pete. Boxer. 1926: 03-13 LJ.

Oiler, John. From East Garland, UT. [OL]. 1923: 10-13 LJ; 1926: 04-03 LJ.

Ond-Baby, Johny. From Fort Hall. [OL]. 1916: 10-21 LJ.

Otahgary, Peter. Born ca. 1820 on the Snake River, probably in ID, to Beaver and an unknown mother. Peter married Sots-Ze-ump (or Sarah, b. ca. 1843, WY. Saw-to-zep, a variant of Sots-Ze-ump, means "blossom."). Number and names of children unclear due to varied accounts. According to USFC 1880, his wife was Sarah (b. ca. 1850) and their children included Mania (b. ca. 1864), Willie (b. ca. 1872), Water Lizard (b. ca. 1876), Walter J. (b. ca. 1879). According to IGI and BAPT records, Peter's wife was Sots-Ze-ump (b. ca. 1843, WY) and their children were Thomas (b. ca. 1863, WY), Eberhart (Eberheart, or Eberhard, b. ca. 1865, WY), Eliza Pat-Sookah (b. 1867, WY), Willie (b. ca. 1869), Pabigee (son b. Mar. 20, 1868, Box Elder, UT, d. Feb. 20, 1877), and Willard (b. ca. 1867, WY, d. Aug. 13, 1883, listed as a half brother). Sarah (or Sots-Ze-ump) either died or they divorced. The 1900 census notes that Peter was married to Can-nan-zo (or Kanajo, b. ca. 1831) and that they had been married for ten years and had eight children, only two of whom were still living. Willie and his sister, Eliza, contested this marriage when Wm. E. Davis and Kanzo (or Can-nan-zo) petitioned for the land of O-Ti-Cot-i who died intestate. Willie was named administrator. Another Peter Ottogary (b. Feb. 18, 1900) is listed, but it is not known whether he was the son of Peter or Willie. Since this child is not mentioned in the Ottogary Family Record Book, it is possible that the entry is erroneous, the issue of Peter and Can-nan-zo, or should have been recorded as Pearly Ottogary, who was listed as being born Feb. 18, 1900. Peter, Willie's father, died Nov. 9, 1909 (at about 89 years old). He was a farmer [Willie Ottogary v. Nancy West Ottogary, First Judicial District Court, probate case no. 194, Box Elder County, 1918; INF Parry, Mae Timbimboo; OFRB; USFC 1880; USFC 1900; VRDC; WCR E-1931]. 1907: 05-30 TT; 1909: 11-20 LJ.

O-Ti-Cot-i. This means "he sits and plays in the fine dust." The name was probably given to Peter Otahgary because, as a child, he enjoyed sitting and playing in the fine grey dust. This name spawned numerous forms—Otahgary, Opah garry, Ottoger, Ottagary, Ottohgary—and eventually led to the most-often used form, Ottogary.

Ottogary, Chester Revoir (Revior). Born Jan. 30, 1908 (Washakie, UT) to Willie Ottogary and Nancy Smith, Chester earned considerable renown in the Intermountain area as a boxer. He boxed under the name of "Kickapoo Dan" (Kickipoo Dan, Kick-boo Dan, or Kick-boo-dan). A farmer, he served an LDS mission to Albuquerque, NM, from 1971 to 1973. His children with his first wife, Vida Pubigee (b. Apr. 30, 1913, Washakie, UT, d. Feb. 12, 1935) were Ernie Steele (Dec. 16, 1927—Aug. 22, 1928), Clyde Selvin (b. Dec. 23, 1929, Washakie, married Cecelia Moon), Effie (b. Sept. 27, 1931, Washakie), Ernest (b. May 24, 1934, Fort Hall, ID, d. Nov. 7, 1987, Bannock Creek, ID). After Vida died, Chester married Bessie Nannekay, but they later divorced. [FGR; INF Ottogary, Clyde; LDS Missionary Index, Church Archives; WCR E-1931]. 1911: 05-11 BEN; 1924: 03-08 LJ, 09-27-A LJ; 1925: 01-24 LJ; 1926: 01-30 LJ, 01-30 LJ, 02-06 LJ, 02-13 LJ, 02-17 LJ, 02-27 LJ, 03-06 LJ, 03-13 LJ, 03-20 LJ, 04-03 LJ, 04-17 LJ, 05-01 LJ, 05-08 LJ, 05-29 LJ,

06-19 LJ, 09-04 LJ, 09-18 LJ, 10-02 LJ, 10-16 LJ, 10-23 LJ, 10-30 LJ, 11-27 LJ, 12-11 LJ; *1927:* 01-29 LJ, 02-05 LJ, 02-19 LJ, 03-19 LJ, 03-26 LJ, 04-09 LJ, 04-16 LJ, 04-30 LJ, 06-18 LJ, 07-02 LJ, 07-09 LJ, 07-23 LJ, 07-30 LJ, 08-06 LJ, 08-20 LJ, 09-03 LJ, 09-17 LJ, 11-05 LJ, 11-26 LJ, 12-03 LJ]; *1928:* 01-28 LJ, 02-04 LJ, 02-11 LJ, 03-03 LJ, 03-24 LJ, 04-28 LJ, 05-19 LJ, 08-13 LJ, 08-18 LJ, 09-01 LJ, 10-27 LJ, 11-03 LJ, 12-06 LJ]; *1929:* 01-19 LJ, 02-23 LJ, 03-05 LJ, 03-09 LJ.

Ottogary, Custer Ernie (Ern). Willie Ottogary's son, Custer, was born Apr. 4, 1910, and his occupation was listed as pugalist. He fought under the name of "General Custer." He never married. Church records note that he achieved the office of priest and that he was nineteen years and eleven months old when he died of pneumonia. In his obituary, the *Oneida County Enterprise* said that Custer was an active church member who had been a home missionary to other LDS wards, and that "formal Indian ceremonies were performed after funeral services." According to Clyde S. Ottogary, Willie named his son Custer because he didn't want whites to feel any hard feelings existed between him and them. Apparently, the name was intended to illustrate positive relations between Indians and whites. [CR 375 8; FGR; INF Ottogary, Clyde; OCE 20 March 1930, p. 1; OL; WCR E-1931]. *1924:* 03-08 LJ; *1926:* 02-17 LJ, 03-06 LJ, 03-13 LJ, 03-20 LJ, 05-08 LJ, 09-04 LJ; *1927:* 03-19 LJ, 04-09 LJ, 04-16 LJ, 04-30 LJ, 07-02 LJ, 07-09 LJ, 07-30 LJ, 08-06 LJ, 09-03 LJ, 09-17 LJ, 11-05 LJ, 11-26 LJ]; *1928:* 03-12 LJ, 07-07 LJ, 09-08 LJ, 10-27 LJ, 11-03 LJ, 11-10 LJ]; *1929:* 01-12 LJ, 02-11 LJ.

Ottogary, Louise Myreth (Murdock). Born Dec. 30, 1912, Elwood, UT, to Willie Ottogary and Nancy Smith. She married Henry Woonsook July 4, 1927, but they later divorced. She married Lynn Perry of Washakie Sept. 24, 1928 at Brigham City. Their children were Glenn Leroy (b. July 4, 1929, Brigham City), Daniel Webster (b. May 26, 1931, Bannock Creek, ID), and Lorene. Louise and Lynn divorced July 19, 1935. Louise then married Evan Ingatuah, Mar. 1937. Louise died ca. Sept. 1992. [INF Ottogary, Clyde, Dianne; OFRB; VRML; WCR E-1931]. *1913:* 01-09 LJ; *1920:* 10-23 LJ, 11-13 LJ; *1923:* 04-14 LJ, 04-28 LJ; *1927:* 02-12 LJ, 03-26 LJ, 11-26 LJ; *1928:* 03-24 LJ.

Ottogary, Nancy. Born Jan. 10, 1883 (Dempsey, ID) to Za-Ko-Na-Cok-Paw (Bob Smith) and Tek-Shu-Yah (Tex-Shu, b. Apr. 20, 1856, ID, d. Dec. 28, 1901). Married to Dick West (b. ca. 1875, Box Elder, UT, d. May 6, 1903) and had at least two children by him, Une (b. Sept. 12, 1900, Washakie, d. Apr. 10, 1901) and Margrate (b. Aug. 16, 1901, Washakie, d. Sept. 9, 1901). She then married Willie Ottogary, Oct. 26, 1903, Brigham City. For their children, see Willie Ottogary. She divorced Willie July 11, 1917 and moved to Idaho. She later married Pierce Youpe with whom she shared twenty years of marriage before he died. She then married Stanquitch Jack, who died in the 1960s. Nancy died ca. 1980s. [BAPT; Willie Ottogary v. Nancy West Ottogary, First Judicial District Court, Civil Case No. 2211, Box Elder County, 1917; Elwood Ward Church Records, LDS Family History Library, Logan branch, film 025,634; FGR; IGI; INF Ottogary, Clyde; OFRB; SLNGS CTP; SLNGS LV]. *1911:* 05-11 BEN; *1913:* 07-03 LJ; *1916:* 06-24 LJ, 08-15 BEN, 08-22 LJ, 11-11 LJ; *1929:* 03-05 LJ.

Ottogary, Willie (William, or Billy). Born July 6, 1869, Mantua, UT, to Peter Ottogary and Sots-Ze-ump. Married Alice (Allis, or Alace) Pishey-boo-ey (meaning: "rotten eyes" or "mucus eyes," or *pisi-puih:* "infected eye"). Alice was born June 1873, NV, and died Nov. 5, 1902. Children of Willie and Alice were Bertha (b. Nov. 30, 1898, Washakie, UT, d. June 29, 1902), Pearl (or Pearly, b. Feb. 18, 1900 or July 29, 1901, Washakie, UT, d. Dec. 5, 1909 of typhoid fever). Willie married Nancy Za-Ko-Na-Cok-Paw (Zako-Nankey, or Smith) Oct. 26, 1903, Brigham City. Children of this marriage were a son (b. ca. 1902, UT), Melton (b. Mar. 1, 1905, Washakie, UT, d. Mar. 30, 1905), Florence Christina (b. Aug. 14, 1906, Elwood, UT, d. Feb. 11, 1907), Chester Revoir (or Revior, b. Jan. 30,

1908, Washakie, UT, d. Nov. 7, 1987), Custer Ernie (or Ern, b. Apr. 4, 1910, Elwood, UT, d. Mar. 13, 1930), Louise Myreth (b. Dec. 30, 1912, Elwood, UT, d. ca. Sept. 1992). He was a farmer, journalist, leader, and died Mar. 18, 1929 of "Acute dilaton of heart." [BAPT; FGR; IGI; INF Crapo, Richley; INF Ottogary, Clyde; INF Parry, Mae Timbimboo; INF Pubigee, Leland; OFRB; SLNGS CTP; VRDC; WCR E-1931]. 1906: 09-20 TT; 1907: 01-10 TT, 05-30 TT, 06-13 TT, 07-18 TT; 1908: 02-06-A TT; 1909: 07-27 LJ; 1910: 01-22 LJ; 1911: 04-25 LJ, 05-11 BEN, 07-13 LJ, 07-13 BEN, 12-21 BEN; 1912: 03-14 LJ, 03-21-B LJ, 03-28 LJ, 03-30 LJ, 04-02 LJ, 04-06 LJ, 05-23 LJ, 06-06 LJ; 1913: 01-09 LJ, 01-30 BEN, 02-08 LJ, 02-13 BEN, 03-06 BEN, 04-22 LJ, 04-22 LJ, 04-24 BEN, 06-12 BEN; 1914: 01-01 BEN, 01-29-A LJ, 01-31 LJ, 07-14 LJ; 1915: 01-18 BEN, 02-26 BEN, 05-06 LJ, 12-23 LJ; 1916: 10-21 LJ, 11-11 LJ, 12-08 BEN, 12-08 BEN; 1917: 01-18 LJ, 03-30 LJ; 1918: 03-19 LJ, 03-19 LJ, 01-24 LJ; 1919: 06-04 LJ, 07-05 LJ, 07-25 LJ, 07-26 LJ, 11-10 LJ, 11-10 LJ; 1920: 05-29 LJ, 10-23 LJ; 1921: 02-11 LJ, 03-22 LJ, 03-25 BEN, 04-27 LJ, 05-18 LJ, 09-05 LJ, 09-05 LJ; 1922: 02-25 LJ, 02-25 LJ, 03-18-A LJ, 03-25 LJ, 04-01 LJ, 05-06 LJ, 06-03 LJ, 06-13 BEN, 06-30 BEN, 07-11 BEN, 07-18 BEN, 09-23 LJ, 09-28 LJ, 09-30 LJ, 10-03 BEN, 10-06 BEN, 11-04-B LJ, 11-18 LJ, 12-02 LJ, 12-15 BEN, 12-30-A LJ; 1923: 03-03 LJ, 03-17 LJ, 04-07 LJ, 05-05 LJ, 06-23 LJ, 06-23 LJ, 07-07 LJ, 07-14 LJ, 08-04 LJ, 08-11 LJ, 08-18 LJ, 09-08 LJ, 09-15 LJ, 09-22 LJ, 09-29 LJ, 10-06 LJ, 12-08 LJ; 1924: 03-08 LJ, 04-26 LJ, 05-03 LJ, 06-05 OCE, 07-05 LJ, 07-26 LJ, 08-16 LJ, 09-20 LJ, 09-27-B LJ, 10-18-A LJ, 10-18-B LJ, 11-29 LJ, 12-04 LJ; 1925: 02-07 LJ, 02-17 LJ, 02-21 LJ, 02-21 LJ, 03-10 LJ, 03-27 BEJ, 03-27 BEJ, 03-28 LJ, 04-11 LJ, 05-16 LJ, 05-22 BEJ, 06-13 LJ, 06-20 LJ, 06-20 LJ, 06-23 BEJ, 06-29 LJ, 07-25 LJ, 08-04 BEJ, 08-15 LJ, 08-29 LJ, 09-05 LJ, 09-12 LJ, 09-18 BEJ, 09-19 LJ, 09-19 LJ, 09-26 LJ, 09-26 LJ, 10-16 BEJ, 10-17 LJ, 12-12 LJ, 12-28 LJ; 1926: 01-02 LJ, 01-02 LJ, 01-30 LJ, 02-06 LJ, 02-13 LJ, 03-06 LJ, 03-13 LJ, 03-27 LJ, 03-27 LJ, 04-17 LJ, 05-01 LJ, 05-15 LJ, 05-15 LJ, 05-29 LJ, 06-19 LJ, 07-26 LJ, 07-31 LJ, 08-07 LJ, 10-02 LJ, 10-16 LJ, 10-23 LJ, 10-30 LJ, 12-04 LJ; 1927: 01-08 LJ, 01-15 LJ, 01-22 LJ, 02-05 LJ, 03-26 LJ, 07-02 LJ, 07-09 LJ, 08-20 LJ, 08-20 LJ, 09-03 LJ, 09-17 LJ, 10-01 LJ, 10-22 LJ, 10-29 LJ, 10-29 LJ, 11-05 LJ, 11-12 LJ, 11-19 LJ, 11-26 LJ, 12-03 LJ, 12-24 LJ; 1928: 01-28 LJ, 02-04 LJ, 02-11 LJ, 02-11 LJ, 02-25 LJ, 03-03 LJ, 03-12 LJ, 03-17 LJ, 03-24 LJ, 04-04 LJ, 04-07 LJ, 04-07 LJ, 04-28 LJ, 05-19 LJ, 06-02 LJ, 06-30 LJ, 06-30 LJ, 07-07 LJ, 07-28 LJ, 08-18 LJ, 09-01 LJ, 09-15 LJ, 09-22 LJ, 10-13 LJ, 11-03 LJ, 12-06 LJ, 12-26 LJ; 1929: 01-12 LJ, 02-04 LJ, 02-11 LJ, 02-23 LJ, 03-09 LJ, 03-20 LJ, 03-23 LJ.

Pabawena (Pabowena, Paboweana, or Pab-a-wonah), David. Traditional meaning of Pabawena: *pa*, "water," *wena*, "to stand." The Pabawenas came to Washakie from Elko, Wells, and other places in Nevada. Katie Neaman and Tom Elk are half sister and half brother to the Pabawena brothers. They have the same mother, but different fathers. [INF Parry, Mae Timbimboo]. Born Aug. 7, 1892, Washakie, UT, to Thomas Sr. (b. ca. 1855, NV) and Jane (or Yam-bah-Gup, b. 1846, WY). David's infant son died fall of 1924. His wife died near the same time, due to blood poison. David did some mining and prospecting in Nevada. [FGR; IGI; INF Crapo, Richley; OL]. 1924: 04-10 OCE, 11-08 LJ; 1925: 02-21 LJ, 04-11 LJ; 1927: 05-28 LJ, 08-06 LJ, 11-19 LJ; 1928: 04-04 LJ, 04-28 LJ, 06-02 LJ, 10-13 LJ, 11-03 LJ.

Pabawena, Emmaline (Emmeline, Emeline, Emmiline, or Emoline). Emmaline was probably born Apr. 4, 1908, Deeth, Elko, NV, to John Spencer Pabawena and Ida North Peter (or Ida Northfork Pete), but lived most of the time with Jane Pabawena (probably her aunt). This is why she is listed with Jane in AICR documents. Married Jim John Neaman ca. June 1924. See Jim John Neaman. [AICR 1917 & 1920; IGI; OL]. 1924: 07-05 LJ.

Pabawena, Herbert M. Born ca. 1908, to Thomas Pabawena (b. 1886, UT) and Julia Tospanguitch (b. ca. 1889). [AICR; IGI]. 1919: 05-15 LJ; 1925: 05-16 LJ, 05-22 BEJ; 1926: 01-11 LJ, 01-23 LJ; 1927: 11-05 LJ, 12-24 LJ.

Pabawena, James (Jim, or Jimmy). Born Dec. 1880, NV, to Thomas Pabawena Sr. and Jane (or Yam-bah-gup). Died 1967. [USFC 1900; WASHCEM]. *1922:* 06-30 BEN, 07-11 BEN, 09-01 BEN; *1923:* 03-10 LJ; *1924:* 01-19 LJ, 02-21 OCE, 06-05 OCE, 08-16 LJ, 08-23 LJ; *1925:* 02-21 LJ, 03-28 LJ, 11-06 BEJ; *1926:* 04-10 LJ, 06-05 LJ, 10-02 LJ; *1927:* 01-08 LJ, 02-05 LJ, 05-28 LJ, 07-23 LJ, 09-17 LJ, 10-22 LJ, 10-29 LJ, 11-12 LJ, 12-03 LJ, 12-24 LJ; *1928:* 02-04 LJ, 02-11 LJ, 02-25 LJ, 03-03 LJ, 03-12 LJ, 04-14 LJ, 04-28 LJ, 05-19 LJ, 05-26 LJ, 06-02 LJ, 07-28 LJ, 09-15 LJ, 09-22 LJ, 10-20 LJ]; *1929:* 01-19 LJ, 02-23 LJ, 03-20 LJ.

Pabawena, Jane (Yam-bah-Gup, Yam-Ba-Cal-Noa, or Yumba-Gorbuyap Jane). Born ca. 1836 or 1846, WY, d. Nov. 16 or 18, 1926. Married Elk or Alex (b. ca. 1836, Deeth, Elko, NV, d. Dec. 18, 1932). Their children were Thomas or Tom (b. Feb. 13, 1872, Deeth, Elko Co., NV), Katie (b. Sept. 10, 1874, Star Valley, Elko, NV). [FGR; OL]. *1926:* 11-27 LJ.

Pabawena, John (or John Spencer, or Johny). Born ca. 1882, UT. First marriage to Ida North Peter (or Ida Northfork Pete). Children of this marriage: Emeline (or Emmiline, b. Apr. 4, 1908, Deeth, Elko, NV), Lillian (or Lilian, b. Nov. 27, 1910, Deeth, Elko, NV). Second marriage to Nellie Thompson. Children of this marriage: Bill (Buffalo) Calf (Billy, or Bill Bufflio Calf, b. Nov. 27, 1916, Oneil, Elko, NV), Grace Irene (b. Dec. 18, 1922, Moor, Elko, NV), Verna Ella (b. Jan. 15, 1932, Washakie, UT). [FGR; IGI; WWROM]. *1923:* 10-27 LJ; *1924:* 02-09 LJ, 03-06 OCE, 03-15 LJ, 04-03 OCE, 04-10 OCE, 04-26 LJ, 05-03 LJ, 05-03 LJ, 05-24 LJ, 06-19 OCE, 12-06 LJ]; *1925:* 04-11 LJ, 04-18 LJ, 05-22 BEJ; *1927:* 05-28 LJ, 09-17 LJ, 11-26 LJ]; *1928:* 04-28 LJ, 05-19 LJ, 05-26 LJ, 06-02 LJ, 08-13 LJ, 09-01 LJ, 09-08 LJ, 09-15 LJ, 10-20 LJ, 11-10 LJ, 12-20 LJ.

Pabawena, Julia. (Julia Tospanguitch). Born 1889. Married Thomas Pabawena Jr. See Thomas Pabawena Jr. [AICR]. *1913:* 01-16 LJ, 01-16 BEN; *1928:* 09-22 LJ, 10-20 LJ; *1929:* 02-11 LJ, 02-16 LJ, 03-05 LJ.

Pabawena, Kate (Katie). Born Sept. 10, 1874, Star Valley, Elko, NV, to Elk or Alex and Yumba-Gorbuyap Jane (Jane Pabawena). Married Moses Neaman July 15, 1910. See Moses Neaman. [CCF 113732-15-SB-150; FGR; USFC 1910]. *1907:* 07-18 TT; *1925:* 02-17 LJ.

Pabawena, Thomas (or Tom), Jr. Born Mar. 1886, UT, to Thomas Sr. and Jane Yam-bah-Gup. Married Julia Tospanguitch (b. 1889) Nov. 24, 1904. Children: Herbert M. (b. ca. 1908, UT), Etheline (b. 1916), Albert Glen (b. June 5, 1920, Washakie, UT), Lucille (b. 1923, UT), Ben Benson (b. Oct. 5, 1926, Washakie, UT). In CCF 15804-25-Western Shoshone-174.1, a document appears which is signed by Thomas Pabawena. Near the signature is a note that reads, "I one of Chief Tosowitze descendents." In *The Shoshoni Frontier and the Bear River Massacre*, Madsen notes that Tosowitz was one of the 10 band chiefs who signed the Treaty of Box Elder in 1863. [AICR; CCF 15804-25-Western Shoshone-174.1; IGI; USFC 1910; VRML; WCR E-1931]. *1911:* 12-21 LJ; *1913:* 01-16 LJ, 01-16 BEN, 08-07 LJ, 08-14-B BEN, 08-14 LJ; *1914:* 07-14 LJ; *1916:* 08-22 LJ; *1919:* 06-26 LJ; *1922:* 03-18-B LJ, 04-08 LJ, 04-22 LJ, 05-20 LJ, 06-03 LJ, 06-30 BEN, 07-11 BEN, 07-25 BEN, 08-12 LJ, 09-01 BEN, 11-04-B LJ, 11-04-B LJ, 11-18 LJ, 11-25 LJ; *1923:* 06-16 LJ, 06-23 LJ, 06-30 LJ, 09-29 LJ, 10-27 LJ, 12-08 LJ, 12-24 LJ; *1924:* 01-12 LJ, 02-09 LJ, 04-10 OCE, 04-26 LJ, 05-03 LJ, 05-24 LJ, 06-19 OCE, 11-08 LJ, 11-29 LJ, 12-06 LJ; *1925:* 02-07 LJ, 02-17 LJ, 02-17 LJ, 09-19 LJ]; *1926:* 03-27 LJ, 05-15 LJ, 05-29 LJ, 09-18 LJ, 12-11 LJ; *1927:* 07-09 LJ, 07-23 LJ, 08-06 LJ, 09-03 LJ, 09-17 LJ, 10-01 LJ, 10-29 LJ, 11-19 LJ, 11-26 LJ, 12-03 LJ]; *1928:* 02-11 LJ, 03-03 LJ, 06-02 LJ, 09-01 LJ, 09-15 LJ, 10-20 LJ, 11-03 LJ, 11-03 LJ, 11-17 LJ]; *1929:* 01-12 LJ, 03-05 LJ.

Pabawena, Tom (Thomas Sr., the father of Thomas). Born ca. 1850 or 1855, Elko, NV, to Zit-O-Bee (or Geet-O-Bay, b. ca. 1830, Elko, NV) and Na-Wats-Zee (or Na-Wat-Zee, b. ca. 1835, Elko, NV). Tom married (was sealed) Mar. 4, 1885 to Ho-Tim-A-Sow-Wop (b. 1848, Elko, NV). It is unclear if this woman is also Jane Yam-Bah-Gup. If not, Tom later married Jane Yam-Bah-Gup (b. ca. 1836 or 1846). Children: Alex or Elex (b. Oct. 1861 [sic], NV), James (or Jimmy, b. Dec. 1880, NV), John Spencer (b. Dec. 1882, UT), Thomas (b. Mar. 1886, UT), Lizzie (b. May 1889, UT), David (b. Aug. 7, 1892, Washakie, UT). [FGR; IGI; SLNGS LV; USFC 1900]. *1926:* 11-27 LJ.

Pabayou, Miss. From Ogden. [OL]. *1928:* 03-03 LJ.

Pabboo (or Pooboo), Mr. *1926:* 12-04 LJ, 12-11 LJ.

Pa-da-Zya, Mrs. *1918:* 06-01 LJ.

Pah-Wea, Mr. From Oklahoma. [OL]. *1925:* 07-18 LJ.

Paniboo (Piniboo, Baniboo, or Pamboo), Joseph (Joe). Traditional meaning of Paniboo: "bumble bee eyes." Born ca. 1856. Married three times. The 1910 census records Joseph's present marriage to Pirdisa (b. ca. 1850, ID). The marriage to Joseph was Pirdisa's second. The couple had been married for twenty-five years and had three children though none were still living. Joseph was a small grain farmer. In 1915, documents record that Mary Piniboo was a sixty-five-year-old widow of Joseph Piniboo. [CCF 113732-15-SB-150; INF Parry, Mae Timbimboo; OL; USFC 1910]. *1913:* 01-16 LJ, 01-16 BEN, 02-13 BEN; *1915:* 12-23 LJ.

Panquitch, Sam. From Fort Hall Res., ID. Born to Pompy-ge-me-ni and Dun-mo-no (b. 1834, Box Elder Co., UT, d. 1873). Married Yamba Mink Panquitch. Children: Sarah Mink Bear. [MTPFHR]. *1921:* 10-31 LJ.

Paregosam (Parahgosam, or Parago-Sam). See Sam, George P.

Parry, Dan. *1921:* 10-24 LJ; *1922:* 05-27 LJ, 06-06 BEN.

Parson, Frank. A well-known horse trader from Malad, ID. [OL]. *1923:* 03-17 LJ, 04-28 LJ.

Pawee, Mr. (Pawnee?). *1925:* 09-05 LJ.

Paxman, J. W. Spoke on dry farming at Agriculture Round Up. [OL]. *1914:* 02-03 LJ.

Pa-zo-quita, Mr. From Fort Washakie, WY. [OL]. *1927:* 01-15 LJ.

Perdash (or Purdash), Charlie (Charles, Charley). Traditional meaning of Perdash: "singing runner." Born Mar. 1864, Logan or Washakie, UT, to Hobeyea-Nuk, or Perdash, and Noquida (or No-que-tha). Married Eunice Moemberg (b. 1865, dau. of John Moemberg and Po-Be-Hup). Their children were Augee (b. 1882, UT), Tiemus (or Timus, b. 1888, Washakie, UT), a child (b. 1886, UT), a child (b. 1891, UT), Nephi (b. June 9, 1892, Washakie, UT), a daughter (b. ca. 1893, UT), Mamie (b. Jan. 3, 1895), Stephen (b. Sept. 26, 1900, Washakie, UT), Juanita (b. June 26, 1903, Washakie, UT), Edwin (b. Apr. 9, 1909, Washakie, UT). The 1910 census notes Charlie and Eunice had been married for thirty years and had eleven children, but only four were still living. A daughter named Woscetts, age six (b. ca. 1904) was living with Charlie and Eunice. Charlie farmed grain and beets. [AICR; CCF 113732-15-SB-150; IGI; INF Parry, Mae Timbimboo; USFC 1910]. *1916:* 07-18 LJ; *1919:* 02-26 LJ; *1922:* 09-28 LJ, 11-04-A LJ, 11-04-A LJ; *1923:* 02-17 LJ, 02-17 LJ; *1926:* 09-18 LJ; *1927:* 05-28 LJ, 09-03 LJ; *1928:* 07-07 LJ, 09-01 LJ, 09-15 LJ.

Perdash, Ethel Eliza. Born Mar. 23, 1911, Washakie, UT, to Nephi Perdash and Jessie Zundel. See Nephi Perdash. [IGI]. *1926:* 08-28 LJ, 09-18 LJ; *1927:* 12-03 LJ; *1928:* 02-04 LJ, 10-20 LJ, 11-03 LJ.

Perdash, Margaret. Born Aug. 11, 1913, Washakie, UT, to Nephi Perdash and Jessie Zundel. Married Linford Neaman (b. May 1911, Washakie, UT). [IGI; OL]. *1928:* 12-26 LJ.

Perdash, May. Infant who died after a week-long illness. [OL]. *1927:* 07-02 LJ.

Perdash, Nephi. Born June 9, 1892, Washakie, UT, to Charlie Perdash and Eunice Moemberg. Married Jessie Annapooey (also known as Jessie Zundel, Jessie Fly, or Jessie Cota) Feb. 7, 1910 at Brigham City. Nephi was 18 and his bride 15. Consent to marry was given by Con (Miss Cohn) Zundel, Jessie's mother. Children: Ethel Eliza (b. Mar. 23, 1911, Washakie, UT, d. June 24, 1929), Margaret (b. Aug. 11, 1913, Washakie, UT), a daughter (b. ca. 1915), Fern (b. ca. 1920), Stephen Harold (b. Mar. 23, 1923, d. Mar.

15, 1988; WWII veteran) Devere (Nephi Devere Perdash, b. Apr. 4, 1930, d. Sept. 5, 1982; Korean War veteran), and Devon (b. ca. 1933). The 1910 census lists the occupation of Nephi Perdash as farm labor, working out. [CCF 113732-15-SB-150; IGI; INF Parry, Mae Timbimboo; MTPFHR; USFC 1910; VRML; WASHCEM]. *1922:* 09-23 LJ; *1923:* 04-07 LJ; *1924:* 05-03 LJ, 07-05 LJ, 09-27-A LJ, 11-08 LJ, 12-06 LJ; *1925:* 04-18 LJ, 06-13 LJ, 09-26 LJ, 11-21 LJ; *1926:* 07-31 LJ, 08-28 LJ, 09-04 LJ, 12-21 LJ; *1927:* 02-12 LJ, 02-26 LJ, 04-09 LJ, 06-18 LJ, 07-09 LJ, 11-19 LJ, 11-26 LJ, 12-03 LJ, 12-24 LJ; *1928:* 01-28 LJ, 02-04 LJ, 04-14 LJ, 05-19 LJ, 06-30 LJ, 07-07 LJ, 09-08 LJ, 09-15 LJ, 10-20 LJ, 11-10 LJ, 12-26 LJ, 12-29 LJ.

Perdash, Rachel. Born Jan. 18, 1858, Logan, UT, to Hobeyea-Nuk (Hobeyea-Muk, or Perdash) and Noquida (or No-que-tha). Although she was married, no record of her spouse has been found. The 1910 census lists Rachel as a fifty-five year old widow with five children, none living. [IGI; INF Parry, Mae Timbimboo; USFC 1910]. *1925:* 09-26 LJ.

Perdash, Timus (Tiemus, or Timas). Born 1888, Washakie, UT, to Charlie Perdash and Eunice Moemberg. Married Emily Zundel (b. ca. 1897, daughter of Cohn Zundel, father's name unknown). Timus and his brother Nephi married Cohn Zundel's daughters. Timus and Emily divorced in the fall of 1926. Timus married another woman but she soon ran away. No record of children exists from either marriage. Timus took sick with influenza and died July 4, 1928. No occupation was listed in census of 1910. [CCF 113732-15-SB-150; IGI; OL; USFC 1910]. *1914:* 01-29-A LJ; *1919:* 03-13 LJ; *1923:* 05-12 LJ, 09-29 LJ, 10-06 LJ, 11-03 LJ; *1924:* 04-10 OCE, 08-23 LJ, 09-27-B LJ; *1925:* 04-18 LJ, 05-02 L; *1926:* 08-14 LJ, 08-28 LJ, 09-18 LJ, 10-23 LJ; *1928:* 02-04 LJ, 05-19 LJ, 06-30 LJ, 07-07 LJ, 11-17 LJ.

Perdash, Mrs. Timus. Emily Zundel Perdash. See Timus Perdash. *1922:* 03-18-A LJ.

Perry, Lyn. This could be the Lynn F. Perry who married Louise Ottogary, fathered three children by her, and then separated from or divorced her. *1928:* 09-15 LJ.

Perry, Tom. Bishop from Logan. [OL]. 1928-03-03 LJ, *1928:* 04-04 LJ.

Perwhat, Susan. See Purdawat, Susie.

Petersen, Miss. School teacher at Washakie Day School. [OL]. *1922:* 04-22 LJ.

Peterson, Charlie. *1926:* 05-15 LJ.

Peterson, Nick. From Union, UT. [OL]. *1926:* 05-29 LJ.

Peterson, Mr. Spoke on dry farming at Agriculture Round Up. [OL]. *1914:* 02-03 LJ.

Peterson, Pross (Ross) W. Spoke on dairying at Agriculture Round Up. [OL]. *1914:* 02-07 LJ.

Peterson, Reed. Boxer from Tremonton, UT. [OL]. *1928:* 11-10 LJ.

Peterson, W. Spoke on county road business at Agriculture Round Up. [OL]. *1914:* 02-10 LJ.

Peyope, Evans. Born ca. 1911 to Jacob Peyope and Lucy Cojoe. Traditional meaning of Peyope: "sugar." Traditional meaning of Cojoe: "pony tail." [IGI; INF Crapo, Richley; INF Parry, Mae Timbimboo]. *1927:* 11-12 LJ, 11-26 LJ; *1928:* 03-03 LJ, 03-17 LJ, 11-17 LJ.

Peyope, Fosy. *1926:* 02-27 LJ.

Peyope, George. Born Apr. 20, 1881, Garland, UT, to Enoch Peyope (b. 1856, UT) and Panzy-pipe (or Pan-zo-pipe) Hootchew (b. ca. 1856, Ruby Valley, NV). Married Nancy Mary (b. June 1881, WY), but the marriage ended sometime before 1903 when George married Lucy Zundel (b. ca. 1887). In an article titled "An Indian Wedding," *The Box Elder News* reported, "George Peyope, an athletic appearing Indian, aged 22, and Lucy Zundle [sic], a dainty Indian maid, who gave her age as 16 . . . were married last Saturday at the Court House. . . . Mother of the bride Corn Zundle [sic] was present to give her consent to the ceremony as the young lady was under legal age. . . ." Children born to George and Lucy were Esther (b. ca. 1903), Steven (b. ca. 1906), and Wilford (b. ca. 1910). George died in 1911. After George's death, Lucy married Tom Elk, see

Tom Elk. [1903-01-29 BEN; CCF 113732-15-SB-150; IGI; OL; SLNGS LV; USFC 1900; USFC 1900, 1910; VRML]. *1907:* 05-09 TT; *1911:* 04-25 LJ.

Peyope, Jacob (Jake). Born Jan. 16, 1876, Garland, UT, to Enoch Peyope (b. 1856, UT) and Panzy-pipe (or Pan-zo-pipe) Hootchew (b. ca. 1856, Ruby Valley, NV). Married Poo-Janey ca. 1899. The 1900 census lists "keeps tepee" as the occupation for Poo-Janey. In about 1903, Jacob married Lucy Cojoe (or Kojo, b. 1890, Box Elder County), daughter of Joe Cojoe (b. ca. 1867) and Pone-zets Paregosam (b. ca. 1870, Box Elder County. Traditional meaning of Pone-zets: "skunk.") Children of Jacob and Lucy were Jennie (or Jenny, b. 1904), Sadie Ann (b. ca. 1909), Evans (b. ca. 1911), Carlandus (b. Sept. 19, 1914, Washakie, UT), Griffin (b. July 18, 1916, Washakie, UT), Leona (b. ca. 1919), and Esther (b. ca. 1926). The 1920 census lists only three children in the household: Sadie, Evans, and Griffin. Jacob worked as a farmer and did odd jobs. He also did a considerable amount of trapping. Jacob died in 1956 and Lucy in 1964. [CCF 113732-15-SB-150; IGI; INF Parry, Mae Timbimboo; OL; USFC 1900, 1910, 1920; WASHCEM; WWROM]. *1913:* 06-12 BEN; *1916:* 05-23 LJ; *1919:* 03-13 LJ, 06-26 LJ; *1921:* 02-08 LJ; *1922:* 02-18 LJ, 07-25 BEN, 08-12 LJ, 12-15 BEN; *1923:* 01-13 LJ, 01-23 BEN, 04-14 LJ; *1924:* 01-12 LJ, 01-10 OCE, 05-03 LJ, 11-08 LJ; *1925:* 02-17 LJ, 05-09 LJ, 05-23 LJ, 06-02 LJ, 06-06 LJ, 12-28 LJ; *1926:* 03-06 LJ, 04-03 LJ, 05-29 LJ, 12-11 LJ; *1927:* 08-06 LJ, 10-01 LJ, 11-05 LJ, 11-12 LJ, 11-12 LJ, 12-24 LJ; *1928:* 02-25 LJ, 02-25 LJ, 03-03 LJ, 03-17 LJ, 03-24 LJ, 04-04 LJ, 04-21 LJ, 05-19 LJ, 05-26 LJ, 06-02 LJ, 08-13 LJ, 09-08 LJ, 09-15 LJ, 10-27 LJ, 12-20 LJ, 12-26 LJ, 12-29 LJ; *1929:* 01-12 LJ, 03-09 LJ.

Peyope, Jim (Jacob?). *1926:* 04-03 LJ.

Peyope, Stephen. Born ca. 1906 to George Peyope and Lucy Zundel. Died of consumption May 1918. [CCF 113732-15-SB-150; IGI; OL]. *1918:* 06-01 LJ.

Peyope, Wilford. Born ca. 1910 to George Peyope and Lucy Zundel. [CCF 113732-15-SB-150; IGI]. *1922:* 11-25 LJ, 12-26 BEN; *1928:* 01-28 LJ, 02-04 LJ, 03-12 LJ, 09-08 LJ, 11-10 LJ, 12-29 LJ.

Phillip (or Phelps), John. From Wind River Reservation, WY. John Phelps was Alene Menta's uncle. Evans Peyope's wife was John Phelps's sister. [INF Menta, Alene]. *1927:* 07-09 LJ, 07-23 LJ.

Piah-namp (or Pian-nanp). Ute Ottogary met in the Uinta Basin, 1919. [OL]. *1919:* 11-10 LJ.

Pingree, James. Probably from Fort Washakie Reservation, WY. Noted as cousin of Willie Ottogary. [OL]. *1925:* 06-20 LJ.

Pingree, Peter. Probably from Fort Washakie Reservation, WY. [OL]. *1925:* 08-15 LJ.

Pin-upe, Mr. (also called Proup, Peyupe). From Fort Hall Reservation, ID. *1911:* 04-25 LJ, 05-11 BEN, 05-25 BEN.

Pittman, Key. Key Pittman was a U.S. senator (Democrat) from Nevada. He was born 1872, d. 1940. He served in the Senate from 1913 to 1940. [SENATEUS]. *1922:* 03-18-B LJ, 03-25 LJ, 04-04 BEN.

Pocatello, Elno. From west of Pocatello, ID. [OL]. *1923:* 01-06 LJ.

Pocatello, Garfield. From Fort Hall Reservation, ID. [OL]. *1912:* 03-02 LJ; *1928:* 09-22 LJ.

Pocatello, Mule. Mooda means "mule." His European surname name was Lasalle. His children were Venus, Carmelita, and Lucille. [INF Menta, Alene]. *1926:* 02-27 LJ; *1927:* 11-05 LJ.

Pocatello, Washington. Listed as Pocatello Washington. [OL]. *1911:* 04-25 LJ.

Poncho (Broncho, or Proncho), Sear. Traditional meaning of Seah: "eagle feather." From Fort Hall, ID. Married Esther Peyope, daughter of George Peyope and Lucy Zundel. [INF Menta, Alene, Parry, Mae Timbimboo; OL]. *1926:* 02-27 LJ; *1927:* 11-05 LJ.

Poncho, Mrs. Sear. Esther Peyope Poncho. Died in childbirth along with her baby boy in 1926. [INF Parry, Mae Timbimboo; OL]. *1924:* 07-05 LJ; *1926:* 01-23 LJ, 01-30 LJ, 02-27 LJ.

Ponco (Ponzo), Ben. From Pocatello, ID. Rides bucking horses. [OL]. *1924:* 02-23 LJ, 03-15 LJ, 06-05 OCE.

Portage, Mr. From Austin, NV. [OL]. *1928:* 11-03 LJ.

Porter, C. W. Spoke on women and work at Agriculture Round Up. [OL]. *1914:* 02-10 LJ.

Posspia, Miss. Buying deer hides at Salt Lake City. [OL]. *1923:* 12-24 LJ.

Preacher, Harry (Preacher Harry). Ghost Dance leader from Wells, NV. He was involved in Western Shoshone tribal politics in the late 19th century and early 20th century. [ROAD, 62, 75, 76]. *1912:* 01-11 BEN; *1919:* 11-10 LJ.

Puape, Johnny. From Fort Hall Reservation, ID. [OL]. *1907:* 11-21 TT.

Pubigee (Pabigee), Traditional meaning of Pubigee: "weasel." It is unclear which Pubigee is the subject of Ottogary's letter. [INF Parry, Mae Timbimboo]. *1911:* 12-21 BEN; *1916:* 05-23 LJ.

Pubigee, Alice. Born ca. 1910, NV. Alice Pubigee's maiden name was Smith until she married James (Chip) Brown. After they divorced, Alice married Elias Pubigee. See Elias Pubigee. [Alice Brown v. James Brown Jr. also known as Chip Brown, et al. First Judicial District Court, Box Elder County, civil case 2386, default entered Mar. 22, 1919; INF Parry, Mae Timbimboo; WCR E-1931; WWROM]. *1927:* 02-05 LJ, 11-26 LJ, 12-03 LJ.

Pubigee, Ammon. Born Nov. 16, 1865, Green River, WY, to Ma-We-Un-Gah and Che-Un-Gah. Married Eliza Pat-Sookah (Patzonah, or Pats-un-gwa, Willie Ottogary's sister). Their children were Seth (b. ca. 1889), Enos Sam (or Eneas, b. July 2, 1897, Washakie, UT), and Elias (b. Mar. 13, 1900, Washakie, UT). The 1910 census notes Ammon and Eliza had eight children, only three of whom were living. Ammon and Willie spent a considerable amount of time together and shared many experiences. Eliza Ottogary died ca. Apr. 1919. Ottogary's letters suggest that Ammon married again years after Eliza's death, but it is not known to whom. [CCF 113732-15-SB-150; IGI; OL; SLNGS LV]. *1907:* 05-30 TT, 07-18 TT, 11-28 TT; *1908:* 02-06-A TT; *1911:* 12-21 BEN; *1912:* 03-28 LJ, 04-16 LJ; *1913:* 04-24 BEN; *1914:* 01-01 LJ; *1916:* 02-03 BEN; *1919:* 05-15 LJ, 06-04 LJ; *1920:* 02-16 LJ, 05-29 LJ; *1921:* 10-31 LJ; *1922:* 03-18-B LJ, 04-29 LJ, 05-27 LJ, 06-30 BEN, 07-18 BEN, 08-08 BEN, 08-19 LJ, 09-01 BEN, 09-19 BEN, 11-04-B LJ, 11-18 LJ, 11-25 LJ; *1923:* 05-12 LJ, 10-06 LJ, 12-08 LJ; *1924:* 02-23 LJ, 03-15 LJ, 04-03 OCE, 04-14 LJ, 04-26 LJ, 06-12 OCE, 07-05 LJ, 08-16 LJ, 08-23 LJ, 09-20 LJ, 09-27-B LJ, 11-08 LJ, 11-29 LJ, 12-06 LJ, 12-27 LJ; *1925:* 01-17-A LJ, 01-17-B LJ, 02-07 LJ, 03-28 LJ, 04-11 LJ, 05-02 LJ, 06-20 LJ, 09-19 LJ, 09-26 LJ, 11-28 LJ, 12-12 LJ; *1926:* 04-03 LJ, 06-19 LJ, 08-07 LJ, 08-28 LJ, 09-04 LJ, 10-23 LJ, 10-30 LJ; *1927:* 02-12 LJ, 02-19 LJ, 04-30 LJ, 08-06 LJ, 09-03 LJ, 09-17 LJ, 10-29 LJ, 12-24 LJ; *1928:* 02-11 LJ, 03-12 LJ, 05-19 LJ, 05-26 LJ, 06-02 LJ, 06-30 LJ, 11-03 LJ, 11-10 LJ; *1929:* 01-19 LJ, 03-20 LJ.

Pubigee, Elias. Born Mar. 13, 1900, Washakie, UT, to Ammon Pubigee (b. Nov. 16, 1865, WY) and Eliza Pat-Sookah Ottogary (b. 1867, WY). Married Alice [Smith] Brown. See Pubigee, Alice. Their children were Catherine (b. July 5, 1926, Washakie, UT, d. Oct. 1926), Aaron (b. Sept. 8, 1927, Washakie, UT), Selma (b. ca. 1929), Lila (b. ca. 1931), Stanley (b. ca. 1932), Asael (b. ca. 1935), Alfaed (Alfred, b. ca. 1938). According to Ottogary, in Oct. 1923, a daughter of Elias died. In 1938, Ammon (father of Elias) was living in this household. [IGI; OL; WWROM]. *1919:* 05-15 LJ; *1921:* 05-18 LJ; *1922:* 06-30 BEN, 07-11 BEN; *1923:* 10-20 LJ, 10-27 LJ; *1924:* 04-14 LJ, 07-05 LJ, 09-27-A LJ, 09-27-B LJ, 12-06 LJ; *1925:* 03-28 LJ, 06-20 LJ, 10-06 BEJ, 10-16 BEJ, 12-28 LJ; *1926:* 06-19 LJ, 10-30 LJ, 12-24 LJ; *1927:* 04-30 LJ, 07-23 LJ, 09-17 LJ, 10-29 LJ, 11-26 LJ, 12-03 LJ; *1928:* 03-12 LJ, 06-30 LJ, 07-28 LJ, 09-15 LJ, 11-17 LJ; *1929:* 03-20 LJ.

Pubigee, Enos. Enos (or Eneas) Sam. Born July 2, 1897, Washakie, UT, to Ammon Pubigee (b. Nov. 16, 1865, WY) and Eliza Pat-Sookah Ottogary (b. 1867, WY). Married Amy (b. 1891). They had one child, Leo Sylvester (b. 1917). Married Lillian Pabawena (b. Nov.

27, 1910, Deeth, NV). Their children were Maurine (b. ca. 1924), Ervin Andrew (b. May 19, 1926), Helen (b. ca. 1928, she later married Frank Warner), Leland (b. Sept. 24, 1930). Court records note other wives, including May L. (no children, divorced Mar. 18, 1938), and Marjorie A. (one child, divorce filed Mar. 27, 1939). [AICR; First Judicial District Court, Box Elder County, civil case 5604 (Enos S. Pubigee v. May L. Pubigee) and 5731 (Marjorie A. Pubigee v. Enos Pubigee); IGI; INF Parry, Mae Timbimboo; INF Pubigee, Leland]. *1912*: 04-16 LJ; *1916*: 10-10 LJ; *1921*: 02-03 LJ; *1922*: 04-04 BEN, 07-18 BEN, 07-25 BEN, 09-19 BEN, 09-23 LJ, 11-14 BEN, 11-18 LJ, 11-25 LJ; *1923*: 06-02 LJ, 06-30 LJ, 10-13 LJ, 11-17 LJ; *1924*: 02-21 OCE, 02-23 LJ, 03-08 LJ, 04-14 LJ, 05-17 LJ, 05-24 LJ, 09-27-A LJ, 09-27-B LJ, 11-08 LJ, 12-06 LJ; *1925*: 05-02 LJ, 05-16 LJ, 05-22 BEJ, 06-29 LJ, 09-12 LJ, 10-16 BEJ, 10-17 LJ, 11-28 LJ, 12-12 LJ, 12-28 LJ; *1926*: 01-16 LJ, 01-23 LJ, 01-30 LJ, 02-06 LJ, 02-27 LJ, 03-06 LJ, 03-13 LJ, 05-29 LJ, 08-07 LJ, 09-18 LJ, 10-16 LJ; *1927*: 01-29 LJ, 01-29 LJ, 04-09 LJ, 04-30 LJ, 05-28 LJ, 06-18 LJ, 07-02 LJ, 07-09 LJ, 07-23 LJ, 07-30 LJ, 08-06 LJ, 08-20 LJ, 09-03 LJ, 09-17 LJ, 10-22 LJ, 10-29 LJ, 11-05 LJ, 11-12 LJ, 12-03 LJ, 12-24 LJ; *1928*: 03-12 LJ, 03-24 LJ, 04-07 LJ, 04-21 LJ, 05-19 LJ, 06-30 LJ, 09-08 LJ, 09-15 LJ, 09-22 LJ, 12-06 LJ, 12-29 LJ.

Pubigee, Mrs. Enos (perhaps Lillian Pabawena Pubigee). *1928*: 09-15 LJ.

Pubigee, Mrs. This is probably Eliza Pat-Sookah Ottogary, Willie's sister. Born 1867, WY, to Peter Ottogary and Sots-Ze-ump. Died ca. spring 1919. [IGI; OL]. *1907*: 03-28 TT, 04-04 TT, 05-30 TT, 07-18 TT, 11-28 TT; *1919*: 05-15 LJ.

Pubigee, Seth. Born May 1, 1884, Washakie, UT, to Ammon Pubigee (b. Nov. 16, 1865, WY) and Eliza Pat-Sookah Ottogary (b. 1867, WY). Married Ivy (Iva, Ivai, or Jennie) Pojennie Woonsook (b. ca. 1886, to Joseph Woonsook and Mary, daughter of Susan Purdawat) on Nov. 24, 1904. Seth filed for divorce on Nov. 14, 1911, but the couple apparently stayed together. Their children were Tessia (Tena, or Lena) Jack (b. ca. 1901, step daughter of Seth, daughter of Pojennie Woonsook and Jim Jack), Wyte (or Wyatt, b. ca. 1906), Vida (b. Apr. 30, 1913), a daughter (b. ca. 1914), Fred (b. ca. 1916), Frank L. (b. 1917), Luella (b. 1922), and Anne Dorothy (b. Oct. 18, 1927). Ottogary said Seth had at least two more children (see 1912-04-04 LJ and 1915-12-23 LJ). Seth's occupations in 1910 were listed as farm laborer and odd jobs. He changed his name from Seth Pubigee to Seth Eagle (sometimes retaining Pubigee; thus, Seth Eagle Pubigee). Ottogary first refers to him as Seth Eagle in 1927. [AICR; Seth Pubigee v. Jennie Wanswook Pubigee, First Judicial District Court, Box Elder County, civil case 1423; CCF 113732-15-SB-150; IGI; INF Parry, Mae Timbimboo; OL; USFC 1910; WWROM]. *1911*: 11-30 BEN, 12-21 LJ; *1912*: 03-14 LJ, 03-21-A LJ, 04-04 LJ; *1915*: 12-23 LJ; *1919*: 05-15 LJ; *1920*: 02-16 LJ, 02-26 LJ; *1921*: 02-03 LJ, 02-11 LJ; *1922*: 01-06 LJ, 04-22 LJ, 05-27 LJ, 08-08 BEN, 08-19 LJ, 10-03 BEN; *1923*: 04-21 LJ, 10-20 LJ, 11-17 LJ; *1924*: 04-14 LJ, 08-16 LJ, 10-18-B LJ, 11-08 LJ, 11-29 LJ, 12-06 LJ; *1925*: 03-10 LJ, 03-28 LJ, 09-26 LJ, 10-03 LJ, 12-28 LJ; *1926*: 02-27 LJ, 03-20 LJ, 05-01 LJ, 05-15 LJ, 05-22 LJ, 05-29 LJ, 06-05 LJ, 08-07 LJ, 10-02 LJ, 10-16 LJ, 10-30 LJ, 10-30 LJ, 11-27 LJ, 12-11 LJ, 12-21 LJ, 12-24 LJ; *1927*: 01-01 LJ, 01-08 LJ, 01-15 LJ, 01-29 LJ, 02-05 LJ, 02-19 LJ, 02-26 LJ, 04-09 LJ, 04-30 LJ, 04-30 LJ, 06-18 LJ, 07-02 LJ, 07-02 LJ, 07-23 LJ, 07-30 LJ, 08-20 LJ, 09-03 LJ, 10-01 LJ, 10-29 LJ, 11-12 LJ, 11-19 LJ, 12-03 LJ, 12-24 LJ; *1928*: 01-28 LJ, 02-04 LJ, 02-11 LJ, 02-25 LJ, 03-03 LJ, 03-24 LJ, 04-07 LJ, 04-14 LJ, 04-21 LJ, 04-28 LJ, 05-19 LJ, 05-26 LJ, 06-30 LJ, 08-18 LJ, 09-08 LJ, 10-27 LJ, 11-03 LJ, 11-10 LJ, 12-06 LJ; *1929*: 01-12 LJ, 01-19 LJ, 02-04 LJ, 02-11 LJ, 02-16 LJ, 02-23 LJ.

Pubigee, Tiny Jack Pajanna (Lena Jack). See Seth Pubigee and Jim Wagon. *1919*: 05-15 LJ.

Purdawat, (Perwhat, Purdawot, Poawhat, or Putterwat), Susie (Susan). Traditional meaning of Purdawat: "without arms," Perwhat may mean "no eyes," or possibly, "blind." Her Indian name was An-zie (or Anzi Chee). Born ca. 1840. Married Charles (Chas)

Ahbuck. Susie was the mother of Mary Woonsook (b. ca. 1864, wife of Joseph Woonsook), and Idumea Toyahdook (b. Dec. 10, 1866, wife of Catch Lion Toyahdook). Susan Purdawat was listed in the 1910 census as a mother-in-law, age eighty, married three times (five children, two living), living in the household of Catch Toyahdook. When Susie died at age ninety (Dec. 22, 1928) Ottogary wrote, "She was a good church member. She was a well known all the country . . . she was older woman in our town. She left two daughter, and several grandchildren, etc. and many great grandchildren." [AICR; CCF 113732-15-SB-150; FGR; INF Parry, Mae Timbimboo; OL; USFC 1910; WASHCEM]. *1923:* 11-03 LJ; *1928:* 12-26 LJ, 12-29 LJ.

Quinney, Joseph Jr. Spoke on sugar beet culture at Agriculture Round Up. [OL]. *1914:* 01-29-B LJ.

Quinney, Mrs. Samuel. Appears to have managed the day-care facilities at the Agriculture Round Up. [OL]. *1914:* 02-03 LJ.

Quintain, Laura. From Pocatello, ID. [OL]. *1912:* 01-11 BEN.

Quipitch, Catch. See: Toyahdook, Catch.

Ramsey, Jack. From Pocatello, ID. [OL]. *1923:* 10-13 LJ, 12-08 LJ; *1925:* 11-28 LJ.

Rassmussen, Miss. School teacher from Bear River City, UT. [OL]. *1922:* 10-21 LJ.

Redcap. Ute met by Ottogary in the Uinta Basin, 1919. [OL]. *1919:* 11-10 LJ.

Redfoot, Mr. Ute met by Ottogary in the Uinta Basin, 1919. [OL]. *1919:* 11-10 LJ.

Reeve, John. From Hinckley, UT. Spoke on the dairy business at Agriculture Round Up. [OL]. *1914:* 02-07 LJ.

Rich, Dr. Physician who attended to Eliza Wongan. [OL]. *1912:* 05-23 BEN.

Richards, Pres. Malad Stake president who attended Ward Conference at Washakie. [OL]. *1912:* 03-21-A LJ.

Riter, Benjamin F. Born Aug. 31, 1859, to Levi Evans Riter and Rebecca Dilworth. Married Maria Inez Corlette July 8, 1882. Founder of Riter Bros. Rexall Drug Store in Logan. A good friend of Ottogary's, Riter was a lover of Western history with an extensive collection of Western Americana in his office. The depth of their friendship was illustrated in 1921 when Riter, on a "big medicine trip," wrote to Ottogary three times while he was away. Each promoted the other's career. Ottogary often gave space in his column to advertise Riter's store. Riter died July 21, 1925, while Ottogary was on a business trip in Wyoming and Idaho. In his next letter, Ottogary wrote, "While I was over to Logan and miss my old pal Mr. B. F. Riter, and feel sorry about him." [OL; Family History Library film 183527, p. 205, ord. 7216, Salt Lake City Temple]. *1913:* 12-18 LJ; *1915:* 01-09 LJ, 12-23 LJ; *1917:* 03-23 LJ; *1921:* 05-18 LJ; *1922:* 07-18 BEN; *1924:* 06-12 OCE; *1925:* 04-11 LJ, 09-26 LJ.

Roberts, Mr. Minister from Fort Washakie, WY. [OL]. *1925:* 08-15 LJ.

Rods, Jeff. *1924:* 05-24 LJ.

Roots, Arb. *1928:* 10-20 LJ.

Ross, Ernie Kid. Boxer from Casper, WY. [OL]. *1927:* 02-05 LJ.

Ross, Jim. Boxer. *1926-*02-13 LJ, *1926:* 02-17 LJ.

Sactlar, Ben (Saintclair). From Wyoming Reservation. [OL]. *1924:* 06-05 OCE, 07-05 LJ.

Sam (Paregosam, Parahgosam, or Parago-Sam), George P. Tribal leader. Born 1881, Washakie, UT, to Parago-Sam and Nau-Weatuts. Married Pompy-woritze (Pompy Worritch, or Pampy Woritch, b. 1870, Rich county, UT, to Perdash and No-Quida). Marriage later solemnized (Aug. 1925) in Logan Temple. Their children were Nookeyshem (b. July 24, 1904, Washakie, UT, d. Jan. 30, 1916) and Rose (b. Oct. 13, 1906, Washakie, UT, d. June 17, 1919). George Sam was a farmer of grain who lived in an aboriginal dwelling. He and Ottogary spent considerable time working for the benefit of the Northwestern Shoshone and to maintain positive relations with other Shoshone groups. Sam was probably a descendent (possibly a son) of Pahragoosahd, one of the Shoshone signers of the Box Elder Treaty of 1863. [BEN Aug. 6, 1925; CCF 113732-15-SB-150; FGR; INF Parry, Mae Timbimboo; KAPPLER; ROAD, 77, 121; USFC 1910]. *1912*: 01-30 LJ; *1914*: 01-01 LJ, 01-15 BEN, 07-14 LJ; *1915*: 12-23 LJ; *1916*: 01-29 LJ, 02-03 BEN, 10-21 LJ; *1918*: 01-24 LJ, 01-24 LJ; *1919*: 03-13 LJ, 06-26 LJ, 07-26 LJ; *1920*: 12-24 LJ; *1921*: 01-10 LJ, 01-22 LJ, 02-03 LJ, 12-08 LJ; *1922*: 02-25 LJ, 03-18-A LJ, 04-22 LJ, 04-29 LJ, 05-20 LJ, 05-27 LJ, 06-03 LJ, 06-06 BEN, 06-30 BEN, 08-12 LJ, 08-19 LJ, 09-19 BEN, 09-23 LJ, 09-28 LJ, 10-21 LJ, 11-04-A LJ, 11-04-B LJ, 11-14 BEN, 11-18 LJ, 12-15 BEN, 12-30-A LJ; *1923*: 03-17 LJ, 04-02 LJ, 05-05 LJ, 06-16 LJ, 06-23 LJ, 06-30 LJ, 07-07 LJ, 12-08 LJ, 12-08 LJ, 12-24 LJ; *1924*: 02-09 LJ, 02-23 LJ, 02-28 OCE, 04-26 LJ, 05-03 LJ, 08-23 LJ; *1925*: 01-17-A LJ, 01-17-B LJ, 02-17 LJ, 02-21 LJ, 03-28 LJ, 05-09 LJ, 05-16 LJ, 06-02 LJ, 06-06 LJ, 09-12 LJ, 10-03 LJ, 10-06 BEJ, 11-07 LJ; *1926*: 04-03 LJ, 04-17 LJ, 06-19 LJ, 07-26 LJ, 09-18 LJ, 10-23 LJ, 11-27 LJ, 12-11 LJ, 12-21 LJ, 12-24 LJ; *1927*: 02-05 LJ, 02-12 LJ, 06-18 LJ, 08-20 LJ, 09-17 LJ, 10-29 LJ, 12-03 LJ, 12-24 LJ; *1928*: 03-03 LJ, 03-12 LJ, 03-17 LJ, 04-07 LJ, 11-10 LJ, 12-26 LJ.

Sam, Mrs. George P. See Sam, George P. *1908*: 02-06-B TT, *1922*: 03-18-B LJ, 03-25 LJ, 08-12 LJ; *1925*: 04-11 LJ; *1926*: 03-27 LJ, 04-03 LJ.

Samboo (or Somboo). From Bannock Creek, ID. Uncle to Mrs. Thomas Pabawena. [OL]. *1927*: 09-17 LJ; *1928*: 09-22 LJ, 10-20 LJ, 12-20 LJ.

Samie. An "old pal" of Ottogary's from Nevada. [OL]. *1920*: 10-23 LJ.

Sandvattes Bros. Sold hay to Washakie residents. [OL]. *1920*: 02-16 LJ.

Saylor, E. (Albert). From Seattle, Washington. Saylor wanted to purchase Indian land. *1917*: 01-18 LJ; *1918*: 03-19 LJ, 06-01 LJ.

Scobby, Albert. Nephew of George P. Sam. *1928*: 03-12 LJ.

Sherman, Mr. Probably editor of the *Tremont Times*. [OL]. *1906*: 08-23 TT, 08-30 TT, 09-20 TT.

Shippack, Mrs. *1923*: 04-21 LJ.

Shoemaker, Dr. F. Sent by Indian Affairs Office to provide eye treatments for Shoshone at Washakie, Deep Creek, and possibly other locations. His assistant was Philene Hall from Portage, UT. [OL]. *1915*: 12-23 LJ; *1916*: 02-03 BEN.

Shorty, Bill. From Nevada. [OL]. *1920*: 10-23 LJ.

Shoshone Bob. From White Rock Reservation, UT. Visited his daughter at Fort Washakie, WY. [OL]. *1925*: 08-22 LJ, 08-29 LJ.

Shuty, Any. From Plymouth, UT. Brought steam thresher to Washakie. [OL]. *1922*: 09-01 BEN.

Skidmore, Charlie. Superintendent of schools who visited Washakie Day School. [OL]. *1929*: 02-16 LJ.

Skidmore, George W. Manager of the Union Knitting Mill in Logan. [OL]. *1912*: 04-02 LJ; *1922*: 05-06 LJ.

Smiling Sun, Miss. An Indian girl who competed in a dogsled race. Ottogary hoped she would defeat the Idaho boys. [OL]. *1924*: 02-21 OCE.

Smith, David A. Spoke on getting clean milk to cities at Agriculture Round Up. [OL]. *1914*: 02-07 LJ.

Smith, Charley. Brought a steam thresher into Washakie. [OL]. *1916*: 08-22 LJ.

Smith, George A. Apostle of the LDS Church. Visited at Garland Stake Conference. [OL]. *1922*: 03-18-A LJ.

Smith, Mr. From Ogden. [OL]. *1927*: 06-18 LJ; *1928*: 10-20 LJ, 11-17 LJ.

Smooks, Walter. From Bannock Creek, ID. [OL]. *1928*: 07-07 LJ.

Smoot, Reed. U.S. senator (Republican) from Utah. Born 1862, died 1941. Served from 1903 to 1933. Ottogary met him at an LDS Church service while in Washington, D.C. [OL; SENATEUS]. *1921*: 03-22 LJ.

Soaker, John. Boxer. [OL]. *1926:* 03-13 LJ.

Soldier, Martin. From Deep Creek Reservation, UT. Spent his early childhood at Washakie. [OL]. *1927:* 01-22 LJ, 01-29 LJ, 04-30 LJ.

Soquitch, Wren. According to Ottogary, this individual died sometime between late 1906 and early 1907. [OL]. *1907:* 01-31 TT.

Spry, Wm. Served two terms as governor of Utah (1909–1917). Born Jan. 11, 1864, Windsor, Berkshire, England. Gave a welcoming address at the Agriculture Round Up and discussed cattle raising. [OL; WARRUM]. *1914:* 02-03 LJ; *1921:* 03-22 LJ.

Stayner, Ralph. Ford dealer from whom several Washakie residents purchased automobiles. [OL]. *1922:* 05-20 LJ; *1926:* 08-28 LJ.

Steed, George. From Fielding, UT. [OL]. *1923:* 06-30 LJ; *1924:* 01-19 LJ; *1927:* 11-19 LJ.

Steed, Harry. *1922:* 06-06 BEN, 09-05 BEN.

Steed, Jim. *1927:* 11-19 LJ.

Steel, Ell (Al). From Nevada. [OL]. *1920:* 10-23 LJ; *1928:* 04-07 LJ.

Steele brothers. Boxers. [OL]. *1926:* 05-08 LJ.

Stevens, Frank. Spoke on market cooperation at Agriculture Round Up. [OL]. *1914:* 01-31 LJ.

Stoney, Harry. From Logan, sold baseball uniforms in Washakie. [OL]. *1921:* 02-11 LJ.

Stueler, Wm. New convert to the LDS faith, Ottogary met him while in New York. [OL]. *1921:* 03-25 BEN.

Swab, Mr. Indian. Baptist (or Presbyterian) minister on a mission at Owyhee, NV. [OL]. *1923:* 08-11 LJ.

Taba, Mr. Grandfather of George Moody of Skull Valley. Taba (or Tab-ba) was a great warrior in the early days. He made peace treaties with U.S. government at Tooele, UT, 1863. [OL; see Madsen's *The Shoshoni Frontier and the Bear River Massacre*, 66]. *1920:* 01-02 LJ.

Talbot, Doab. Boxer. [OL]. *1928:* 07-07 LJ.

Terna Pitch (or Te na-pa-ch), Miss. Da Na Pa ch, means "man." Ottogary notes in 1914 that she was the oldest woman in town. [INF Parry, Mae Timbimboo; OL]. *1914:* 01-15 BEN.

Thomas, (Thomas Bros). Farmers. Seth Pubigee made a peach contract with them. [OL]. *1922:* 08-19 LJ.

Thomas, Pres. Spoke on women and work at Agriculture Round Up. [OL]. *1914:* 02-10 LJ.

Thompson, Jim. Possibly father, or uncle, of Nellie Thompson Pabawena. [OL]. *1928:* 05-26 LJ, 06-02 LJ.

Thompson, Johnny (or John). Born ca. 1850. Married Mary (b. ca. 1870). Thompson was the son of Poongorah (or Po-on-go-sah), one of the signers of the Treaty of Ruby Valley in 1863. A medicine man from Wells, NV, Thompson practiced his healing art for a time in Washakie. [KAPPLER; Edna B. Patterson, Louise A. Ulph, and Victor Goodwin, *Nevada's Northeast Frontier* (Sparks, NV: Western Printing and Publishing Co., 1969), 34]; OL; USFC 1920, NV, Elko, Wells Precinct]. *1926:* 06-19 LJ; *1928:* 09-01 LJ, 09-01 LJ, 09-08 LJ, 09-15 LJ, 09-22 LJ, 11-03 LJ, 11-17 LJ; *1929:* 01-12 LJ, 02-11 LJ, 02-16 LJ, 03-09 LJ, 03-20 LJ.

Thompson, Mr. Used to play baseball with Ottogary. [OL]. *1926:* 06-05 LJ.

Thompson, Miss Mone. *1929:* 01-12 LJ.

Thornton, William. Bought cedar posts cut by Washakie men. [OL]. *1922:* 04-29 LJ.

Thornley, Wm. Spoke on preparing horse's feet for shoes at Agriculture Round Up. [OL]. *1914:* 02-03 LJ.

Timbimboo (Timpimboo, or Timboo, and other variations), Amy. Traditional meaning of Timbimboo: "rock writer." Born 1893 to Don Carlos Hootchew (b. 1870, Logan, UT, md. Annie Feb. 3, 1915, d. May 3, 1898, Washakie, UT) and Annie Cah Mase Vah (b. Sept. 3, 1871, Elko, NV, d. June 28, 1925). Married Moroni Timbimboo Nov. 29, 1910. Amy died May 1999. See Moroni Timbimboo. [CCF 113732-15-SB-150; INF Parry, Mae Timbimboo; MTPFHR; OL; VRML]. *1927:* 07-23 LJ.

(Timbimboo), Frank Warner. Also known as Beshup "Red Clay" Timbimboo. Born ca. 1860, to Sagwitch "Speaker, or Orator," and Dadabaychee, "The Sun" (Tanlabitche, or Tan-lob-Itche). His mother was killed at the Bear River Massacre, Jan. 29, 1863. Young Beshup was sold by his uncle, One Eyed Tom, to the Warner family, who raised him as Frank Warner. Frank had two half-brothers, Yeager Timbimboo and Soquitch Timbimboo, who were living at Washakie. Frank married Edna Davis. Census of 1880 notes Frank's occupation as school teacher. He died Jan. 1919. [SAG, 239; INF Parry, Mae Timbimboo; OL; USFC 1880 Utah, Box Elder, Plymouth Precinct]. *1912:* 03-28 LJ, 03-30 LJ; *1925:* 09-18 BEJ, 09-19 LJ.

Timbimboo, Joana L. (Joanna). Born ca. 1912, to Moroni Timbimboo and Amy Hootchew. Joana spent some time at the Chemawa School at Forest Grove, OR. [CCF 113732-15-SB-150; OL]. *1927:* 01-29 LJ, 02-05 LJ.

Timbimboo, Moroni. Born 1888, UT, to Yeager (Yeagah, Yeaga, or Yeahgat) Timbimboo (b. 1848, WY) and Yampitch (or Yampatch) Wongan (b. 1863, d. June 24, 1929). Moroni married Phoebe Shoshonitze in the summer of 1906. They had one daughter, Edna (b. Jan. 1907). Moroni and Phoebe later divorced. He then married Amy Hootchew, Nov. 29, 1910, when he was 21 and Amy 17. Amy's mother, Annie Hootchew, consented to the marriage. Children of Moroni and Amy were Joana L. (Joanna, b. ca. 1912), Hazel Evaline (b. 1914), Moroni Jr. (b. 1916, d. 1916), Mary I. (b. 1917, d. 1918), Mae (b. 1919), Frankie (b. 1922), Kimball (b. 1924, d. 1924), Grace (b. 1925), and Katherine Ivy (or Catherine Ivy, b. 1927). [CCF 113732-15-SB-150; IGI; INF Parry, Mae Timbimboo; OL; WASHCEM; WWROM]. *1907:* 01-31 TT; *1912:* 01-11 BEN; *1914:* 01-29-A LJ; *1916:* 05-23 LJ, 11-11 LJ, 12-08 BEN; *1919:* 05-15 LJ; *1920:* 11-13 LJ; *1921:* 09-05 LJ, 10-10 LJ, 12-30 LJ; *1922:* 01-06 LJ, 05-20 LJ, 06-06 BEN, 10-21 LJ, 11-04-A LJ, 11-18 LJ, 12-02 LJ, 12-09 LJ, 12-15 BEN; *1923:* 02-06 BEN, 04-02 LJ, 04-07 LJ, 10-06 LJ, 12-08 LJ; *1924:* 01-12 LJ, 01-10 OCE, 03-08 LJ, 03-08 LJ, 04-14 LJ, 06-05 OCE, 06-12 OCE, 08-16 LJ, 08-23 LJ; *1925:* 03-10 LJ, 03-27 BEJ, 06-29 LJ, 10-24 LJ, 12-28 LJ; *1926:* 01-16 LJ, 01-23 LJ, 01-30 LJ, 05-15 LJ, 07-31 LJ, 08-14 LJ, 08-21 LJ, 08-28 LJ, 09-04 LJ, 09-18 LJ, 10-23 LJ, 12-24 LJ; *1927:* 01-01 LJ, 01-15 LJ, 01-22 LJ, 01-29 LJ, 02-26 LJ, 03-19 LJ, 06-18 LJ, 07-23 LJ, 07-30 LJ, 09-03 LJ, 10-29 LJ, 12-24 LJ, 12-24 LJ; *1928:* 02-04 LJ, 03-03 LJ, 03-12 LJ, 04-04 LJ, 05-19 LJ, 06-30 LJ, 09-08 LJ, 09-22 LJ, 11-10 LJ, 12-06 LJ; *1929:* 02-11 LJ, 03-09 LJ.

Timbimboo, Miss/Mrs. Moroni (Amy, or Eving). See Timbimboo, Amy. *1912:* 01-11 BEN, *1918:* 03-19 LJ, *1920:* 01-02 LJ.

Timbimboo, Mr. *1912:* 04-06 LJ.

Timbimboo, Phoebe. See Timbimboo, Moroni. *1907:* 01-31 TT.

Timbimboo, Soquitch ("Many Buffaloes," or Tuinipucci, "Young Man"). Born ca. 1846, Blue Creek area, Box Elder County, UT, to Sagwitch, "Speaker, or Orator," and Egypitcheeadaday, "Coyote's Niece" (or An ne sua). Sealed to To-an-cy (Towange, Twenge, or Tooange, b. 1846, d. 1935) Apr. 5, 1875. Also sealed to Ahdzeek Dec. 7, 1882. One child listed for Soquitch and Towange: Phoebe (b. Dec. 1886, d. ca. 1900). Soquitch and his wife spent a lot of time at Ottogary's home in Elwood. When Soquitch died in 1927, Ottogary noted that his uncle, Soquitch, had died. This relationship is unclear, but it may be through Towange. In 1915, Jones Neaman (son of Mose Neaman) was living with Soquitch and Towange and was listed as Soquitch's grandson. [CCF 113732-15-SB-150; INF Parry, Mae Timbimboo; OL; SAG p. 237; USFC 1900; WASHCEM]. *1907:* 01-10 TT, 05-09 TT, 09-19 TT; *1909:* 06-15 LJ; *1910:* 01-22 LJ; *1911:* 09-12 LJ, 12-21 BEN; *1912:* 03-28 LJ; *1913:* 02-13 BEN, 08-07 LJ, 08-14-B BEN; *1916:* 05-23 LJ, 07-18 LJ, 08-15 BEN, 09-12 BEN; *1922:* 08-08 BEN, 09-05 BEN, 09-23 LJ, 12-15 BEN; *1923:* 02-10 LJ, 04-07 LJ, 06-23 LJ, 10-06 LJ, 12-24 LJ; *1924:* 05-17 LJ, 05-24 LJ, 07-05

LJ, 08-16 LJ, 08-23 LJ, 09-27-B LJ; *1925*: 03-27 BEJ, 04-18 LJ, 05-16 LJ, 05-22 BEJ, 06-06
LJ, 06-20 LJ, 06-23 BEJ, 06-29 LJ, 09-18 BEJ, 10-03 LJ; *1926*: 01-11 LJ, 01-16 LJ, 02-06 LJ,
02-13 LJ, 03-13 LJ, 04-10 LJ, 05-08 LJ, 05-15 LJ, 06-05 LJ, 09-04 LJ, 12-21 LJ; *1927*: 01-01
LJ, 01-15 LJ, 01-29 LJ, 02-12 LJ, 02-19 LJ, 03-19 LJ, 03-26 LJ, 03-26 LJ.

Timbimboo, (Mrs. Soquitch) Towange. *1907*: 04-25 TT; *1926*: 01-23 LJ.

Timbimboo, Yeager (Yeagah, Niegah, or Taputsi, "Little Cottontail"). Born ca. 1848, Green
   River area, WY, to Sagwitch "Speaker, or Orator," and Hewechee, "Mourning Dove" (or
   Ew-wach). Married Yampitch (Yampatch, or Yam-pits-zah, b. 1865, Brigham City, to
   James Wongan and Lucy Honevah or Horace). Yeager and Yampitch were sealed Feb.
   10, 1886. Among their children were Moroni (b. 1888), So-go-re-ets (b. Sept. 1892),
   Nellie (b. Oct. 1894), Tomy (b. Oct. 1898). The 1910 census says the couple lived in an
   aboriginal dwelling and had eleven children, only one of whom was living. His occupation was farm laborer, grain farmer. Others listed in the household were Lucy (ninety
   years old, mother-in-law), Yogoboy (relationship looks like aunt), eighty-year-old widow
   from NV, Edna (three-year-old granddaughter [dau. of Moroni and Phoebe]). [CCF
   113732-15-SB-150; IGI; INF Parry, Mae Timbimboo; SAG p. 238; SLNGS LV; USFC
   1900, 1910]. *1909*: 07-27 LJ; *1911*: 05-25 BEN, 07-13 LJ, 09-12 LJ, 10-12 BEN; *1912*:
   03-28 LJ, 04-16 LJ; *1913*: 01-16 LJ, 01-16 BEN; *1915*: 12-23 LJ; *1916*: 08-15 BEN,
   12-08 BEN; *1920*: 02-26 LJ, 10-20 LJ; *1922*: 04-29 LJ, 05-20 LJ, 06-03 LJ, 08-08
   BEN, 12-09 LJ, 12-15 BEN, 12-30-A LJ; *1923*: 01-06 LJ, 02-06 BEN, 02-10 LJ, 02-24
   LJ; *1924*: 01-10 OCE, 04-14 LJ, 09-20 LJ, 09-27-A LJ, 09-27-B LJ; *1925*: 02-02 LJ,
   04-18 LJ, 09-18 BEJ, 09-19 LJ; *1926*: 02-06 LJ, 09-04 LJ, 09-18 LJ, 12-21 LJ; *1927*:
   01-22 LJ, 02-12 LJ, 03-19 LJ, 09-17 LJ, 10-01 LJ; *1928*: 02-11 LJ, 05-26 LJ, 06-02 LJ,
   09-01 LJ, 09-22 LJ; *1929*: 02-11 LJ, 03-09 LJ.

Tinchee, [?]. *1927*: 10-01 LJ.

To-de-neda, Mr. Reporting from Fort Washakie, WY, Ottogary notes To-de-neda was killed
   by lightning. [OL]. *1925*: 08-22 LJ.

Tommy, Annies. Born 1871. Married Topsy (b. 1871). Their children were Mishie (Mary,
   b. 1900) and Canada (son, b. 1909). Ottogary spent considerable time with Tommy and
   traveled with him to Washington, D.C., in 1915. [AICR Goshute of Ibapah 1919 &
   1920; OL]. *1913*: 03-06 BEN; *1915*: 02-26 BEN; *1925*: 07-18 LJ, 08-01 LJ, 08-04 BEJ,
   11-06 BEJ, 11-07 LJ; *1928*: 02-11 LJ; *1929*: 02-16 LJ, 02-23 LJ.

Tommy, Clyde. Participant in a church meeting at Deep Creek. [OL]. *1913*: 04-24 BEN.

Tommy, Harry. Participant in a church meeting at Deep Creek. [OL]
1913: 04-24 BEN.

Tommy, Johny. Participant in a church meeting at Deep Creek. [OL]. *1913*: 04-24 BEN.

Tommy, Kenniatra. Participant in a church meeting at Deep Creek. [OL]. *1913*: 04-24 BEN.

Tommy, Nessia. Participant in a church meeting at Deep Creek. [OL]. *1913*: 04-24 BEN.

Tommy, Rachel. Participant in a church meeting at Deep Creek. [OL]. *1913*: 04-24 BEN.

Tomock (Timock, or Temoke), George. Traditional meaning of Tomock: "rope." Father-in-
   law to George Mose. [INF Parry, Mae Timbimboo; OL]. *1911*: 11-30 BEN; *1916*: 07-18
   LJ; *1917*: 11-24 LJ; *1922*: 09-28 LJ; *1924*: 09-27-B LJ; *1925*: 02-17 LJ, 03-28 LJ, 10-03
   LJ, 10-06 BEJ; *1926*: 09-04 LJ, 12-11 LJ; *1927*: 12-03 LJ; *1928*: 01-28 LJ, 05-19 LJ,
   06-02 LJ, 09-22 LJ.

Tomock, Mrs. George. *1928*: 02-25 LJ, 09-08 LJ, 09-15 LJ.

Tomock, Irene (Miss). *1927*: 12-03 LJ; *1928*: 09-15 LJ, 11-03 LJ.

Tomock, John (Johnny). Possibly from Idaho Reservation. Born ca. 1865. Married Annie
   Deweywatz (b. ca. 1865, mother of Lucy and Willie Neaman; see Neaman, Mose). The
   child of John Tomock and Annie Deweywatz was Kingbury (b. ca. 1905). In 1915, Lucy
   Neaman Drinks was living with this family. She was married to a man named Drinks

from Fort Hall, ID, and was eighteen years old at the time. [CCF 113732-15-SB-150; WWROM]. *1913:* 06-12 BEN; *1916:* 05-23 LJ; *1920:* 10-20 LJ.

Tonhee, Mr. Reporting from Fort Hall, Ottogary notes a rabbit hunting venture with Tonhee. [OL]. *1926:* 01-02 LJ.

Tonnywhom, Mr. Reporting from Elko, NV, Ottogary said Tonnywhom was a long-time Indian interpreter. [OL]. *1923:* 09-15 LJ.

Toogan, Bond. Speaker at a church meeting in Deep Creek. [OL]. *1913:* 04-24 BEN.

Toogan, Gus. Presented a reading at a church meeting in Deep Creek. [OL]. *1913:* 04-24 BEN.

Toogan, Twiney. Recites first three verses of "America" at a church meeting in Deep Creek. [OL]. *1913:* 04-24 BEN.

Tootiaina, Harry Dixon. See Dixon, Harry.

Tospanguitch, George. Traditional meaning of Tospanguitch: "white fish." Born ca. 1845, ID. According to 1910 census he was married six times, twenty years in present marriage to Annie (b. ca. 1865, NV). Her marrige to George was her second. The couple had three children, only one still living. George was a farmer of grain and beets. He was listed as Bannock, not Shoshone. [CCF 113732-15-SB-150; INF Parry, Mae Timbimboo; USFC 1910]. *1907:* 09-12 TT; *1909:* 05-29 LJ; *1916:* 08-22 LJ; *1917:* 11-24 LJ; *1919:* 05-15 LJ, 07-26 LJ; *1922:* 04-08 LJ; *1923:* 04-02 LJ, 04-28 LJ; *1924:* 01-12 LJ, 02-09 LJ, 07-05 LJ, 09-27-B LJ; *1925:* 02-17 LJ, 05-02 LJ, 05-16 LJ, 05-23 LJ, 09-26 LJ; *1926:* 10-23 LJ, 12-04 LJ; *1927:* 06-18 LJ, 07-02 LJ, 07-09 LJ, 11-12 LJ.

Tovier, Jim. See Dioves, Jim.

Towhee, Mr. From near Tah-hee Station, Idaho. [OL]. *1927:* 04-16 LJ, 11-26 LJ.

Toyahdook (Tire-took, Toar-rook, Dortook, or Tooksook), Catch (or Ketch) Lion. Traditional meaning of Toyahdook: "mountain lion." Catch Impitch, Catch Quipitch (or Queyembitch), and Catch Lion/Toyahdook were the same person. Ottogary's cursive "Q" was probably misread as an "I," hence Impitch. Catch was born Jan. 25, 1870, Logan, UT, to Toyahdook (from NV) and Pan-Zoa-Vitche (from OR). Married Iduma (or Idumea, b. Dec. 10, 1866, Paradise, UT, to Sauk-zia-yimaka [or So-p-ky-ge; this individual may also be known as Charles Ahbuck] and Susan Purdawat). Catch and Iduma married ca. 1892. The couple had no children, though in 1928 they adopted Ed Wagon (b. June 17, 1916, Cache, UT, to Jim Wagon and Teannie Jack). Ed died Oct. 3, 1935. Catch was a farmer of grain and beets. In 1910 his mother-in-law, Susan Purdawat (eighty years old), was living with his family. In 1923, he was called to be a counselor to Bishop George M. Ward in the Washakie Ward bishopric. Catch died Dec. 18, 1948, his wife, Iduma, died Aug. 23, 1940. [FGR; INF Menta, Alene, and Parry, Mae Timbimboo; MTPFHR; NOSHOS, 100; OL; USFC 1910]. *1917:* 11-24 LJ; *1920:* 01-02 LJ; *1921:* 01-22 LJ; *1922:* 03-18-A LJ, 04-08 LJ, 04-22 LJ, 12-30-B LJ; *1924:* 01-12 LJ, 07-05 LJ, 11-08 LJ, 11-29 LJ; *1925:* 02-02 LJ, 09-12 LJ, 09-18 BEJ, 09-19 LJ, 09-26 LJ; *1926:* 01-02 LJ, 01-11 LJ, 01-16 LJ, 01-30 LJ, 04-03 LJ, 04-17 LJ, 05-15 LJ, 07-26 LJ, 07-31 LJ, 08-07 LJ, 08-14 LJ, 08-21 LJ, 10-02 LJ, 10-16 LJ, 10-30 LJ, 12-04 LJ, 12-11 LJ, 12-21 LJ; *1927:* 07-30 LJ, 08-20 LJ, 10-29 LJ; *1928:* 02-25 LJ, 03-03 LJ, 03-17 LJ, 03-24 LJ, 04-07 LJ, 04-21 LJ, 04-28 LJ, 05-19 LJ, 05-26 LJ, 06-02 LJ, 08-13 LJ, 09-01 LJ, 09-08 LJ, 09-15 LJ, 10-13 LJ, 10-20 LJ, 10-27 LJ, 11-03 LJ, 12-29 LJ; *1929:* 01-19 LJ, 02-23 LJ.

Toyahdook, Eddie. See Wagon, Eddie.

Trim, Joe. Born 1851. Married Susie (b. 1861). [AICR Ibapah]. *1919:* 07-26 LJ.

Tyboatz (Tyboats, or Tybots), Thomas. Traditional meaning of Tyboatz: "white man." Born 1870. Married Phoebe Hootchew (b. 1881, to William and Julia Hootchew). Children: Sylvia (b. 1899), May (b. 1904), Lilly (or Lily, b. 1906), Martha (b. 1909), Vera (b. 1916). Ottogary notes that a baby boy was also born Nov. 1916, but he died after a few days. [CCF 113732-15-SB-150; INF Parry, Mae Timbimboo; OL]. *1914:* 01-15 BEN; *1916:* 05-23 LJ, 12-08 BEN; *1921:* 10-31 LJ.

Tyboatz, Mrs. See Tyboatz, Thomas. *1907:* 03-28 TT; *1919:* 03-13 LJ.

Tyler, Mr. Schools official who visited Washakie Day School with Superintendent Charlie Skidmore. [OL]. *1929:* 02-16 LJ.

Valentine, Mr. *1925:* 01-17-B LJ.

Wagon (Wagoner or Wagen), Eddie (Ed). Born June 17, 1916 to Jim Wagon and Teannie (or Lena) Jack. Adopted by Catch Toyahdook 1928. Eddie died Oct. 3, 1935. [FGR; INF Parry, Mae Timbimboo; OL]. *1926:* 03-27 LJ, 04-03 LJ; *1928:* 01-28 LJ, 03-03 LJ, 03-17 LJ, 04-07 LJ, 09-08 LJ, 11-17 LJ.

Wagon (Wagoner, or Wagen), Jim (or Jim John). Called Jim John Wagon (b. 1898, Box Elder, UT), his father was also listed as Jim Wagon. This would explain why Ottogary reports later of "Jim" and "John" Wagon. This was apparently the same person. He married Teanie (Tenie, Tena, or Lena) Jack (b. June 10, 1902, Box Elder, UT, to Jim Jack and Ivai Pojenney Woonsook). Their children were all born at Washakie, UT, except for Walter Roy, who was born in Riverside, UT. They were Ed (Eddie, or Eddy, b. June 17, 1916, d. Oct. 3, 1935), unnamed daughter (b. ca. 1917), Johnson (b. Dec. 10, 1907, d. Nov. 16, 1918), Walter Roy (b. Oct. 21, 1919, d. Mar. 22, 1922), Ralph (b. June 6, 1921), Lavern (b. Jan. 16, 1923), Herman (b. Sept. 13, 1924, d. Oct. 17, 1925), Milton (b. May 7, 1926, d. 1947), Edith Lydia (b. Feb. 14, 1928), Eleanor (b. June 17, 1929, d. June 23, 1929), and Josephine (b. May 6, 1930, d. May, 16, 1930). [AICR; FGR; INF Parry, Mae Timbimboo; OL]. *1918:* 01-24 LJ; *1922:* 04-01 LJ, 04-08 LJ, 05-27 LJ, 07-11 BEN, 07-18 BEN, 08-08 BEN; *1923:* 04-14 LJ, 04-28 LJ, 06-16 LJ; *1924:* 06-12 OCE, 07-05 LJ, 09-27-B LJ, 12-27 LJ; *1925:* 01-17-A LJ, 03-10 LJ, 04-18 LJ, 05-16 LJ, 06-06 LJ, 06-13 LJ, 07-06 LJ, 08-01 LJ, 08-22 LJ, 09-05 LJ, 11-06 BEJ; *1926:* 01-16 LJ, 01-30 LJ, 04-03 LJ, 05-22 LJ, 06-05 LJ, 08-21 LJ, 10-23 LJ, 10-30 LJ, 11-27 LJ, 12-21 LJ; *1927:* 02-05 LJ, 06-18 LJ, 10-29 LJ, 11-26 LJ, 12-24 LJ; *1928:* 02-04 LJ, 03-17 LJ, 04-07 LJ, 04-14 LJ, 04-21 LJ, 04-28 LJ, 05-19 LJ, 05-26 LJ, 06-02 LJ, 08-18 LJ, 09-22 LJ, 10-20 LJ, 11-17 LJ, 12-26 LJ, 12-29 LJ, 12-29 LJ; *1929:* 02-11 LJ, 03-20 LJ.

Wagon, Roger. From Fort Washakie, WY. [OL]. *1925:* 09-05 LJ

Wah-ah-gun-to (or Wah-Hah-Gun-Ta). Ottogary reported on a Blackfoot man who was said to be 131 years old, the oldest man in the world. [OL]. *1913:* 01-23 BEN.

Walker, Moody. From Skull Valley, UT, Goshute Reservation. [OL]. *1912:* 05-23 BEN, 05-25 LJ.

War Bonnet, Mr. From Idaho Reservation. [OL]. *1922:* 12-30-B LJ; *1923:* 01-06 LJ, 10-06 LJ; *1925:* 10-03 LJ.

Ward, George M. Bishop of Washakie Ward from 1902 to 1929. [MALADSTKHST]. *1907:* 04-04 TT, 06-06 TT; *1909:* 06-15 LJ; *1910:* 02-15 LJ; *1912:* 03-21-A LJ, 05-23 BEN, 05-25 LJ, 09-12 LJ; *1913:* 01-02 LJ, 01-09 LJ, 02-08 LJ, 06-10 LJ, 08-14-B BEN, 12-18 LJ; *1916:* 01-29 LJ; *1919:* 03-13 LJ; *1920:* 02-26 LJ; *1922:* 04-08 LJ, 04-22 LJ; *1923:* 10-20 LJ, 12-08 LJ; *1924:* 04-14 LJ, 05-03 LJ, 05-24 LJ, 06-19 OCE, 08-16 LJ, 10-18-B LJ; *1925:* 03-10 LJ, 03-27 BEJ, 03-28 LJ, 04-14 BEJ, 04-25 LJ, 10-16 BEJ; *1926:* 02-06 LJ, 04-10 LJ; *1927:* 02-19 LJ, 03-26 LJ, 12-24 LJ; *1928:* 03-03 LJ, 09-01 LJ, 09-01 LJ, 11-10 LJ, 12-26 LJ, 12-29 LJ.

Ward, John M. Son of George M. Ward. [OL]. *1924:* 04-14 LJ.

Ward, Moroni. Father of George M. Ward. Moroni was bishop of the Washakie Ward from 1890 to 1902. Ottogary noted that he taught the Indians how to farm, worked among them for forty years, was a great friend to the Indian, and was also an Indian interpreter. He died Mar. 1927. [MALADSTKHST; OL]. *1916:* 10-21 LJ; *1927:* 02-19 LJ, 02-26 LJ, 03-26 LJ.

Ward, Miss Vida. School teacher at Washakie Day School. She taught about twenty children. [OL]. *1922: 12-30-A* LJ; *1923: 05-05* LJ.

Ward, Miss (Vida?). *1926: 12-24* LJ.

Warner, Frank. See (Timbimboo), Frank Warner.

Warner, Mr. From Willard, UT. [OL]. *1925: 09-18* BEJ.

Warner, Wayne. Cousin of Moroni Timbimboo. [OL]. *1924: 08-16* LJ; *1926: 01-23* LJ.

Washakie, Chief. Chief of Eastern Shoshone. [OL]. *1925: 01-24* LJ.

Washington, George (Western Shoshone). Born ca. 1853, NV. Married Sallie W. (b. ca. 1873, NV). The 1910 census notes the couple had been married seven years and had three children, all still living. The record lists six individuals living at the residence, besides George and Sallie. Of these, two were grandsons: John Adams (b. ca. 1882), and Major Washington (b. ca. 1896). The others were Frank Fish (age forty, nephew), Maggie (Fish? age fifty, possibly step niece), Harry Marsh (age twenty-seven, visitor), and Battle Mountain Sam (age twenty-eight, possibly servant). George's occupation was stock farmer. [USFC 1910 Nevada, Elko, Duck Valley Indian Reservation]. *1923: 07-14* LJ, *07-28* LJ.

Washington, George. U.S. President. *1921: 03-25* BEN; *1923: 03-03* LJ.

Welling, M. (Milton) H. Utah congressman seen by Ottogary during a trip to Washington, D.C. [OL]. *1921: 03-22* LJ.

Wells, John. From East Portage, UT. [OL]. *1922: 04-29* LJ; *1923: 03-17* LJ.

West, Frank. Born ca. 1845, NV. Married to Satonsip (or Teahtonsip, b. ca. 1855, NV). The couple had been married for ten years at the 1910 census (both had been married previously). No children were listed, though a granddaughter, Eva (b. ca. 1899) was living with them. Frank was a grain farmer. According to Ottogary, West was killed by an automobile in Oct. 1927. [CCF 113732-15-SB-150; OL; USFC 1910]. *1912: 01-30* LJ, *03-02* LJ; *1916: 05-23* LJ, *06-24* LJ; *1927: 10-22* LJ.

Whaney, Tomy. Born and raised in Utah (probably Washakie), Whaney died at Elko, Nevada. He was a cousin to Susie Highyou. [OL]. *1926: 01-16* LJ.

Wheelon, Mr. Spoke on the Bear River Valley before the Great Canal at Agriculture Round Up. [OL]. *1914: 01-31* LJ.

White, Dr. Doctor at Tremonton Hospital. [OL]. *1929: 01-19* LJ, *02-04* LJ, *02-23* LJ.

White, Jim. From Owyhee Reservation, NV, a friend of Henry Woonsook. [OL]. *1922: 03-18-A* LJ, *03-18-B* LJ, *05-27* LJ, *08-08* BEN.

Whitney, Samuel. Samuel A. Whitney was born Nov. 10, 1840, Palmyra, OH, to Alonzo Wells Whitney and Henrietta Keyes. Sam married Fanny Mariah Oct. 18, 1863 (marriage solemnized in Salt Lake Endowment House Oct. 29, 1867). Sam took a second wife, Polly Ann (or Pauline) Campbell Jan. 27, 1878. Sam was an Indian interpreter and was referred to by Ottogary as an old friend. [OL; SAW]. *1912: 03-14* LJ, *03-21-B* LJ; *1922: 05-06* LJ.

Whitt, F. F. From Lewiston, UT. [OL]. *1916: 09-12* LJ.

Widtsoe, John A. President of the Utah Agricultural College, Logan, from 1907 to 1916. He served as president of the University of Utah from 1916 to 1921. In 1921 he was appointed as an apostle of the LDS Church. Spoke on irrigation at Agriculture Round Up. [OL; Widtsoe, John A., *In a Sunlit Land: The Autobiography of John A. Widtsoe* (Salt Lake City: Deseret News Press, 1953), 88, 98, 163]. *1914: 01-31* LJ, *02-10* LJ.

Widtsoe, Mrs. J. A. Wife of John A. Widtsoe. Spoke on proper dress for young girls at Agriculture Round Up. [OL]. *1914: 02-03* LJ.

William, Mr. It is unclear as to whether William is the first or last name. [OL]. *1916: 10-10* LJ.

Williams, Bill (Bile, or Bell). From Skull Valley, UT. Bill died suddenly in the fall of 1926. [OL]. *1923: 04-02* LJ, *04-07* LJ; *1926: 10-16* LJ; *1927: 04-16* LJ.

William[s], Ed. From Malad, ID. [OL]. *1907: 08-01* TT.

William[s], Lewis. Resided in Boise, ID. Was once a "school chum" of Ottogary's. [OL].
1926: 10-02 LJ.

Williams, Mr. From Twin Falls, ID. Driver of auto that crashed into Nephi Perdash's car.
[OL]. *1928*: 12-26 LJ.

Wilson, Woodrow. U.S. president. *1916*: 09-12 LJ.

Wongan, Eliza (Mrs. Quarretze Wongan). Traditional meaning of Wongan: "pine tree-
possessor of." Wongan comes from wonko-kan(tyn), the final n is not pronounced. See
Quarretz Wongan. [INF Crapo, Richley]. *1912*: 05-23 BEN, 05-25 LJ, 06-06 LJ.

Wongan, Quarretz (or Quarretze). Born 1873, UT, to James Wongan and Minnie (or Yah-
gotse). Married Eliza (b. 1875) ca. 1891. Their children were a daughter (b. 1890), Auh-
Sige-Ep (b. 1891), a daughter (b. 1893), Sylvia (b. 1894), a child (b. 1895), Tish-E-A-
Wipe (or Iona, b. May 1896), Warren (b. Apr. 1898), Thomas (b. 1901), Eunice (b.
1905), Zina (b. 1907), and Luvene (Luvina, or Lavinia, b. 1910). Census of 1910 lists
Eliza as having nine children, only three (Iona, Warren, and Eunice) living. [IGI; USFC
1900, 1910]. *1911*: 05-25 BEN; *1912*: 03-02 LJ; *1913*: 06-12 BEN; *1914*: 01-15 BEN.

Wongan, Warren. Born Apr. 1898, to Quarretz Wongan and Eliza. Married Mamie Perdash
(b. Jan. 3, 1895, to Charlie Perdash and Eunice Moemberg). The couple were sealed in
the Logan Temple Jan. 1926. Their children were (William) Willis Wayne (b. 1916), Ivy
Violet (b. 1918), Clifford Edwin (or Edwin Clifford, b. 1921, d. 1934), Harold (or
Howard Thomas, b. 1926), Ruby Eunice (b. 1928), Kenneth Ross (b. 1930), and a child
(b. 1933). Warren died in 1934. His wife, Mamie, died in 1956. [CCF 113732-15-SB-150;
IGI; OL; WASHCEM]. *1915*: 12-23 LJ; *1916*: 11-11 LJ; *1922*: 04-08 LJ, 04-29 LJ, 05-27
LJ, 06-06 BEN, 07-18 BEN, 09-23 LJ; *1923*: 12-24 LJ; *1924*: 05-17 LJ, 05-24 LJ, 06-05
OCE; *1925*: 01-17-B LJ, 04-11 LJ, 04-18 LJ, 09-12 LJ; *1926*: 01-16 LJ, 01-23 LJ, 08-28
LJ, 09-04 LJ, 12-24 LJ; *1927*: 07-02 LJ, 07-09 LJ, 07-09 LJ, 07-23 LJ, 08-20 LJ, 09-03 LJ,
10-29 LJ, 11-12 LJ, 12-24 LJ; *1928*: 02-11 LJ, 02-25 LJ, 03-03 LJ, 03-17 LJ, 03-24 LJ,
04-21 LJ, 05-19 LJ, 06-30 LJ, 07-07 LJ, 09-08 LJ, 12-06 LJ, 12-29 LJ; *1929*: 01-19 LJ, 02-23
LJ, 03-20 LJ.

Wongan, Mrs. Warren (Mamie Perdash Wongan). See Wongan, Warren. *1915*: 12-23 LJ.

Wongsaw (Wongasaw, Wong-Ge-Shew, Wongsawa, or Wongasow), Hyrum. Born 1848, ID,
to Wong-Ge-Shew. Married Belle (Isabel, Bell, Wyah-Tung, Wyah Ta gup, or Wyah tun-
gup, b. ca. 1850). Traditional meaning of Wyah Ta gup: "burned knee." Their child was
Eunice (b. 1906, d. Apr. 1, 1920). Census of 1910 notes that Hyrum was a farmer of
grain, and that he lived in an aboriginal dwelling. [AICR, CCF 113732-15-SB-150; IGI,
INF Parry, Mae Timbimboo; USFC 1910, 1920]. *1911*: 05-25 BEN; *1916*: 05-23 LJ; *1919*:
05-15 LJ, 06-26 LJ; *1923*: 04-14 LJ, 11-17 LJ; *1924*: 04-10 OCE, 09-20 LJ, 09-27-A LJ;
1926: 05-01 LJ, 09-18 LJ, 12-21 LJ; *1927*: 08-20 LJ; *1928*: 09-15 LJ, 11-10 LJ, 11-17 LJ;
1929: 03-20 LJ.

Wongsaw, Jim. *1923*: 05-05 LJ.

Woonsook (Wansook, Wonsook, Woonsock, or Woonsooka), Frankie. Listed as Frankie
Wontook in 1911. He died during the spring of that year. [OL]. *1911*: 04-25 LJ.

Woonsook, Henry. Born Feb. 3, 1895, Washakie, UT, to Joseph Woonsook (or Woonsooka)
and Mary Neayes. Married several times. First wife appears to be Elsie (Elice or Alice)
Low. They had one child: Inez (b. Mar. 2, 1920). Second marriage to Lillie (or Lilly)
Tybots (or Tyboatz, b. 1901 or 1906, to Tom Tybots and Phoebe Hootchew) Sept. 21,
1920, Brigham City. Child: Dwight (or Dewit, or Dewight, b. 1921). He also married
Rhoda, and their children were Emily (b. ca. 1928), Wendall Norman (b. 1930), Gary
L. (or Legrand, b. 1943). Henry was also married to Louise Ottogary for a short time.
[AICR; CCF 113732-15-SB-150; INF Parry, Mae Timbimboo; VRML; WWROM].
1911: 02-11 LJ; *1914*: 01-29-A LJ; *1919*: 05-15 LJ, 06-26 LJ; *1922*: 01-06 LJ, 03-18-A

LJ, 05-20 LJ, 05-27 LJ, 06-06 BEN, 07-11 BEN, 07-25 BEN, 10-21 LJ; *1923:* 02-24 LJ, 09-29 LJ, 10-06 LJ; *1924:* 02-21 OCE, 07-05 LJ, 08-23 LJ, 09-20 LJ, 12-06 LJ, 12-27 LJ; *1925:* 12-28 LJ; *1926:* 01-23 LJ, 01-30 LJ, 02-06 LJ, 02-27 LJ, 03-20 LJ, 05-01 LJ, 05-29 LJ, 06-19 LJ, 07-26 LJ, 08-28 LJ, 10-30 LJ, 12-24 LJ; *1927:* 08-20 LJ; *1928:* 02-04 LJ, 10-27 LJ, 11-03 LJ, 12-20 LJ, 12-29 LJ, *1929:* 02-23 LJ.

Woonsook (Wan-tzook-Tin-dap, or Woonsooka), Joseph. Born 1864, Raft River, Cassia, ID. His father was Tank-So-Go-Gee. Married Mary Neayes (b. 1866, Logan, UT, daughter of Susan Purdawat). Their children were Nisha (Nessie, b. 1883 or 1893), Ivy Pojenny (or Pojennie, b. 1886), Maggie (b. 1888), a child (b. Feb. 7, 1894), Henry (b. Feb. 3, 1895), Minnie (b. 1898, spouse of Henry Hootchew and mother of Daisy Pubigee who was born ca. 1925), Frank (or Frankie, b. 1900, d. spring of 1911), a child (b. Aug. 30, 1903), and Ruth Ann (b. 1905). Census of 1910 notes Joseph and Mary married thirty years (husband's second marriage, wife's first). Mother (Mary presumably) has had twelve children, five living. Joseph's occupation was listed as farmer, small grain. [CCF 113732-15-SB-150; IGI; OL; USFC 1910]. *1916:* 05-23 LJ; *1920:* 02-16 LJ, 02-26 LJ; *1921:* 09-05 LJ; *1922:* 04-08 LJ, 04-29 LJ; *1923:* 04-07 LJ; *1924:* 09-27-A LJ, 09-27-B LJ, 11-08 LJ; *1925:* 02-02 LJ, 02-07 LJ, 04-11 LJ, 04-14 BEJ, 04-25 LJ, 05-16 LJ, 12-28 LJ; *1926:* 02-06 LJ; *1927:* 01-01 LJ, 07-23 LJ, 08-20 LJ.

Woonsook, Mrs. Joseph. See Woonsook, Joseph. *1914:* 07-14 LJ.

Woonsook, Minnie. See Woonsook, Joseph. *1919:* 05-15 LJ.

Woonsook, Mrs. It is unclear which Mrs. Woonsook this is. *1908:* 02-06-B TT.

Yamp-Sia-Tick, Mr. From Fort Washakie, WY. Married Minnie Horn from Fort Hall, Reservation, ID. Traditional meaning of Yamp-Sia-Tick: the first syllable is from *iampy*, "wild carrot." Tick may be from *tykka*, "to eat something", Sia might be from *suaih*, "to want, to desire, to need." The meaning might then be "greedy for wild carrots," perhaps a nickname given a child. [INF Crapo, Richley; OL]. *1925:* 07-17 BEJ, 07-18 LJ.

Yorup, Jim. *1920:* 12-04 LJ.

Young, Bob ("colored boy"). Boxer. [OL]. *1926:* 03-13 LJ.

Youpe, Julius. From Idaho, visited at Mose Neaman's place. [OL]. *1922:* 09-19 BEN, 09-23 LJ.

Zundel, Cohn (Kohn, Corn, Conn, or Con), Miss. Born 1863 to Shoshonitze and Dakamodakey (or Nabenocha), died Nov. 17, 1949, Washakie, UT. Married twice, first to Mironi (Moroni) Zundel (b. ca. 1855). Their children were Nephi (b. 1875, later md. Minnie James) and Lucy (Cojo; b. ca. 1883, later md. to George Peyope). Sometime before the 1900 census, Mironi died. Second marriage, Jan. 14, 1893, Washakie, UT, to Johnny Annepooey Quedup (Johnny Fly, or Indian Johnny, b. ca. 1867, NV, d. Washakie, UT). Cohn was Johnny's third wife. Johnny's first wife was Wonk ga de a chee (they divorced, no children); his second wife was See Doe Broom (they had one child: Hu No boi chee); his third wife was Cohn Shoshonitz. They had three children, See Saw (b. Nov. 1893, d. very young), Jessie (b. Mar. 13, 1896, Washakie, UT, later md. Nephi Perdash, d. Nov. 10, 1920, Pocatello, ID); Emily (b. ca. 1897, later md. Timus Perdash). Jessie and Emily sometimes used the name Zundel, though Moroni Zundel was their stepfather. The census of 1910 notes Cohn was married twice, had nine children, four living. She was appointed as a counselor in the Washakie Ward Relief Society, June 18, 1883. Cohn died in 1949. [BEN 29 Jan. 1903; CCF 113732-15-SB-150; INF Parry, Mae Timbimboo; JRNLH; MTPFHR; USFC 1880, 1900, 1910; WASHCEM; WWROM]. *1919:* 05-15 LJ; *1924:* 09-27-A LJ, 11-29 LJ; *1926:* 08-28 LJ; *1927:* 01-15 LJ.

Zundel, Ida. See Zundel, Nephi. *1922:* 04-22 LJ; *1928:* 10-20 LJ, 11-03 LJ.

Zundel, John. County sheriff called in to arrest the thieves who had robbed Grouse Creek Jack and Sam Jack. [OL]. *1915:* 12-23 LJ.

Zundel, Nephi. Born 1875, to Moroni Zundel and Cohn Shoshonitz Zundel. Married Minnie James (b. 1874). Both had been married before. Their children were Melvin (b. ca. 1908), Ida (b. ca. 1910, md. a Ballard, and later md. a man named Boise), Wallace (b. ca. 1913, md. Hazel Timbimboo, d. June 14, 1999). Nephi died in 1951, his wife, Minnie, died in 1920. Census of 1910 lists Nephi's occupation as mail carrier United States. [CCF 113732-15-SB-150; MTPFHR; USFC 1910; WASHCEM; WWROM]. *1908:* 02-06-A TT; *1909:* 11-20 LJ; *1913:* 01-02 LJ; *1916:* 05-23 LJ; *1919:* 06-26 LJ; *1920:* 05-29 LJ; *1921:* 01-22 LJ; *1922:* 10-03 BEN; *1923:* 09-29 LJ, 10-06 LJ; *1924:* 02-09 LJ, 04-26 LJ, 07-05 LJ, 08-23 LJ, 09-27-B LJ; *1925:* 06-20 LJ; *1926:* 05-22 LJ, 06-19 LJ; *1927:* 06-18 LJ, 07-09 LJ, 07-23 LJ, 10-01 LJ, 11-19 LJ, 12-03 LJ; *1928:* 04-14 LJ, 06-02 LJ, 07-28 LJ, 09-08 LJ, 09-22 LJ, 12-29 LJ; *1929:* 02-11 LJ, 02-23 LJ, 03-09 LJ.

Zundel, Wallace. See Zundel, Nephi, for more information. *1928:* 03-03 LJ.

Subject Index